The Princeton Review®

PSAT/ NMSQT®

PREP

with 3 Practice Tests,
2021 Edition

The Staff of The Princeton Review

PrincetonReview.com

Penguin
Random
House

The Princeton Review
110 East 42nd Street, 7th Floor
New York, NY 10017
E-mail: editorialsupport@review.com

Published in the United States by Penguin Random House LLC, New York, and
in Canada by Random House of Canada, a division of Penguin Random House
Ltd., Toronto.

Terms of Service: The Princeton Review Online Companion Tools ("Student
Tools") for retail books are available for only the two most recent editions
of that book. Student Tools may be activated only once per eligible book
purchased for a total of 24 months of access. Activation of Student Tools more
than once per book is in direct violation of these Terms of Service and may
result in discontinuation of access to Student Tools Services.

ISBN: 978-0-525-57028-8
eBook ISBN: 978-0-525-57032-5
ISSN: 2687-8755

PSAT/NMSQT is a registered trademark of the College Board and the National
Merit Scholarship Corporation, which are not affiliated with, and do not
endorse, this product.

The Princeton Review is not affiliated with Princeton University.

Permission has been granted to reprint portions of the following:

"Jumping Spiders Can Think Ahead, Plan Detours" by Michael Greshko. Copyright ©
2016 National Geographic Creative. Originally published January 21, 2016.

"Living in an Imaginary World" by Josie Glausiusz. *Scientific American,* MIND Special
Edition. January 2014. Reproduced with permission. Copyright © 2014 Scientific
American, a division of Nature America, Inc. All rights reserved.

The Botany of Desire: A Plant's-Eye View of the World by Michael Pollan, copyright
© 2001 by Michael Pollan. Used by permission of Random House, an imprint and
division of Penguin Random House LLC. All rights reserved.
© Michael Pollan, 2001. *Botany of Desire.* Bloomsbury Publishing Plc.

Never a City So Real: A Walk in Chicago by Alex Kotlowitz. Copyright © 2004 by Alex
Kotlowitz. Used by permission of Crown Journeys, an imprint of the Crown Publishing Group, a division of Penguin Random House LLC. All rights reserved.

"A Wandering Mind Reveals Mental Processes and Priorities." Copyright © University of Wisconsin-Madison. March 2012. Reprinted with permission.

"Bacterium counteracts 'coffee ring effect.'" Copyright © KU Leuven. Full text of study
published in Nature Communications 4, Article number 1757, April 2013. Reprinted
with permission.

"Physicists undo the 'coffee ring effect.'" Copyright © University of
Pennsylvania. August 2011. Reprinted with permission.

"A Third of All Food Never Gets Eaten. How Can we Fix This?" by Elizabeth Royte.
Copyright © 2016 National Geographic Creative. Originally published
October 26, 2016.

"These 'Indestructible' Animals Would Survive a Planet-Wide Apocalypse" by Casey
Smith. Copyright © 2018 National Geographic Creative. Originally published April
23, 2018.

"Tardigrades Become First Animals to Survive Vacuum of Space" by Ed Yong. Copyright © 2008 Ed Yong.

"The Ability to Discriminate Paintings Found in Mice" by Keio University.
Released in 2013.

Editorial
Rob Franek, Editor-in-Chief
David Soto, Director of Content Development
Stephen Koch, Student Survey Manager
Deborah Weber, Director of Production
Gabriel Berlin, Production Design Manager
Selena Coppock, Managing Editor
Aaron Riccio, Senior Editor
Meave Shelton, Senior Editor
Chris Chimera, Editor
Anna Goodlett, Editor
Eleanor Green, Editor
Orion McBean, Editor
Patricia Murphy, Editorial Assistant

Penguin Random House Publishing Team
Tom Russell, VP, Publisher
Alison Stoltzfus, Publishing Director
Amanda Yee, Associate Managing Editor
Ellen Reed, Production Manager
Suzanne Lee, Designer

The material in this book is up-to-date at the time of publication. However,
changes may have been instituted by the testing body in the test after this book
was published. If there are any important late-breaking developments, changes,
or corrections to the materials in this book, we will post that information online
in the Student Tools. Register your book and check your Student Tools to see if
there are any updates posted there.

Editor: Eleanor Green
Production Editors: Liz Dacey and Emily Epstein White
Production Artist: Kris Ogilvie

Printed in the United States of America.

10 9 8 7 6 5 4 3 2 1

2021 Edition

Acknowledgments

Special thanks to Sara Kuperstein, Amy Minster, and Cynthia Ward for their contributions to this edition, as well as Aaron Lindh for his expert guidance.

Thanks also to Anne Bader, Kevin Baldwin, Gabby Budzon, Grace Cannon, Nicole Cosme, April Davis, Anne Goldberg-Baldwin, Brian Hong, Brad Kelly, Jomil London, Dave MacKenzie, Amanda Nowotny, Scott O'Neal, Danielle Perrini, Xander Posner, Jess Thomas, Christina Torturo, and Jimmy Williams.

The Princeton Review would also like to thank Kris Ogilvie, Liz Dacey, and Emily Epstein White for their time and attention to each page.

Special thanks to Adam Robinson, who conceived of and perfected the Joe Bloggs approach to standardized tests, and many other techniques in this book.

Contents

Get More (Free) Content.. vi

Part I: Orientation 1

1   What Is the PSAT/NMSQT? 3

2   All About the National Merit Scholarships 13

3   General Strategies 19

Part II: Practice Test 1 27

4   Practice Test 1 29

5   Practice Test 1: Answers and Explanations 81

Part III: PSAT/NMSQT Prep 115

6   Reading Comprehension... 117

7   Introduction to Writing and Language Strategy 157

8   Punctuation... 167

9   Words... 187

10 Questions 201

11 Math Basics 219

12 Math Techniques.. 273

13 Advanced Math 309

14 Additional Math Topics 345

Part IV: Drill Answers and Explanations.................................... 383

Part V: Practice Test 2 427

15 Practice Test 2 429

16 Practice Test 2: Answers and Explanations 487

Practice Test 3 ....online

Practice Test 3: Answers and Explanations ....online

Get More (Free) Content
at **PrincetonReview.com/prep**

As easy as 1·2·3

1 Go to PrincetonReview.com/prep and enter the following ISBN for your book:

9780525570288

2 Answer a few simple questions to set up an exclusive Princeton Review account. *(If you already have one, you can just log in.)*

3 Enjoy access to your **FREE** content!

Once you've registered, you can...

- Access and print out one more full-length practice test as well as the corresponding answers and explanations

- Get valuable advice about the college application process, including tips for writing a great essay and where to apply for financial aid

- If you're still choosing between colleges, use our searchable rankings of The Best 386 Colleges to find out more information about your dream school

- Access printable resources, including a score conversion table, a study guide, and extra bubble sheets for the practice tests in this book

- Check to see if there have been any corrections or updates to this edition

Need to report a potential **content** issue?

Contact **EditorialSupport@review.com** and include:

- full title of the book
- ISBN
- page number

Need to report a **technical** issue?

Contact **TPRStudentTech@review.com** and provide:

- your full name
- email address used to register the book
- full book title and ISBN
- Operating system (Mac/PC) and browser (Firefox, Safari, etc.)

Look For These Icons Throughout The Book

 ONLINE ARTICLES

 PROVEN TECHNIQUES

 APPLIED STRATEGIES

 STUDY BREAK

 **MORE GREAT BOOKS**

Part I
Orientation

1 What Is the PSAT/NMSQT?
2 All About the National Merit Scholarships
3 General Strategies

Chapter 1
What Is the PSAT/NMSQT?

The PSAT/NMSQT—from now on, we'll just call it the PSAT—is a standardized test given primarily to high school juniors to give them a "preliminary" idea of how well they could do on SAT question types. The test is also used to determine which students are eligible for National Merit Scholar recognition. This chapter will give you a general overview of the test and how it is used, along with the basics to start your preparation. First, a glimpse at the other tests in the College Board's Suite of Assessments: the PSAT 8/9 and the PSAT 10.

PSAT 8/9

Just like the SAT and PSAT, the PSAT 8/9, which is designed for eighth and ninth graders, contains a Reading Test, a Writing and Language Test, and a Math Test. The content of each subject is comparable to the content on the PSAT and SAT.

According to the College Board, the "Evidence-Based Reading and Writing section asks you to interpret, synthesize, and use evidence found in a wide range of sources." The bottom line: be prepared to justify your selected answer with evidence from the passage and/or graph provided. This test is still not about making up anything, but finding the correct answer based on the text.

The College Board also claims that the "Math Test focuses in-depth on two essential areas of math: Problem Solving and Data Analysis, and Heart of Algebra." The bottom line: expect to see Algebra I and II, some Geometry, as well as questions that have charts, graphs, data tables, scatterplots, or other form of data display provided.

Psst...
There's the PSAT 8/9, the PSAT 10, and PSAT/NMSQT. But when we refer to just the plain old "PSAT" in this book, we're referring to the PSAT/NMSQT.

The Math Test is split into two sections: one in which a calculator may be used and one in which it may not be used. Even though a calculator is allowed in one section, it is up to the test-taker to determine whether the calculator will be a benefit in solving a question. According to the College Board, "students who make use of structure or their ability to reason will probably finish before students who use a calculator." The bottom line: show your work and use the calculator for tedious calculations, but a calculator most likely will not be necessary to solve a majority of the questions.

All questions in the Evidence-Based Reading and Writing section are multiple choice. Most of the Math Test questions are multiple choice, with 18 percent of all Math Test questions in the grid-in, or student-produced, format. For each question answered correctly, one raw point is earned, and there is no penalty for an incorrect response or a question left blank. The bottom line: don't leave anything blank!

PSAT 10

Though this test is called the PSAT 10, it is identical to the structure of the PSAT/NMSQT in terms of both number of questions and time limits per section. The major differences are who takes the test and when: 10th-graders and schools choose a date in the spring. Additionally, this test does not qualify you for National Merit Scholarship consideration.

Just as with the SAT and the PSAT, the PSAT 10 includes an Evidence-Based Reading and Writing section and a Math Test. The Evidence-Based Reading and Writing section tests the ability to select, among the choices provided, the answer that is best evidenced in the provided passage and/or informational graphics that accompany select passages. The Math Test is divided into two sections: one in which a calculator may be used and one in which it may not be used. Even though the calculator is allowed in one section, it is up to the test-taker to determine whether or not the calculator will prove necessary.

WHAT'S WITH ALL THESE SCORES?

The PSAT (and the PSAT 8/9, PSAT 10, and SAT) is designed (according to College Board) to reflect how prepared you are for college and the working world. While we at The Princeton Review may take issue with that claim, this idea does inform both how College Board recommends you prepare and why there are so many different scores on your score report.

The College Board maintains that the best way to prepare for the test is to:

- take challenging courses
- do your homework
- prepare for tests and quizzes
- ask and answer lots of questions

College admissions advisors wanted a more "well-rounded" picture of the applicant, so the College Board did its best to meet the demand. The test provides a measurement of four Evidence-Based Reading and Writing Subscores (Command of Evidence, Words in Context, Standard English Conventions, and Expression of Ideas), and three Math Subscores (Heart of Algebra, Problem Solving and Data Analysis, and Passport to Advanced Math).

In addition to the seven subscores reported, the College Board now provides two cross-test scores to offer more insight: one score for Analysis in History/Social Studies and another for Analysis in Science. Remain calm; these scores are gathered only from select questions that deal with appropriate subject matter and are not actual entire test sections. We will go into PSAT scoring in more detail later.

> **How Do You Pronounce PSAT/NMSQT, Anyway?**
> Ah, yes—first things first. Well, to be honest, we're not really sure. You can pronounce it *pee-sat-nim-squit* if you want. However, we think it's easier just to call it the PSAT.

When Is the PSAT Given?

The PSAT is officially administered twice each year, typically on a Wednesday and Saturday of the same week in October. Your school will announce the exact dates at the beginning of the school year, or you can find out at <u>PrincetonReview.com</u>, or through the College Board at <u>CollegeBoard.org</u>.

> **Keep on Schedule**
> You'll officially take the PSAT in the fall of your junior year. Plan to take the SAT anytime between the winter of your junior year and the fall of your senior year.

How Do I Sign Up for the PSAT?

You don't have to do anything to sign up for the PSAT; your school will do all the work for you. Test registration fees can vary from school to school, so be sure to check with your school counselor if you have questions about how much the PSAT will cost you.

What About Students with Special Needs?

If you have a diagnosed learning difference, you will probably qualify for accommodations on the PSAT. However, it's important that you get the process started early. The first step is to speak to your school counselor who handles learning differences. Only he or she can file the appropriate paperwork. You'll also need to gather some information (documentation of your condition) from a licensed practitioner and some other information from your school. Then your school counselor will file the application for you.

You will need to apply for accommodations only once; with that single application you'll qualify for accommodations on the PSAT, SAT, SAT Subject Tests, and AP Exams. The one exception to this rule is that if you change school districts, you'll need to have a counselor at the new school refile your paperwork.

Does the PSAT Play a Role in College Admissions?

No! The PSAT plays no role in college admissions. It's really just a practice test for the SAT.

The one exception is for that very small group of students, about 4 percent of all students nationwide, whose PSAT scores qualify them for National Merit recognition. (We'll tell you more than you ever wanted to know about that in the next chapter.) Recognition as a commended scholar, semifinalist, or finalist for National Merit is a fairly impressive addition to your college admissions portfolio, and is something that you should certainly pursue if you are seriously in contention for it.

What Happens to the Score Report from the PSAT?

Only you, your high school, and the National Merit Scholarship Corporation (which co-sponsors the PSAT) will receive copies of your score reports. They won't be sent to colleges.

WHAT DOES THE PSAT TEST?

As you begin your prep, it's useful to remember that the PSAT is not a test of aptitude, how good of a person you are, or how successful you will be in life. The PSAT simply tests how well you take the PSAT. That's it. And performing well on the PSAT is a skill that can be learned like any other. The Princeton Review was founded 40 years ago on this very simple idea, and—as our students' test scores show—our approach is the one that works.

All of these changes to tests that you hear could heavily influence your college admission strategy can be extremely daunting. However, remember that any standardized test is a coachable test. A beatable test. Just remember:

The PSAT doesn't measure the stuff that matters. It measures neither intelligence nor the depth and breadth of what you're learning in high school. It doesn't predict college grades as well as your high school grades do. Colleges know there is more to you as a student—and as a person—than what you do on a single test.

Who Writes the PSAT?

The PSAT is written and administered by the College Board and used for scholarships by National Merit Scholarship Corporation. You might think that the people at the College Board are educators, professors of education, or teachers. They're not. They are people who just happen to make a living writing tests. In fact, they write hundreds of tests, for all kinds of organizations.

The folks at the College Board aren't really paid to educate; they're paid to write and administer tests. And even though you'll be paying them to take the PSAT, you're not their customer. The actual customers the College Board caters to are the colleges, which get the information they want at no cost. This means that you should take everything that the College Board says with a grain of salt and realize that its testing "advice" isn't always the best advice. (Getting testing advice from the College Board is a bit like getting baseball advice from the opposing team.)

Every test reflects the interests of the people who write it. If you know who writes the test, you will know a lot more about what kinds of answers will be considered "correct" answers on that test.

WHAT IS THE PRINCETON REVIEW?

The Princeton Review is the nation's leading test-preparation company. In just a few years, we became the nation's leader in SAT preparation, primarily because our techniques work. We offer courses and private tutoring for all of the major standardized tests, and we publish a series of books to help in your search for the right school. If you'd like more information about our programs or books, give us a call at 800-2-Review, or check out our website at PrincetonReview.com.

> **Shortcuts**
> The Princeton Review's techniques are the closest thing there is to a shortcut to the PSAT. However, there is no shortcut to learning these techniques.

HOW TO USE THIS BOOK

This book is divided into five parts. The first three parts of the book contain Practice Test 1 and general testing strategies and question-specific problem-solving instruction. Use the first practice test as a diagnostic to see which sections of the test you need to work when you read through the content chapters. The last two parts of the book contain Practice Test 2 and drill answers and explanations. After working through the content chapters and checking your answers and the explanations to the chapter drills, take Practice Test 2 and apply everything you've learned to improve your score. The "Session-by-Session Study Guide" starting on page 9 will give you a plan of attack for these tests and the rest of the book. There is no single plan that will fit everyone, so be prepared to adapt the plan and use it according to your own needs. For additional practice, you can download one more practice test online by registering your book on our website and following the steps to access your online resources. (See "Get More (Free) Content on pages vi–vii.)

Practice Test 1 will give you an idea of your strengths and weaknesses, both of which can be sources of improvement. If you're already good at something, additional practice can make you great at it; if you're not so good at something, what you should do about it depends on how important it is. If the concept is one that frequently appears on the test, you should spend a lot of time on it; if it comes up only once in a while, you should spend very little time working on it and remember that it's something you should either put off until you've completed easier things or skip it entirely.

How do you know what's important? We'll tell you throughout this book, when we discuss techniques like Plugging In and so forth, but you can also get an idea of what to focus on simply by observing how this book is laid out. The most important concepts in each section appear first in the corresponding section of this book. For example, if you're shaky on critical reading, you know you'll need to devote some time to Reading questions because there are a total of 47 such questions on the test. And if you're not so confident when it comes to geometry, don't panic: geometry questions appear only in the Advanced Math chapter, which tells you that this topic isn't as much of a priority as Plugging In or Math Basics.

Time Management

To manage your PSAT preparation, make use of the study guide on the following pages. This guide will break down the seemingly daunting task of PSAT prep into bite-sized pieces we call "sessions." We have mapped out tasks for each session to be sure you get the most out of this book. The tests will be the first and last sessions, so you should be sure to plan to have about three hours for these sessions. Most other sessions will last between an hour and two hours, so plan to take a short break in the middle, and if it looks like the session is going to exceed two hours, feel free to stop and pick up where you left off on the next day.

When You Take a Practice Test

You'll see when to take practice tests in the session outlines. Here are some guidelines for taking these tests:

- Time yourself strictly. Use a timer, watch, or stopwatch that will ring, and do not allow yourself to go over time for any section. If you try to do so at the real test, your scores will probably be canceled.
- Take a practice test in one sitting, allowing yourself breaks of no more than two minutes between sections. You need to build up your endurance for the real test, and you also need an accurate picture of how you will do. However, do take 5-minute breaks after the Reading and Math (No Calculator) sections. On the real test you will have a break, so it's important not to skip it on the practice tests.
- Always take a practice test using an answer sheet with bubbles to fill in, just as you will for the real test. For the practice tests in the book, use the answer sheets provided at the back of this book. You need to be comfortable transferring answers to the separate sheet because you will be skipping around a bit.
- Each bubble you choose should be filled in thoroughly, and no other marks should be made in the answer area.
- As you fill in the bubble for a question, check to be sure you are on the correct number on the answer sheet. If you fill in the wrong bubble on the answer sheet, it won't matter if you've worked out the problem correctly in the test booklet. All that matters to the machine scoring the test is the No. 2 pencil mark.

Session-by-Session Study Guide

Session Zero   You're involved in this session right now. Finish reading the first chapter so you'll know what the test is about, why it is important for you to take, and what to expect from the rest of the book. This step probably won't take you long, so if you have about three hours after you complete Chapter 1, you can go on to Session One and take the first practice test.

Session One   Take Practice Test 1 and score it. You'll use this result to get an idea of how many questions on each section you should attempt before guessing strategically, and the parts of each section you should concentrate on. Note that our explanations refer to concepts discussed elsewhere in this book, so you may want to wait until after Session Four before reviewing this test.

Session Two   Work through Chapters 2 and 3 of the Orientation and Chapter 6, Reading Comprehension.

Session Three   Read Chapter 7, Introduction to Writing and Language Strategy, along with Chapter 8, Punctuation.

Session Four   Work through the Math Basics in Chapter 11 and the corresponding drills.

Session Five   Work through the Math Techniques section in Chapter 12 and associated drills. Take a look at Chapter 9, Words.

Session Six   Review Advanced Math, Chapter 13. As you work through this chapter, be sure to apply techniques like Plugging In that you learned in Chapter 12. Since these techniques are central to doing well on the math sections, you can never practice them too much. If there's time, start Chapter 14.

Session Seven   Work through the Additional Math Topics in Chapter 14. When you finish, read through Chapter 10, Questions. This will give you a good idea of how the PSAT will put together all the things you've gone over for the Writing and Language section of the test.

Session Eight   Take Practice Test 2. Use the techniques you've been practicing throughout the book. Score your test and go through the explanations, focusing on where you may have missed the opportunity to use a technique and your decisions about whether you should have attempted a question or not, given your pacing goals and Personal Order of Difficulty.

Some of the terminology in the study guide may be unfamiliar to you now, but don't worry, you'll get to know it soon. Also, you'll want to refer back to this study guide at each session to keep yourself on track. Don't forget to download Practice Test 3 from your online student tools for more prep!

One important note: In this book, some sample questions do not appear in numerical order within a chapter. For example, you might see a question 4 followed by a question 14. This is because on the Math sections of PSAT, a higher question number generally indicates a higher level of difficulty (this is not the case with Reading or Writing and Language). Chapter 3 has great advice on how to crack some of the most difficult questions.

> **...The Less to Study**
> While higher-level math may sound scary at first, stay tuned for further information from us on the most effective techniques to use on the PSAT that can, sometimes, drastically reduce the math complexity for many questions.

HOW IS THE PSAT STRUCTURED AND SCORED?

Category	PSAT/NMSQT
Time	2 hours and 45 minutes

Components	• Evidence-Based Reading and Writing:
	  – Reading
	  – Writing and Language
	• Math (Calculator and No Calculator)

Number of Questions, Time by Section	• Reading: 47 questions over 5 passages, 60 minutes • Writing and Language: 44 questions over 4 passages, 35 minutes • Math (No Calculator): 17 questions (13 multiple-choice, 4 grid-in), 25 minutes • Math (Calculator): 31 questions (27 multiple-choice, 4 grid-in), 45 minutes
Important Features	• Emphasis on reasoning and a strong focus on the knowledge, skills, and understandings important to college and career readiness and success • Emphasis on the meaning of words in extended contexts and on how word choice shapes meaning, tone, and impact • Rights-only scoring (a point for a correct answer but no deduction for an incorrect answer; blank responses have no impact on score)
Score Reporting	• Scored on a scale of 320–1520 that will be the sum of the two section scores (Evidence-Based Reading and Writing and Math) that range from 160–760
Subscore Reporting	• Subscores for every test, providing added insight for students, parents, educators, and counselors
Answer Choices	• 4 answer choices for multiple-choice questions

According to the College Board, the PSAT redesign of 2015 raised the complexity of questions across the board. For the Reading and Writing and Language Tests, this refers in part to the way in which all questions are now connected to full passages, which are written at the same level as writing expected in introductory college and vocational training programs. This means that there will be a good amount of history- and science-based reading material. Additionally, there are no longer any fill-in-the-blank sentence completion questions or stand-alone sentence-editing questions. Instead, the PSAT tests your ability to demonstrate a full understanding of a source's ideas.

Moreover, the scope of math content focuses on a specific set of problem-solving and analytical topics, and it includes high-level content like trigonometry. You will also encounter more grid-in questions, and you will face topics that are both specifically geared to test your ability to use a calculator and for which calculators are not permitted.

The Math Test is divided into two sections, one without a calculator, with 17 questions over the course of 25 minutes, followed by one with a calculator, with 31 questions administered in

45 minutes. Because of the tight time limit, particularly in the No Calculator section, you should work as efficiently as possible. To help you do this, even if you answer a question correctly, we recommend that you review the explanations for the questions in the drills and the practice tests. You may discover techniques that help to shave seconds from your solutions. A large part of what's being tested is your ability to use the appropriate tools in a strategic fashion, and while there may be multiple ways to solve a given problem, you'll want to focus on the most efficient.

Scoring on the PSAT

The PSAT is scored on a scale of 320–1520, which is the sum of the two section scores that range from 160–760. The two sections are the Evidence-Based Reading and Writing section and the Mathematics section. Wrong answers to multiple-choice questions are not penalized, so you're advised never to leave a question blank—even if that means blindly picking a letter and bubbling it in for any uncompleted questions before time runs out.

In addition to the overall total score and the section scores, you'll find several sub-scores on your PSAT score report.

Analysis in History/Social Studies and **Analysis in Science** cross-test scores are generated based on questions from all three of the subject tests (Math included!). These cross-test scores assess the cross-curricular application of the tested skills to other contexts. Relax! This doesn't mean that you have to start cramming dates and anatomy—every question can be answered from the context of a given reading passage or the data included in a table or figure. The only changes have to do with the content of the passages and questions themselves.

Additionally, the Math Test is broken into several categories, as we've done in this book. The **Heart of Algebra** subscore looks specifically at how well students understand how to handle algebraic expressions, work with a variety of algebraic equations, and relate real-world scenarios to algebraic principles. **Problem Solving and Data Analysis** focuses more on interpretation of mathematical expressions, graphical analysis, and data interpretation. Your ability to understand what the question is asking will come in handy here. **Passport to Advanced Mathematics** questions showcase the higher-level math that's been added to the test, from quadratics and their graphs to the creation and translation of functions. Finally, there is an **Additional Topics** domain that's filled with what you might consider wild-card material. Although these questions might not correlate directly to a subscore, two of these miscellaneous types will show up on the redesigned test.

In the Verbal portions of the test, the **Command of Evidence** subscore measures how well you can translate and cite specific lines that back up your interpretation, while the **Words in Context** subscore ensures that you can select the best definition for how a word is used in a passage. The Writing and Language Test additionally measures **Expression of Ideas**, which deals with revising language in order to make more logical and cohesive arguments, and **Standard English Conventions**, which assesses your ability to conform to the basic rules of English structure, punctuation, and usage.

Scoring Your Practice Tests
As you can see, scoring is a little tricky. That's why we provide scoring tables to help you determine your approximate score. When we say that the score is "approximate," we mean that the score is accurate for that particular test. However, the number of questions you need to get right or wrong to earn a certain score can vary depending on the PSAT's scale from test to test. For example, if you miss 10 Math questions and get a 680 on a practice test, that does not necessarily mean that 10 missed Math questions on the actual exam will result in a 680 as well; you may get that score from missing 8 questions or 12 questions.

HOW DOES THE SAT DIFFER FROM THE PSAT?

The SAT does not differ significantly from the PSAT in structure and timing! Indeed, the PSAT's Reading Test, which contains 5 fewer questions, is only 5 minutes shorter than the SAT's Reading Test. The Writing and Language Test is the same in terms of length and timing for both tests. The PSAT's Math Test has only 10 fewer total questions as compared to those of the SAT's Math Test. The tables below summarize the differences—or actually, the similarities!—of the two tests.

Here's a breakdown of how the tests differ:

	SAT	PSAT
Structure	4 (+ optional Essay) sections	4 sections
Length	3 hours (+ 50 minutes for Essay)	2 hours 45 minutes
Purpose	College admissions	NMSQT
Scoring	400–1600	320–1520

Are You Ready for the SAT?

If you want to start preparing for the SAT, pick up a copy of our *SAT Premium Prep*, which is chock full of content review, strategy, and realistic practice!

What Does the PSAT Score Mean for My SAT Score?

The SAT is scored on a 1600 scale, whereas the PSAT is scored on a 1520 scale. However, because the PSAT and SAT are aligned by the College Board to be scored on the same scale, your PSAT score indicates the approximate SAT score you would earn were you to have taken the SAT on that same day.

How Much Should I Prepare for the PSAT?

If you're in that very small percentage of students who are in contention for National Merit recognition, it may be worth your while to put in a good deal of time to prepare for this test. After all, your extra hard work may well put you in a better position for National Merit recognition. Otherwise, you should prepare enough so that you feel more in control of the test and have a better testing experience. (Nothing feels quite as awful as being dragged through a testing experience feeling like you don't know what you're being tested on or what to expect—except perhaps dental surgery.) The other reason to prepare for the PSAT is that it will give you some testing skills that will help you begin to prepare for the tests that actually count, namely the SAT and SAT Subject Tests.

The bottom line is this: the best reason to prepare for the PSAT is that it will help you get an early start on your preparation for the SAT.

Study

If you were getting ready to take a biology test, you'd study biology. If you were preparing for a basketball game, you'd practice basketball. So, if you're preparing for the PSAT (and eventually the SAT), study the PSAT. The PSAT can't test everything, so concentrate on learning what it *does* test.

Chapter 2
All About the National Merit Scholarships

The NMSQT part of the name PSAT/NMSQT stands for National Merit Scholarship Qualifying Test. That means that the PSAT serves as the test that will establish whether or not you are eligible for National Merit recognition. This chapter will help you figure out what that may mean for you and even other scholarships you may qualify for.

WHAT IS THE NATIONAL MERIT SCHOLARSHIP PROGRAM?

You might think that the PSAT is simply a warm-up for the SAT, but the National Merit Scholarship Program makes the PSAT an important test in its own right.

The mission of National Merit Scholarship Corporation (NMSC) is to recognize and honor the academically talented students of the United States. NMSC accomplishes this mission by conducting nationwide academic scholarship programs. The enduring goals of NMSC's scholarship programs are the following:

- to promote a wider and deeper respect for learning in general and for exceptionally talented individuals in particular
- to shine a spotlight on brilliant students and encourage the pursuit of academic excellence at all levels of education
- to stimulate increased support from organizations that wish to sponsor scholarships for outstanding scholastic talent

The National Merit Scholarship Program is an academic competition for recognition and scholarships that began in 1955. High school students enter the National Merit Program by taking the Preliminary SAT/National Merit Scholarship Qualifying Test (PSAT/NMSQT) and by meeting published program entry and participation requirements.

HOW DO I QUALIFY FOR NATIONAL MERIT?

To participate in the National Merit Scholarship Program, a student must:

1. take the PSAT/NMSQT in the specified year of the high school program and **no later than** the third year in grades 9 through 12, regardless of grade classification or educational pattern;
2. be enrolled as a high school student (traditional or homeschooled), progressing normally toward graduation or completion of high school, and planning to enroll full time in college no later than the fall following completion of high school; and
3. be a citizen of the United States; or be a U.S. lawful permanent resident (or have applied for permanent residence, the application for which has not been denied) and intend to become a U.S. citizen at the earliest opportunity allowed by law.

The Index

How does your PSAT score qualify you for National Merit? The National Merit Scholarship Corporation uses a selection index, which is the sum of your Reading, Writing and Language, and Math Test scores that are each on a scale of 8–38. Those three test scores are added together and then multiplied by 2 to calculate your Selection Index score that has a range of 48–228. Qualifying scores for National Merit recognition will vary from state to state, so check with your school counselor as to what the cutoff score is that year for your particular state. For instance, if your PSAT scores were 24 Math, 22 Reading, and 30 Writing and Language, your index would be 152.

$$\text{Math} \quad + \quad \text{Reading} \quad + \quad \text{Writing and Language} \quad = \quad \text{Test Scores Total}$$
$$24 \quad + \quad 22 \quad + \quad 30 \quad = \quad 76$$

National Merit Selection Index

$$76 \times 2 = 152$$

The Awards and the Process

In the fall of their senior year, about 50,000 students will receive one of two letters from NMSC (National Merit Scholarship Corporation): either a Letter of Commendation or a letter stating that they have qualified as semifinalists for National Merit.

Commended Students   Roughly two-thirds of these students (about 34,000 total students each year) will receive a Letter of Commendation by virtue of their high scores on the test. This looks great on your college application, so if you have a reasonable chance of getting one, it's definitely worth your time to prepare for the PSAT. Make no mistake, though, these letters are not easy to get. They are awarded to students who score between the 95th and the mid-99th percentiles—that means to the top four to five percent in the country.

If you receive this honorable mention from NMSC, you should be extremely proud of yourself. Even though you won't continue in the process for National Merit scholarships, this commendation does make you eligible for special scholarships sponsored by certain companies and organizations, which vary in their amounts and eligibility requirements.

Semifinalists   The other third of these students—those 16,000 students who score in the upper 99th percentile in their states—will be notified that they are National Merit semifinalists. If you qualify, you'll get a letter announcing your status as a semifinalist, along with information about the requirements for qualification as a finalist. These include maintaining high grades, performing well on your SAT, and getting an endorsement from your principal.

Becoming a National Merit semifinalist is quite impressive, and if you manage it, you should certainly mention it on your college applications.

What does "scoring in the upper 99th percentile in the state" mean? It means that you're essentially competing against the other people in your state for those semifinalist positions. Since some states have higher average scores than others, this means that if you're in states like New York, New Jersey, Maryland, Connecticut, or Massachusetts, you need a higher score to qualify than if you live in other states.

Finalists The majority of semifinalists (more than 90 percent) go on to qualify as finalists. Students who meet all of the eligibility requirements will be notified in February of their senior year that they have qualified as finalists. This means that they are now eligible for scholarship money, though it doesn't necessarily mean that they'll get any. In fact, only about half of National Merit finalists actually win scholarships through NMSC. What determines whether a student gets money or not? There is a final screening process, based on criteria that NMSC doesn't release to the public, to determine who actually gets these scholarships. 2,500 finalists earn $2,500 one-time scholarships from NMSC, and approximately 1,000 more win corporate-sponsored merit scholarships, which are typically given to children of the sponsors' employees, residents of certain communities, and students who plan to study or work in specific fields. The monetary amount of corporate-sponsored scholarships can be anywhere from $500–$10,000, and some are one-time scholarships while others are given for each year of study. Some students who meet the corporation's qualifications but aren't finalists will also earn Special Scholarships. Approximately an additional 4,000 students will be offered college-sponsored scholarships from the schools they plan to attend. These awards range from $500 to $2,000 and are renewable for four years.

Though the amounts of money may not be huge, every little bit helps. One other point to keep in mind is that while most of the scholarships through NMSC are relatively small, many universities seek out National Merit finalists because of their academic abilities and (who are we kidding?) because the universities like to brag about how many such students chose them. For this reason, a number of state schools and less elite universities offer significant scholarships to National Merit finalists and sometimes semifinalists as well. Some schools offer full tuition for National Merit finalists, including the University of Alabama, University of Central Florida, University of Kentucky, University of Mississippi, Washington State University, Baylor University, and quite a few others. Many more schools award incomplete but large scholarships to National Merit finalists and semifinalists.

Aside from the possibility of winning a scholarship, the award itself looks great in your portfolio. So if you think you are in contention for National Merit recognition, practice diligently and smartly! If not, don't sweat it too much, but prepare for the PSAT anyway because it is good practice for the SAT.

If you're willing to forego the name-brand recognition of an Ivy, a state school can be an excellent choice—and if it offers you a National Merit scholarship, the trade-off can be more than worth it. Check out our mega-guide, *The Complete Book of Colleges,* for well-researched profiles of over 1,000 public and private schools.

But I'm Not a Junior in High School Yet...

If you are not yet a junior, and you're interested in National Merit, you will have to take the test again your junior year in order to qualify.

A certain number of schools give the PSAT to students in their sophomore year—and sometimes even earlier. These schools hope that earlier exposure to these tests will help their students perform better in later years. If you're not yet in your junior year, the PSAT won't count for National Merit scholarship purposes, so it's really just a trial run for you. It's still a good idea to go into the test prepared in order to feel and perform your best. After all, there's nothing more unpleasant than an unpleasant testing experience, except maybe having a tooth drilled or watching the sad downward spiral of certain pop stars.

What If I'm in a Three-Year or Other Nonstandard Course of Study?

If you're going to spend only three years in secondary school, you have two options for when to take the PSAT for National Merit purposes: you can take it either in your next-to-last year or in your last year of secondary school. However, our advice is this: if you're in any program other than a usual four-year high school, be sure to talk to your school counselor. He or she will consult with NMSC and help ensure that you take the PSAT at the right time. This is important, because not taking the PSAT at the right time can disqualify you from National Merit recognition.

What If I Miss the PSAT Administration My Junior Year?

If you aren't concerned about National Merit scholarships, there's no reason to do anything in particular—except, perhaps, to obtain a few PSAT booklets to practice with, just to see what fun you missed.

However, if you want to be eligible for National Merit recognition, then swift action on your part is required. If an emergency arises that prevents you from taking the PSAT, you should write to the National Merit Scholarship Corporation *immediately* to request alternate testing dates. If your request is received soon enough, it should be able to accommodate you. (NMSC says that this kind of request must absolutely be received by April 1 following the missed PSAT administration.) You'll also need a signature from a school official.

For More Information

If you have any questions or problems, the best person to consult is your school counselor, who can help make sure you're on the right track. If you need further help, contact your local Princeton Review office at 800-2-REVIEW or PrincetonReview.com. Or, you can contact National Merit directly:

National Merit Scholarship Corporation
1560 Sherman Avenue, Suite 200
Evanston, IL 60201-4897
(847) 866-5100
NationalMerit.org

WHAT OTHER SCHOLARSHIPS CAN I APPLY TO?

In addition to the National Merit Scholarships, you can also apply to College Board's new Opportunity Scholarships and their partner scholarships. If you opt in the free Student Search Service® when you take the PSAT/NMSQT, the College Board will further connect you to scholarship partners who offer over $300 million annually in scholarships to qualifying students!

College Board Opportunity Scholarships

Beginning with the 2020 class, the College Board is offering a new scholarship program with $5 million scholarships each year to qualifying high school juniors in the United States, Puerto Rico, and other U.S. territories. The program consists of six different scholarships designed to help students divide the process of applying to college from start to finish. Completing each step gives students the opportunity to earn a certain amount of scholarship money, and students who complete all the steps are finally eligible for a $40,000 scholarship. The six-step scholarships are:

1. **Build Your College List:** $500
2. **Practice for the SAT:** $1,000
3. **Improve Your Score:** $2,000
4. **Strengthen Your College List:** $500
5. **Complete the FAFSA:** $1,000
6. **Apply to Colleges:** $1,000

For information regarding the official rules on how to qualify for each scholarship and deadlines, visit the College Board's Opportunity Scholarships website: https://opportunity.collegeboard.org/

Other Partner Scholarships

Hispanic Scholarship Fund
When to apply: accepting applications for class of 2022 in January 2021–February 2021
https://www.hsf.net/scholarship

United Negro College Fund (UNCF)
When to apply: Anytime
https://www.uncf.org/

American Indian Graduate Center
When to apply: Anytime
http://www.aigcs.org/

Asian Pacific Islander American Scholars
When to apply: September 2020–January 2021
https://apiascholars.org/

Children of Fallen Patriots
When to apply: Anytime
https://www.fallenpatriots.org/

For more partner scholarship programs, please visit: https://collegereadiness.collegeboard.org/psat-nmsqt-psat-10/scholarships-and-recognition/scholarship-partners-programs

Chapter 3
General Strategies

The first step to cracking the PSAT is to know how best to approach the test. The PSAT is not like the tests you've taken in school, so you need to learn to look at it in a different way. This chapter will show test-taking strategies that immediately improve your score. Make sure you fully understand these concepts before moving on to the following chapters. Good luck!

BASIC PRINCIPLES OF CRACKING THE TEST

What the College Board Is Good At

The folks at the College Board have been writing standardized tests for more than 80 years, and they write tests for all sorts of programs. They have administered the test so many times that they know exactly how you will approach it. They know how you'll attack certain questions, what sort of mistakes you'll probably make, and even what answer you'll be most likely to pick. Freaky, isn't it?

However, the College Board's strength is also a weakness. Because the test is standardized, the PSAT has to ask the same type of questions over and over again. Sure, the numbers or the words might change, but the basics don't. With enough practice, you can learn to think like the test-writers. But try to use your powers for good, okay?

The PSAT Isn't School

Our job isn't to teach you math or English—leave that to your supersmart school teachers. Instead, we're going to teach you what the PSAT is and how to crack the PSAT. You'll soon see that the PSAT involves a very different skill set.

> **No Penalty for Incorrect Answers!**
> You will NOT be penalized on the PSAT for any wrong answers. This means you should always guess, even if this means choosing an answer at random.

Be warned that some of the approaches we're going to show you may seem counterintuitive or unnatural. Some of these strategies may be very different from the way you learned to approach similar questions in school, but trust us! Try tackling the questions using our techniques, and keep practicing until they become easier. You'll see a real improvement in your score.

Let's take a look at the questions.

Cracking Multiple-Choice Questions

What's the capital of Azerbaijan?

Give up?

Unless you spend your spare time studying an atlas, you may not even know that Azerbaijan is a real country, much less what its capital is. If this question came up on a test, you'd have to skip it, wouldn't you? Well, maybe not. Let's turn this question into a multiple-choice question—just like all the questions on the PSAT Reading Test and Writing and Language Test, and the majority of questions you'll find on the PSAT Math Test—and see if you can figure out the answer anyway.

1

The capital of Azerbaijan is

A) Washington, D.C.

B) Paris.

C) London.

D) Baku.

The question doesn't seem that hard anymore, does it? Of course, we made our example extremely easy. (By the way, there won't actually be any questions about geography on the PSAT that aren't answered by the accompanying passage.) But you'd be surprised by how many people give up on PSAT questions that aren't much more difficult than this one just because they don't know the correct answer right off the top of their heads. "Capital of Azerbaijan? Oh, no! I've never heard of Azerbaijan!"

These students don't stop to think that they might be able to find the correct answer simply by eliminating all of the answer choices they know are wrong.

You Already Know Almost All of the Answers

All but a handful of the questions on the PSAT are multiple-choice questions, and every multiple-choice question has four answer choices. One of those choices, and only one, will be the correct answer to the question. You don't have to come up with the answer from scratch. You just have to identify it.

How will you do that?

Look for the Wrong Answers Instead of the Right Ones

Why? Because wrong answers are usually easier to find than the right ones. After all, there are more of them! Remember the question about Azerbaijan? Even though you didn't know the answer off the top of your head, you easily figured it out by eliminating the three obviously incorrect choices. You looked for wrong answers first.

In other words, you used the Process of Elimination, which we'll call POE for short. This is an extremely important concept, one we'll come back to again and again. It's one of the keys to improving your PSAT score. When you finish reading this book, you will be able to use POE to answer many questions that you may not understand.

It's Not About Circling the Right Answer

Physically marking in your test booklet what you think of certain answers can help you narrow down choices, take the best possible guess, and save time! Try using the following notations:

- ✔ Put a check mark next to an answer you like.
- ~ Put a squiggle next to an answer you kinda like.
- ? Put a question mark next to an answer you don't understand.
- A̶ Cross out the letter of any answer choice you KNOW is wrong.

You can always come up with your own system. Just make sure you are consistent.

The great artist Michelangelo once said that when he looked at a block of marble, he could see a statue inside. All he had to do to make a sculpture was to chip away everything that wasn't part of it. You should approach difficult PSAT multiple-choice questions in the same way, by chipping away everything that's not correct. By first eliminating the most obviously incorrect choices on difficult questions, you will be able to focus your attention on the few choices that remain.

PROCESS OF ELIMINATION (POE)

There won't be many questions on the PSAT in which incorrect choices will be as easy to eliminate as they were on the Azerbaijan question. But if you read this book carefully, you'll learn how to eliminate at least one choice on almost any PSAT multiple-choice question, if not two or even three choices.

What good is it to eliminate just one or two choices on a four-choice PSAT question?

Plenty. In fact, for most students, it's an important key to earning higher scores. Here's another example:

2

The capital of Qatar is

A) Paris.

B) Dukhan.

C) Tokyo.

D) Doha.

On this question you'll almost certainly be able to eliminate two of the four choices by using POE. That means you're still not sure of the answer. You know that the capital of Qatar has to be either Doha or Dukhan, but you don't know which.

Should you skip the question and go on? Or should you guess?

Close Your Eyes and Point

There is no guessing penalty on the PSAT, so you should bubble something for every question. If you get down to two answers, just pick one of them. There's no harm in doing so.

You're going to hear a lot of mixed opinions about what you should bubble or whether you should bubble at all. Let's clear up a few misconceptions about guessing.

FALSE: Don't answer a question unless you're absolutely sure of the answer.

You will almost certainly have teachers and school counselors who tell you this. Don't listen to them! While the SAT used to penalize students for wrong answers prior to 2016, no tests in the current "Suite of Assessments" do this now. Put something down for every question: you might get a freebie.

FALSE: If you have to guess, guess (C).

This is a weird misconception, and obviously it's not true. As a general rule, if someone says something really weird-sounding about the PSAT, it's safest not to believe that person. (And we at The Princeton Review have gone through every PSAT and SAT and found that there isn't a "better" letter to guess, so just pick your favorite!)

FALSE: Always pick the [fill in the blank].

Be careful with directives that tell you that this or that answer or type of answer is always right. It's much safer to learn the rules and to have a solid guessing strategy in place.

As far as guessing is concerned, we do have a small piece of advice. First and foremost, make sure of one thing:

> Answer every question on the PSAT. There's no penalty.

LETTER OF THE DAY (LOTD)

Sometimes you won't be able to eliminate any answers, and other times there will be questions that you won't have time to look at. For those, we have a simple solution. Pick a "letter of the day," or LOTD (from A to D), and use that letter for all the questions for which you weren't able to eliminate any choices.

This is a quick and easy way to make sure that you've bubbled everything. It also has some potential statistical advantages. If all the answers show up about one-fourth of the time and you guess the same answer every time you have to guess, you're likely to get a couple of freebies.

LOTD should absolutely be an afterthought; it's far more important and helpful to your score to eliminate answer choices. But for those questions you don't know at all, LOTD is better than full-on random guessing or no strategy at all.

Get Ready...
Check out *Are You Ready for the SAT and ACT?, 2nd Edition* to brush up on essential skills for these exams and beyond.

PACE YOURSELF

LOTD should remind us about something very important: there's a very good chance that you won't answer every question on the test. Instead, work at a pace that lets you avoid careless mistakes, and don't stress about the questions you don't get to.

Think about it this way. There are 5 passages and 47 questions on the Reading Test. You have 60 minutes to complete those questions. Now, everyone knows that the Reading Test is super long and boring, and 47 questions in 60 minutes probably sounds like a ton. The great news is that you don't have to work all 47 of these questions. After all, do you think you read most effectively when you're in a huge rush? You might do better if you worked only four of the passages and LOTD'd the rest. There's nothing in the test booklet that says that you can't work at your own pace.

Let's say you do all 47 Reading questions and get half of them right. How many questions do you get correct? That's right: 23 or 24. On the PSAT, the number of correct answers you earn in a test (Reading, Writing and Language, or Math) is known as your *raw* score.

Now, let's say you do only three of the 10-question Reading passages and get all of them right. It's conceivable that you could because you've now got all this extra time. What raw score would you earn from this method? You bet: 30—and maybe even a little higher because you'll get a few freebies from your Letter of the Day.

In this case, and on the PSAT as a whole, slowing down can get you more points. Unless you're currently scoring in the 650+ range on the two sections, you shouldn't be working all the questions. We'll go into this in more detail in the later chapters, but for now remember this:

Slow down, score more. You're not scored on *how many questions you do*. You're scored on *how many questions you answer correctly*. Doing fewer questions can mean more correct answers overall!

EMBRACE YOUR POOD

Embrace your what now? POOD! It stands for "Personal Order of Difficulty." One of the things that PSAT has dispensed with altogether is a strict Order of Difficulty—in other words, an arrangement of questions that puts easy ones earlier in the test than hard ones. In the absence of this Order of Difficulty (OOD), you need to be particularly vigilant about applying your *Personal* Order of Difficulty (POOD).

Think about it this way. There's someone writing the words that you're reading right now. So what happens if you are asked, *Who is the author of PSAT/NMSQT Prep?* Do you know the answer to that question? Maybe not. Do we know the answer to that question? Absolutely.

So you can't exactly say that that question is "difficult," but you can say that certain people would have an easier time answering it.

As we've begun to suggest with our Pacing, POE, and Letter of the Day strategies, The Princeton Review's strategies are all about making the test your own, to whatever extent that is possible. We call this idea POOD because we believe it is essential that you identify the questions that you find easy or hard and that you work the test in a way most suitable to your goals and strengths.

As you familiarize yourself with the rest of our strategies, keep all of this in mind. You may be surprised to find out how you perform on particular question types and sections. This test may be standardized, but the biggest improvements are usually reserved for those who can treat the test in a personalized, nonstandardized way.

Summary

o   When you don't know the right answer to a multiple-choice question, look for wrong answers instead. They're usually easier to find.

o   When you find a wrong answer choice, eliminate it. In other words, use Process of Elimination, or POE.

o   There's no penalty for wrong answers, so there's no reason NOT to guess.

o   There will likely be at least a few questions you simply don't get to or where you're finding it difficult to eliminate even one answer choice. When this happens, use the LOTD (Letter of the Day) strategy.

o   Pace yourself. Remember, you're not scored on the number of questions you answer, but on the number of questions you answer correctly. Take it slow and steady.

o   Make the test your own. When you can work the test to suit your strengths (and use our strategies to overcome any weaknesses), you'll be on your way to a higher score.

Part II
Practice Test 1

4   Practice Test 1
5   Practice Test 1: Answers and Explanations

Chapter 4
Practice Test 1

Reading Test

60 MINUTES, 47 QUESTIONS

Turn to Section 1 of your answer sheet to answer the questions in this section.

Questions 1–9 are based on the following passage.

The following passage is excerpted from E.C. Bentley, *Trent's Last Case*. First published in 1913, this novel tells the story of a detective who attempts to solve the murder of a wealthy financier.

Between what matters and what seems to matter, how should the world we know judge wisely?

When the scheming, indomitable brain of Sigsbee
Line Manderson was scattered by a shot from an unknown
5 hand, that world lost nothing worth a single tear. It
gained something memorable in a harsh reminder of
the vanity of such wealth as this dead man had piled
up—without making one loyal friend to mourn him,
without doing an act that could help his memory to
10 the least honour. But when the news of his end came, it
seemed to those living in the great vortices of business
as if the earth, too, shuddered under a blow.

In all the lurid commercial history of his country
there had been no figure that had so imposed itself upon
15 the mind of the trading world. He had a niche apart
in its temples. Financial giants, strong to direct and
augment the forces of capital, and taking an approved
toll in millions for their labour, had existed before; but
in the case of Manderson there had been this singularity,
20 that a pale halo of piratical romance, a thing especially
dear to the hearts of his countrymen, had remained
incongruously about his head through the years when
he stood in every eye as the unquestioned guardian of
stability, the stamper-out of manipulated crises, the foe
25 of the raiding chieftains that infest the borders of Wall
Street.

The fortune left by his grandfather, who had been
one of those chieftains on the smaller scale of his day,
had descended to him with accretion through his father
30 who during a long life had quietly continued to lend
money and never had margined a stock. Manderson,
who had at no time known what it was to be without
large sums to his hand, should have been altogether
of that newer American plutocracy which is steadied
35 by the tradition and habit of great wealth. But it was
not so. While his nurture and education had taught
him European ideas of a rich man's proper external
circumstance; while they had rooted in him an instinct
for quiet magnificence, the larger costliness which does
40 not shriek of itself with a thousand tongues; there had
been handed on to him nevertheless much of the Forty-
Niner and financial buccaneer, his forbear. During
that first period of his business career which had been
called his early bad manner, he had been little more
45 than a gambler of genius, his hand against every man's—
an infant prodigy—who brought to the enthralling
pursuit of speculation a brain better endowed than any
opposed to it. At St. Helena it was laid down that war
is a beautiful occupation; and so the young Manderson
50 had found the multitudinous and complicated dog-fight
of the Stock Exchange of New York.

Then came his change. At his father's death, when
Manderson was thirty years old, some new revelation
of the power and the glory of the god he served seemed
55 to have come upon him. With the sudden, elastic
adaptability of his nation he turned to steady labour
in his father's banking business, closing his ears to the

CONTINUE →

sound of the battles of the Street. In a few years he
came to control all the activity of the great firm whose
50 unimpeached conservatism, safety, and financial
weight lifted it like a cliff above the angry sea of the
markets. All mistrust founded on the performances of
his youth had vanished. He was quite plainly a different
man. How the change came about none could with
55 authority say, but there was a story of certain last words
spoken by his father, whom alone he had respected and
perhaps loved.

1

The main purpose of the passage is to

A) discuss the life of a powerful financier and explain
the impact of his death.

B) reveal the motivations behind a sudden change in
the life of a tycoon.

C) outline the reasons that a wealthy businessman
made few friends.

D) argue that prosperity is more likely to result from
hard work than from risky speculations.

2

Based on the information in the passage, Manderson
was known chiefly for his

A) sharp business practices and harsh manner toward
those he thought inferior.

B) vast wealth and willingness to lend money at low
interest rates.

C) European habits and unusual good fortune as a
gambler.

D) power and determination to protect the security
of the financial sector.

3

Which choice provides the best evidence for the
answer to the previous question?

A) Lines 13–15 ("In all . . . world")

B) Lines 23–26 ("he stood . . . Street")

C) Lines 27–31 ("The fortune . . . stock")

D) Lines 42–45 ("During . . . genius")

4

The passage suggests which of the following about
Manderson's death?

A) Its cause was unknown, but news of it spread
quickly throughout the financial world.

B) It served as a reminder that financial prosperity is
not more valuable than health.

C) It had a greater impact on Manderson's business
connections than on his personal connections.

D) It occurred when Manderson was only thirty years
old, at a time when many distrusted him.

5

Which choice provides the best evidence for the
answer to the previous question?

A) Lines 3–5 ("When . . . tear")

B) Lines 5–12 ("It gained . . . blow")

C) Lines 16–18 ("Financial . . . before")

D) Lines 52–55 ("At his . . . him")

6

As used in line 39, "quiet" most nearly means

A) silent.

B) still.

C) understated.

D) secluded.

7

In lines 48–51, the reference to St. Helena serves
primarily to

A) introduce a comparison illustrating Manderson's
view of his work.

B) present a dilemma that perplexed Manderson's
coworkers.

C) describe a significant event in the history of the
Stock Exchange.

D) suggest a potential career path dismissed by
Manderson.

CONTINUE

8

Which choice best describes Manderson's "change" (line 52)?

A) Supporter of a business to rival taking over that business

B) Soldier at St. Helena to powerful business magnate

C) Disrespectful prodigy to trusted clerk

D) Clever speculator to steadfast banker

9

As used in line 55, "elastic" most nearly means

A) rubbery.

B) flexible.

C) expandable.

D) looped.

CONTINUE

Questions 10–18 are based on the following passage and supplementary material.

This passage is adapted from "A Third of All Food Never Gets Eaten. How Can We Fix This?" by Elizabeth Royte, NG Image Collection. Published 2016.

With governments fretting over how to feed more than nine billion people by 2050, a dominant narrative calls for increasing global food production by 70 to 100 percent. But agriculture already represents one of the greatest threats to planetary health. It is responsible for 70 percent of the planet's freshwater withdrawals, 80 percent of the world's tropical and subtropical deforestation, and 30 to 35 percent of human-caused greenhouse gas emissions.

Meanwhile, nearly 800 million people worldwide suffer from hunger. But according to the Food and Agriculture Organization of the United Nations, we squander enough food—globally, 2.9 trillion pounds a year—to feed every one of them more than twice over. Where's all that food—about a third of the planet's production—going?

In developing nations much is lost postharvest for lack of adequate storage facilities, good roads, and refrigeration. In comparison, developed nations waste more food farther down the supply chain, when retailers order, serve, or display too much and when consumers ignore leftovers in the back of the fridge or toss perishables before they've expired.

Wasting food takes an environmental toll as well. Producing food that no one eats—whether sausages or snickerdoodles—also squanders the water, fertilizer, pesticides, seeds, fuel, and land needed to grow it. The quantities aren't trivial.

Globally a year's production of uneaten food guzzles as much water as the entire annual flow of the Volga, Europe's most voluminous river.

If food waste were a country, it would be the third largest producer of greenhouse gases in the world, after China and the U.S. On a planet of finite resources, with the expectation of at least two billion more residents by 2050, this profligacy, Tristram Stuart argues in his book *Waste: Uncovering the Global Food Scandal*, is obscene.

Every year some 2.9 trillion pounds of food—about a third of all that the world produces—never get consumed. Along the supply chain fruits and vegetables are lost or wasted at higher rates than other foods. Easily bruised and vulnerable to temperature swings en route from farm to table, they're also usually the first to get tossed at home.

Others have been making similar arguments for years, but reducing food waste has become a matter of international urgency. Some U.S. schools, where children dump up to 40 percent of their lunches into the trash, are setting up sharing tables, letting students serve themselves portions they know they'll eat, allotting more time for lunch, and scheduling it after recess—all proven methods of boosting consumption. Countless businesses, such as grocery stores, restaurants, and cafeterias, have stepped forward to combat waste by quantifying how much edible food isn't consumed, optimizing their purchasing, shrinking portion sizes, and beefing up efforts to move excess to charities. Stuart himself has made a specialty of investigating conditions farther up the supply chain, where supermarket standards and ordering practices lead to massive, but mostly hidden, dumps of edible food.

By the end of 2015 the UN and the U.S. had pledged to halve food waste by 2030. The exact mechanisms of this ambitious goal haven't been spelled out. But already countries and companies are devising and adopting standardized metrics to quantify waste. If the target is met, enough food could be saved to feed at least one billion people.

CONTINUE

Figure 1
Global Dairy Waste for Developed and
Developing Nations (per year)

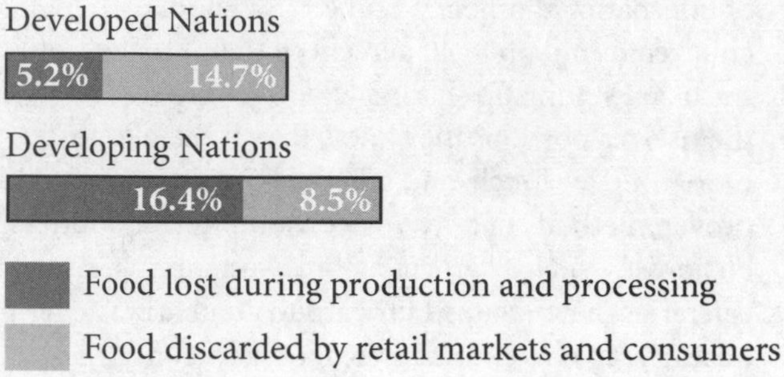

Developed Nations

| 5.2% | 14.7% |

Developing Nations

| 16.4% | 8.5% |

◼ Food lost during production and processing

◼ Food discarded by retail markets and consumers

Figure 2
World Food Waste by Type (per year)

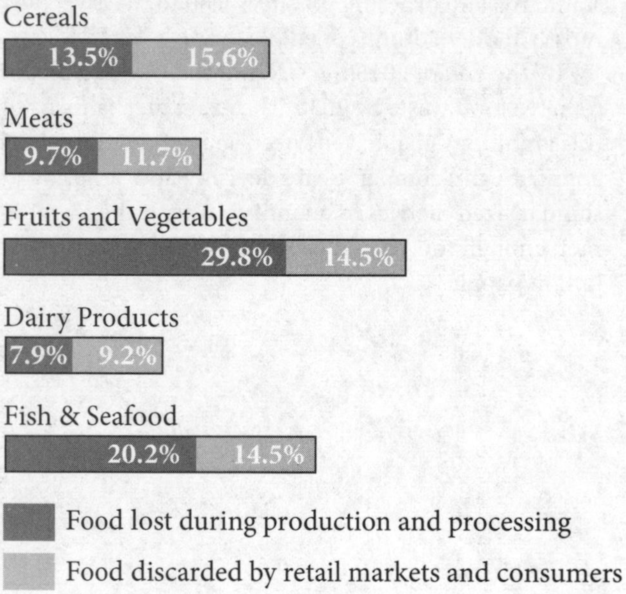

Cereals

| 13.5% | 15.6% |

Meats

| 9.7% | 11.7% |

Fruits and Vegetables

| 29.8% | 14.5% |

Dairy Products

| 7.9% | 9.2% |

Fish & Seafood

| 20.2% | 14.5% |

◼ Food lost during production and processing

◼ Food discarded by retail markets and consumers

10

As used in line 2, "dominant" most nearly means

A) aggressive.

B) forceful.

C) outstanding.

D) prominent.

11

According to the passage, agriculture has led to an increase in the

A) flow of Europe's drinkable river water.

B) cost of postharvest perishable goods.

C) strain placed on the environment.

D) number of people suffering from hunger.

12

Which choice provides the best evidence for the answer to the previous question?

A) Lines 5–9 ("It is . . . emissions")

B) Lines 17–19 ("In developing . . . refrigeration")

C) Lines 29–31 ("Globally a . . . river")

D) Lines 32–34 ("If food . . . U.S.")

13

The author indicates that the amount of food wasted annually across the globe

A) has steadily decreased since industrialization.

B) could feed every starving person in the world.

C) is the leading cause of malnutrition worldwide.

D) is not given sufficient attention.

CONTINUE

Which choice provides the best evidence for the answer to the previous question?

A) Lines 10–11 ("Meanwhile . . . hunger")

B) Lines 11–14 ("But according . . . over")

C) Lines 63–64 ("By the . . . 2030")

D) Lines 65–67 ("But already . . . waste")

5

In lines 25–26, the author includes the phrase "whether sausages or snickerdoodles" in order to

A) distinguish between the perceived values of food groups.

B) identify the food waste that environmentalists object to most strongly.

C) caution her readers against consuming particularly wasteful foods.

D) highlight the gravity of the overall effects of food waste.

16

As used in line 38, "obscene" most nearly means

A) censored.

B) improper.

C) vulgar.

D) outrageous.

17

Which idea is supported by both the passage and the information in figure 1?

A) Retail markets and consumers are responsible for a greater percentage of food waste in developed nations than in developing nations.

B) In developed nations, a lack of adequate food storage is responsible for the majority of post-production food waste.

C) Each year, developed and developing nations account for roughly the same amount of food waste.

D) A smaller percentage of food is lost during production and processing in developing nations than in developed nations.

18

Figure 2 most directly supports which statement from the passage?

A) Lines 1–4 ("With governments . . . percent")

B) Lines 19–23 ("In comparison . . . expired")

C) Lines 41–45 ("Along the . . . home")

D) Lines 53–58 ("Countless . . . charities")

CONTINUE

Questions 19–28 are based on the following passage and supplementary material.

This passage is adapted from "The Ability to Discriminate Paintings Found in Mice," a 2013 press release by Keio University

Keio University Professor Emeritus Shigeru Watanabe has reported the ability to discriminate paintings in pigeons and Java Sparrows in the past, but
Line his latest experiments have identified that this same
5 ability exists in mice. He began by examining if the mice stayed longer in front of paintings by Kandinsky or Mondrian. He found that most mice did not display any discrepancy in staying time (painting preference). They did not show a preference for paintings when shown
10 Renoir vs. Picasso, either. However, when mice were injected with morphine while viewing one painting and injected with saline solution when viewing the other, the mice clearly began to stay for longer periods near the paintings associated with morphine injection. In
15 the second experiment, mice were able to discriminate between pictures after training them to touch one of the pictures displayed on a touch screen in order to receive milk. Mice have been generally considered non-visual animals, but this research indicates that mice are
20 capable of higher-order visual perception.

Two types of apparatuses were used for the experiments. The first was an apparatus with three compartments. An iPod was installed on either side of the apparatus, and slide shows of pictures of paintings
25 were shown in sequence. Sensors recorded the staying time of mice in the compartments with their respective paintings. Next, mice were confined in one of the compartments with a painting immediately after receiving an injection of morphine (3mg/kg). During
30 this confinement, paintings were displayed on the iPod. The next day, mice received saline injections and were confined in another compartment and shown different paintings. After this procedure repeating three times, mice were allowed to walk freely around
35 the apparatus without any injection. As mice know that morphine causes pleasure, they should stay longer near the painting associated with the morphine injection if able to discriminate between paintings (Experiment 1).

40 The second apparatus was a touch screen on which a pair of paintings was displayed. If the mice touched one of the paintings—one of Kandinsky's paintings, for example—the mice would be rewarded with milk. If they touched the other painting (Mondrian's painting,
45 in this case), they would not receive milk. If mice are capable of discrimination, they should touch the painting associated with the milk reward (Experiment 2).

The first experiment, in which a slide show program
50 on the iPod displayed 10 paintings each of Kandinsky and Mondrian to the mice, did not indicate a longer staying time for either artist's paintings. Analysis of individual mice revealed only one mouse out of the twenty stayed longer near Kandinsky's paintings. The
55 mice did not indicate a preference for Picasso or Renoir either, although one mouse out of the twelve stayed longer near Renoir's painting. In the experiment which used morphine (conditioning in Experiment 1), mice stayed longer at the painting shown to them after the
60 morphine injection for both the Kandinsky/Mondrian and Picasso/Renoir pairs. In short, they were able to discriminate between the paintings. When mice were shown a number of the 10 paintings after the morphine injection (e.g. five Kandinsky paintings), they recorded
65 a longer staying time with the remaining paintings of the same artist, even when those paintings had not previously been shown to them (e.g. the five remaining Kandinsky paintings). This is a phenomenon called "generalization" and indicates that the mice were able
70 to categorize a certain style of painting into a group. In the touch screen experiment (Experiment 2), once mice could correctly discriminate the pairs of Kandinsky and Mondrian paintings, they were trained with different pairs. After repeating this four times, mice were able
75 to correctly choose the artist's painting in pairs of paintings never shown to them around 80% of the time. However, when the paintings were switched to Picasso-Renoir pairs, the mice were unable to choose correctly. This means that the mice were discriminating
80 or categorizing a painting style as a single group.

Among mammals, humans place importance on their sense of sight. Birds generally have excellent vision. Mice have excellent senses of smell and hearing, but it has been thought that they are non-visual
85 animals. This is understandable considering the fact that mice are nocturnal and burrowing creatures. This experiment demonstrates that mice have much better visual perception abilities than previously thought. Additionally, it means that perception of complex visual
90 stimuli like paintings extend to non-human animals.

CONTINUE

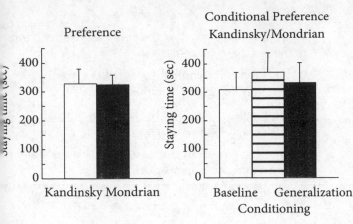

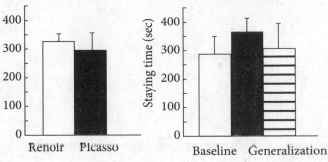

19

Which choice best reflects the overall structure of the passage?

A) An overview of an observed behavior is followed by two hypotheses that attempt to explain the behavior.

B) A discussion of a perceived scientific truth is followed by an alternative model.

C) The results of two experiments are followed by a description of the two experiments.

D) An outcome of a study is followed by an extension of the outcome to another field.

20

As used in line 12, "solution" most nearly means

A) mixture.

B) answer.

C) resolution.

D) key.

21

Which choice is an underlying assumption Professor Watanabe makes regarding "staying time?"

A) If mice stay longer with a painting, then it must be due to an association with the reward used.

B) If mice are given rewards, they will have better vision and therefore be better equipped to differentiate between paintings.

C) If mice spend more time viewing the paintings they saw when receiving a reward, then they are experiencing the same pleasure derived from the reward.

D) If mice stay with a painting for as long as pigeons and Java Sparrows, then the mice have the ability to discriminate between paintings.

22

Which choice provides the best evidence for the answer to the previous question?

A) Lines 1–5 ("Keio . . . in mice")

B) Lines 18–20 ("Mice have . . . perception")

C) Lines 33–35 ("After this . . . injection")

D) Lines 35–38 ("As mice . . . paintings")

23

As used in line 46, "discrimination" most nearly means

A) prejudice.

B) differentiation.

C) bias.

D) insight.

24

It can reasonably be inferred that Professor Watanabe showed the paintings to the mice prior to the conditioning experiments in order to

A) prove that the staying times increased by 80%.

B) familiarize them with the artists.

C) heighten their sense of anticipation for rewards.

D) establish a lack of preference without training.

25

Which choice best supports the claim that mice are more visually adept than they were conventionally believed to be?

A) Lines 54–57 ("The mice . . . painting")

B) Lines 77–79 ("However . . . correctly")

C) Lines 83–85 ("Mice have . . . animals")

D) Lines 86–88 ("This . . . thought")

26

The primary purpose of the final paragraph (lines 81–90) is to

A) explain the source of an error.

B) justify an experiment's methods.

C) discuss implications of a study's results.

D) suggest a topic for further research.

27

What main purpose does the figure serve in relation to the passage as a whole?

A) It resolves the conflicting conclusions of the various experiments in the passage.

B) It quantifies results of the first experiment discussed in the passage.

C) It offers a possible source of error that casts doubt on Professor Watanabe's conclusions.

D) It suggests a different interpretation than that presented in the passage.

28

Based on information in the passage and in the figure the mice, in general,

A) showed an ability to generalize from paintings to art of other media by the same artist.

B) had a greater appreciation for Picasso than Renoir before the conditioning.

C) exhibited increased staying times following conditioning with morphine.

D) were influenced less by the milk reward than by the morphine reward.

CONTINUE

Questions 29–38 are based on the following passage.

This passage is adapted from *The Federalist Papers,* written by Alexander Hamilton, John Jay, and James Madison in 1788. In this piece, John Jay discusses maintaining the United States as a single nation or dividing the country into a collection of small independent sovereignties.

To the People of the State of New York:

When the people of America reflect that they are now called upon to decide a question, which, in its consequences, must prove one of the most important that ever engaged their attention, the propriety of their taking a very comprehensive, as well as a very serious, view of it, will be evident.

Nothing is more certain than the indispensable necessity of government, and it is equally undeniable,
10 that whenever and however it is instituted, the people must cede to it some of their natural rights in order to vest it with requisite powers. It is well worthy of consideration therefore, whether it would conduce more to the interest of the people of America that they
15 should, to all general purposes, be one nation, under one federal government, or that they should divide themselves into separate confederacies, and give to the head of each the same kind of powers which they are advised to place in one national government.

20 It has until lately been a received and uncontradicted opinion that the prosperity of the people of America depended on their continuing firmly united, and the wishes, prayers, and efforts of our best and wisest citizens have been constantly directed to that object.
25 But politicians now appear, who insist that this opinion is erroneous, and that instead of looking for safety and happiness in union, we ought to seek it in a division of the States into distinct confederacies or sovereignties. However extraordinary this new doctrine may appear,
30 it nevertheless has its advocates; and certain characters who were much opposed to it formerly, are at present of the number. Whatever may be the arguments or inducements which have wrought this change in the sentiments and declarations of these gentlemen, it
35 certainly would not be wise in the people at large to adopt these new political tenets without being fully convinced that they are founded in truth and sound policy.

It has often given me pleasure to observe that
40 independent America was not composed of detached and distant territories, but that one connected, fertile, wide-spreading country was the portion of our western

sons of liberty. Providence has in a particular manner blessed it with a variety of soils and productions, and
45 watered it with innumerable streams, for the delight and accommodation of its inhabitants. A succession of navigable waters forms a kind of chain round its borders, as if to bind it together; while the most noble rivers in the world, running at convenient
50 distances, present them with highways for the easy communication of friendly aids, and the mutual transportation and exchange of their various commodities. With equal pleasure I have as often taken notice that Providence has been pleased to give this
55 one connected country to one united people—a people descended from the same ancestors, speaking the same language, professing the same religion, attached to the same principles of government, very similar in their manners and customs, and who, by their
60 joint counsels, arms, and efforts, fighting side by side throughout a long and bloody war, have nobly established general liberty and independence.

This country and this people seem to have been made for each other, and it appears as if it was the
65 design of Providence, that an inheritance so proper and convenient for a band of brethren, united to each other by the strongest ties, should never be split into a number of unsocial, jealous, and alien sovereignties.

29

The position that Jay takes in this essay can best be described as that of

A) an impartial onlooker pointing out both sides of an issue.

B) a leader arguing for a particular outcome.

C) an intellectual studying a historical decision.

D) a spokesperson seeking a reasonable compromise.

30

As used in line 12, "vest" most nearly means

A) clothe.

B) abandon.

C) endow.

D) belong.

31

According to Jay, which of the following questions about the American political system arose shortly before the passage was written?

A) Whether it is truly necessary for the people to give up some of their rights to the government

B) Whether it is better for America to be governed as one nation or for each state to be governed independently

C) Whether it is best to give all authority to the federal government or to reserve some powers for the states

D) Whether the American people should share one common language and religion

32

Which choice provides the best evidence for the answer to the previous question?

A) Lines 8–12 ("Nothing . . . powers")

B) Lines 25–28 ("But politicians . . . sovereignties")

C) Lines 43–46 ("Providence . . . inhabitants")

D) Lines 53–62 ("With equal . . . independence")

33

Jay indicates that those who choose to support dividing the country into separate confederacies

A) are contradicting the wishes, prayers, and efforts of the majority of its citizens.

B) value independence over safety and happiness.

C) should not do so without first examining the issue thoroughly.

D) are threatening the prosperity of the nation by encouraging political turmoil.

34

Which choice provides the best evidence for the answer to the previous question?

A) Lines 20–22 ("It has . . . united")

B) Lines 29–32 ("However . . . number")

C) Lines 32–38 ("Whatever . . . policy")

D) Lines 39–43 ("It has . . . liberty")

35

In lines 39–43, Jay makes a distinction between

A) self-reliance and liberty.

B) secluded provinces and a unified domain.

C) deserted marketplaces and lush farmland.

D) division and independence.

36

In the context of the passage as a whole, Jay's references to "innumerable streams" (line 45), "navigable waters" (line 47), and "noble rivers" (line 49) primarily serve to

A) endorse the protection of natural resources.

B) inspire an adventurous spirit.

C) summarize a complicated position.

D) support an argument through comparison.

37

In saying "with equal pleasure" (line 53), Jay suggests that he

A) finds the unity among the country's people as satisfying as the connections in the country's geography.

B) would be just as happy to have the states unified as he would to have them divided.

C) would enjoy meeting new people if he had the opportunity to travel more.

D) would prefer traveling by water as much as he would prefer traveling by land.

38

The list in lines 55–59 ("a people . . . customs") primarily serves to

A) outline a method that Jay has endorsed.

B) summarize the points that Jay has dismissed.

C) provide support for a claim Jay has made.

D) restate the key issues Jay's audience must settle.

CONTINUE →

Questions 39–47 are based on the following passages.

Passage 1 is adapted from "Tardigrades become first animals to survive vacuum of space" by Ed Yong © 2016. Passage 2 is adapted from "These 'Indestructible' Animals Would Survive a Planet-Wide Apocalypse" by Casey Smith, NG Image Collection. Published 2018.

Passage 1

In September last year, a team of scientists launched a squad of tiny animals into space aboard a Russian satellite. Once in orbit, the creatures were shunted into
5 ventilated containers that exposed them to the vacuum of space. In this final frontier, they had no air and they were subjected to extreme dehydration, freezing temperatures, weightlessness and lashings of both cosmic and solar radiation. It's hard to imagine a more inhospitable environment for life but not only did the critters survive,
10 they managed to reproduce on their return to Earth. Meet the planet's toughest animals – the tardigrades. Tardigrades are small aquatic invertebrates that are also known as "water bears", after their impossibly cute shuffling walk. They also happen to be nigh-invincible and
15 can tolerate extreme environments that would kill almost any other animal. They can take temperatures close to absolute zero, punishing doses of radiation and prolonged periods of drought. And now, they have become the only animals to have ever survived the raw vacuum of space.
20 Their stellar adventure began with Ingemar Jonsson from Kristianstad University, who really wanted to test the limits of their resilience. To that end, he launched adults from two species (*Richtersius coronifer* and *Milnesium tardigradum*) into space aboard the
25 FOTON-M3 spacecraft, as part of a mission amusingly known as TARDIS (Tardigrades In Space). The tardinauts spent ten days in low Earth orbit, about 270km above sea level. The tardigrades were sent into orbit in a dry, dormant state called a "tun" and it's this
30 dessicated form that is the key to their extraordinary levels of endurance. By replacing almost all of the water in their bodies with a sugar called trehalose, they can escape many of the things that would otherwise kill them. Jonsson says, "Environmental agents that rely
35 on water or the respiratory system don't work. You can put a dry tardigrade in pure alcohol and expose them to poisonous gases without killing them."

The ability to dry out completely is an adaptation to the tardigrades' precarious environment – damp pools
40 or patches of water on moss or lichen that can easily

evaporate. They have evolved to cope with sporadic drought and can stay dormant for years. All it takes to revive them is a drop of water, and that's exactly what happened when the TARDIS astronauts returned to Earth.

Passage 2

45 The world's most robust animals may very well survive until the sun stops shining. Tardigrades are tiny water-dwelling creatures famed for their resiliency. The eight-legged invertebrates can survive for up to 30 years without food or water and can endure wild temperature
50 extremes, radiation exposure, and even the vacuum of space. At a minimum, all of Earth's oceans would have to boil away to completely wipe out all life on the planet. Although tardigrades are only known to survive high temperatures when dry—and those species living in the
55 sea would likely die before the waters boiled—tardigrades are still expected to avoid extinction until our sun swells up and becomes a red giant roughly six billion years from now, according to researchers who investigated the effects of various doomsday scenarios, and who described the
60 results in the journal Scientific Reports.

Astrophysical events such as asteroid strikes have been fingered as the causes of past mass extinctions on Earth. Such violent cataclysms could easily wipe out humans: We belong to a sensitive species, and subtle
65 changes in the environment impact us dramatically, notes study co-author Rafael Alves Batista of the University of Oxford.

Intrigued by the resilience of tardigrades, Alves Batista and his colleagues wanted to explore the effects
70 of potential astrophysical catastrophes on more than just human life. There are asteroids out there that do pose collision risks and are large enough to trigger an "impact winter," blotting out sunlight and causing temperatures to drop. This would be catastrophic for
75 many life-forms on the surface, but tardigrades would have a refuge.

"Tardigrades can live around volcanic vents at the bottom of the ocean, which means they have a huge shield against the kind of events that would be catastrophic
80 for humans," Sloan says. In essence, the researchers say, only the death of the sun will ultimately lead to the total extinction of life on Earth, including tardigrades.

Tardigrades are as close to indestructible as it gets on Earth," Alves Batista says, "but it's possible that
85 there are other resilient species examples elsewhere in the universe."

39

In Passage 1, which choice provides the best support for the author's statement that space is an "inhospitable environment for life"?

A) Lines 3–5 ("Once in . . . space")

B) Lines 5–8 ("In this . . . radiation")

C) Lines 18–19 ("And now . . . space")

D) Lines 26–28 ("The tardinauts . . . level")

40

As used in line 15, "tolerate" most nearly means

A) permit.

B) indulge.

C) endure.

D) ignore.

41

The author of Passage 1 indicates that tardigrades can survive in hostile environments due to which unique trait?

A) Shuffling walk

B) Tolerance for famine

C) Small size

D) Ability to replace water with sugar

42

Which choice provides the best evidence for the answer to the previous question?

A) Lines 1–3 ("In September . . . satellite")

B) Lines 12–16 ("Tardigrades . . . animal")

C) Lines 31–34 ("By replacing . . . them")

D) Lines 42–44 ("All it . . . Earth")

43

As used in line 45, "robust" most nearly means

A) round.

B) tough.

C) flavorful.

D) healthy.

44

A student claimed that tardigrades would likely face extinction before humans. Would the author of Passage 2 most likely agree with the student's claim?

A) Yes, because the author states that tardigrades are nearly indestructible and can go long periods without food or water.

B) Yes, because the author states that tardigrades are vulnerable to both asteroid impacts and the death of the sun.

C) No, because the author states that tardigrades may be protected from cataclysmic events that would be highly destructive for humans.

D) No, because the author states that tardigrades are vulnerable to astrophysical events such as asteroid strikes.

45

The main purpose of both Passage 1 and Passage 2 is to

A) examine the methods of testing the resiliency of invertebrates in space.

B) claim that invertebrates living in water are less able to withstand extreme environments.

C) describe the high level of resiliency of a particular invertebrate.

D) imagine invertebrates in different catastrophic scenarios.

CONTINUE

46

Based on the information provided in Passage 2, the "water bears" referred to in line 13

A) belong to the subphylum of vertebrates.

B) are related to tuns.

C) are made of trehalose.

D) have eight legs.

47

Based on Passages 1 and 2, which of the following is most likely a natural habitat of the "water-dwelling creatures" (line 47)?

A) Volcanic lava domes

B) Vacuum of space

C) Water pipes in homes

D) Patches of lichen

STOP
**If you finish before time is called, you may check your work on this section only.
Do not turn to any other section in the test.**

Writing and Language Test

35 MINUTES, 44 QUESTIONS

Turn to Section 2 of your answer sheet to answer the questions in this section.

DIRECTIONS

Each passage below is accompanied by a number of questions. For some questions, you will consider how the passage might be revised to improve the expression of ideas. For other questions, you will consider how the passage might be edited to correct errors in sentence structure, usage, or punctuation. A passage or a question may be accompanied by one or more graphics (such as a table or graph) that you will consider as you make revising and editing decisions.

Some questions will direct you to an underlined portion of a passage. Other questions will direct you to a location in a passage or ask you to think about the passage as a whole.

After reading each passage, choose the answer to each question that most effectively improves the quality of writing in the passage or that makes the passage conform to the conventions of standard written English. Many questions include a "NO CHANGE" option. Choose that option if you think the best choice is to leave the relevant portion of the passage as it is.

Questions 1–11 are based on the following passage.

The Nobel Prize and the School of...

The Nobel Prize has been awarded in a variety of categories since 1901. There aren't many **1** exceptions on the list. As one would expect, the early prizes were given mostly to Americans and **2** people who hailed from Europe, but the committee has since become more international. The winners of the prizes have aged alongside increasing life expectancy. In the early days, the average winner of the Nobel Prize in Physics was in **3** their early 50s. Nowadays it's fairly surprising to see a winner in any category who is younger than 60.

1

A) NO CHANGE
B) surprises
C) outliers
D) abominations

2

A) NO CHANGE
B) those of European descent,
C) people from Europe,
D) Europeans,

3

A) NO CHANGE
B) one's
C) his or her
D) they're

CONTINUE

4 The winners in most categories come from the elite research institutions in the United States and abroad: Harvard, MIT, Stanford, Caltech, Cambridge, Columbia, and Berkeley. Not, however, the winners of the Nobel Prize in Literature. These winners share an average age (64) and geographical diversity with those in other **5** categories, though they have not attended the same schools—not by a long shot. Eugene O'Neill, one of the first American laureates, did spend one year at Princeton, but he did not finish, completing the "education" that would inspire his great works while working as a seaman and an active member of the Marine Transport Workers Union. The most **6** recent prize went to Toni Morrison earned her undergraduate degree at Howard University in Washington, D.C.

Which choice most effectively establishes the main topic of the paragraph?

A) Old as they are, nevertheless, winners in all categories tend to be affiliated with the same universities.

B) One surprise in the list of Nobel Prize winners, however, has to do with the educational backgrounds of some winners.

C) Most of the best research is done by college students and their professors.

D) It will shock no one that all Nobel prize winners are highly intelligent in one way or another.

A) NO CHANGE

B) categories; though

C) categories however

D) categories. Though

A) NO CHANGE

B) choice in literature was Toni Morrison

C) recent winner, whose name was Toni Morrison,

D) recent recipient of the prize, Toni Morrison,

[1] This trend should remind us that creativity can strike anywhere, and one of the Nobel committee's great merits is that that **7** <u>they have</u> been willing to identify great talent outside of the typical places. [2] Work in economics, medicine, or the sciences **8** <u>requires</u> a vibrant, collaborative atmosphere, with the best minds in the field working together toward solutions. [3] The elite universities of the world provide just such an atmosphere. [4] Literary labor requires the mind and circumstances of a great writer, plus a healthy dose of imagination and courage. [5] While the other fields celebrate great **9** <u>accomplishments, discoveries, and new findings,</u> the Nobel Prize in Literature celebrates great individual minds, those that contain all there is to know and more. [6] Work in literature, however, needs no such place. **10**

These trends show that great thinkers and scholars do not live only at the big research universities. Anyone with an open mind can do great things, **11** <u>and it's not unreasonable to expect that you'd find the most open minds at the best schools.</u> The trends among Nobel laureates in literature teach us much the same lesson that literature itself does. There is an endless supply of wonder in our infinitely diverse world, and those with the willingness to see it will always be rewarded.

7
A) NO CHANGE
B) we are
C) it has
D) they might've

8
A) NO CHANGE
B) require
C) do require
D) has required

9
A) NO CHANGE
B) accomplishments, findings, and new discoveries
C) accomplishments and finding discoveries
D) accomplishments and new discoveries

10
For the sake of the logic and coherence of this paragraph, sentence 6 should be placed
A) where it is now.
B) after sentence 2.
C) after sentence 3.
D) after sentence 4.

11
Which choice would most effectively support the assertion made in this sentence and paragraph as a whole?
A) NO CHANGE
B) whether that's in a high-end graduate program, a community college, or the workforce.
C) although here, too, the Literature laureates are an exception.
D) but obviously an author of fiction needs to have a very open mind to begin with.

CONTINUE

Questions 12–22 are based on the following passage and supplementary material.

I'd Rather Be With An Animal

Many children dream of being veterinarians. Working all day with animals just like one's dog, cat, **12** fish or horse seems, like a dream come true. For some reason, though, kids seem to grow out of this fantasy as they get older, with **13** fewer than 3,000 veterinary school graduates each year in the United States. It may be time, however, to bring the dream back: the U.S. Bureau of Labor Statistics predicts that, between 2010 and 2020, **14** the U.S. economy will see some slow growth. The need for veterinary technicians is predicted to grow even more quickly, **15** although the data show that other professions will grow even more quickly.

Veterinary Technologists and Technicians
Percent change in employment, projected 2010–20

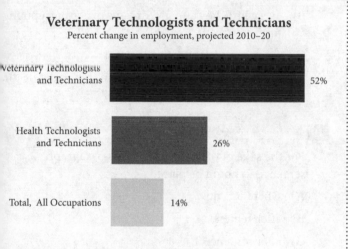

Veterinary Technologists and Technicians — 52%

Health Technologists and Technicians — 26%

Total, All Occupations — 14%

Note: All Occupations include all occupations in the U.S. Economy.
Source: U.S. Bureau of Labor Statistics, Employment Projections program

12
A) NO CHANGE
B) fish, or, horse seems
C) fish, or horse seems
D) fish or, horse seems

13
A) NO CHANGE
B) less than
C) fewer then
D) less then

14
Which of the following true statements best supports the statement made earlier in this sentence?
A) NO CHANGE
B) many children will be born in the United States.
C) some veterinarians will retire.
D) the veterinary profession will grow by 36 percent.

15
Which choice completes the sentence with accurate data based on the graph?
A) NO CHANGE
B) at over three times the rate of all occupations in the United States.
C) but being a health technician has equally positive job prospects.
D) largely because these positions can be filled by those who have not gone to veterinary school.

CONTINUE

For many years, veterinarians have provided a series of basic services for household **16** pets. From basic check-ups and shots to neutering and defanging. Today, however, pets have a longer life expectancy than in the past, and **17** they are required to perform more and more procedures involving animal cancers, skin abscesses, and torn ligaments and cartilage. Medical expenses are now a significant factor in the cost of pet ownership, and companies offering Veterinary Pet Insurance (VPI) are sprouting up all over the country.

[1] If this seems to resemble medical care for humans, it's not mere coincidence. [2] In fact, the word "owners" may itself be a misnomer: **18** some pets are shared between friends. [3] There are many cultural factors leading to this increase in attention and intimacy. [4] The main one may be that as young men and women are getting married and starting families later in life, they are more likely to own pets as new college graduates and young professionals. [5] For many pet owners, dogs and cats are more "human" than ever before. **19**

16

A) NO CHANGE
B) pets—from
C) pets; from
D) pets from,

17

A) NO CHANGE
B) we
C) veterinarians
D) all of them

18

Which choice best emphasizes that many pet owners consider their pets to be more human than animal?

A) NO CHANGE
B) every little boy and girl dreams of getting a puppy for Christmas.
C) many now self-identify as pet "parents."
D) pets are a great way to teach children about death.

19

For the sake of the cohesion of this paragraph, sentence 5 should be placed

A) where it is now.
B) after sentence 1.
C) after sentence 2.
D) after sentence 3.

CONTINUE

As pets continue to take on a new symbolic importance, the need for veterinary specialization is increasing. There is a huge **20** demand, for instance, for the work of specialists in veterinary dentistry and animal behaviorism as these fields become better understood. In the latter particularly, there is an obvious correlation between the humanity of pets and the perceived complexity of **21** their minds and of the way they think. There have also been significant increases in the very "human" procedures of hip replacements, blood transfusions, and organ transplants.

Veterinary advocates have been quick to point out that increases in animal health correlate directly with increases in human health. Given the increase in people living alone and the decrease in the average number of children per family, an animal's companionship can provide **22** stuff that is often attributed to the traditional nuclear family. The grandeur of childhood dreams may not be so unreasonable after all: as the veterinary profession grows, veterinary science will increasingly become a part of how we understand the human experience.

20

A) NO CHANGE
B) demand for instance
C) demand for, instance,
D) demand for instance,

21

A) NO CHANGE
B) the way they think about things.
C) what they mind.
D) their minds.

22

A) NO CHANGE
B) one of the things
C) all
D) the stability

Questions 23–33 are based on the following passage.

Veterans in School

23 It may seem commonplace today for many people to go to college, this is a relatively recent development. For much of American history, a university education was reserved only for the very wealthy, but all of that changed with the G.I. Bill.

The Servicemen's Readjustment Act, the G.I. Bill's official name, was signed into law in 1944. More than twenty years earlier, **24** after the conclusion of World War I, the veterans of the bloodiest war on record were more or less forgotten by the U.S. government. Many of them were given little more than a $60 allowance and a train ticket home. While **25** they're was some talk of military bonuses, those bonuses were not easily obtained. As a result, **26** a group of 1932 veterans marched into Washington to achieve its bonus demands. The march ended bitterly: no bonuses were paid, and many protesters were chased off by armed military.

23

A) NO CHANGE

B) Because it

C) While it

D) Really, it

24

Which of the following true choices provides the information most consistent with the rest of the sentence?

A) NO CHANGE

B) so that would be around 1924,

C) two decades into the twentieth century,

D) when the G.I. Bill hadn't been written yet,

25

A) NO CHANGE

B) it

C) their

D) there

26

A) NO CHANGE

B) Washington invited the bonus veterans to march in 1932 on it.

C) in 1932, a group of veterans marched on Washington to demand the bonuses.

D) a group of veterans planned to march on 1932 bonuses for Washington.

CONTINUE

As World War II neared its end, though, the U.S. government sought to avoid another such standoff. Indeed, for many, the goal was less idealistic: the 27 tremendous unemployment, among World War I veterans, was seen as accelerating the economic collapse of the Great Depression. 28 Hoping to avoid either or both of these catastrophes, Congress passed the Servicemen's Readjustment Act, which included provisions for education, home loans, and unemployment insurance.

27

A) NO CHANGE

B) tremendous unemployment among World War I veterans

C) tremendous, unemployment among, World War I veterans

D) tremendous unemployment among World War I veterans,

28

Which of the following choices best agrees with the ideas discussed in this paragraph?

A) NO CHANGE

B) In 1944, a year before World War II ended officially,

C) Almost three years after the Japanese attack on Pearl Harbor,

D) Perhaps for other reasons that historians don't understand,

CONTINUE

One of the perhaps unintended consequences **29** in university education was a revolution in the United States. In 1947, veterans on the G.I. Bill accounted for 49 percent of college admissions. By 1956, of the 16 million World War II veterans, nearly half had used the G.I. Bill for some kind of training. Therefore, by the early 1960s, college training **30** had changed drastically. For the first time in American history, college was truly democratic: it was not limited to the very wealthy. Instead, **31** college could be a new springboard for the upwardly mobile. Interestingly, in this same span, the least utilized of all benefits was that of unemployment: while veterans came in droves to attend colleges and get help financing their homes, very few used the unemployment subsidy.

32 Some years are better for the G.I. Bill than others. In 2008, for instance, the bill was expanded to include more support for servicemen and women, including the ability to transfer unused benefits to husbands, wives, and children. We may not expect a piece of wartime legislation to have been so **33** good, but the G.I. Bill changed the face of education as we know it, and we feel its effects all around us.

29

The best placement for the underlined portion would be

A) where it is now.

B) at the beginning of the sentence (adjusting punctuation and capitalization accordingly).

C) after the word *was.*

D) after the word *revolution.*

30

A) NO CHANGE

B) changes

C) changing

D) would change

31

Which of the following choices best supports the idea presented in the previous sentence?

A) NO CHANGE

B) most of the beneficiaries were still pretty wealthy.

C) the criteria for selection were not based on income.

D) few could hope to reach the economic status of earlier college graduates.

32

Which of the following best introduces the topic of this paragraph?

A) NO CHANGE

B) The benefits of the bill continue to this day.

C) G.I.s can do many things with their degrees.

D) The home subsidy is an underappreciated part of the bill.

33

A) NO CHANGE

B) educational

C) influential

D) intelligent

CONTINUE ➡

Questions 34–44 are based on the following passage and supplementary material.

The Ecological Recovery of Detroit

The borderland between the United States and Canada was **34** hotly contested in its early history. Fighting between the English, the French, the Native Americans, and the newly independent Americans made the region one of the most volatile of the early 1800s. While many humans and animals have influenced the history of the region, one **35** animals influence, the beavers, has been as significant as it is overlooked. Although Michigan eventually became a powerhouse in the later part of the Industrial Revolution, it was initially attractive to settlers who wanted to cash in on the fur trade, and beaver pelts were some of the hottest commodities.

The city of Detroit was founded on *le détroit,* **36** which is where the name obviously comes from. Antoine Laumet de la Mothe, sieur de Cadillac, and his fellow settlers saw this "*détroit*" as the perfect place to build a fort to protect their fur interests. Their plans were successful, and within a very short **37** span. Furs had become the dominant trade items in the region. By the mid-1700s, after the British had seized control of the region, beaver skins had become almost universally accepted as currency, and the Hudson Bay Company issued beaver-shaped tokens that were valued at one skin each.

34

Which of the following most effectively supports the ideas in this paragraph?
A) NO CHANGE
B) bitterly cold
C) primarily enforested
D) boldly international

35

A) NO CHANGE
B) animal influence, the beaver,
C) animals' influence, the beaver's,
D) animal's influence, the beaver's,

36

Which of the following true statements best clarifies the information given in the first part of this sentence?
A) NO CHANGE
B) the "strait" of the river connecting Lake St. Clair to Lake Erie.
C) on the borderland between southern Canada and the northern United States.
D) just across the river from modern-day Windsor, Ontario.

37

A) NO CHANGE
B) span; furs
C) span, furs
D) span, but furs

38 Finite resources built the unfortunate universal popularity of it. For instance, beaver skins were popular in the stylish clothes of the day, particularly hats. Although silks had become more popular than animal skins in the early 1800s, by that time the beaver had been hunted to the point that **39** it was nearly eliminated from the region altogether. In addition, the region around Detroit had grown in population, and much of the beaver habitat around the rivers had been replaced by homes and would soon be replaced by factories. **40** Then, in the twentieth century, Detroit became the "Motor City," the main producer of automobiles in the United States, certainly not a place where wildlife could **41** think about living anymore.

38

A) NO CHANGE
B) The unfortunate resources were also universally finite in popularity.
C) Unfortunately, this universal popularity was built on finite resources.
D) Universal popularity came with the unfortunate finitude of resources.

39

A) NO CHANGE
B) it's
C) they were
D) one was

40

The writer is considering deleting the phrase "by factories" from the previous sentence and adjusting the punctuation accordingly. Should the phrase be kept or deleted?

A) Kept, because it helps to emphasize that the auto industry is largely to blame for the extinction of the beaver.
B) Kept, because it clarifies what in addition to houses has replaced the beaver habitat.
C) Deleted, because it repeats information given earlier in the sentence.
D) Deleted, because it paints an unnecessarily negative portrait of the Industrial Revolution in Detroit.

41

A) NO CHANGE
B) migrate to with the seasons.
C) be enjoyed by all.
D) continue to thrive.

CONTINUE ▶

Detroit's population peaked in the 1950s, but since the 1960s, the auto industry and population have declined precipitately. [42] Between 1990 and 2010 alone, the population of Detroit was reduced by over half. Large parts of the city are now abandoned, and thousands of abandoned houses and lots are overgrown with nature, earning them the title "urban prairies." Although Detroit [43] may have long been seen as a hotbed of urban blight, it is now becoming a place of new beginnings. Where one might see urban decay, for instance, many have come to see a resurgence of the wilderness, emblematized by, of all things, the return of the beaver. [44] Unlike other cities, parts of Detroit, it seems, may be returning to something like a "natural state." Josh Hartig, with the U.S. Fish and Wildlife Service, has called the renaturalization of the area "one of the most dramatic ecological recovery stories in North America."

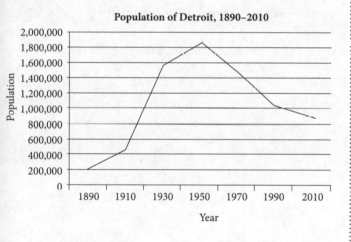

Population of Detroit, 1890–2010

42

Which choice completes the sentence with accurate data based on the graph?

A) NO CHANGE

B) Throughout the twentieth century,

C) Between 1890 and 1950,

D) From 1950 to 2010,

43

A) NO CHANGE

B) may of

C) might of

D) would have

44

A) NO CHANGE

B) As is not the case in other cities,

C) Dissimilar to some parts,

D) Different from other cities,

STOP
**If you finish before time is called, you may check your work on this section only.
Do not turn to any other section in the test.**

Math Test – No Calculator

25 MINUTES, 17 QUESTIONS

Turn to Section 3 of your answer sheet to answer the questions in this section.

For questions 1–13, solve each problem, choose the best answer from the choices provided, and fill in the corresponding circle on your answer sheet. **For questions 14–17**, solve the problem and enter your answer in the grid on the answer sheet. Please refer to the directions before question 14 on how to enter your answers in the grid. You may use any available space in your test booklet for scratch work.

NOTES

1. The use of a calculator **is not permitted**.
2. All variables and expressions used represent real numbers unless otherwise indicated.
3. Figures provided in this test are drawn to scale unless otherwise indicated.
4. All figures lie in a plane unless otherwise indicated.
5. Unless otherwise indicated, the domain of a given function f is the set of all real numbers x for which $f(x)$ is a real number.

REFERENCE

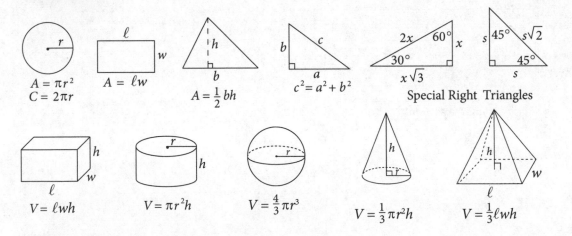

$A = \pi r^2$
$C = 2\pi r$

$A = \ell w$

$A = \frac{1}{2} bh$

$c^2 = a^2 + b^2$

Special Right Triangles

$V = \ell wh$

$V = \pi r^2 h$

$V = \frac{4}{3}\pi r^3$

$V = \frac{1}{3}\pi r^2 h$

$V = \frac{1}{3}\ell wh$

The number of degrees of arc in a circle is 360.
The number of radians of arc in a circle is 2π.
The sum of the measures in degrees of the angles of a triangle is 180.

CONTINUE

1

Which of the following are the solutions to the equation $3x^2 - 48 = 0$?

A) $-\dfrac{\sqrt{48}}{3}$ and $\dfrac{\sqrt{48}}{3}$

B) -4 and 4

C) $-\sqrt{48}$ and $\sqrt{48}$

D) -16 and 16

2

At an organic farm, a 2.6 square kilometer plot of soybeans is being harvested. If the farm workers can harvest 23 hectares a day, which of the following functions can be used to estimate how many <u>hectares</u>, $H(d)$, will remain to be harvested after d days?

(Note: 100 hectares = 1 square kilometer)

A) $H(d) = 2.6 \quad 0.23d$

B) $H(d) = 2.6 - 23d$

C) $H(d) = 260 - 23d$

D) $H(d) = 2,300 - 260d$

3

$$13 - \frac{3}{4}x = \frac{3}{8}x - 5$$

What is the value of x in the equation above?

A) 8

B) 9

C) 16

D) $\dfrac{81}{4}$

4

$$y < \frac{1}{4}(3y - 2)$$

Which of the following values of y would make the above inequality true?

A) -3

B) -2

C) 0

D) 3

5

Which of the following is equivalent to the expression $ab^2 - 3ab + 2b - 6$?

A) $(a + 2)(b - 3)$

B) $(ab + 2)(b - 3)$

C) $b(a + 3)(b - 3)$

D) $b(ab - 3a) + 2(b - 6)$

6

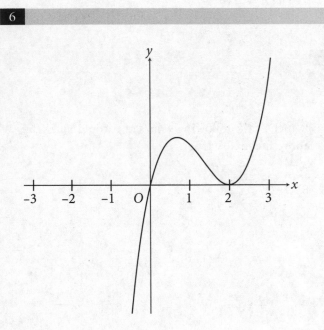

The function f is shown in the xy-plane above. Which of the following could be $f(x)$?

A) $f(x) = x(x + 2)$

B) $f(x) = x(x - 2)$

C) $f(x) = x(x + 2)^2$

D) $f(x) = x(x - 2)^2$

7

Line a is given by the equation $y = 2x - 3$. Which of the following equations represents a line that intersects line a in the xy-plane at the point $\left(\dfrac{5}{2}, 2\right)$?

A) $4x - 3y = 4$

B) $2x + 3y = 5$

C) $y - 2x = 1$

D) $y = -\dfrac{1}{2}x - 3$

8

Which of the following expressions is equivalent to $(x + 2)(x - 5) - 18$?

A) $(x - 4)(x + 7)$

B) $x^2 - 3x - 8$

C) $x^2 - 3x - 25$

D) $(x - 7)(x + 4)$

CONTINUE

9

$$\cfrac{1}{\cfrac{1}{2y} - \cfrac{1}{y+3}}$$

For all $y > 3$, which of the following is equivalent to the expression above?

A) $3 - y$

B) $\dfrac{2y^2 + 6y}{3 - y}$

C) $\dfrac{3 - y}{2y^2 + 6y}$

D) $2y^2 + 6y$

10

$$h(x) = 9 - |x - 3|$$

In the equation above, $h(n) = h(-3)$. Which of the following could be the value of n ?

A) -6

B) 3

C) 9

D) 12

11

$$C = 0.08(B - x)$$

A new county regulation requires that a school system spend a certain amount of its discretionary budget each month on curriculum-based activities and a certain percentage of the remainder on after-school clubs. The equation above gives the amount, C dollars, that a school must spend on after-school clubs based on B dollars, the discretionary budget that month, and x dollars, the amount that must be spent on curriculum-based activities. If a school with a monthly discretionary budget of $9,000 must spend $320 on after-school clubs, what is the school required to spend on curriculum-based activities?

A) $4,000

B) $5,000

C) $8,000

D) $8,680

12

$$P = 2,500 + 135x$$

The population of County Y, <u>in thousands</u>, can be modeled by the above equation, in which x represents the number of years since the 2010 census. What does the number 135 represent in this equation?

A) Every year the population of County Y increases by 135 people.

B) Every 135 years that passes, the population of County Y increases by 2,500 people.

C) Every 135 years that passes, the population of County Y increases by 250,000 people.

D) Every year the population of County Y increases by 135,000 people.

CONTINUE

13

$$\frac{\sqrt{x^5}}{\sqrt[4]{x^3}} = x^b$$

If the expression above is true for all values of x where $x > 0$, what is the value of b ?

A) $\dfrac{1}{4}$

B) $\dfrac{5}{3}$

C) $\dfrac{7}{4}$

D) $\dfrac{10}{3}$

CONTINUE

DIRECTIONS

For questions 14–17, solve the problem and enter your answer in the grid, as described below, on the answer sheet.

1. Although not required, it is suggested that you write your answer in the boxes at the top of the columns to help you fill in the circles accurately. You will receive credit only if the circles are filled in correctly.

2. Mark no more than one circle in any column.

3. No question has a negative answer.

4. Some problems may have more than one correct answer. In such cases, grid only one answer.

5. **Mixed numbers** such as $3\frac{1}{2}$ must be gridded as 3.5 or 7/2. (If  is entered into the grid, it will be interpreted as $\frac{31}{2}$, not as $3\frac{1}{2}$.)

6. **Decimal Answers:** \ If you obtain a decimal answer with more digits than the grid can accommodate, it may be either rounded or truncated, but it must fill the entire grid.

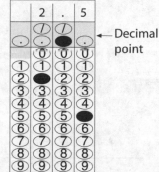

Answer: $\frac{7}{12}$

Write answer in boxes. — Fraction line

Grid in result. —

Answer: 2.5 — Decimal point

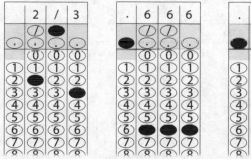

Acceptable ways to grid $\frac{2}{3}$ are:

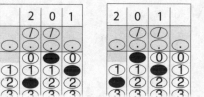

Answer: 201 – either position is correct

NOTE: You may start your answers in any column, space permitting. Columns you don't need to use should be left blank.

14

$$4s + 2t = 7$$

$$3s - 2t = 14$$

In the system of equations above, what is the value of s ?

15

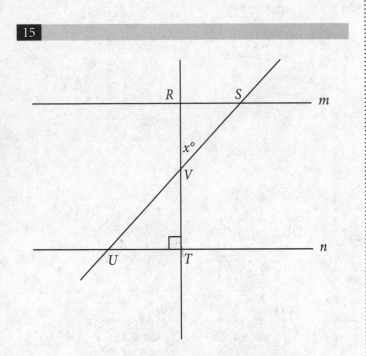

In the figure above, lines m and n cross the lines containing segments $\overline{RT}$ and $\overline{SU}$ such that angle RSV is congruent to angle TUV. If angle UVT is a right angle, and angle TUV measures 65°, what is the value of x ? (Disregard the degree sign when gridding your answer.)

16

A theater sells student tickets to a play for $24 and regular admission tickets for $36. If the theater sells out the 100-seat theater for opening night and has total ticket sales of $3,144, how many of the tickets sold were student tickets?

17

If $x \neq 0$ and $5x = 7y$, what is the value of $\dfrac{x - y}{x}$?

STOP
If you finish before time is called, you may check your work on this section only.
Do not turn to any other section in the test.

No Test Material On This Page

Math Test – Calculator

45 MINUTES, 31 QUESTIONS

Turn to Section 4 of your answer sheet to answer the questions in this section.

DIRECTIONS

For questions 1–27, solve each problem, choose the best answer from the choices provided, and fill in the corresponding circle on your answer sheet. **For questions 28–31,** solve the problem and enter your answer in the grid on the answer sheet. Please refer to the directions before question 28 on how to enter your answers in the grid. You may use any available space in your test booklet for scratch work.

NOTES

1. The use of a calculator **is permitted**.
2. All variables and expressions used represent real numbers unless otherwise indicated.
3. Figures provided in this test are drawn to scale unless otherwise indicated.
4. All figures lie in a plane unless otherwise indicated.
5. Unless otherwise indicated, the domain of a given function f is the set of all real numbers x for which $f(x)$ is a real number.

REFERENCE

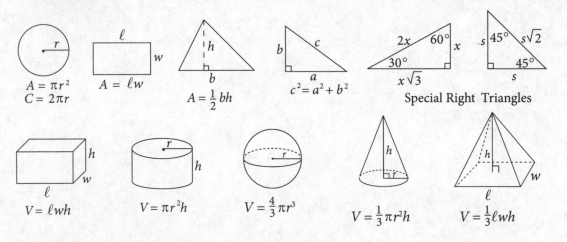

The number of degrees of arc in a circle is 360.
The number of radians of arc in a circle is 2π.
The sum of the measures in degrees of the angles of a triangle is 180.

CONTINUE ➔

1

Which of the following expressions is equivalent to $2(x - 5) + 3$?

A) $2x - 7$

B) $2x - 2$

C) $5x - 2$

D) $10x + 3$

2

A small glass tube used in a scientific lab can hold no more than 8.50 milliliters of liquid needed for a certain experiment. Approximately how many <u>teaspoons</u> can the beaker hold? (1 teaspoon ≈ 4.93 milliliters)

A) 1.72

B) 3.57

C) 6.78

D) 41.91

3

Every fifteen minutes, a lab assistant can centrifuge 3 vials of blood. If she continues at this rate, how many vials of blood will she centrifuge in 4 <u>hours</u>?

A) 12

B) 20

C) 32

D) 48

CONTINUE

4

A company that produces sports drinks wants to test the effects of its new electrolyte-infused water on athletic performance. One of the runners in the study drinks a bottle of the company's new water before his 1,500-meter run and keeps track of his speed throughout the run. The figure below graphs his speed, in meters per second, on the y-axis and the distance, in meters, along the x-axis.

Runner's Speed During Study

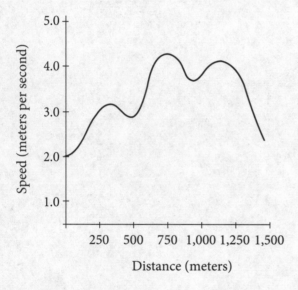

Distance (meters)

Based on the graph, which of the following statements is true?

A) The x-intercept of the graph represents the runner's starting speed.

B) The runner's slowest speed during his run occurs during the last 250 meters.

C) The runner increases his speed steadily until he reaches a distance of 1,000 meters.

D) The runner reaches his fastest speed at a distance of 750 meters.

5

What is the value of $5\left(a - \dfrac{1}{2}\right)$ if $10a = 13$?

A) $\dfrac{13}{5}$

B) 4

C) 6

D) $\dfrac{13}{2}$

6

$$(x - 3)^2 = 16$$

Which of the following values of x satisfies the equation above?

A) -7

B) -1

C) 3

D) 4

CONTINUE

Questions 7–9 refer to the following information.

High School Students' Summer Plans

	Male	Female	Total
Travel	15	25	40
Summer Job	17	13	30
Relax	33	21	54
Sports	13	9	22
Volunteer	11	14	25
Other	16	13	29
Total	105	95	200

The table above shows the results of a survey of a random sample of 200 high school students. The students were asked to indicate the option that best represented their summer plans.

If one of the females is selected at random, what is the approximate probability that the student indicated volunteering as her summer plans?

A) 0.07

B) 0.15

C) 0.25

D) 0.56

How many males in the survey plan to either work a summer job, relax, or volunteer over the summer?

A) 15

B) 41

C) 48

D) 61

The high school has a total of 1,200 students. Based on the data in the table, what is the predicted number of female students in the entire school who would indicate travel as their summer plans?

A) 240

B) 180

C) 150

D) 25

CONTINUE

10

Dana buys a shirt, a pair of shoes, and a purse at the store. Her bill is $81, and the shoes cost 25 percent more than the purse and shirt combined. How much were the shoes?

A) $26

B) $36

C) $45

D) $54

Questions 11 and 12 refer to the following information.

The Manor Hill Parent Teacher Association ordered some prizes as a class reward; the bill is shown below.

Quantity	Item	
14	Pendants	
11	T-shirts	
5	Hats	
9	Frisbees	
Shipping:		$ 15.65
Grand Total:		$211.30

There is no tax on the order. The shipping charge is calculated as a percent of the order cost. The grand total is the sum of the cost of the order and the shipping charge.

11

What is the percent value used to calculate the shipping charge on the order?

A) 8%

B) 10%

C) 12%

D) 16%

12

The total cost of the frisbees and hats is $72, and the cost of two hats and a frisbee is $14.50. What is the cost of a frisbee?

A) $3.22

B) $4.50

C) $5.50

D) $5.78

CONTINUE

13

$$3x + 2y = 4$$

$$y = \frac{2}{3}x - 2$$

The two equations in the system of equations above each form a line when graphed in the *xy*-plane. Which of the following statements is true regarding these two lines?

A) The lines are the same line.

B) The lines are perpendicular.

C) The lines are parallel.

D) The lines intersect at (3, 2).

14

Stephen takes out an interest-free loan from his friend. Each month he makes a payment to his friend. The amount of money that Stephen still owes his friend is given by the equation $y - 1{,}200 - 75m$, in which m is the number of months since the loan was made and y is the money, in dollars, that Stephen still owes. Which of the following best describes the meanings of the constant and coefficient in this equation?

A) The number 75 is the rate of decrease, in dollars per month, in the amount Stephen owes his friend, which started at $1,200.

B) The number 75 is the number of months it will take Stephen to pay off the loan, which was for $1,200.

C) The number 75 is the rate of increase, in dollars per month, that Stephen owes his friend for the loan, which started at $1,200.

D) The number 75 is the rate of increase, in dollars per month, of Stephen's payments on the loan, which was for $1,200.

Questions 15 and 16 refer to the following information.

A catering company offers three meal options when it caters weddings. There is no additional charge for guests that indicate a food allergy, and there is no price difference among the meal selections. Children's meals are provided at a discounted price. The company collected data on all the dish selections for the weddings that it catered over the past year.

	Children	Male Adults	Female Adults
Chicken	924	1,143	1,237
Fish	710	2,345	1,892
Vegetarian	241	862	1,451
Total meals	1,875	4,350	4,580
Cost of meals ($)	24,750	111,447	117,248
Indicated food allergy	134	542	632

15

What is the average cost of a child's meal?

A) $26.80

B) $23.45

C) $13.20

D) $7.90

16

Based on the table, what is the approximate probability that a guest will be an adult, if the guest orders the chicken?

A) 0.28

B) 0.49

C) 0.53

D) 0.72

CONTINUE

17

As an object moves through a fluid, the object experiences a force known as drag. For a given projected object area in meters squared and fluid density in kilograms per meter cubed, drag can be modeled by the equation $R = \frac{1}{2}Cv^2$, where R is drag force in Newtons, C is the coefficient of drag, and v is velocity in meters per second. Which of the following is equivalent to two Newtons? (Assume the object is moving at a constant speed.)

A) The drag on an object with a coefficient of drag of 1 and a velocity of 2 meters per second

B) The drag on an object with a coefficient of drag of 2 and a velocity of 1 meter per second

C) The drag on an object with a coefficient of drag of 2 and a velocity of 2 meters per second

D) The drag on an object with a coefficient of drag of 4 and a velocity of 0.25 meter per hour

18

A shoe store is having a sale in which a customer receives a 30 percent discount on a second pair of shoes after purchasing the first at regular price. The tax rate of 6 percent is applied to the whole purchase. If s represents the regular price of each pair of shoes at the store, which of the following expressions gives the total amount that a customer would pay for two pairs during this sale?

A) $1.06(s + 0.7s)$

B) $1.06(s - 0.3s)$

C) $1.06s + 0.7s$

D) $1.7s + 0.06$

19

A high school class is selling barrels of popcorn to raise money. The histogram below shows the number of students that sold each quantity of barrels.

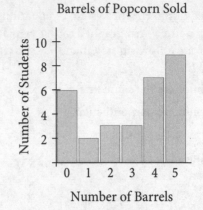

Barrels of Popcorn Sold

Which of the following is true?

I. The mode number of barrels sold is equal to the median number of barrels sold.

II. The median number of barrels sold is equal to the mean number of barrels sold.

III. The mode number of barrels sold is equal to the range of the number of barrels sold.

A) I only

B) III only

C) I and II only

D) II and III only

CONTINUE

20

Sam's Sunscreen Shop makes two kinds of sunscreen: Sunscreen A and Sunscreen B. Sunscreen A contains 8% of the active ingredient, and Sunscreen B has 12.5% of the same active ingredient. Sam wants to create a new sunscreen by blending the two sunscreens to make a new product that has a concentration of more than 10% active ingredient. The sunscreen should be in a tube containing at least 12 ounces, but no more than 16 ounces. If a represents the ounces of Sunscreen A in the blend and b represents the ounces of Sunscreen B in the blend, which of the following systems can be used to solve for all the values of a and b that fit these requirements?

A) $\begin{cases} 6 \leq a \leq 8 \\ 6 \leq b \leq 8 \\ \dfrac{0.08a + 0.125b}{a + b} > 0.10 \end{cases}$

B) $\begin{cases} a > 0 \\ b > 0 \\ 0.08a + 0.125b < 0.10 \\ a + b = 12 \end{cases}$

C) $\begin{cases} a > 0 \\ b > 0 \\ 0.08a + 0.125b > 0.10 \\ 12 \leq a + b \leq 16 \end{cases}$

D) $\begin{cases} a > 0 \\ b > 0 \\ 0.08a + 0.125b > 0.10(a + b) \\ 12 \leq a + b \leq 16 \end{cases}$

21

Types of Pets	Percent of pets
Dogs	40%
Cats	25%
Fish	15%
Birds	20%
Total	100%

The table above shows the distribution of pets at a pet shop. How many pets are at the pet shop if there are 36 more dogs than cats?

A) 240

B) 120

C) 60

D) 48

CONTINUE

22

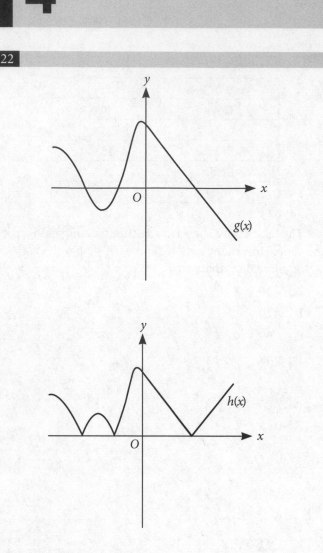

The graphs of the functions *g* and *h* are shown above. Which of the following defines *h* in terms of *g*?

A) $h(x) = -g(x)$

B) $h(x) = |g(x)|$

C) $h(x) = g(x) + 3$

D) $h(x) = g(x - 3)$

23

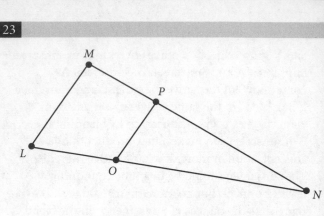

Note: Figure not drawn to scale.

In triangle *LMN* above, angle *NPO* is congruent to angle *MLN*, *NP* = 7, and *LN* = 18. If the length of $\overline{MN}$ is 1 unit less than 3 times the length of $\overline{NO}$, what is the length of side $\overline{NO}$?

A) 11

B) 5

C) $\dfrac{7}{3}$

D) $\dfrac{1}{3}$

24

The membership of a sports fan group increases by 10 percent each month during the season. What type of relationship exists between the size of the fan group and the number of months since the start of the season?

A) Exponential relationship in which higher membership numbers correspond to earlier dates in the season

B) Linear relationship whose graph has a slope greater than 0

C) Exponential relationship in which higher membership numbers correspond to later dates in the season

D) Linear relationship whose graph has a slope less than 0

CONTINUE

25

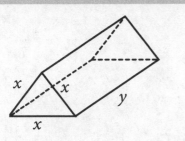

The total surface area of the triangular prism shown above can be calculated using the following formula, where x is the length of the sides of the triangular ends and y is the length of the rectangular faces.

$$SA = 2\left(\frac{\sqrt{3}}{4}x^2\right) + 3xy$$

What must the expression $\frac{\sqrt{3}}{2}x^2$ represent?

A) The area of one triangular end

B) The area of one rectangular face and one triangular end

C) The sum of the areas of the rectangular faces

D) The sum of the areas of the triangular ends

26

$$(3 - y)^2 - (3 - y)$$

Which of the following is an equivalent form of the expression above?

A) $3 - y$

B) $y^2 - 7y + 6$

C) $(3 - y)(2 - y)$

D) $9 - y^2$

27

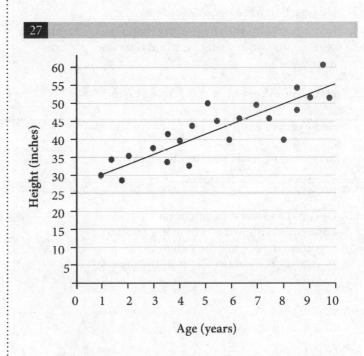

Age (years)

A pediatrician's office collects data on the heights of all its patients. The scatterplot above shows the heights of the male patients seen by the office at various ages less than 10 years. A linear model best describes the data, and the line of best fit is shown. For the patient that is exactly 8 years old, which of the following best estimates the percent increase from his actual height to the height that the model predicts?

A) 20%

B) 25%

C) 75%

D) 80%

CONTINUE

DIRECTIONS

For questions 28–31, solve the problem and enter your answer in the grid, as described below, on the answer sheet.

1. Although not required, it is suggested that you write your answer in the boxes at the top of the co lumns to help you fill in the circles accurately. You will receive credit only if the circles are filled in correctly.

2. Mark no more than one circle in any column.

3. No question has a negative answer.

4. Some problems may have more than one correct answer. In such cases, grid only one answer.

5. **Mixed numbers** such as $3\frac{1}{2}$ must be gridded as 3.5 or 7/2. (If 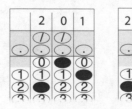 is entered into the grid, it will be interpreted as $\frac{31}{2}$, not as $3\frac{1}{2}$.)

6. **Decimal Answers:** If you obtain a decimal answer with more digits than the grid can accommodate, it may be either rounded or truncated, but it must fill the entire grid.

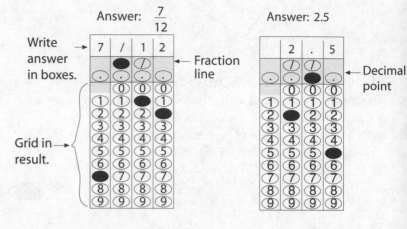

Answer: $\frac{7}{12}$ Answer: 2.5

Write answer in boxes. → Fraction line

Grid in result. → Decimal point

Acceptable ways to grid $\frac{2}{3}$ are:

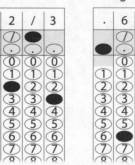

Answer: 201 – either position is correct

NOTE: You may start your answers in any column, space permitting. Columns you don't need to use should be left blank.

CONTINUE

28

A certain box has a width that is 2 inches more than its length and a height that is 5 inches less than its length. If each of the two smallest faces of the box has an area of 36 square inches, what is the volume of the box?

29

$$5x - 3y = 7$$
$$2x + y = 5$$

If (x, y) is the solution to the system of equations above, what is the value of y ?

Questions 30 and 31 refer to the following information.

In a certain marathon, 45 percent of the runners were men and the rest were women. The official timekeeper determined that 64 percent of the men and 68 percent of the women completed the marathon in under four hours.

30

What percent of the runners who completed the marathon in under four hours were women? (Ignore the percent symbol when entering your answer. For example, if the answer is 35.2%, enter 35.2.)

31

What percent of the runners completed the marathon in under four hours? (Ignore the percent symbol when entering your answer. For example, if the answer is 35.2%, enter 35.2.)

STOP
If you finish before time is called, you may check your work on this section only.
Do not turn to any other section in the test.

The Princeton Review®

EXAMPLES OF

COMPLETE MARK ● **INCOMPLETE MARKS** ⊘ ⊗ ⊖ ◉ ● ◐ ◓ ◑

It is recommended that you use a No. 2 pencil. It is very important that you fill in the entire circle darkly and completely. If you change your response, erase as completely as possible. Incomplete marks or erasures may affect your score.

■ TEST NUMBER

ENTER TEST NUMBER
For instance, for Practice Test #1, fill in the circle for 0 in the first column and for 1 in the second column.

⊔⊔

0 ○○
1 ○○
2 ○○
3 ○○
4 ○○
5 ○○
6 ○○
7 ○○
8 ○○
9 ○○

■ SECTION 1

	A B C D		A B C D		A B C D		A B C D
1	○○○○	13	○○○○	25	○○○○	37	○○○○
2	○○○○	14	○○○○	26	○○○○	38	○○○○
3	○○○○	15	○○○○	27	○○○○	39	○○○○
4	○○○○	16	○○○○	28	○○○○	40	○○○○
5	○○○○	17	○○○○	29	○○○○	41	○○○○
6	○○○○	18	○○○○	30	○○○○	42	○○○○
7	○○○○	19	○○○○	31	○○○○	43	○○○○
8	○○○○	20	○○○○	32	○○○○	44	○○○○
9	○○○○	21	○○○○	33	○○○○	45	○○○○
10	○○○○	22	○○○○	34	○○○○	46	○○○○
11	○○○○	23	○○○○	35	○○○○	47	○○○○
12	○○○○	24	○○○○	36	○○○○		

PSAT/NMSQT PRACTICE TEST ANSWER SHEET

COMPLETE MARK ●
EXAMPLES OF
INCOMPLETE MARKS ○⊗⊖◉ ●◔◑◐

It is recommended that you use a No. 2 pencil. It is very important that you fill in the entire circle darkly and completely. If you change your response, erase as completely as possible. Incomplete marks or erasures may affect your score.

■ SECTION 2

	A B C D		A B C D		A B C D		A B C D		A B C D
1	○○○○	10	○○○○	19	○○○○	28	○○○○	37	○○○○
2	○○○○	11	○○○○	20	○○○○	29	○○○○	38	○○○○
3	○○○○	12	○○○○	21	○○○○	30	○○○○	39	○○○○
4	○○○○	13	○○○○	22	○○○○	31	○○○○	40	○○○○
5	○○○○	14	○○○○	23	○○○○	32	○○○○	41	○○○○
6	○○○○	15	○○○○	24	○○○○	33	○○○○	42	○○○○
7	○○○○	16	○○○○	25	○○○○	34	○○○○	43	○○○○
8	○○○○	17	○○○○	26	○○○○	35	○○○○	44	○○○○
9	○○○○	18	○○○○	27	○○○○	36	○○○○		

PSAT/NMSQT PRACTICE TEST ANSWER SHEET

| COMPLETE MARK ● | EXAMPLES OF INCOMPLETE MARKS ⬭ ⊗ ⊖ ◉ ◐ ◔ ◑ ◕ | It is recommended that you use a No. 2 pencil. It is very important that you fill in the entire circle darkly and completely. If you change your response, erase as completely as possible. Incomplete marks or erasures may affect your score. |

■ SECTION 3

1 Ⓐ Ⓑ Ⓒ Ⓓ   4 Ⓐ Ⓑ Ⓒ Ⓓ   7 Ⓐ Ⓑ Ⓒ Ⓓ   10 Ⓐ Ⓑ Ⓒ Ⓓ   13 Ⓐ Ⓑ Ⓒ Ⓓ

2 Ⓐ Ⓑ Ⓒ Ⓓ   5 Ⓐ Ⓑ Ⓒ Ⓓ   8 Ⓐ Ⓑ Ⓒ Ⓓ   11 Ⓐ Ⓑ Ⓒ Ⓓ

3 Ⓐ Ⓑ Ⓒ Ⓓ   6 Ⓐ Ⓑ Ⓒ Ⓓ   9 Ⓐ Ⓑ Ⓒ Ⓓ   12 Ⓐ Ⓑ Ⓒ Ⓓ

Only answers that are gridded will be scored. You will not receive any credit for anything written in the boxes.

14

15

16

17

NO CALCULATOR ALLOWED

PSAT/NMSQT PRACTICE TEST ANSWER SHEET

COMPLETE MARK ● EXAMPLES OF INCOMPLETE MARKS ⊘ ⊗ ⊖ ◉ ◖ ◔ ◑ ◒

It is recommended that you use a No. 2 pencil. It is very important that you fill in the entire circle darkly and completely. If you change your response, erase as completely as possible. Incomplete marks or erasures may affect your score.

■ SECTION 4

1 A B C D
2 A B C D
3 A B C D
4 A B C D
5 A B C D
6 A B C D

7 A B C D
8 A B C D
9 A B C D
10 A B C D
11 A B C D
12 A B C D

13 A B C D
14 A B C D
15 A B C D
16 A B C D
17 A B C D
18 A B C D

19 A B C D
20 A B C D
21 A B C D
22 A B C D
23 A B C D
24 A B C D

25 A B C D
26 A B C D
27 A B C D

Only answers that are gridded will be scored. You will not receive any credit for anything written in the boxes.

28

29

30

31

/ ○ ○
. ○ ○ ○ ○
0 ○ ○ ○ ○
1 ○ ○ ○ ○
2 ○ ○ ○ ○
3 ○ ○ ○ ○
4 ○ ○ ○ ○
5 ○ ○ ○ ○
6 ○ ○ ○ ○
7 ○ ○ ○ ○
8 ○ ○ ○ ○
9 ○ ○ ○ ○

**CALCULATOR
ALLOWED**

Chapter 5
Practice Test 1:
Answers and
Explanations

PRACTICE TEST 1 ANSWER KEY

	Section 1: Reading				Section 2: Writing and Language				Section 3: Math (No Calculator)				Section 4: Math (Calculator)		
1.	A	25.	D	1.	B	23.	C	1.	B	11.	B	1.	A	16.	D
2.	D	26.	C	2.	D	24.	A	2.	C	12.	D	2.	A	17.	A
3.	B	27.	B	3.	C	25.	D	3.	C	13.	C	3.	D	18.	A
4.	C	28.	C	4.	B	26.	C	4.	A	14.	3	4.	D	19.	B
5.	B	29.	B	5.	A	27.	B	5.	B	15.	25	5.	B	20.	D
6.	C	30.	C	6.	D	28.	A	6.	D	16.	38	6.	B	21.	A
7.	A	31.	B	7.	C	29.	D	7.	A			7.	B	22.	B
8.	D	32.	B	8.	A	30.	A	8.	D	17. $\frac{2}{7}$,		8.	D	23.	C
9.	B	33.	C	9.	D	31.	A	9.	B	.285,		9.	C	24.	C
10.	D	34.	C	10.	C	32.	B	10.	C	or		10.	C	25.	D
11.	C	35.	B	11.	B	33.	C			.286		11.	A	26.	C
12.	A	36.	D	12.	C	34.	A					12.	C	27.	B
13.	B	37.	A	13.	A	35.	D					13.	B	28.	396
14.	B	38.	C	14.	D	36.	B					14.	A	29.	1
15.	D	39.	B	15.	B	37.	C					15.	C	30.	56.4 or
16.	D	40.	C	16.	B	38.	C								56.5
17.	A	41.	D	17.	C	39.	A							31.	66.2
18.	C	42.	C	18.	C	40.	B								
19.	C	43.	B	19.	B	41.	D								
20.	A	44.	C	20.	A	42.	D								
21.	A	45.	C	21.	D	43.	A								
22.	D	46.	D	22.	D	44.	B								
23.	B	47.	D												
24.	D														

PRACTICE TEST 1 EXPLANATIONS

Section 1—Reading

1. **A** The question asks about the *main purpose of the passage*. Because this is a general question, it should be done after all of the specific questions. The beginning of the passage describes the death of a wealthy financier and the impact of his death, stating that he died *without making one loyal friend to mourn him*, but *that it seemed to those living in the great vortices of business as if the earth too shuddered under a blow*. The following paragraphs discuss Manderson's life and his rise to power in the financial world. Choice (A) matches this structure, so keep it. The passage mentions a change in Manderson's life, but it also says that *how the change came about none could with authority say*, so eliminate (B). The passage does mention that Manderson died without making any loyal friends, but the focus of the passage as a whole is not why he failed to make friends, so (C) can also be eliminated. While the passage does explain that Manderson was more successful after he changed from *a gambler of genius* to one who worked with *steady labour,* the passage focuses on Manderson specifically, not on the advantages of hard work over risky speculations in general. Eliminate (D). The correct answer is (A).

2. **D** This question asks what *Manderson* was chiefly *known* for. Notice that it's the first question in a paired set, so it can be done in tandem with Q3. Start with the answers to Q3. The lines for (3A) state that Manderson *imposed [himself] upon the mind of the trading world* in a way that hadn't been done before. While these lines do describe Manderson, they don't support any of the specific answers in Q2. Eliminate (3A). The lines for (3B) say that Manderson was the *unquestioned guardian of stability, the stamper-out of manipulated crises, the foe of the raiding chieftains that infest the borders of Wall Street.* These lines support choice (2D) (*power and determination to protect*), so connect those two choices. The lines for (3C) refer to the origin of Manderson's family money, which doesn't support any of the answers for Q2. Eliminate (3C). Choice (3D) talks about his early career, which is not how Manderson was *chiefly* known, nor does it support any of the choices in Q2. Eliminate (3D). Without any support from Q3, choices (2A), (2B), and (2C) can be eliminated. The correct answers are (2D) and (3B).

3. **B** (See explanation above.)

4. **C** This question asks what the passage suggests *about Manderson's death*. Notice that it's the first question in a paired set, so it can be done in tandem with Q5. Look at the answers for Q5 first. The lines for (5A) say that when Manderson was killed, the world *lost nothing worth a single tear*. These lines don't support any of the answers for Q4, so eliminate (5A). The lines in (5B) say that his death was a *harsh reminder of the vanity of such wealth* and that even though he didn't have *one loyal friend to mourn him*, the news of his death caused *those living in the great vortices of business* to feel as if *the earth…shuddered under a blow.* These lines support (4C), so draw a line to connect those two answer choices. The lines in (5C) don't reference Manderson's death at all, and therefore do not support any of the answers for Q4. Eliminate (5C). The lines in (5D) discuss Manderson's change after his father's death, which doesn't support any of the answers for Q4. Without support from Q5, (4A), (4B), and (4D) can be eliminated. The correct answers are (4C) and (5B).

5. **B**   (See explanation above.)

6. **C**   The question asks what the word *quiet* most nearly means in line 39. Go back to the text, find the word *quiet*, and underline it. Then read the window carefully, using context clues to determine another word that would fit in the text. The text says that *they had rooted in him an instinct for quiet magnificence, the larger costliness which does not shriek of itself with a thousand tongues.* The word *quiet* is contrasted with the phrase *shriek of itself with a thousand tongues.* Therefore, *quiet* must mean something like "subtle" or "reserved." *Silent, still,* and *secluded* are all possible definitions of the word *quiet,* but none of them is consistent with the prediction. Eliminate (A), (B), and (D). *Understated* is consistent with "subtle" and "reserved." The correct answer is (C).

7. **A**   The question asks what the *reference to St. Helena* serves to do in the passage. Find the line reference and carefully read the window to figure out what the reference to St. Helena does within the context of the passage. Lines 46–49 state that *at St. Helena it was laid down that war is a beautiful occupation and so the young Manderson had found the…dogfight of the Stock Exchange.* The reference to St. Helena introduces a comparison between war and work at the Stock Exchange, so eliminate any answer choices that are not consistent with this prediction. Choice (A) matches the prediction, so keep it. There is no *dilemma* nor mention of *coworkers,* so eliminate (B). The sentence does not refer to an *event in the history of the Stock Exchange,* so (C) can be eliminated. The lines about St. Helena do not suggest that Manderson rejected war as a *career path,* so eliminate (D). The correct answer is (A).

8. **D**   The question asks what best describes *Manderson's change* in line 52. Carefully read the window to find evidence about the change. The passage states that after his father's death, Manderson *turned to steady labour in his father's banking business, closing his ears to the sound of the battles of the Street.* The correct answer should have something to do with Manderson becoming a serious banker after his earlier days at the Stock Exchange. He did not become a *rival* taking over a business, so eliminate (A). Although the window mentions *battles,* he was never a *soldier,* so eliminate (B). He becomes a powerful businessman, not a *trusted clerk,* so eliminate (C). Choice (D) is consistent with the prediction. The correct answer is (D).

9. **B**   The question asks what the word *elastic* most nearly means in line 55. Go back to the text, find the word *elastic,* and underline it. Carefully read the window and use context clues to determine another word that would fit in the text. The sentence as a whole discusses the fact that Manderson changed from *a gambler of genius* to one who *worked with steady labour.* Therefore, the missing word must mean something like "adaptable." *Rubbery, expandable,* and *looped* are all possible definitions of the word *elastic,* but none of them is consistent with the prediction. Eliminate (A), (C), and (D). *Flexible* is consistent with "adaptable." The correct answer is (B).

10. **D**   The question asks what the word *dominant* most nearly means in line 2. Go back to the text, find the word *dominant,* and underline it. Then read the window carefully, using context clues to determine another word that would fit in the text. The text says, *With governments fretting over how to feed more than nine billion people by 2050, a dominant narrative calls for increasing global food production by 70 to 100 percent.* Therefore, the word *dominant* could be replaced with something like "major." Neither *aggressive, forceful,* nor *outstanding* matches "major." These are all Could Be True trap answers based

on other meanings of "dominant" that are not supported by the text. Eliminate (A), (B), and (C). Choice (D), *prominent*, matches "major," so keep (D). The correct answer is (D).

11. **C** The question asks what has increased as a result of *agriculture*. This is the first question in a paired set, but it is easy to find, so it can be done on its own. Use lead words and the order of the questions to find the window. Q10 asks about line 2, so the window for Q11 most likely begins after that line. Look for the lead word *agriculture*. Lines 4–9 state that *agriculture already represents one of the greatest threats to planetary health. It is responsible for 70 percent of the planet's freshwater withdrawals, 80 percent of the world's tropical and subtropical deforestation, and 30 to 35 percent of human-caused greenhouse gas emissions.* Therefore, agriculture has led to an increase in environmental problems. Eliminate the answers that don't match this prediction. Choice (A) is a Right Answer, Wrong Question trap answer: the passage does mention the flow of a European river, but it is not mentioned as something that increased due to agriculture, so eliminate (A). The passage doesn't discuss the *cost of goods*, so eliminate (B). Keep (C) because it matches the prediction. Choice (D) is a Right Answer, Wrong Question trap answer: the passage mentions the number of people who *suffer from hunger*, but it does not say the number increased as a result of agriculture; eliminate (D). The correct answer is (C).

12. **A** The question is the best evidence question in a paired set. Since Q11 was easy to find, simply look at the lines used to answer Q11. The prediction for Q11 came from lines 4–9. Part of this window is included in (A). The correct answer is (A).

13. **B** The question asks what the author indicates about *the amount of food wasted annually across the globe*. Notice that this is the first question in a paired set, so it can be done in tandem with Q14. Look at the answers for Q14 first. The lines for (14A) say that *nearly 800 million people worldwide suffer from hunger*. These lines don't discuss *the amount of food wasted*, so eliminate (14A). The lines for (14B) state that *we squander enough food—globally, 2.9 trillion pounds a year—to feed every one of [the people suffering from hunger] more than twice over*. Check the answers for Q13 to see if this information supports any of the answers; it supports (13B), so draw a line connecting (13B) with (14B). The lines for (14C) say, *By the end of 2015 the UN and the U.S. had pledged to halve food waste by 2030*. This information doesn't support any of the answers to Q13, so eliminate (14C). The lines for (14D) say that *countries and companies are devising and adopting standardized metrics to quantify waste*. These lines don't support any of the answers for Q13, so eliminate (14D). Without any support in the answers from Q14, (13A), (13C), and (13D) can be eliminated. The correct answers are (13B) and (14B).

14. **B** (See explanation above.)

15. **D** The question asks for the purpose of the phrase *whether sausages or snickerdoodles*. Use the given line reference to find the window. Lines 24–28 state, *Wasting food takes an environmental toll as well. Producing food that no one eats—whether sausages or snickerdoodles—also squanders the water, fertilizer, pesticides, seeds, fuel, and land needed to grow it. The quantities aren't trivial.* The main point of this paragraph is that the environmental harm caused by food waste is significant, and the phrase *whether sausages or snickerdoodles* helps the author illustrate this point. Eliminate answers that don't match this prediction. Eliminate (A) because the author does not compare *values* of different *food groups*. Eliminate (B) because the author does not state that *environmentalists object to* the waste of

these two foods *most strongly*. Eliminate (C) because sausages and snickerdoodles are not given as examples of *particularly wasteful foods*, nor does the author try to *caution her readers against consuming* any type of food. Keep (D) because it matches the prediction. The correct answer is (D).

16.　**D**　The question asks what the word *obscene* most nearly means in line 38. Go back to the text, find the word *obscene*, and underline it. Then read the window carefully, using context clues to determine another word that would fit in the text. The text says that if *food waste were a country, it would be the third largest producer of greenhouse gases in the world* and that *on a planet of finite resources, with the expectation of at least two billion more residents by 2050*, this waste *is obscene*. Therefore, the word *obscene* could be replaced by something like "appalling." *Censored* means "suppressed;" it does not match "appalling," so eliminate (A). *Improper* means "inappropriate" and does not match "appalling," so eliminate (B). *Vulgar* means "lacking good taste" and does not match "appalling," so eliminate (C). *Outrageous* matches "appalling," so keep (D). Note that (A), (B), and (C) are Could Be True trap answers based on alternate meanings of obscene that are not supported by the text. The correct answer is (D).

17.　**A**　The question asks which idea is supported by both the passage and the information in Figure 1. First, work through each answer using the figure. Choice (A) is supported by Figure 1: in developed nations, *food discarded by retail markets and consumers* accounts for 14.7% of dairy waste, while in developing nations, waste by retail markets and consumers accounts for only 8.5% of waste. Keep (A). Choice (B) is not supported by Figure 1, because the figure does not include information about *a lack of adequate food storage*. Eliminate (B). Choice (C) is not supported by the figure. Figure 1 only shows what percent of the food within each region is wasted; it doesn't give a basis for comparing the actual amounts of food wasted in developing versus developed nations. Eliminate (C). Choice (D) is not supported by the figure. Figure 1 shows that 16.4% of food is lost during production and processing in developing nations, while only 5.2% of food is lost during production and processing in developed nations. Eliminate (D). Check to see whether (A) is supported by the passage. Lines 17–23 indicate that in comparison with developing nations, *developed nations waste more food farther down the supply chain, when retailers order, serve, or display too much and when consumers ignore leftovers in the back of the fridge or toss perishables before they've expired*. This information supports (A). The correct answer is (A).

18.　**C**　The question asks which *statement from the passage* is most directly supported by *Figure 2*. Work through each answer choice using the figure. The lines for (A) state, *With governments fretting over how to feed more than nine billion people by 2050, a dominant narrative calls for increasing global food production by 70 to 100 percent*. Figure 2 does not include information about *increasing global food production*. Eliminate (A). The lines for (B) state, *developed nations waste more food farther down the supply chain* due to the actions of *retailers* and *consumers*. Figure 2 doesn't include information about the ways *developed nations* in particular waste food, so eliminate (B). The lines for (C) state, *Along the supply chain fruits and vegetables are lost or wasted at higher rates than other foods. Easily bruised and vulnerable to temperature swings en route from farm to table, they're also usually the first to get tossed at home*. Figure 2 supports this statement, since it shows a higher percentage of waste for *fruits and vegetables* than for the other types of food in the graph. Keep (C). The lines for (D) state, *Countless businesses, such as grocery stores, restaurants, and cafeterias, have stepped forward to combat waste by* *quantifying how much edible food isn't consumed, optimizing their purchasing, shrinking portion sizes, and beefing up efforts to move excess to charities.* Figure 2 doesn't include information about measures businesses are taking to combat food waste, so eliminate (D). The correct answer is (C).

19. **C**   The question asks about the overall structure of the passage. Since this is a general question, it should be answered after the specific questions. The passage begins by summarizing and describing the results of two *experiments* that address *higher-order visual perception in mice*. The following paragraphs describe those experiments in more detail. Eliminate answers that don't match this prediction. Though the first paragraph does contain an *overview* of the experiments and their results, the rest of the text does not discuss *two hypotheses*. Eliminate (A). Choice (B) uses ideas from the passage but answers the wrong question: the last sentence of the first paragraph presents *a perceived scientific truth* (that mice were thought to be *non-visual*) and then an *alternative* conclusion based on the experiments described. However, this only describes the structure of the end of the first paragraph, not that of the whole passage. Eliminate (B). Keep (C) because it matches the prediction. Eliminate (D), which is a Mostly Right, Slightly Wrong trap answer: the beginning of the passage does describe the *outcome of a study*, but this is not *followed by an extension of the outcome to another field*. The correct answer is (C).

20. **A**   The question asks what the word *solution* most nearly means in line 12. Go back to the text, find the word *solution*, and cross it out. Then read the window carefully, using context clues to determine another word that would fit in the text. The text says that *mice* were *injected with saline solution*. Therefore, *solution* must refer to a liquid that contains saline and other components, so it must mean something like "composite liquid." *Mixture* matches "composite liquid," so keep (A). *Answer* does not match "composite liquid," so eliminate (B). *Resolution* means "solution to a problem," which does not match "composite liquid," so eliminate (C). *Key* does not match "composite liquid," so eliminate (D). Note that (B), (C), and (D) are Could Be True trap answers based on other meanings of *solution* that are not supported by the text. The correct answer is (A).

21. **A**   The question asks for *an underlying assumption* that *Professor Watanabe makes regarding "staying time."* This is the first question in a paired set, but it is easy to find, so it can be done on its own. Since there is no line reference, use lead words and the order of the questions to find the window for the question. Q20 asks about line 12, so the window for Q21 most likely begins after line 12. Scan the second paragraph, looking for the lead words *staying time*. The paragraph says that *staying time* is a measure of how long the mice stayed *in the compartments with their respective paintings*. The last sentence of the paragraph says, *As mice know that morphine causes pleasure, they should stay longer near the painting associated with the morphine injection if able to discriminate between paintings.* Therefore, Professor Watanabe assumes that the mice are able to associate paintings with pleasure, or reward, and that this results in them staying longer near a particular painting. Eliminate answers that don't match this prediction. Keep (A) because it matches the prediction. Eliminate (B), because it is a Right Words, Wrong Meaning trap answer: the passage does not suggest that giving the mice *rewards* will give them *better vision*. Eliminate (C) for the same reason: the passage does not suggest that *mice spend more time viewing the paintings they saw when receiving a reward* because they are *experiencing the same pleasure derived from the reward*. There is no measure of whether the mice are experiencing pleasure again or to what degree they might. Eliminate (D) because the passage does not compare the *staying time* of *mice* with those of *pigeons and Java Sparrows*. The correct answer is (A).

22.　**D**　The question is the best evidence question in a paired set. Because Q21 was a specific question, simply look at the lines used to answer the previous question. Two different lines were used in the prediction: *Sensors recorded the staying time of mice in the compartments with their respective paintings* and *As mice know that morphine causes pleasure, they should stay longer near the painting associated with the morphine injection if able to discriminate between paintings.* Of these two lines, only the second one is an answer choice. The correct answer is (D).

23.　**B**　The question asks what the word *discrimination* most nearly means in line 46. Go back to the text, find the word *discrimination*, and cross it out. Then read the window carefully, using context clues to determine another word that would fit in the text. The text says, *If mice are capable of discrimination, they should touch the painting associated with the milk reward.* In other words, a mouse capable of *discrimination* would be able to recognize and choose the painting associated with the milk. Therefore, *discrimination* must mean something like "noticing the difference between things." *Prejudice* means "preconceived judgement;" it does not match "noticing the difference between things," so eliminate (A). *Differentiation* means "noticing the difference between things," which matches the prediction, so keep (B). *Bias* means "favoring something without considering other options," which does not match "noticing the difference between things," so eliminate (C). *Insight* does not match "noticing the difference between things," so eliminate (D). Note that (A), (C), and (D) are Could Be True trap answers based on other meanings of *discrimination* that are not supported by the text. The correct answer is (B).

24.　**D**　The question asks for an inference that explains why *Professor Watanabe showed the paintings to the mice prior to the conditioning experiments.* Since there is no line reference, use lead words and the order of the questions to find the window for the question. Q23 asks about line 46, so the window for Q24 most likely begins after that line. Scan the fourth paragraph, looking for the lead word *conditioning*. The paragraph says that the *conditioning in Experiment 1* was the injection of *morphine* into the mice when they viewed certain paintings, encouraging them to associate pleasure with a specific painting. Prior to this, the paragraph discusses the *first experiment* without morphine, in which mice that were shown paintings from multiple artists did not show a preference for a particular painting or artist. Therefore, mice were shown paintings without any pleasure reward first to make sure they did not have a preference for a particular painting or artist before beginning the experiment with the morphine. Eliminate answers that don't match this prediction. Eliminate (A) because it is a Right Words, Wrong Meaning trap answer: Professor Watanabe did not show paintings to the mice first in order to *prove that the staying times increased by 80%.* Eliminate (B) because the passage does not say that the mice were shown paintings first to *familiarize them with the artists.* Eliminate (C) because the passage does not discuss the mice's *sense of anticipation for rewards.* Keep (D) because it matches the prediction. The correct answer is (D).

25.　**D**　The question asks for evidence that *supports the claim that mice are more visually adept than they were conventionally believed to be.* Use the line references given in the answer choices to find a statement that supports this claim. Choices (A) and (B) discuss a lack of *preference* for *Picasso or Renoir* and the mice's inability to discriminate between the two artists, but neither discusses a conventional belief. Eliminate (A) and (B). Choice (C) discusses a conventional understanding about mice (*it has been thought that they are non-visual animals*), but it does not mention anything about them being *more* *visually adept* than this belief suggests. Eliminate (C). Choice (D) says that the *experiment demonstrates that mice have much better visual perception abilities than previously thought*, which supports the idea that *mice are more visually adept than they were conventionally believed to be*. The correct answer is (D).

26. **C** The question asks for the *primary purpose of the final paragraph*. Read the final paragraph, which says, *This experiment demonstrates that mice have much better visual perception abilities than previously thought*. It then broadens the significance of this idea, saying that the *perception of complex visual stimuli like paintings extends to non-human animals*. Eliminate answers that don't match this prediction. Eliminate (A) because the final paragraph does not describe an *error*; it describes a change in understanding. Eliminate (B) because the last paragraph does not *justify* the methods described earlier in the passage. Keep (C) because it matches the prediction. Eliminate (D) because, though the paragraph mentions the broad significance of the findings, it does not suggest a *topic for future research*. The correct answer is (C).

27. **B** The question asks for the purpose that *the figure* serves *in relation to the passage as a whole*. The passage describes a recent study and discusses the significance of that study's findings. The figure shows data from the "staying time" experiment, which was Experiment 1. Eliminate answers that are inconsistent with either the passage or the figure. Eliminate (A) because the passage does not indicate that the two *experiments* had *conflicting conclusions*. Keep (B) because it is consistent with both the purpose of the figure and information from the passage. Eliminate (C) because the figure does not introduce a *possible source of error* or cast *doubt on Professor Watanabe's conclusions*. Eliminate (D) because the figure agrees with the results in the passage; it does not *suggest a different interpretation than that presented in the passage*. The correct answer is (B).

28. **C** The question asks for a conclusion about *mice, in general,* based on *information in the passage and in the figure*. Since this is a general question, it should be answered after the specific questions. The figure shows data from Experiment 1, and the passage says that Experiment 1 showed that mice stayed longer at paintings that they associated with pleasure from a morphine injection. Eliminate answers that are inconsistent with either the passage or the figure. Choice (A) is a Right Answer, Wrong Question trap answer: it uses words from the description of Experiment 2, but the figure only relates to Experiment 1. Eliminate (A). Eliminate (B) because the figure and the passage both support the idea that the mice did not have a *greater appreciation* for either *Picasso* or *Renoir* before *conditioning*, which contradicts (B). Keep (C) because the figure and the passage both show that the mice had *increased staying times following conditioning with morphine*. Eliminate (D) because it is a Right Words, Wrong Meaning trap answer: the passage does not compare the degrees to which *milk* and *morphine* influenced the mice's actions. The correct answer is (C).

29. **B** The question asks about the *position that Jay* (the author) takes in the essay. Since this is a general question, it should be answered after the specific questions. Over the course of the passage, Jay, a Founding Father, argues that the United States should not be split into smaller, separate nations. Eliminate answers that don't match this prediction. Choice (A) can be eliminated because Jay is definitely not *an impartial onlooker pointing out both sides of an issue*. Choice (B) matches the prediction, so keep it. Choice (C) can be eliminated because, for Jay, this is not a *historical decision* but rather a current event. Choice (D) can also be eliminated because Jay argues for a particular side in his essay. He is not looking for a compromise. The correct answer is (B).

30. **C** The question asks what the word *vest* most nearly means in line 12. Go back to the text, find the word *vest*, and underline it. Then read the window carefully, using context clues to determine another word that would fit in the text. The text says that *nothing is more certain than the indispensable necessity of government, and…the people must cede to it some of their natural rights in order to vest it with requisite powers.* In other words, the people must give over to the government some of their natural rights in order to "provide" or "give" the government its necessary power. Therefore, *vest* must mean something like "provide" or "give." Choice (A) might initially look attractive because a vest is also an article of clothing, but that does not match the prediction. Choice (A) is a Could Be True trap answer that is based on another meaning of *vest* that is not supported by the passage. Eliminate (A). Choice (B), *abandon*, doesn't match "provide" or "give," so eliminate (B). Choice (C), *endow*, means "to give," which is consistent with the prediction. Choice (D), *belong*, does not match the prediction. The correct answer is (C).

31. **B** The question asks *which of the following questions about the American political system arose shortly before the passage was written.* Notice that this is the first question in a paired set, so it can be done in tandem with Q32. Look at the answers for Q32 first. The lines for (32A) say that *nothing is more certain than the indispensable power of government,* and that *the people must cede to it some of their natural rights in order to* provide it with necessary powers. These lines do not address Q31, so eliminate (32A). The lines for (32B) say that *politicians now appear who insist that* a previously stated opinion is *erroneous,* and that instead *we ought to seek [safety and happiness] in a division of the States into distinct* parts. The previously stated opinion (lines 20–24) was *that the prosperity of the people of America depended on their continuing firmly unified,* and the author states that this opinion was *uncontradicted* until recently. In other words, the debate mentioned in the lines for (32B) arose shortly before the passage was written. Therefore, check the answers for Q31 to see whether any of the answers are supported by these lines. This information matches (31B), whether America should *be governed as one nation* or as independent states. Draw a line connecting (31B) and (32B). The lines for (32C) say that America has been *blessed…with a variety of soils and productions…for the delight and accommodation of its inhabitants.* These lines do not address Q31, so eliminate (32C). The lines for (32D) say that America is *one connected country* with *one united people,* claiming that its people are bound by common language, religion, principles, and customs as well as the history of *a long and bloody war.* This information does not address a political question or debate that would have occurred before the passage was written. Eliminate (32D). Without support from Q32, (31A), (31C), and (31D) can be eliminated. The correct answers are (31B) and (32B).

32. **B** (See explanation above.)

33. **C** The question asks what Jay *indicates about those who support dividing the country into separate confederacies.* Notice that this is the first question in a paired set, so it can be done in tandem with Q34. Look at the answers for Q34 first. The lines for (34A) say that *the prosperity of the people of America depended on their continuing firmly united.* While this answer might initially seem to connect with (33A), there is no evidence in the text that he believes those who support dividing the country are *encouraging political turmoil.* Eliminate (34A). The lines for (34B) simply say that division *has its advocates,* but there is no mention of Jay's belief about those advocates. Eliminate (34B). The lines

for (34C) warn that it would not be wise to advocate for division *without being fully convinced that [separating the country is] founded in truth and sound policy.* These lines support (33C). Connect those two answers. Choice (32D) describes how *independent America was not composed of detached and distant territories, but…connected, fertile, wide-spreading country.* There is nothing about those who advocate for dividing the county, so these lines don't support any of the answers for Q33. Eliminate (34D). Without support from Q34, (33A), (33B), and (33D) can be eliminated. The correct answers are (33C) and (34C).

34. **C** (See explanation above.)

35. **B** The question asks about a *distinction* Jay makes in the passage. Use the given line reference to find the window. The text states that it gives [Jay] pleasure *to observe that independent America was not composed of detached and distant territories, but that one connected, fertile, wide-spreading country was the portion of our western sons of liberty.* The correct answer should be consistent with the distinction between detached territories and one connected country. Choice (A) is not consistent with this prediction, so it can be eliminated. Choice (B) is a solid paraphrase of the prediction, so keep it. There is nothing in the text about *deserted marketplaces,* so eliminate (C). Choice (D) can also be eliminated because Jay's distinction here is about detached and connected physical space, not the ideas of *division* and *independence.* The correct answer is (B).

36. **D** The question asks about the purpose of Jay's reference to *innumerable streams…navigable waters…* and *noble rivers.* Use the given line reference to find the window. Jay first describes the benefits of the streams *(for the delight and accommodation of its inhabitants),* the waters *(a kind of chain round its borders, as if to bind it together),* and the rivers *(highways for the easy communication of friendly aids).* For Jay, these waters are beneficial. He continues by saying that *[w]ith equal pleasure I have as often taken notice that Providence has been pleased to give this one connected country to one united people.* He then goes on to describe how the people are also connected. Therefore, the correct answer must have something to do with Jay using the examples to represent the connectedness of the people of the country. Choice (A) can be eliminated because Jay isn't arguing to protect natural resources. Choice (B) can be eliminated because there is no evidence that the references to water are meant to get people out exploring. Choice (C) can be eliminated because the references to water aren't summarizing anything; they are representing something. Choice (D) is consistent with the prediction, as Jay uses the description of the waters as a comparison that supports his argument about the connectedness of the people. The correct answer is (D).

37. **A** The question asks what Jay means when he says *with equal pleasure.* Use the given line reference to find the window. Notice that this line reference is from the same window as the previous question. The text states that Jay likes both the connectedness of the land and the connectedness of the people of the United States. Eliminate any answer choices that aren't consistent with this prediction. Choice (A) is a paraphrase of the prediction, so keep it. Choice (B) can be eliminated because Jay does not feel equally happy about unification and division. Although (C) might seem logical, there is no evidence for it in the text, and it can be eliminated. Choice (D) might also make sense, but again, there is no direct evidence for it in the text, so it can be eliminated. The correct answer is (A).

38. **C**   The question asks for the purpose of the list in lines 55–59. Use the given line reference to find the window. In lines 53–55, Jay states that *Providence has been pleased to give this one connected country to one united people.* He then goes on to list the ways in which the people are united: Jay states that the people of the United States are *a people descended from the same ancestors, speaking the same language, professing the same religion, attached to the same principles of government, very similar in their manners and customs.* In other words, the list supports Jay's argument that the people of the United States are a unified people. Choice (A) mentions a *method*, but there is no discussion about a method in the window, so eliminate (A). Choice (B) says that the list is summarizing *points that Jay has dismissed*, but this list is related to a claim that Jay supports, so (B) can be eliminated. Choice (C) is consistent with the text, so keep it. Choice (D) mentions *issues* that *Jay's audience must settle*, but the list is a set of examples that support a claim, not a list of undecided issues. Eliminate (D). The correct answer is (C).

39. **B**   The question asks for evidence from Passage 1 that supports the claim that *space is an "inhospitable environment for life."* Use the line references given in the answer choices to find a statement that supports this claim. The lines for (A) say that the tardigrades were *exposed to the vacuum of space.* These lines do not describe the space environment, so eliminate (A). The lines for (B) say that the tardigrades had *no air* and *were subjected to extreme dehydration, freezing temperatures, weightlessness and lashings of both cosmic and solar radiation.* These lines support the claim that space is an *inhospitable environment*, so keep (B). The lines for (C) say that the tardigrades *survived the raw vacuum of space*, but they do not describe the space environment, so eliminate (C). The lines for (D) state that the tardigrades spent time in *low Earth orbit*, but they don't describe the space environment, so eliminate (D). The correct answer is (B).

40. **C**   The question asks what the word *tolerate* most nearly means in line 15. Go back to the text, find the word *tolerate*, and underline it. Then read the window carefully, using context clues to determine another word that would fit in the text. The text says that tardigrades *can tolerate extreme environments that would kill almost any other animal.* Therefore, *tolerate* must mean something like "survive." *Permit* does not match "survive," so eliminate (A). *Indulge* does not match "survive," so eliminate (B). *Endure* matches "survive," so keep (C). *Ignore* does not match "survive," so eliminate (D). Note that (A), (B), and (D) are Could Be True trap answers based on other meanings of *tolerate* that are not supported by the text. The correct answer is (C).

41. **D**   The question asks which *unique trait* allows *tardigrades to survive in hostile environments.* Notice that this is the first question in a paired set, so it can be done in tandem with Q42. Look at the answer choices for Q42 first. The lines for (42A) say that *a team of scientists launched a squad of tiny animals into space aboard a Russian satellite.* These lines do not address Q41, so eliminate (42A). The lines for (42B) state that tardigrades are *aquatic invertebrates* and that they are *nigh-invincible.* Although the lines mention the tardigrades' *shuffling walk*, they do not say that the *shuffling walk* helps tardigrades survive in hostile environments. Eliminate (43B). The lines for (42C) say that tardigrades survive *by replacing almost all of the water in their bodies with a sugar called trehalose.* This information matches (41D). Draw a line connecting (42C) and (41D). The lines in (42D) state that tardigrades can be revived by *a drop of water.* Check the answers for Q41 to see whether any of the answers are supported by these lines. None of the answers in Q41 match the information in (42D), so eliminate

(42D). Without any support in the answers from Q42, (41A), (41B), and (41C) can be eliminated. The correct answers are (41D) and (42C).

42. **C** (See explanation above.)

43. **B** The question asks what the word *robust* most nearly means in line 45. Go back to the text, find the word *robust*, and underline it. Then read the window carefully, using context clues to determine another word that would fit in the text. The text says that the *world's most robust animals may very well survive until the sun stops shining* and that tardigrades are *famed for their resiliency*. Therefore, *robust* must mean something like "resilient." *Round* does not match "resilient," so eliminate (A). *Tough* matches "resilient," so keep (B). *Flavorful* does not match "resilient," so eliminate (C). *Healthy* does not match "resilient," so eliminate (D). Note that (C) and (D) are Could Be True trap answers based on other meanings of *robust* that are not supported by the text. The correct answer is (B).

44. **C** The question asks whether the author of Passage 2 would agree with a student's claim that *tardigrades would likely face extinction before humans*. Since there is no line reference, use lead words to find the window. Look for the lead words *extinction, humans*, and *tardigrades*. The second paragraph mentions *humans* and *extinction*. The paragraph states, *Astrophysical events such as asteroid strikes have been fingered as the causes of past mass extinctions on Earth. Such violent cataclysms could easily wipe out humans.* The third paragraph states that an asteroid collision with earth *would be catastrophic for many lifeforms on the surface, but tardigrades would have a refuge.* The next paragraph adds, *"Tardigrades can live around volcanic vents at the bottom of the ocean, which means they have a huge shield against the kind of events that would be catastrophic for humans."* Therefore, the author would probably not agree that tardigrades are likely to face extinction before humans. Eliminate answers that don't match this prediction. Eliminate (A) and (B). Keep (C) because it matches the prediction. Eliminate (D) because the passage indicates that tardigrades are **not** vulnerable to *asteroid strikes*. The correct answer is (C).

45. **C** The question asks for the *main purpose of both Passage 1 and 2*. Consider one passage at a time. Passage 1 discusses a study that found that tardigrades can survive in space. Eliminate answers that don't match this prediction. Eliminate (B) because Passage 1 focuses on only one *invertebrate*, and tardigrades are more *able to withstand extreme environments* than other species. Eliminate (D) because Passage 1 does not discuss *catastrophic scenarios*, and it only discusses one *invertebrate*, the tardigrade. Passage 2 discusses what phenomena could lead to the extinction of the tardigrade. No method of testing is discussed in Passage 2, so eliminate (A). Keep (C) because it matches the predictions for both passages. The correct answer is (C).

46. **D** The question asks what is true of "water bears" (line 13) based on information in Passage 2. Use the given line reference to find the window in Passage 1. The lines say, *Tardigrades are small aquatic invertebrates that are also known as "water bears."* Since *water bears* is another name for *tardigrades*, the answer should include a statement that is true of tardigrades. Use lead words from the answers to find the relevant information, and eliminate answers that are not supported. Eliminate (A) because both passages state that tardigrades are *invertebrates*, not *vertebrates*. Choice (A) is a Mostly Right, Slightly Wrong trap answer. Eliminate (B) because *tuns* is mentioned only in Passage 1 and describes the *dormant state* of tardigrades; the passage does not state that tardigrades *are related to tuns*. Choice (B) is a Right Words, Wrong Meaning trap answer. Eliminate (C) because *trehalose* is only mentioned

in Passage 1, and the text indicates that tardigrades can replace *almost all of the water in their bodies with…trehalose*; it doesn't say that tardigrades are *made of trehalose*. Keep (D) because line 48 describes tardigrades as *eight-legged*. The correct answer is (D).

47.   **D**   The question asks which environment could be the *natural habitat of the "water-dwelling creatures"* mentioned in line 47, based on Passages 1 and 2. Use the given line reference to find the window in Passage 2. Lines 46–47 state, *Tardigrades are tiny water-dwelling creatures famed for their resiliency.* Therefore, the *water-dwelling creatures* are *tardigrades*, so the correct answer should give a possible natural habitat of tardigrades, based on the passages. Use lead words from the answers to find the relevant information, and eliminate answers that aren't supported. Lines 77–80 suggest that some species of tardigrades live *around volcanic vents* in the ocean; however, the passage doesn't say that they live in *volcanic lava domes*, so (A) is a Right Words, Wrong Meaning trap answer. Eliminate (A). Lines 1–3 say that *scientists launched* the tardigrades into space, so space is not their *natural habitat*. Eliminate (B). *Water pipes* are not mentioned in either passage, so eliminate (C). Lines 39–40 mention the *tardigrades' precarious environment*, which are *damp pools or patches of water on moss or lichen*, which support (D). The correct answer is (D).

Section 2—Writing and Language

1.   **B**   The vocabulary is changing in the answer choices, so the question is testing word choice. Look for a word whose definition is consistent with the other ideas in the sentence. The sentence discusses what *aren't* on the list, and the next sentence uses the phrase *As one would expect*. Therefore, the definition should mean "something unexpected." *Exceptions* means " exclusion or objections," so eliminate (A). *Surprises* means "unexpected," so keep (B). *Outliers* means "those outside of the norm," so eliminate (C). *Abominations* means "greatly disliked," so eliminate (D). The correct answer is (B).

2.   **D**   The number of words is changing in the answer choices, so the question is testing concision. First, determine whether the extra words are necessary. In this case, all the answers mean the same thing, so the shortest answer is probably going to be the best. To confirm, the choice should be consistent with the rest of the sentence. The sentence lists two things. The second should be consistent with the first, so *Americans and Europeans* would be consistent. The correct answer is (D).

3.   **C**   Pronouns are changing in the answer choices, so the question is testing consistency of pronouns. A pronoun must be consistent with the noun it is replacing. The pronoun refers to the noun *winner*, which is singular. To be consistent, the pronoun in the answer choice must also be singular. *Their* and *they're* are plural, so eliminate (A) and (D). While *one's* is singular, it is only consistent with the word "one," which does not appear in the sentence, so eliminate (B). *His or her* is singular and is consistent with *winner*. The correct answer is (C).

4.   **B**   Note the question! The question asks for the *main topic of the paragraph,* so it's testing consistency of ideas. Determine the topic discussed in the paragraph and select the choice that is consistent with that idea. The paragraph discusses how *winners in most categories come from the elite research institutions*, yet *winners of the Nobel Prize in Literature…have not attended the same schools*. The correct answer will be consistent with the topic of *winners from different institutions* or *schools*. Stating that

the *winners in all categories tend to be affiliated with the same universities* is the opposite, so eliminate (A). *One surprise…with the educational backgrounds of some winners* is consistent, so keep (B). The *best research is done by college students and their professors* is not consistent, so eliminate (C). Stating that the *winners are highly intelligent* is not consistent, so eliminate (D). The correct answer is (B).

5. **A** The punctuation is changing in the answer choices, so the question is testing STOP and GO punctuation. Use the Vertical Line Test and identify the ideas as complete or incomplete. Draw the vertical line between the words *categories* and *though*. The phrase *These winners share an average age (64) and geographical diversity with those in other categories* is a complete idea. The phrase *though they have not attended the same schools* is an incomplete idea. To connect a complete idea to an incomplete idea, GO or HALF-STOP punctuation is needed. The semicolon and the period are STOP punctuation, so eliminate (B) and (D). The words *though* and *however* are changing in (A) and (C). Both words indicate a separate idea that contrasts with the previous idea. The word *however* makes the second part of the sentence complete, which does not work with GO punctuation. Eliminate (C). The correct answer is (A).

6. **D** The entire phrases are changing in the answer choices, so the question is testing concision and precision. Also, the commas are changing in the answer choices, so the question is testing the four ways to use a comma. In this sentence, the commas are used to separate out unnecessary info. Both (A) and (B) use the name *Toni Morrison* as both the object of the prize (it went *to* her) and the subject of the verb *earned*. The name cannot do both jobs, so eliminate (A) and (B). Both (C) and (D) correctly separate out *Toni Morrison* as she is already identified as the *winner* or the *recipient*. Since (C) and (D) are both grammatically correct, choose the more concise answer. The phrase *whose name was* is not needed, so eliminate (C). The correct answer is (D).

7. **C** Both the pronouns and the verbs are changing in the answer choices, so the question is testing consistency. A pronoun must be consistent in number with the noun it is replacing. The pronoun refers to the noun *committee*, which is singular. To be consistent, the pronoun in the answer choice must also be singular. The pronouns *they* and *we* are plural, so eliminate (A), (B), and (D). The pronoun *it* is singular. The correct answer is (C).

8. **A** Verbs are changing in the answer choices, so the question is testing consistency of verbs. A verb must be consistent with its subject and with the other verbs in the sentence. The subject of the verb is *Work*, which is singular. To be consistent, the verb in the answer choices must also be singular. Eliminate (B) and (C) because they are plural. *Requires* is in the present tense and *has required* is in the present perfect. Since there are no other verbs in the sentence, select the choice that is consistent with the verb in the following sentence. The following sentence uses the verb *provide*, which is present tense. Eliminate (D). The correct answer is (A).

9. **D** One thing that is changing in the answer choices is the number of words, so the question is testing concision. Both *findings* and *discoveries* mean the same thing, so it is redundant to list both. Eliminate (A), (B), and (C). The correct answer is (D).

10. **C** Note the question! The question asks where sentence 6 should be placed, so it's testing consistency. Determine the subject matter of the sentence, and find the other sentence that also discusses that information. Sentence 6 mentions *literature needs no such place*, and uses the word *however*. For

consistency, sentence 6 should be placed after a discussion of *place* and before a discussion of *literature*. Sentences 2 and 3 discuss *an atmosphere* for *economics, medicine, and the sciences* and sentence 4 discusses literature. Therefore, sentence 6 should be placed between sentences 3 and 4. The correct answer is (C).

11. **B** Note the question! The question asks for the choice that would *most effectively support the assertion made in this sentence and paragraph*, so it's testing consistency of ideas. The main idea of the paragraph is that *great thinkers and scholars do not live only at the big research universities*, so the correct answer will be consistent with this idea. The claim that *you'd find the most open minds at the best schools* is not consistent, so eliminate (A). Discussing different educational sources such as a *high-end graduate program, a community college, or the workforce* is consistent, so keep (B). Claiming that *Literature laureates are an exception* is not consistent, so eliminate (C). Discussing an *author of fiction* is not consistent, so eliminate (D). The correct answer is (B).

12. **C** Commas are changing in the answer choices, so the question is testing the four ways to use a comma. The sentence contains a list of four things: 1) dog, 2) cat, 3) fish, and 4) horse. There should be a comma after each item in the list before the word *and* or *or*. Therefore, there must be a comma after *fish*. Eliminate (A) and (D). There is no need for a comma after *or*, so eliminate (B). The correct answer is (C).

13. **A** The vocabulary is changing in the answer choices, so the question is testing word choice. Use *fewer* when comparing concrete, countable items. Use *less* when comparing uncountable nouns. The sentence is comparing the number of *graduates*, which is countable, so use *fewer*. Eliminate (B) and (D). Next, *than* indicates a comparison while *then* indicates time. The sentence is comparing the graduates each year, so eliminate (C). The correct answer is (A).

14. **D** Note the question! The question asks for the statement that best supports the statement made earlier in this sentence, so it's testing consistency of ideas. The beginning of the sentence states that *it may be time to bring the dream back*. The *dream* is the *dream of being veterinarians* from the first sentence. Thus, the underlined portion must be consistent with the idea of fulfilling the dream of becoming a vet. The *U.S. economy* is not consistent, so eliminate (A). The number of *children born* is not consistent, so eliminate (B). That *some veterinarians will retire* does not necessarily mean there will be an increase in the number of jobs typically available, so eliminate (C). Stating that *the veterinary profession will grow* is consistent, so keep (D). The correct answer is (D).

15. **B** Note the question! The question asks for the choice that has *accurate data based on the graph*, so it's testing consistency. First, understand the labels and the data from the graph. The graph shows the *percent change in employment, projected 2010–20* and lists three groups of jobs. Next, read each choice and determine whether it's consistent with the data in the graph. *Other professions will grow even more quickly* is not consistent because the veterinary technicians have the highest percent change; eliminate (A). Veterinary technicians will *grow at over three times the rate of all occupations in the United States* is consistent with the data because 52% is greater than 3 × 14% = 42%; keep (B). *A health technician has equally positive job prospects* is not consistent because the bar for veterinary technicians is at 52% and the bar for health technicians is at 26%; eliminate (C). *Those who have not gone to veterinary school* are not mentioned on the graph, so eliminate (D). The correct answer is (B).

16. **B** The punctuation is changing in the answer choices, so the question is testing STOP and GO punctuation. Use the Vertical Line Test and identify the ideas as complete or incomplete. Draw the vertical line between the words *pets* and *from*. The first phrase is a complete idea, and the second phrase is an incomplete idea. Therefore, either GO or HALF-STOP punctuation is needed. The period and the semicolon are STOP punctuation, so eliminate (A) and (C). The dash is a HALF-STOP, so keep (B). The comma in (D) has been moved between the words *from* and *basic*, which separates the meaning of the ideas incorrectly; eliminate (D). The correct answer is (B).

17. **C** The pronouns and nouns are changing in the answer choices, so the question is testing precision. Determine the subject of the pronoun, and choose an answer that makes the meaning consistent and precise. The subject of *are required to perform more and more procedures* should be the veterinarians, but that isn't clearly implied by a pronoun such as *they* or *them*. Since the veterinarians are not mentioned in the sentence, the noun *veterinarians* must be used to precisely state the correct subject. The correct answer is (C).

18. **C** Note the question! The question asks for the choice that *emphasizes that many pet owners consider their pets to be more human than animal*, so it's testing consistency of ideas. Showing that *pets are shared between friends* is not consistent with *more human than animal*, so eliminate (A). *Getting a puppy for Christmas* is not consistent, so eliminate (B). Owners who *self-identify as pet "parents"* is consistent, so keep (C). *Pets are a great way to teach children about death* is not consistent, so eliminate (D). The correct answer is (C).

19. **B** Note the question! The question asks where sentence 5 should be placed, so it's testing consistency. Determine the subject matter of the sentence, and find the other sentence that also discusses that information. Sentence 5 discusses *pet owners* believing their pets *are more "human" than ever before*. Sentence 2 discusses the *owners*. Since it starts with the phrase *In fact*, it indicates a continuation of the idea. Therefore, sentence 5 should be placed before sentence 2. The correct answer is (B).

20. **A** Commas are changing in the answer choices, so the question is testing the four ways to use a comma. The sentence does not contain a list, so look for unnecessary information. The phrase *for instance* is unnecessary information, so it should be surrounded by commas. The correct answer is (A).

21. **D** The number of words is changing in the answer choices, so the question is testing concision. The sentence must be about pets' minds or the way they think, but it does not need to reference both. Eliminate (A) because it contains a repetition of the ideas of *minds* and *the way they think*. Eliminate (C) because it changes the meaning and therefore is not precise. Between (B) and (D), (B) is wordier and therefore not as concise; eliminate (B). The correct answer is (D).

22. **D** The pronoun and nouns are changing in the answer choices, so this question is testing precision. Look for a word that provides the most precise definition. Eliminate (A), (B), and (C) because they are vague. *The stability* is the most precise. The correct answer is (D).

23. **C** The transition is changing in the answer choices, so the question is testing consistency of ideas. Determine how the ideas in the sentence relate to each other and select the transition that properly links them. The first part of the sentence states that *it may seem commonplace today*, and the second part states that *this is a relatively recent development*. These are opposite ideas, so a transition that

indicates a shift in ideas is needed. A lack of a transition, the word *because*, or the word *really* all indicate a similar idea, so eliminate (A), (B), and (D). *While* indicates a shift in ideas. The correct answer is (C).

24. **A** Note the question! The question asks *for information most consistent with the rest of the sentence*, so it's testing consistency of ideas. Since the sentence starts with *More than twenty years earlier* and the previous sentence gives the year as *1944*, the information in (B) and (C) is redundant, so eliminate (B) and (C). The rest of the sentence discusses *the veterans of the bloodiest war on record*, so the correct answer will be consistent with this idea. The *conclusion of World War I* is consistent, so keep (A). The *G.I. Bill* is not consistent, so eliminate (D). The correct answer is (A).

25. **D** Pronouns are changing in the answer choices, so the question is testing precision and consistency of pronouns. *They're* means "they are," which does not work in the sentence; eliminate (A). *It* is not a precise pronoun, and there is not a noun that *it* would clearly represent; eliminate (B). *Their* indicates possession, but the following word *was* cannot be possessed; eliminate (C). The correct answer is (D).

26. **C** The phrases are changing in the answer choices, so the question is testing precision and consistency. First, the placement of 1932 is changing, which changes the meaning. To be precise, the sentence should state that the march happened in 1932. Eliminate (A), which states that the veterans were from 1932. Eliminate (D), which states that the bonuses were in 1932. To be consistent with the meaning of the paragraph, the veterans went to Washington to demand their bonuses. Eliminate (B), which states that *Washington invited the veterans*. The correct answer is (C).

27. **B** Commas are changing in the answer choices, so the question is testing the four ways to use a comma. The sentence does not contain a list, so look for unnecessary information. All of the phrases are necessary, so there is no need for any commas. The correct answer is (B).

28. **A** Note the question! The question asks for the choice that agrees with the ideas discussed in this paragraph, so it's testing consistency of ideas. The first sentence states that the *government sought to avoid another such standoff*, so the answer will be consistent with this idea. The end of the second sentence mentions *economic collapse. Hoping to avoid...these catastrophes* is consistent, so keep (A). Stating the date *1944* is not consistent, so eliminate (B). *Pearl Harbor* is not consistent, so eliminate (C). *Historians don't understand* is not consistent, so eliminate (D). The correct answer is (A).

29. **D** Note the question! The question asks for the best placement of the underlined portion, so it's testing precision. Place the underlined portion in the correct position to keep the precise meaning of the sentence. The phrase *in university education* must follow the phrase that it's modifying. It is the *revolution* that is *in university education*. The correct answer is (D).

30. **A** Verbs are changing in the answer choices, so the question is testing consistency of verbs. A verb must be consistent with its subject, the other verbs in the sentence, and the time indicators. The time indicator is *by the early 1960s*, so the verb must be in the past tense. Eliminate (B) and (C). The verb in the previous sentence is *had used*, so *had changed* is consistent. The correct answer is (A).

31. **A** Note the question! The question asks for the choice that *best supports the idea presented in the previous sentence*, so it's testing consistency of ideas. The previous sentence states that college *was not limited to the very wealthy*, so the answer will be consistent with this idea. Eliminate (B) and (D) because they

state the opposite idea. The *criteria for selection* is not consistent, so eliminate (C). A *springboard for the upwardly mobile* is consistent because it suggests that people who came from less wealthy backgrounds could attend college and move up in society. The correct answer is (A).

32. **B** Note the question! The question asks for the best introduction for the topic of this paragraph, so it's testing consistency of ideas. The previous paragraph left off in the 1960s. This paragraph introduces 2008 and discusses how the bill was expanded. The correct answer will be consistent with the bill in more recent times. The paragraph indicates that the bill continued to get better, so eliminate (A). The *benefits of the bill continue to this day* is consistent, so keep (B). *G.I.s* and *their degrees* is not consistent, so eliminate (C). The *home subsidy* is not consistent, so eliminate (D). The correct answer is (B).

33. **C** The vocabulary is changing in the answer choices, so this question is testing word choice. Look for a word whose definition is consistent with the other ideas in the sentence. The sentence discusses how the *G.I. Bill changed the face of education as we know it*, so the word should indicate a substantial change. *Good* is positive but does not indicate a change, so eliminate (A). *Educational* means "instructive," so eliminate (B). *Influential* means "having a large effect," so keep (C). *Intelligent* means "smart," so eliminate (D). The correct answer is (C).

34. **A** Note the question! The question asks for the choice that *most effectively supports the ideas in this paragraph*, so it's testing consistency of ideas. The next sentence discusses the *fighting*, so the answer will be consistent with this idea. The correct answer is (A).

35. **D** Apostrophes are changing in the answer choices, so the question is testing apostrophe usage. When used with a noun, the apostrophe indicates possession. In this sentence, the *influence* belongs to the *animal*, so the word *animal* needs an apostrophe. Eliminate (A) and (B). Since *one animal* is singular, the apostrophe must be before the *s*. Eliminate (C). The correct answer is (D).

36. **B** Note the question! The question asks for the choice that *clarifies the information given in the first part of this sentence*, so it's testing consistency of ideas. The part of the sentence that needs *clarification* is the foreign phrase *le détroit*. The correct answer will explain what the phrase means. The correct answer is (B).

37. **C** The punctuation is changing in the answer choices, so the question is testing STOP and GO punctuation. Use the Vertical Line Test, and identify the ideas as complete or incomplete. Draw the vertical line between the words *span* and *furs*. The phrase *within a very short span* is an incomplete idea and the phrase *furs had become the dominant trade items in the region* is a complete idea. Therefore, GO punctuation is needed. The period and the semicolon are STOP punctuation, so eliminate (A) and (B). The comma is GO punctuation, so keep (C). The word *but* is one of the FANBOYS, and a comma plus one of the FANBOYS is STOP punctuation; eliminate (D). The correct answer is (C).

38. **C** The word order in the phrases is changing in the answer choices, so the question is testing precision. Select the choice whose word order makes the most sense. Focus on the phrasing and placement of *unfortunate*. It's not the *popularity* that is unfortunate, so eliminate (A). It's not the *resources* that are unfortunate, so eliminate (B). Choice (C) makes it clear that the situation of *finite resources* being popular is unfortunate, so keep (C). Eliminate (D) because it is not as clear as (C) in indicating that the popularity of finite resources is unfortunate. The correct answer is (C).

39. **A** Pronouns and verb tenses are changing in the answer choices, so the question is testing consistency. A pronoun must be consistent in number with the noun it is replacing, and a verb must be consistent with the verbs around it. The pronoun here refers to the noun *the beaver*, which is singular. To be consistent, the pronoun in the answer choice must also be singular. *They* is plural, so eliminate (C). Although *one* is singular, it is only consistent with the word *one*; eliminate (D). *It's* is a contraction that means "it is." Therefore, *it's* is in the present tense when the past tense is needed. Eliminate (B). The correct answer is (A).

40. **B** Note the question! The question asks whether the phrase should be kept or deleted, so it's testing precision. The phrase should be deleted unless it is needed to keep the precise meaning of the sentence. In this case, if the phrase *by factories* were deleted, it would be unclear what is replacing the homes. Therefore, the phrase should be kept. Eliminate (C) and (D). The *extinction of the beaver* is not consistent with the passage, so eliminate (A). The correct answer is (B).

41. **D** The phrases are changing in the answer choices, so the question is testing consistency of ideas. The previous sentences discuss how homes and factories replaced the beaver habitat. The answer will be consistent with the idea that wildlife no longer has a home there. Eliminate (B) and (C) because they are not consistent. Both (A) and (D) are consistent in meaning. However, (D) uses more precise language and is more concise. Eliminate (A). The correct answer is (D).

42. **D** Note the question! The question asks for *accurate data based on the graph*, so it's testing consistency. First, understand the labels and the data from the graph. The graph shows the *population of Detroit* over time. Then find the information in the sentence to match. The sentence says that *the population of Detroit was reduced by almost half*. Between 1990 and 2010 the population dropped from 1,000,000 to 900,000, which is not half; eliminate (A). *Throughout the twentieth century*, the population rose as well as declined; eliminate (B). Between 1890 and 1950 the population rose, so eliminate (C). From 1950 to 2010 the population dropped from about 1,900,000 to 900,000, which is over half. The correct answer is (D).

43. **A** The vocabulary is changing in the answer choices, so the question is testing precision of language. For each phrase, it is only correct to use the verb *have*, not the preposition *of*. Eliminate (B) and (C). Using the word *would* changes the meaning of the sentence, so eliminate (D). The correct answer is (A).

44. **B** The phrases are changing in the answer choices, so the question is testing consistency. Each choice uses a comparison word, so the items being compared must be consistent. Both (A) and (D) compare *cities* to *parts*, which is not consistent; eliminate (A) and (D). Choice (C) compares *parts* to *parts*, but it is unclear what the first *parts* refers to; eliminate (C). Choice (B) uses the word *as* to compare actions, so the sentence now compares what happens in other cities to what happened in parts of Detroit (*returning to something like a "natural state"*). The comparison is consistent. The correct answer is (B).

Section 3—Math (No Calculator)

1. **B** The question asks for the solutions to an equation. Although the question asks for a specific value and there are numbers in the answer choices, plugging in the answers could be difficult given the lack of calculator use and the square roots. Instead, solve the equation for x. Start by adding 48 to both sides of the equation to get $3x^2 = 48$. Next, divide both sides by 3 to get $x^2 = 16$. Then, take the square root of both sides to get $x = \pm 4$. The correct answer is (B).

2. **C** The question asks for the function that gives the hectares remaining to be harvested after d days. Translate the information in Bite-Sized Pieces and eliminate after each piece. One piece of information says that *the farm workers can harvest 23 hectares a day*. Therefore, each day there are 23 fewer hectares remaining to be harvested, so the function must include $-23d$. Eliminate (A) and (D), which do not contain this term. Compare the remaining choices. Choices (B) and (C) differ by the first term. The question states that the farmers are harvesting *a 2.6 square kilometer plot*, but the question refers to the function in *hectares*. The note after the question indicates that there are 100 hectares in 1 square kilometer, so 2.6 square kilometers is equivalent to $2.6 \times 100 = 260$ hectares. Eliminate (B), which does not contain this number. The correct answer is (C).

3. **C** The question asks for the value of x in the equation. Because the question asks for a specific value and the answers contain numbers in increasing order, plug in the answers. Since 16 is divisible by 4 and 8, it is easier to multiply $\frac{3}{4}$ and $\frac{3}{8}$ by 16 than it is to multiply those fractions by 9, so start with (C). If $x = 16$, the equation becomes $13 - \frac{3}{4}(16) = \frac{3}{8}(16) - 5$. This becomes $13 - 3(4) = 3(2) - 5$, which simplifies to $13 - 12 = 6 - 5$ or $1 = 1$. This is true. The correct answer is (C).

4. **A** The question asks for the value of y that makes the inequality true. Although the question asks for a specific value and there are numbers in the answer choices, plugging in the answers could be difficult given the negative values of some answer choices. Instead, solve the inequality for y. Start by multiplying both sides of the inequality by 4 to eliminate the fraction. The inequality becomes $4y < 3y - 2$. Next, subtract $3y$ from both sides to get $y < -2$. Because the value of y must be less than -2, (B), (C), and (D) are all too large. The correct answer is (A).

5. **B** The question asks for an expression that is equivalent to the one given. There are variables in the question and answer choices, so plug in. Make $a = 3$ and $b = 2$. The expression in the question becomes $(3)(2)^2 - 3(3)(2) + 2(2) - 6$, which simplifies to $(3)(4) - 18 + 4 - 6$ and then to $12 - 20$, which is -8. This is the target value; circle it. Now plug $a = 3$ and $b = 2$ into the answer choices to see which ones matches the target value. Choice (A) becomes $(3 + 2)(2 - 3)$, which is $(5)(-1)$ or -5. This doesn't match the target; eliminate (A). Choice (B) becomes $[(3)(2) + 2](2 - 3)$, which is $(8)(-1)$ or -8. This matches the target; keep (B), but check the remaining answer choices just in case. Choice (C) becomes $2(3 + 3)(2 - 3)$, which is $2(6)(-1)$ or -12. Eliminate (C). Choice (D) becomes $2[(3)(2) - 3(3)] + 2(2 - 6)$, which is $2(6 - 9) + 2(-4)$. This further simplifies to $2(-3) + 2(-4)$, which becomes $-6 - 8 = -14$. Eliminate (D). The correct answer is (B).

6. **D** The question asks for an equation that represents a graph. To find the best equation, plug points from the graph into the equations in the answer choices. It's easiest to start with zeroes, but plugging in the origin often makes more than one equation work. Instead, start with (2, 0). In function notation, $f(x) = y$. Make $x = 2$ and $f(x) = 0$ in each answer choice and eliminate any choice that is not true. Choice (A) becomes $0 = (2)(2 + 2)$, or $0 = (2)(4)$, which is $0 = 8$. Eliminate (A). Choice (B) becomes $0 = (2)(2 - 2)$, which is $0 = (2)(0)$ or $0 = 0$. Keep (B) but check the remaining answers just in case. Choice (C) becomes $0 = (2)(2 + 2)^2$, which is $0 = (2)(4)^2$ or $0 = 32$. Eliminate (C). Choice (D) becomes $0 = (2)(2 - 2)^2$, which is $0 = (2)(0)^2$ or $0 = 0$. Keep (D). Next, plug in another point. It is hard to tell exactly where the line hits when $x = 1$, but it is positive between $x = 0$ and $x = 2$. When $x = 1$, (B) becomes $f(1) = (1)(1 - 2) = (1)(-1) = -1$ and (D) becomes $f(1) = (1)(1 - 2)^2 = (1)(-1)^2 = 1$. The value of $f(1)$ should be positive, so eliminate (B). The correct answer is (D).

7. **A** The question asks for the equation of a line that intersects line *a*. Because the two lines intersect at $\left(\dfrac{5}{2}, 2\right)$, that point must be on the second line. Therefore, plug $x = \dfrac{5}{2}$ and $y = 2$ into each answer choice and eliminate any that is not true. Choice (A) becomes $4\left(\dfrac{5}{2}\right) - 3(2) = 4$, which is $10 - 6 = 4$ or $4 = 4$. This is true, and no information is given about the line other than the point. Since this equation worked, it must be the equation of the line. The correct answer is (A).

8. **D** The question asks for an equivalent form of an expression. There are variables in the answer choices, so plug in. Make $x = 2$. The expression becomes $(2 + 2)(2 - 5) - 18$, which is $(4)(-3) - 18$. This becomes $-12 - 18$ or -30. This is the target value; circle it. Now plug $x = 2$ into the answer choices to see which one matches the target value. Choice (A) becomes $(2 - 4)(2 + 7)$, which is $(-2)(9)$ or -18. This does not match the target, so eliminate (A). Choice (B) becomes $2^2 - 3(2) - 8$, which is $4 - 6 - 8$ or -10. Eliminate (B). Choice (C) becomes $2^2 - 3(2) - 25$, which is $4 - 6 - 25$ or -27. Eliminate (C). Choice (D) becomes $(2 - 7)(2 + 4)$, which is $(-5)(6)$ or -30. This matches the target. The correct answer is (D).

9. **B** The question asks for an equivalent form of an expression. There are variables in the answer choices, so plug in. Since *y* must be greater than 3, make $y = 4$. The expression becomes $\dfrac{1}{\dfrac{1}{2(4)} - \dfrac{1}{4+3}}$, which is $\dfrac{1}{\dfrac{1}{8} - \dfrac{1}{7}}$. To subtract fractions, make the denominators the same. One common denominator of 7 and 8 is 56. Multiply the numerator and denominator of $\dfrac{1}{8}$ by 7 to get $\dfrac{7}{56}$. Multiply the numerator and denominator of $\dfrac{1}{7}$ by 8 to get $\dfrac{8}{56}$. The expression becomes $\dfrac{1}{\dfrac{7}{56} - \dfrac{8}{56}}$, which is $\dfrac{1}{-\dfrac{1}{56}}$. To divide by a fraction, multiply the numerator by the reciprocal of the denominator to get $1 \times \left(-\dfrac{56}{1}\right)$ or -56.

This is the target value; circle it. Now plug $y = 4$ into the answer choices to see which one matches

the target value. Choice (A) becomes $3 - 4$ or -1. This does not match the target, so eliminate (A).

Choice (B) becomes $\dfrac{2(4)^2 + 6(4)}{3-4}$, which is $\dfrac{2(16)+24}{-1}$. Multiplying gives $\dfrac{32+24}{-1}$, which is -56.

Keep (B) but check the remaining answer choices just in case. Choice (C) is the reciprocal of (B), so

it will equal $-\dfrac{1}{56}$. Eliminate (C). Choice (D) is the numerator of (B), so it will equal 56. Eliminate

(D). The correct answer is (B).

10. **C**   The question asks for the value of n given a function definition. Because the question asks for a specific amount and there are numbers in the answer choices, plug in the answers. In function notation, the number inside the parentheses is the x-value that goes into the function, and the value that comes out of the function is the y-value. Before starting with the answers, find $h(-3)$ because that is what the correct answer will equal. Plug $x = -3$ into the h function to get $h(-3) = 9 - |-3 - 3| = 9 - |-6| = 9 - 6 = 3$. The correct answer should give 3 as a value for the function. Start with (B), 3. If $n = 3$, then $h(3) = 9 - |3 - 3| = 9 - |0| = 9$. This doesn't match the result for $h(-3)$, so eliminate (B). It may not be clear if a greater or smaller value of n is needed, so just pick another answer choice to try. Try (A). If $n = -6$, then $h(-6) = 9 - |-6 - 3| = 9 - |-9| = 9 - 9 = 0$. This doesn't match the value for $h(-3)$, so eliminate (A). Try (C). If $n = 9$, $h(9) = 9 - |9 - 3| = 9 - |6| = 9 - 6 = 3$. This matches the value of $h(-3)$. The correct answer is (C).

11. **B**   The question asks for the amount the *school is required to spend on curriculum-based activities*. Start by reading the final question and translate the information in Bite-Sized Pieces. The question states that the amount *spent on curriculum-based activities* is represented as x. The school has a *monthly discretionary budget of $9,000*, and the *discretionary budget that month* is represented as B, so $B = 9,000$. Additionally, the school *must spend $320 on after-school clubs*, and the amount spent on after-school clubs is represented as C, so $C = 320$. The equation becomes $320 = 0.08(9,000 - x)$. Solve for x. Start by multiplying both sides by 100 to get rid of the decimal: $32,000 = 8(9,000 - x)$. Divide both sides by 8 to get $4,000 = 9,000 - x$. Subtract 9,000 from both sides to get $-5,000 = -x$. Multiply both sides by -1 to get $x = \$5,000$. The correct answer is (B).

12. **D**   The question asks for the meaning of a number in context. Start by reading the final question, which asks for the meaning of the number 135. Then label the parts of the equation with the information given. The variable x is *the number of years since the 2010 census*, so P must be the *population of County Y, in thousands*. The equation becomes *population (thousands)* $= 2,500 + 135$(*years since 2010*). Next, use Process of Elimination to get rid of answer choices that are not consistent with the labels. Choice (A) refers to an increase in population per year, and the 135 is multiplied by years in the equation. This is consistent with the labels, so keep (A) but check the remaining answers just in case. Choices (B) and (C) both refer to the population increasing by a certain amount every 135 years, so these answers are not consistent with the labels. Eliminate (B) and (C). Choice (D) also refers to an

increase in population per year, so keep (D). The difference between (A) and (D) is the value of the increase. The equation represents the population *in thousands*, so 135 should be multiplied by 1,000 to give 135,000 as the actual population increase. Eliminate (A). The correct answer is (D).

13. **C**   The question asks for the value of *b* in an equation with exponents. When dealing with questions about exponents, remember the MADSPM rules. The DS part of the acronym indicates that Dividing matching bases means to Subtract the exponents. The bases on the left of the equation do not match, so use fractional exponents to simplify the equation. Radicals can be turned into fractional exponents by the rule *power over root*. Convert the radicals to fractional exponents to get $\dfrac{x^{\frac{5}{2}}}{x^{\frac{3}{4}}} = x^b$. Next, subtract the exponents to get $x^{\frac{5}{2}-\frac{3}{4}} = x^b$. Multiply the numerator and the denominator of the first fraction by 2 to get a common denominator of 4 on the exponents. The equation becomes $x^{\frac{10}{4}-\frac{3}{4}} = x^b$, which is $x^{\frac{7}{4}} = x^b$. The bases are the same, so the exponents must be equal. Therefore, $b = \dfrac{7}{4}$. The correct answer is (C).

14. **3**   The question asks for the value of *s* in a system of equation. To find this, look for a way to eliminate the *t* terms. The *t* terms have the same coefficient with opposite signs, so stack and add the equations to make *t* disappear.

$$\begin{array}{r} 4s + 2t = 7 \\ +\underline{3s - 2t = 14} \\ 7s \quad\quad = 21 \end{array}$$

Divide both sides by 7 to get *s* = 3. The correct answer is 3.

15. **25**   The question asks for the value of *x*, which is a degree measure on a figure. Use the geometry basic approach. Start by labeling the figure with the given information. Mark that $\angle RSV$ is congruent to $\angle TUV$ and that $\angle TUV$ measures 65°. More information is known about triangle *VUT*, so look for a way to use that to find *x*. Opposite angles are equal, so the measure of $\angle UVT$ will also be *x*°. There are 180° in a triangle, so $\angle UVT$ is 180 − 90 − 65 = 25°. Therefore, *x*° also equals 25°. The correct answer is 25.

16. **38**   The question asks for the number of student tickets that were sold. Use Bite-Sized Pieces to translate from English to math and then solve the resulting system of equations. Let *s* represent the number of student tickets sold and *r* represent the number of regular tickets sold. Since the *100-seat theater* sold out, *s* + *r* = 100. *Student tickets* are $24, *regular admission tickets* are $36, and *total ticket sales* are $3,144, so 24*s* + 36*r* = 3,144. The question asks for the number of student tickets sold, so solve for *s*. Start with the first equation. Subtract *s* from both sides to get *r* = 100 − *s*. Substitute this value of *r* into the second equation to get 24*s* + 36(100 − *s*) = 3,144. Distribute the 36 to get 24*s* + 3,600 − 36*s* = 3,144. Combine like terms on the left side by subtracting to get −12*s* + 3,600 = 3,144. Subtract 3,600 from both sides to get −12*s* = −456. Divide both sides by −12 to get *s* = 38. The correct answer is 38.

17. $\dfrac{2}{7}$, **.285, or .286**   The question asks for the value of an expression. There are related variables in the question, so plug in numbers that make the equation 5*x* = 7*y* true. Make *x* = 7 and *y* = 5, so the equation

becomes $5(7) = 7(5)$. Next, plug $x = 7$ and $y = 5$ into the expression to get $\dfrac{7-5}{7} = \dfrac{2}{7}$. The correct answer can be entered as $\dfrac{2}{7}$, .285, or .286.

Section 4—Math (Calculator)

1. **A** The question asks for an equivalent form of the provided expression. Although there are variables in the answer choices, plugging in on this question would be less efficient than simplifying. The expression is not too complicated, though, so simplifying is likely a more efficient approach. Distribute the 2 in front of the parentheses to get $2x - 10 + 3$. Combine like terms to get $2x - 7$. The correct answer is (A).

2. **A** The question asks for the number of teaspoons a glass tube can hold. Begin by reading the question to find information on the glass tube. The question states that a glass tube *can hold the 8.50 milliliters of liquid needed* and that *1 teaspoon ~ 4.93 milliliters*. Set up a proportion to determine the volume, making sure to match up the units: $\dfrac{1 \text{ teaspoon}}{4.93 \text{ milliliters}} = \dfrac{x \text{ teaspoons}}{8.50 \text{ milliliters}}$. Cross-multiply to solve for x: $8.50 = 4.93x$. Divide both sides of the equation by 4.93 to get $x \approx 1.72$ teaspoons. The correct answer is (A).

3. **D** The question asks for the number of vials a lab assistant can centrifuge in a certain amount of time. Begin by reading the question to find information on the centrifuge rate. The question states that *every fifteen minutes, a lab assistant can centrifuge 3 vials of* blood. First, convert hours to minutes. Each hour has 60 minutes, so there are $4(6) = 240$ minutes in 4 hours. Set up a proportion to determine the number of vials she can centrifuge in 4 hours, making sure to match up the units: $\dfrac{3 \text{ vials}}{15 \text{ minutes}} = \dfrac{x \text{ vials}}{240 \text{ minutes}}$. Cross-multiply to solve for x: $15x = 720$. Divide both sides of the equation by 15 to get $x = 48$ vials. The correct answer is (D).

4. **D** The question asks for a true statement based on the graph. The graph gives speed on the vertical axis and distance on the horizontal axis. Read each answer choice carefully and use Process of Elimination. Choice (A) refers to the x-intercept, but the graph never touches the horizontal x-axis; eliminate (A). Choice (B) states that the slowest speed is in the last 250 meters, but the slowest speed is at the beginning of the graph; eliminate (B). Choice (C) states that the runner's speed increases steadily during the first 1,000 meters, but there is a decrease in speed between 250 and 500 meters; eliminate (C). Choice (D) states that the fastest speed is at 750 meters, and the peak of the graph is at that point along the horizontal axis. The correct answer is (D).

5. **B** The question asks for the value of an expression given an equation. Start by finding the value of a from the equation. Divide both sides by 10 to get $a = \dfrac{13}{10}$. Next, substitute $\dfrac{13}{10}$ for a in the expression to get $5\left(\dfrac{13}{10} - \dfrac{1}{2}\right)$. Get a common denominator by multiplying $\dfrac{1}{2}$ by $\dfrac{5}{5}$. The expression becomes

$5\left(\dfrac{13}{10}-\dfrac{5}{10}\right)$. Subtract within the parentheses to get $5\left(\dfrac{8}{10}\right)$. Multiply to get $\dfrac{40}{10}$ or 4. The correct answer is (B).

6. **B** The question asks for the value of x that satisfies the equation. Since the question asks for a specific value and the answers contain numbers in increasing order, plug in the answers. Begin by labelling the answers as "x" and start with (B), –1. If $x = -1$, the equation becomes $(-1 - 3)^2 = 16$. Subtract within the parentheses to get $(-4)^2 = 16$. Square the left side to get $16 = 16$. This is true, so stop here. The correct answer is (B).

7. **B** The question asks for a probability, which is defined as $\dfrac{\text{number of outcomes you want}}{\text{number of possible outcomes}}$. Read the table carefully to find the numbers to make the probability. There are 14 females who indicated volunteering, so that is the *# of outcomes that fit requirement*. There are 95 total females, so that is the *total # of outcomes*. Therefore, the probability is $\dfrac{14}{95}$. The answer choices are expressed as decimals, so divide 14 by 95 to find that this is approximately 0.15. The correct answer is (B).

8. **D** The question asks for the number of males that plan to work, relax, or volunteer over the summer, based on the table. Look up the numbers in the table and add them together. There are 17 males who plan to have a summer job, 33 who plan to relax, and 11 who plan to volunteer, for a total of 17 + 33 + 11 = 61 males who plan to do one of those activities. The correct answer is (D).

9. **C** The question asks for the predicted number of females in the school who plan to travel based on the table. To calculate this, find the percent of the students surveyed who are females planning to travel and multiply that percent by the total population. There are 25 females who plan to travel out of 200 total students surveyed, so the percent is $\dfrac{25}{200} \times 100 = 12.5\%$ of the students are female and plan to travel. There are 1,200 students in the school, so there would be $\dfrac{12.5}{100} \times 1{,}200 = 150$ females in the school who plan to travel. The correct answer is (C).

10. **C** The question asks for the cost of the shoes that Dana purchased. Since the question asks for a specific value and the answers contain numbers in increasing order, plug in the answers. Begin by labelling the answers as "cost of shoes," and start with (B), $36. If the shoes were $36, then the shirt and purse together were the rest of the bill, or $81 – $36 = $45. However, the shoes cost 25 percent *more* than the shirt and purse combined, so this cost of the shoes is too low. Eliminate (A) and (B). Try (C), $45. If the shoes were $45, then the shirt and purse together were $81 – $45 = $36. To see if the shoes were 25 percent more than the other two items, find the difference in the costs, which is $45 – $36 = $9. This amount is 25% of $36, so these values fit the requirements of the question. The correct answer is (C).

11. **A** The question asks for the *percent value used to calculate the shipping charge*. To calculate this, first find the cost of the order before shipping. If the shipping cost is $15.65 and the total with shipping is $211.30, then the order cost $211.30 – $15.65 = $195.65 before shipping. The percent becomes $\dfrac{15.65}{195.65} \times 100 = 0.07999 \times 100 \approx 8\%$. The correct answer is (A).

12. **C** The question asks for the cost of a frisbee. Since the question asks for a specific amount, plugging in the answers is an option. However, there is a lot of information about the cost of hats and frisbees, so this may get confusing. Instead, start by translating English to math, then solve the resulting system for the price of a frisbee. Let f represent the cost of a frisbee and h represent the cost of a hat. The question says that *the total cost of the frisbees and hats is $72*, so $5h + 9f = \$72$. The question also says that *the cost of two hats and a frisbee* is $14.50, so $2h + f = \$14.50$. Next, solve for the price of one frisbee, or the value of f. One way to solve is to stack the equations and add to eliminate the price of hats. Multiply the equations so the coefficients on the price of hats are the same but with opposite signs. Multiply the first equation by 2 to get $10h + 18f = \$144.00$. Multiply the second equation by -5 to get $-10h - 5f = -\$72.50$. Stack and add the equations.

$$\begin{array}{r} 10h + 18f = \$144.00 \\ \underline{-10h - 5f = -\$72.50} \\ 13f = \$71.50 \end{array}$$

Divide both sides by 13 to get $f = \$5.50$. The correct answer is (C).

13. **B** The question asks for a true statement given the equations of two lines. Choices (A), (B), and (C) state that the lines are the same line, perpendicular, or parallel, respectively. To determine whether any of these is true, find the slopes of the two lines. The first equation is in standard form: $Ax + By = C$. The slope of a line in standard form is $-\dfrac{A}{B}$. For this equation, $A = 3$ and $B = 2$, so the slope of this line is $-\dfrac{3}{2}$. The second equation is in slope-intercept form: $y = mx + b$. The slope of a line in slope-intercept form is m, so the slope of the line is $\dfrac{2}{3}$. The two slopes are negative reciprocals, which means the lines are perpendicular. The correct answer is (B).

14. **A** The question asks for the meaning of the constant and coefficient in the equation. Label the parts of the equation with the information given. The question states that m is *the number of months since the loan was made*, and y is the *money, in dollars, that Stephen still owes*. Therefore, the equation is *the money, in dollars, that Stephen still owes* = 1,200 − 75(*the number of months since the loan was made*). Next, use Process of Elimination to get rid of answer choices that are not consistent with the labels. Choice (A) states that 75 is the rate of decrease in dollars per month and $1,200 is the original amount of the loan. Since 75 is multiplied by the number of months since the loan was made, and that term is subtracted from 1,200, this is consistent with the labels; keep (A). Choice (B) says that it will take 75 months to pay off the loan, but 75 is multiplied by the number of months. This is not consistent with the labels, so eliminate (B). Choice (C) states that 75 is the rate of increase in the total amount owed, but 75 × *months since the loan was made* is subtracted from, not added to, the amount owed. Eliminate (C). Choice (D) states that 75 is the rate of increase in the monthly payments, but again, there is not an increase because the equation features subtraction. Eliminate (D). The correct answer is (A).

15. **C** The question asks for the average cost of a child's meal. For averages, use the formula $T = AN$, in which T is the total, A is the average, and N is the number of things. Read the chart carefully to find the correct numbers to use. In the Children column, there are a total of 1,875 meals for a total cost of $24,750. The formula becomes $24,750 = A(1,875)$. Divide both sides by 1,875 to find that $\$13.20 = A$. The correct answer is (C).

16. **D** The question asks for a probability, which is defined as $\frac{\text{number of outcomes you want}}{\text{number of possible outcomes}}$. Read the table carefully to find the numbers to make the probability. There are 1,143 male adults and 1,237 female adults who ordered chicken, so there are 1,143 + 1,237 = 2,380 total adults who ordered chicken. This is the number of outcomes you want. The total possible outcomes includes everyone who ordered chicken. There are also 924 children who ordered chicken, so there are 924 + 2,380 = 3,304 possible outcomes. Therefore, the probability is $\frac{2,380}{3,304}$. The answer choices are expressed as decimals, so divide 2,380 by 3,304 to find that this is approximately 0.72. The correct answer is (D).

17. **A** The question asks for the answer that *is equivalent to two Newtons*. Look through the question to find a mention of Newtons. In the equation, *R* is drag force in Newtons, so the correct answer will make *R* = 2. The other variables are *C* as the coefficient of drag and *v* as velocity in meters per second. Plug the values for *C* and *v* in the answer choices into the equation to determine which gives 2 for *R*. Start with (A). If the coefficient of drag is 1 and velocity in meters per second is 2, then *C* = 1 and *v* = 2. Plug those values into the equation to get $R = \frac{1}{2}(1)(2)^2$, which becomes $R = \frac{1}{2}(4)$ or *R* = 2. This matches the value given in the question, so stop here. The correct answer is (A).

18. **A** The question asks for an expression for the amount a customer would pay for two pairs of shoes during a sale. Translate the information in Bite-Sized Pieces and eliminate after each piece. The question states that *the tax rate of 6 percent is applied to the whole purchase*, so everything should be multiplied by 1.06 to reflect the total (1) plus the additional 6 percent (0.06). Eliminate (C), which only has the 1.06 multiplied by one term, and (D), which does not have 1.06 at all. The question also states that the *customer receives a 30 percent discount on a second pair of shoes after purchasing the first at regular price*, so the price of the second shoe should be added to the first, not subtracted from it. Eliminate (B). The correct answer is (A).

19. **B** The question asks for a true statement based on the data in a histogram. Read the numbered statements carefully and use Process of Elimination. There are various statistical measures in the statements, so start with the easiest to calculate: mode and range. Statement (III) says that the mode is equal to the range. The mode is the most commonly occurring value, so in this case it will be the bar with the most students, which is 5. The range of a list of values is the greatest value minus the least value, so in this case, that is 5 – 0 = 5. Because the mode and range are equal, (III) is true. Eliminate (A) and (C), which do not contain statement (III). Compare the remaining answer choices. Choice (D) includes statement (II), which indicates that the median is equal to the mean. The median is the value in the middle of all the values, when all the values are arranged consecutively. There are 6 students who sold 0 barrels of popcorn, 2 who sold 1 barrel, 3 who sold 2, 3 who sold 3, 7 who sold 4, and 9 who sold 5. Therefore, there are 6 + 2 + 3 + 3 + 7 + 9 = 30 students total. Because there is an even number of students, the median will be average of the 15th and 16th students. Starting from the lower number of barrels of popcorn, there are 6 + 2 + 3 = 11 students who sold 0 to 2 barrels. The next 3 students sold 3 barrels, bringing the list up to 14 students who sold 0 to 3 barrels. Because 7 students sold 4 barrels of popcorn, the 15th and 16th student both sold 4 barrels of popcorn. Therefore, the median is 4. To find the mean or average, use the formula *T* = *AN,* in which *T* is the total, *A* is the average, and *N* is the number of things. To find the total number of barrels, multiply the number

of students who sold a certain number of barrels by the number of barrels they sold and add up the results. This becomes $(6 \times 0) + (2 \times 1) + (3 \times 2) + (3 \times 3) + (7 \times 4) + (9 \times 5)$, which is $0 + 2 + 6 + 9 + 28 + 45 = 90$. Therefore, $T = 90$ and $N = 30$ for the number of students. The average formula becomes $90 = A(30)$. Divide both sides by 30 to get $3 = A$. This does not match the median, so statement (II) is false. Eliminate (D) which contains statement (II). The correct answer is (B).

20. **D** The question asks for a system of inequalities that models a specific situation. Translate the information in Bite-Sized Pieces and eliminate after each piece. One piece of information says that the tube must contain *at least 12 ounces, but no more than 16 ounces*. Because the amount in the tube is $a + b$, the answer should contain $12 \leq a + b \leq 16$. Eliminate (A) and (B) which do not include this inequality. Compare the remaining answer choices. The difference between (C) and (D) is the third inequality: specifically, whether 0.10 should be multiplied by $(a + b)$. The question states that the product should have a *concentration of more than 10% active ingredient*. The active ingredient should be more than 10 percent of the total product, so the correct answer must multiply 0.10 by the total product. Eliminate (C) which does not multiply 0.10 by any other term. The correct answer is (D).

21. **A** The question asks for the number of pets in the pet shop. Since the question asks for a specific value and the answer choices contain numbers in decreasing order, plug in the answers. Begin by labelling the answers as "total pets" and start with (B), 120. If there are 120 total pets and 40% of those pets are dogs, then $120 \times 0.40 = 48$ of the pets are dogs. If 25% of those pets are cats, then $120 \times 0.25 = 30$ of the pets are cats. Therefore, there are $48 - 30 = 18$ more dogs than cats. The question states that there are *36 more dogs than cats*, so eliminate (B). Since the numbers of cats and dogs were too close together, the total number of pets must be too small; eliminate (C) and (D) as well. If this isn't obvious, do the calculations on (A), 240. With 240 total pets, there would be 96 dogs and 60 cats, or 36 more dogs than cats. The correct answer is (A).

22. **B** The question asks for the equation of $h(x)$ in terms of $g(x)$. The graph of $h(x)$ is the same as the graph of $g(x)$ at every point where y is greater than or equal to 0, but for all the points where y is less than 0 on the graph of $g(x)$, the graph is flipped from below the x-axis to above it on the graph of $h(x)$. The transformation that would cause this would be absolute value, which is (B). Choice (A) would flip *all* values of $g(x)$ over the x-axis, but only the negative y-values were flipped. Choice (C) would shift $g(x)$ up three units, but the positive values are not shifted, and the negative values are reflected. Choice (D) would shift $g(x)$ to the right three units, but once again the positive values aren't shifted. The correct answer is (B).

23. **C** The question asks for the length of side $\overline{NO}$ on a figure. Use the geometry basic approach. Start by labeling the figure with the given information. Label NP as 7 and LN as 18. Mark angles NPO and MLN as congruent.

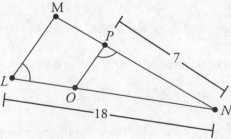

Since the two triangles have a congruent angle and share angle N, the third angles of the triangles will be congruent as well. Therefore, the triangles are similar, with triangle NPO corresponding to triangle NLM. The corresponding sides are difficult to see, since the figure is not drawn to scale and the angle in the lower left of NLM is congruent to the angle at the top of NPO. Redraw the two triangles separately using the description in the question to get the correct scale.

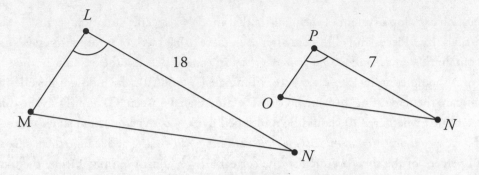

Similar triangles have proportional sides, so set up the proportion with the known sides compared to NO and its corresponding side MN: $\dfrac{NP}{NL} = \dfrac{NO}{MN}$. Plug the information given for the lengths of NP and LN into the proportion to get $\dfrac{7}{18} = \dfrac{NO}{MN}$. The question states that the length of $\overline{MN}$ is *1 unit less than 3 times the length of* $\overline{NO}$, so translate this into $MN = 3(NO) - 1$. Put the right side of this equation into the proportion for MN to get $\dfrac{7}{18} = \dfrac{NO}{3(NO) - 1}$. To solve for NO, cross-multiply to get $18(NO) = 7[3(NO) - 1]$ or $18NO = 21NO - 7$. Subtract $21NO$ from both sides to get $-3NO = -7$, then divide both sides by -3 to get $NO = \dfrac{7}{3}$. The correct answer is (C).

24. **C** The question asks for the relationship between two variables. If the fan group increases by a certain percentage each month, then the actual number of additional members each month increases as the size of the group increases. This is exponential growth, so eliminate (B) and (D), which indicate linear growth. Compare the remaining answer choices. The difference between (A) and (C) is when the higher numbers will occur. Because the size of the group is increasing, later dates will have *higher membership numbers*; eliminate (A). The correct answer is (C).

25. **D** The question asks for the meaning of an expression in context. Start by reading the final question, which asks for the meaning of the expression $\dfrac{\sqrt{3}}{2} x^2$. Then label the parts of the equation with the information given. The question states that x is the *length of the sides of the triangular ends* and y is *the length of the rectangular faces*. The equation becomes $SA = 2 \left(\dfrac{\sqrt{3}}{4} \left(\text{length of sides of triangular ends} \right)^2 \right) + 3 \left(\text{length of sides of triangular ends} \right) \left(\text{length of rectangular faces} \right)$. Next, use Process of Elimination to get rid of answer choices that are not consistent with the labels. Since the expression $\dfrac{\sqrt{3}}{2} x^2$ only includes the sides of the triangular faces as a variable, it doesn't

refer to the rectangular faces; eliminate (B) and (C). Compare the remaining answer choices. The difference between (A) and (D) is the number of triangular faces included. In the equation, the term $\frac{\sqrt{3}}{4}x^2$ is multiplied by 2, which would result in $\frac{\sqrt{3}}{2}x^2$. Therefore, $\frac{\sqrt{3}}{2}x^2$ must represent both the triangular sides. Eliminate (A). The correct answer is (D).

26. **C** The question asks for an equivalent form of an expression. There are variables in the answer choices, so plug in. Make $y = 2$. The expression becomes $(3 - 2)^2 - (3 - 2)$, which is $(1)^2 - 1$ or 0. This is the target value; circle it. Now plug $y = 2$ into the answer choices to see which one matches the target value. Choice (A) becomes $3 - 2$ or 1. This does not match the target, so eliminate (A). Choice (B) becomes $2^2 - 7(2) + 6$, which is $4 - 14 + 6$ or -4; eliminate (B). Choice (C) becomes $(3 - 2)(2 - 2)$, which is $(1)(0)$ or 0; keep (C), but check (D) just in case. Choice (D) becomes $9 - 2^2$, which is $9 - 4$ or 5; eliminate (D). The correct answer is (C).

27. **B** The question asks for the percent increase from a patient's actual height to that predicted by the line of best fit. Percent change is defined as $\frac{\text{difference}}{\text{original}} \times 100$. The child who is *exactly 8 years old* is 40 inches tall, and the line of best fit indicates that someone with an age of 8 will have a height of 50 inches. The difference in heights is $50 - 40 = 10$ inches. Because the question asks for a *percent increase*, use the smaller number as the original. The percent change is $\frac{10}{40} \times 100 = 25\%$. The correct answer is (B).

28. **396** The question asks for the volume of a box. The dimensions of the box are described in the word problem, so start by translating English to math. The question states that the *width is 2 inches more than its length*, so $w = l + 2$. The question also states that the *height is 5 inches less than its length*, so $h = l - 5$. The two smallest dimensions would be the length and the height, because $l + 2$ is greater than l and $l - 5$. The formula for the area of a rectangle is $A = lw$. The area of the smallest face is 36, so the formula becomes $36 = l(l - 5)$. This simplifies to $36 = l^2 - 5l$. Solve by subtracting 36 from both sides to set the quadratic equal to zero to get $0 = l^2 - 5l - 36$. Factor the quadratic; -9 and 4 add to -5 and multiply to -36, so the quadratic factors to $0 = (l - 9)(l + 4)$. The values of l are 9 and -4, but a length cannot be negative, so use $l = 9$. The width is $l + 2 = 9 + 2 = 11$, and the height is $l - 5 = 9 - 5 = 4$. The formula for the volume of a rectangular box is $V = lwh$, so plug in the values to determine the volume of the box. The formula becomes $V = (9)(11)(4) = 396$. The correct answer is 396.

29. **1** The question asks for the value of y in a system of equations, so solve the system for y. Look to eliminate the x terms by making the coefficients on x in the two equations the same but with opposite signs. Multiply the first equation by 2 to get $10x - 6y = 14$, and multiply the second equation by -5 to get $-10x - 5y = -25$. Stack and add the equations.

$$10x - 6y = 14$$
$$\underline{-10x - 5y = -25}$$
$$-11y = -11$$

Divide both sides by -11 to get $y = 1$. The correct answer is 1.

30. **56.4 or 56.5** The question asks for the percent of runners *completing the marathon in under four hours* that *were women*. The question doesn't give an actual number for the runners, but percent information about the unknown total is given. Therefore, plug in for the unknown total. Make the total number of runners 1,000. If *45 percent of the runners were men*, then 0.45 × 1,000 = 450 of the runners were men. If the rest were women, then 1,000 − 450 = 550 of the runners were women. If *64 percent of the men* completed the marathon in under four hours, then 0.64 × 450 = 288 of the men completed the marathon in under four hours. Similarly, if *68 percent of the women completed the marathon in under four hours*, then 0.68 × 550 = 374 women completed the marathon in under four hours. The total number of runners who completed the marathon in under four hours is 288 + 374 = 662, so the percent becomes $\frac{374}{662} \times 100 = 56.49$ percent of the runners who completed the marathon in less than four hours. The correct answer can be expressed as 56.4 or 56.5.

31. **66.2** The question asks for the percent of runners who *completed the marathon in under four hours*. The question doesn't give an actual number for the runners, but percent information about the unknown total is given. Therefore, plug in for the unknown total. Make the total number of runners 1,000. If *45 percent of the runners were men*, then 0.45 × 1,000 = 450 of the runners were men. If the rest were women, then 1,000 − 450 = 550 of the runners were women. If *64 percent of the men* completed the marathon in under four hours, then 0.64 × 450 = 288 of the men completed the marathon in under four hours. Similarly, if *68 percent of the women completed the marathon in under four hours*, then 0.68 × 550 = 374 women completed the marathon in under four hours. The total number of runners who completed the marathon in under four hours is 288 + 374 = 662, so the percent becomes $\frac{662}{1,000} \times 100 = 66.2\%$. The correct answer is 66.2.

RAW SCORE CONVERSION TABLE SECTION AND TEST SCORES

Raw Score (# of correct answers)	Reading Test Score	Writing and Language Test Score	Math Section Score	Raw Score (# of correct answers)	Reading Test Score	Writing and Language Test Score	Math Section Score
0	8	8	160	25	22	26	510
1	9	8	180	26	23	26	520
2	10	9	200	27	23	27	530
3	11	9	210	28	24	28	540
4	12	10	220	29	24	28	550
5	12	10	240	30	25	29	560
6	13	11	260	31	26	29	570
7	13	11	280	32	26	30	580
8	14	12	300	33	27	30	590
9	14	13	320	34	28	31	600
10	15	14	330	35	28	32	610
11	15	15	350	36	29	33	620
12	16	15	370	37	30	33	630
13	16	16	380	38	30	34	640
14	17	17	400	39	31	34	650
15	17	17	410	40	32	35	660
16	18	18	420	41	33	36	670
17	18	19	430	42	33	37	680
18	19	20	440	43	34	37	690
19	19	21	450	44	35	38	700
20	20	22	460	45	36		710
21	20	22	470	46	37		730
22	21	23	480	47	38		740
23	21	24	490	48			760
24	22	25	500				

CONVERSION EQUATION SECTION AND TEST SCORES

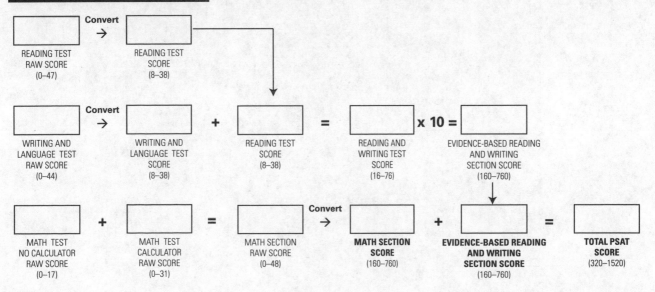

Part III
PSAT/NMSQT
Prep

6 Reading Comprehension
7 Introduction to Writing and Language Strategy
8 Punctuation
9 Words
10 Questions
11 Math Basics
12 Math Techniques
13 Advanced Math
14 Additional Math Topics

Chapter 6
Reading
Comprehension

Half of your Evidence-Based Reading and Writing score comes from the Reading Test, a 60-minute test that requires you to answer 47 questions spread out over five passages. The questions will ask you to do everything from determining the meaning of words in context, to deciding an author's purpose for providing a detail, to finding the main idea of an entire passage, to pinpointing information on a graph. Each passage ranges from 500 to 750 words and has 9 or 10 questions. Time will be tight on this test. The purpose of this chapter is to introduce you to a basic approach that will streamline how you take the test and allow you to focus on only what you need to get your points.

PSAT READING: CRACKING THE PASSAGES

Answering passage-based reading questions is exactly like taking an open-book test: all of the information that you could be asked about is right in front of you, so you never have to worry about any history, literature, or chemistry that you may (or may not) have learned in school. Of course, you will use the passage to answer the questions, but you will *not* need to read the passage from beginning to end, master all its details, and then carefully select the one choice that answers the question perfectly. What you need is a way to get in and get out of this section with as little stress and as many points as possible.

If someone asked you in what year Louis Pasteur invented pasteurization, would you read the Wikipedia entry on Pasteur from the beginning until you found the answer? Or would you quickly scan through it looking for words like "invented" and "pasteurization"—or better yet, look for the numbers that represent a year, which are easy to spot? We're sure his childhood was fascinating, but your job is to answer a specific question, not read an entire text. This is exactly how to approach passage-based reading questions on the PSAT.

Your Mission:

Process five passages and answer 9 or 10 questions for each passage (or pair of passages). Get as many points as you can.

Okay…so how do you get those points? Let's start with the instructions for the Reading Test.

DIRECTIONS

Each passage or pair of passages below is followed by a number of questions. After reading each passage or pair, choose the best answer to each question based on what is stated or implied in the passage or passages and in any accompanying graphics (such as a table or graph).

Notice that the directions clearly state the correct answer is based on "what is stated or implied in the passage." This is great news! You do not have to rely on your outside knowledge here. All the College Board cares about is whether you can read a text and understand it well enough to answer some questions about it. Unlike in the Math or the Writing and Language Tests, there are no formulas to memorize, no comma rules to learn. You just need to know how to efficiently process the text, the questions, and the answer choices in order to maximize your score. A mantra you can use here: Don't think! Just read!

Another benefit of this open-book test format: you can (and should!) flip back and forth between the passage and the questions so that you are reading only what you need in order to answer a given question.

Your POOD and Your Reading Test

You will get all five of the Reading passages at the same time, so use that to your advantage. Take a quick look through the entire section and figure out the best order for you to do the passages. Depending on your target score, you may be able to temporarily skip (don't forget LOTD!) an entire passage or two, so figure out which passages are hardest, and save them for last (or for never).

How do you decide which ones to do and which ones to skip? Consider these concepts:

- **Type of passage:** You'll have one literature passage, two science passages, and two history/social studies passages. If you like to read fiction, the literature passage may be a good place for you to start. If you like to read nonfiction, one of the science or history/social studies passages might be a better starting place for you.
- **Topic and date of passage:** The blurb will give you some basic information about the passage that can help you decide whether to do the passage or skip it.
- **Types of questions:** Do the questions have a good number of Line References and Lead Words? Will you be able to find what you're looking for relatively quickly, or will you have to spend more time wading through the passage to find what you need?

Don't forget: On any questions or passages that you skip, always fill in your LOTD!

Basic Approach for the Reading Test

Follow these steps for every Reading passage. We'll go over these in greater detail in the next few pages.

1. **Read the Blurb**. The little blurb at the beginning of each passage may not contain a lot of information, but it can be helpful for identifying the type of passage.

2. **Select and Understand a Question**. For the most part, do the questions in order, saving the general questions for last and using your LOTD on any questions or passages you want to skip.

3. **Read What You Need.** Don't read the whole passage! Use Line References and Lead Words to find the reference for the question, and then carefully read a window of about 10–12 lines (usually about 5 or 6 lines above and below the Line Reference/Lead Word) to find the answer to the question.

4. **Predict the Correct Answer.** Your prediction should come straight from the text. Don't analyze or paraphrase. Often, you'll be able to find something in the text that you can actually underline to predict the answer.

5. **POE.** Eliminate anything that isn't consistent with your prediction. Don't necessarily try to find the right answer immediately, because there is a good chance you won't see anything that you like. If you can eliminate answers that you know are wrong, though, you'll be closer to the right answer. If you can't eliminate three answers with your prediction, use the POE criteria (which we'll talk about in a few pages).

Where the Money Is

A reporter once asked notorious thief Willie Sutton why he robbed banks. Legend has it that his answer was, "Because that's where the money is." While reading comprehension is safer and slightly more productive than larceny, the same principle applies. Concentrate on the questions and answer choices because that's where the points are. The passage is just a place for the College Board to stash facts and details. You'll find them when you need to. What's the point of memorizing all 67 pesky details about plankton if the College Board asks you about only 10?

Let's see these steps in action!

A sample passage and questions appear on the next few pages. Don't start working the passage right away. In fact…you can't! The answer choices are missing. Just go ahead to page 124, where we will begin going through the steps of the Basic Approach, using the upcoming passage and questions.

SAMPLE PASSAGE AND QUESTIONS

Here is an example of what a reading comprehension passage and questions look like. We will use this passage to illustrate the reading Basic Approach throughout this chapter. You don't need to do the questions now, but you might want to paperclip this page so it's easy to flip back to later.

Questions 21–29 are based on the following passage.

The passage below is adapted from an article discussing minor Elizabethan dramatists. It focuses on the works of Thomas Heywood and Thomas Middleton, two influential playwrights of the early seventeenth century.

Thomas Heywood, of whom little is known, was one of the most prolific writers the world has ever seen. In 1598 he became an actor, or, as
Line Henslowe, who employed him, phrases it, "came
5 and hired himself to me as a covenanted servant for two years." The date of his first published drama is 1601; that of his last published work, a "General History of Women," is 1657. As early as 1633 he represents himself as having had
10 an "entire hand, or at least a main finger," in two hundred and twenty plays, of which only twenty-three were printed. "It is true," he says, "that my plays are not exposed to the world in volumes, as others are: one reason is that many of them,
15 by shifting and change of companies, have been negligently lost; others of them are still retained in the hands of some actors, who think it against their peculiar profit to have them come in print; it was also never any great ambition in me to be in
20 this kind voluminously read." It was said of him, by a contemporary, that he "not only acted every day, but also obliged himself to write a sheet every day for several years; but many of his plays being composed loosely in taverns, occasions them to
25 be so mean." Besides his labors as a playwright, he worked as translator, versifier, and general maker of books. Late in life he conceived the design of writing the lives of all the poets of the world, including his contemporaries. Had this
30 project been carried out, we should have known something about the external life of Shakespeare; for Heywood must have carried in his brain many of those facts which we of this age are most curious to know.
35 Heywood's best plays evince large observation, considerable dramatic skill, a sweet and humane

spirit, and an easy command of language. His style, indeed, is singularly simple, pure, clear, and straightforward; but it conveys the impression of
40 a mind so diffused as almost to be characterless, and incapable of flashing its thoughts through the images of imaginative passion. He is more prosaic, closer to ordinary life and character, than his contemporaries.
45 With less fluency of diction, less skill in fastening the reader's interest to his fable, harsher in versification, and generally clumsier in construction, the best plays of Thomas Middleton are still superior to Heywood's in force of
50 imagination, depth of passion, and fullness of matter. It must, however, be admitted that the sentiments which direct his powers are not so fine as Heywood's. He depresses the mind, rather than invigorates it. The eye he cast on human life
55 was not the eye of a sympathizing poet, but rather that of a sagacious cynic. His observation, though sharp, close, and vigilant, is somewhat ironic and unfeeling. His penetrating, incisive intellect cuts its way to the heart of a character as with a knife;
60 and if he lays bare its throbs of guilt and weakness, and lets you into the secrets of its organization, he conceives his whole work is performed. This criticism applies even to his tragedy of "Women Beware Women," a drama which shows a deep
65 study of the sources of human frailty, considerable skill in exhibiting the passions in their consecutive, if not in their conflicting action, and a firm hold upon character; but it lacks pathos, tenderness, and humanity; its power is out of all
70 proportion to its geniality; the characters, while they stand definitely out to the eye, are seen through no visionary medium of sentiment and fancy.

There is, indeed, no atmosphere to Middleton's
75 mind; and the hard, bald caustic peculiarity of his genius, which is unpleasingly felt in reading any one of his plays, becomes a source of painful weariness as we plod doggedly through his works. This is most powerfully felt in his tragedy of "The

80 Changeling," at once the most oppressive and
impressive effort of his genius. The character
of De Flores in this play has in it a strangeness
such as is hardly paralleled in the whole range
of the Elizabethan drama. The passions of this
85 brute imp are not human. They are such as might
be conceived of as springing from the union of
animal with fiendish impulses, in a nature which
knew no law outside of its own lust, and was as
incapable of a scruple as of a sympathy.

These are the questions for the passage. We've removed the answer choices because, for now, we just want you to see the different question types the PSAT will ask. Don't worry about answering these here. Not all of these questions will have answers. This is just to demonstrate how to read questions in the Reading Comprehension section.

21

The primary purpose of the passage is to

22

According to the information in the passage, the author most likely would agree that Heywood

23

Which choice provides the best evidence for the answer to the previous question?

24

As used in line 9, "represents" most nearly means

25

The author's reaction to Middleton is best described as a mix of

26

According to the information in the passage, one primary difference between Heywood and Middleton is that Heywood

27

Which choice provides the best evidence for the answer to the previous question?

28

As used in line 28, "design" most nearly means

29

The information in lines 58–62 serves primarily to

Step 1: Read the Blurb

You should always begin by reading the blurb (the introductory material above the passage). The blurb gives you the title of the piece, as well as the author and the publication date. Typically the blurb won't have much more information than that, but it'll be enough to let you know whether the passage is literature, history/social studies, or science. It will also give you a sense of what the passage will be about and can help you make a POOD decision about when to do the passage.

Read the blurb at the beginning of the passage on page 121. Based on the blurb, is the passage literature, history/social studies, or science? What will the passage be about?

_____

_____

Step 2: Select and Understand a Question

Select...

Notice that the steps of the Basic Approach have you jumping straight from the blurb to the questions. There is no "Read the Passage" step. You get points for answering questions, not for reading the passage, so we're going to go straight to the questions.

On a test you take in school, you probably do the questions in order. That seems logical and straightforward. However, doing the questions in order on a Reading passage can set you up for a serious time issue. The College Board says the order of the questions "is also as natural as possible, with general questions about central ideas, themes, point of view, overall text structure, and the like coming early in the sequence, followed by more localized questions about details, words in context, evidence, and the like." So to sum it up, the general questions come first, followed by the specific questions.

That question structure works great in an English class, when you have plenty of time to read and digest the text on your own. When you're trying to get through five passages in only an hour, you don't have time for that. Instead of starting with the general questions and then answering the specific questions, we're going to flip that and do the specific questions first.

Look back at the questions on page 123.

What does the first question ask you about?

In order to answer that question, you'd have to read what part of the passage?

And what we don't want to do is read the whole passage! So skip that first question. You'll come back to it, but not until you've done the specific questions. Once you go through and answer all (or most) of the specific questions, you'll have a really good idea what the test-writers think is important. You'll also have read most of the passage, so answering the general questions at the end will be easier than it would be if you had started with them.

Remember we mentioned earlier that the questions are in "natural" order? Look at the Line References in the specific questions. What do you notice about them?

Yep! They're in order through the passage! So work through them as they're given, and you'll work through the passage from beginning to end. Do not get stuck on a hard question, though. If you find yourself stumped, use your LOTD and move on to the next question. You can always come back if you have time.

Based on that logic, let's skip the first question and move on to the second question.

...and Understand

Once you've selected a question, you need to make sure you understand what it's asking. Reading questions are often not in question format. Instead, they will make statements such as, "The author's primary reason for mentioning the gadfly is to," and then the answer choices will follow. Make sure that you understand the question by turning it into a question — that is, back into a sentence that ends with a question mark and begins with What/Why/How.

> **22**
>
> According to the information in the passage, the author most likely would agree that Heywood

What is this question asking?

Notice the phrase *most likely would agree that*. This phrase lets you know that the question can be rephrased as a "what" question. So for this particular question, you want to figure out "What does the author most likely think about Heywood?" Notice also the phrase *according to the information in the passage* at the start of the question. This phrase lets you know that you don't have to be psychic! You just need to find something the author actually said about Heywood, and use that information to answer the question.

> **Rephrase the Question...**
> ...so that it asks:
> What?
> Why?
> How?

Step 3: Read What You Need

Line References and Lead Words

Many questions will refer you to a specific set of lines or to a particular paragraph, so you won't need to read the entire passage to answer those questions. Those are Line References. Other questions may not give you a Line Reference, but may ask about specific names, quotes, or phrases that are easy to spot in the text. We'll call those Lead Words. It's important to remember that the Line Reference or Lead Word shows you where the *question* is in the passage, but you'll have to read more than that single line in order to find the *answer* in the passage.

If you read a window of about five lines above and five lines below each Line Reference or Lead Word, you should find the information you need. It's important to note that while you do not need to read more than these 10–12 lines of text, you usually cannot get away with reading less. If you read only the lines from the Line Reference, you will very likely not find the information you need to answer the question. Read carefully! You should be able to put your finger on the particular phrase, sentence, or set of lines that answers your question.

5 Above, 5 Below
5 is the magic number when it comes to Line Reference questions. Read about 5 lines above the Line Reference and then about 5 lines below it to get all of the information you need in order to answer the question correctly.

> Read a window of about 5 lines above and 5 lines below the Line Reference to get the context for the question.

25

The author's reaction to Middleton is best described as a mix of

What is the Lead Word in this question?

What lines will you need to read to find the answer?

Once you use the Lead Words to find your window, draw a bracket around the window so that you can find it easily. The more you can get out of your brain and onto the page, the better off you'll be. Because the Lead Word is *Middleton*, skip to line 48 and start reading there. In this case, the first half of the third paragraph would be a good window.

Now it's time to read. Even though you're reading only a chunk of the text, make sure you read it carefully.

Step 4: Predict the Answer

The College Board does its best to distract you by creating tempting—but wrong—answers. However, if you know what you're looking for in advance, you will be less likely to fall for a trap answer. Before you even glance at the answer choices, take the time to think about what specific, stated information in your window supplies the answer to the question. Be careful not to paraphrase too far from the text or try to analyze what you're reading. Remember that what might be a good "English class" answer may lead you in the wrong direction on the PSAT! Stick with the text.

As you read the window, look for specific lines or phrases that answer the question. Often what you're looking for will be in a sentence before or after the Line Reference or Lead Word, so it's crucial that you read the full window.

Once you've found text to answer the question, underline it if you can! Otherwise, jot down a prediction for the answer, sticking as close to the text as possible.

Let's keep looking at question 25, this time with the window.

25

The author's reaction to Middleton is best described as a mix of

---

Here's your window from the passage. Read it and see if you can find something that answers the question. Underline your prediction if you can.

> 45　With less fluency of diction, less skill in
> fastening the reader's interest to his fable, harsher
> in versification, and generally clumsier in
> construction, the best plays of Thomas Middleton
> are still superior to Heywood's in force of
> 50　imagination, depth of passion, and fullness of
> matter. It must, however, be admitted that the
> sentiments which direct his powers are not so
> fine as Heywood's. He depresses the mind, rather
> than invigorates it. The eye he casts on human life
> 55　was not the eye of a sympathizing poet, but rather
> that of a sagacious cynic. His observation, though
> sharp, close, and vigilant, is somewhat ironic and
> unfeeling.

Did you underline some negative terms as well as some positive ones? The passage gives you clear evidence that the author's reaction to Middleton involves both a positive and a negative

---

The Strategy
1. Read the Blurb
2. Select and Understand a Question
3. Read What You Need
4. Predict the Answer

judgment. The sentence *His observation, though sharp, close, and vigilant, is somewhat ironic and unfeeling* shows this ambivalence.

Step 5: Use Process of Elimination

A multiple-choice test is a cool thing because you have all the right answers on the page in front of you. All you have to do is eliminate anything that isn't correct. Sometimes, especially on Reading, it's easier to find wrong answers that aren't supported by the passage rather than trying to find the right answer that might not look the way you think it should.

Process of Elimination, or POE, involves two steps. The first step will be the question, "What can I eliminate that doesn't match—or is inconsistent with—my prediction?" For many of the easy and medium questions, this step will be enough to get down to the right answer.

The Strategy
1. Read the Blurb
2. Select and Understand a Question
3. Read What You Need
4. Predict the Answer
5. Use Process of Elimination

25

The author's reaction to Middleton is best described as a mix of

Remember, on the previous page, you used the text to predict that the author reacted to Middleton with a mix of positive and negative judgment. Start by eliminating anything that does not fit that prediction.

	Keep?	Eliminate?
A) admiration for his ingenuity but criticism for his absence of warmth.		
B) disgust for his style but appreciation for his displays of tenderness.		
C) confusion about his use of diction but curiosity about his sentiments.		
D) apathy toward his ability to dishearten readers but dislike of his coldness.		

Did you eliminate (C) and (D) right away? Neither choice involves a mix of positive and negative. That was fast! Now that you're down to two answer choices that fit your prediction, use the text to get the right one. On the negative side, what's the author's criticism? Middleton *depresses* us because he is *unfeeling*. Does that better match (A), criticism, or (B), disgust? Disgust seems too extreme. If you're not sure yet, look at the positive side: What does the author like about Middleton? The *force of imagination, depth of passion, and fullness of matter.* Does that match (A), admiration, for his ingenuity? Maybe. Does that match (B), appreciation, for his displays of tenderness? Not at all. Either way you slice it, (A) is better than (B). Pick (A).

POE Criteria

On most of the easy and medium questions, you'll be able to eliminate three of the four answers simply by using your prediction. On other questions, usually the Harder questions, your prediction will help you get rid of one or two answers, and then you'll need to consider the remaining answers a little more carefully. If you're down to two answers, and they both seem to make sense, you're probably down to the right answer and the trap answer. Luckily, there are some common traps that the College Board will set for you, and knowing them can help you figure out which is the trap answer and which is the right answer. Here are a few of those traps:

> **Predictions and POE**
> Use these criteria after you have eliminated anything that doesn't match your prediction.

- **Mostly Right, Slightly Wrong**: These answers look just about perfect except for a word or two that doesn't match what's in the text.
- **Could Be True**: These answers might initially look good because they make sense or seem logical. You might be able to support these answers in an English class, but they lack the concrete support from the text to make them correct PSAT answers.
- **Right Answer, Wrong Question:** These answer choices are true based on the passage, but they don't answer the question asked.
- **Right Words, Wrong Meaning:** These answer choices say what the passage says, but they don't mean the same thing. These answers are traps for test-takers who are simply matching words from the passage and not looking at the meaning.

QUESTION TYPES AND FORMATS

Now that you know the steps of the Basic Approach, let's consider the different types of questions you'll be answering. It's not important that you can identify the question types by the names we give them. But it is extremely important that you can read a question and know how to respond. Is the question asking you WHAT the author says, WHAT the author means, WHAT a particular word means, WHAT evidence supports a point, etc.? The next section of this chapter will help you decode those question types and formats. The final section will help you make sense of WHY or HOW an author does something, as well as the General WHAT questions. Your score will depend on your ability to figure out if a question is asking you WHAT, WHY, or HOW.

> Question Types and Formats:
>
> - Detail
> - Vocabulary in Context
> - Infer/Imply/Suggest
> - Paired Questions
> - General

DETAIL (*What?*)

When you see a question that contains the phrase *according to the passage* or *according to the author*, your job is fairly simple. Get to that part of the text, find the detail that tells you WHAT the passage or the author is saying, and then use POE to get rid of wrong answers. Carefully read the window and do not simply rely on your memory. The question writers are really good at tricking people who use their memories rather than their eyes.

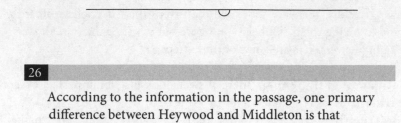

26

According to the information in the passage, one primary difference between Heywood and Middleton is that Heywood

A) displayed a more cynical attitude toward humanity.

B) had fewer of his works published.

C) was a more disciplined writer.

D) showed less powerful creativity in his writing.

Here's How To Crack It

First, you need to go back to the text and find a *primary difference* between the two writers. Since paragraphs 1 and 2 are about Heywood only, and paragraph 4 is about Middleton only, focus on paragraph 3. Since the second half of paragraph 3 is about only Middleton, focus on the first half, which contrasts both writers. As you read that window, underline whatever is true about Heywood but not Middleton. You should notice that, compared to Middleton, Heywood has more *fluency of diction* and *skill in fastening the reader's interest to his fable*, better *versification* and *construction*, but has less *force of imagination, depth of passion, and fullness of matter*. Once you have this prediction—based completely on the text, not on your opinion and not on your memory—use POE to work through the answer choices. Choice (A) doesn't match the prediction (and actually fits Middleton, rather than Heywood), so eliminate it. Choice (B) might seem logical, but it's not in the text and does not match the prediction. Eliminate it. Choice (C) could be true because the text says he had more fluency and skill and better construction. If he's better at the technical parts of writing, it might make sense that he's a more disciplined writer. However, nothing in the text actually supports that. Watch out for answers that you might be able to justify in an essay. There has to be support in the text! Choice (C) does not have that support, and it does not match the prediction. Eliminate it. Choice (D) totally matches the prediction. Remember: don't think—read! Put another way: don't remember —underline!

VOCABULARY IN CONTEXT (*What?*)

Another way that the College Board will test your reading comprehension is with Vocabulary-in-Context (VIC) questions. The most important thing to remember is that these are *IN CONTEXT!* Gone are the days of "SAT Vocabulary" when you had to memorize lists of obscure words like *impecunious* and *perspicacious*. Now the test-writers want to see that you can understand what a word means based on context. You'll see words that look familiar but may be used in ways that are a little less familiar. Do not try to answer these questions simply by defining the word in your head and looking for that definition. You have to go back to the text and look at the context for the word.

28

As used in line 28, "design" most nearly means

A) draft.

B) pattern.

C) biography.

D) intention.

Here's How To Crack It

With VIC questions, you don't need to read a full 10–12-line window. Typically a few lines before and a few lines after will give you what you need. Go to line 28 and find the word *design*. Underline it. When you read a bit before and after the word, say lines 25 through 29, the text says: *Besides his labors as a playwright, he worked as translator, versifier, and general maker of books. Late in life he conceived the design of writing the lives of all the poets of the world, including his contemporaries.* Now read the sentence and put in a different word than "design" that means the same thing. Did you use a word like "plan"? Compare your prediction to the four answer choices, and you can quickly eliminate (A), (B), and (C).

Do not give in to the temptation to simply answer the question without looking at the text. Did you notice that at least two of the wrong answer choices do legitimately mean *design*? If you don't go back to the text, you can easily fall for such a wrong answer. But if you make a prediction based on the text, you will avoid these tricky answers. Don't think—just read!

Now try this one.

```
24
```

As used in line 9, "represents" most nearly means

A) supports.

B) portrays.

C) elects.

D) acts.

Here's How To Crack It

Here are lines 8–12: *As early as 1633 he represents himself as having had an "entire hand, or at least a main finger," in two hundred and twenty plays, of which only twenty-three were printed.*

The sentence discusses how Heywood described his accomplishments, so you could replace the word *represents* with "describes." Does the word *supports* have the same meaning as "describes?" No. Does *portrays*? Yes—to portray something in a certain way means to describe it that way. What about *elects* or *acts*? No, and no. Using your prediction based on the meaning of *represents* in context, (A), (C), and (D) are out. You may have noticed that some of the wrong answers are related to other definitions of the word *represents*, but none of them fit your prediction nor the way the word is used in the passage. The correct answer is (B).

INFER/IMPLY/SUGGEST (*What?*)

When you see a question that contains the word *infer*, *imply*, or *suggest*, be extra careful. In real life, those words often signify a question asking your interpretation. You may think that the test-writers want you to do some English-class-level reading between the lines. In actuality, though, they don't. It's still just a straight reading comprehension question. There may be a tiny bit of reading between the lines, because the answer may not be as directly stated in the text as it will with a detail question, but there will still be plenty of evidence in the text to support the correct answer.

A few pages ago, we discussed this question:

25

The author's reaction to Middleton is best described as a mix of

A) admiration for his ingenuity but criticism for his absence of warmth.

B) disgust for his style but appreciation for his displays of tenderness.

C) confusion about his use of diction but curiosity about his sentiments.

D) apathy toward his ability to dishearten readers but dislike of his coldness.

Recall how we solved it by going back to the text, finding relevant evidence, predicting an answer, and then using POE to eliminate answer choices that didn't fit the prediction. If you rely on this procedure, you will improve your performance with these sorts of questions.

Whereas Detail questions ask WHAT the author says, Inference questions ask WHAT the author really means. The correct answer will have the same *meaning* as the text, even though the *words* may be different.

BEST EVIDENCE QUESTIONS (*What?*)

Remember the full name of this section of the test? It's the PSAT Evidence-Based Reading Test. Throughout this chapter, you've been using evidence to answer all of these questions, so this next step won't come as a complete surprise. In fact, once you get a hold of the best way to manage evidence questions, you'll be glad. You can do the work for one question and get points for two.

Best Evidence: Easy-to-Find Paired Questions

We discussed question 26 earlier. Here it is:

26

According to the information in the passage, one primary difference between Heywood and Middleton is that Heywood

---

The correct answer was (D): *showed less powerful creativity in his writing*. Recall that we based this answer on the part of the text that said Heywood had less *force of imagination, depth of passion, and fullness of matter*.

So now you encounter the following question:

27

Which choice provides the best evidence for the answer to the previous question?

A) Lines 8–12 ("As early . . . printed")

B) Lines 20–25 ("It was . . . mean")

C) Lines 45–51 ("With . . . matter")

D) Lines 54–56 ("The eye . . . cynic")

Here's How to Crack It

What to do? Since the text you already used to answer question 26 (*force of imagination, depth of passion, and fullness of matter*) was in lines 49–51, simply pick (C) and move on! Buy one, get one free.

We're not kidding: Easy-to-Find best evidence questions are like free points. Get them all!

Best Evidence
Not sure where to find the answer? Let the "best evidence" lines help!

Best Evidence: Harder-to-Find Paired Questions

Sometimes, though, the best evidence question follows a question that is harder to find in the passage. The first question may have no Line References or Lead Words, and the order of the questions might leave you with a long section of the passage to search. You might think that you have to answer the first question by reading a long section of the passage and then answer the evidence question based on that exhaustive research. But luckily, there's a time-saving and accuracy-improving alternative: a strategy that we call Parallel POE.

Using Parallel POE, you'll be able to work through the questions at the same time! When you find yourself faced with a set of paired questions, you can start with the second question (the "best evidence" question) if (1) you aren't sure where to look for the answer, or (2) the first question is a general question about the whole passage. Because the second question in the pair asks which lines provide the *best evidence* for the previous question, you can use those lines to help work through the answers for the previous question. Let's take a look.

22

According to the information in the passage, the author most likely would agree that Heywood

A) could have contributed more to our knowledge of influential seventeenth-century writers than he actually did.

B) was more involved in professions other than playwriting than many authorities today believe.

C) was an actor in more than two hundred plays, although only slightly more than twenty became popular productions.

D) would have been the most talented playwright of his day had he possessed more imagination and passion.

23

Which choice provides the best evidence for the answer to the previous question?

A) Lines 3–12 ("In 1598 . . . printed")

B) Lines 20–27 ("It was . . . books")

C) Lines 27–34 ("Late . . . know")

D) Lines 37–44 ("His style . . . contemporaries")

Here's How to Crack It

Heywood is discussed throughout most of the passage. That's a pretty big window! What to do? That's where Parallel POE comes in. Notice that question 23 gives you the only possible lines for your evidence. Choice (23A) references 10 lines, (23B) references 8 lines, (23C) references 8 lines, and (23D) references 8 lines. So what would you rather do: read the entire passage hoping you might find an answer somewhere or read these tiny chunks one at a time to see if they answer the question? We hope you answered the latter!

What's great about Parallel POE is that, in the first instance, the original question does not even matter. Think for a moment about how paired questions operate. The correct answer to the first question *must* be supported by an answer to the best evidence question, and the correct answer to the best evidence question *must* support an answer to the first question. In other words, if there is a best evidence answer that doesn't support an answer to the first question, it is wrong. Period. Likewise, if there is an answer to the first question that isn't supported by a best evidence answer, it too is wrong. Period.

Let's use this to our advantage! Rather than worry about what the first question is asking and what the answer might be, just start making connections between the two answer sets. If a best evidence answer supports a first question answer, physically draw a line connecting them. You should not expect to have four connections. If you are lucky, you will have only one connection, and you will have your answer pair. Otherwise, you might have two or three connections and will then (and only then) worry about the first question. The important thing to remember is that any answer choice in the first question that isn't physically connected to a best evidence answer—and any best evidence answer that isn't connected to an answer in the first question—must be eliminated.

Let's take a look at how this first Parallel POE pass would look. (The paired questions have been arranged in two columns for your convenience. This does not represent what you will see on the official test.)

22. According to the information in the passage, the author most likely would agree that Heywood	23. Which choice provides the best evidence for the answer to the previous question?
A) could have contributed more to our knowledge of influential seventeenth-century writers than he actually did.	A) Lines 3–12 ("In 1598 . . . printed")
B) was more involved in professions other than playwriting than many authorities today believe.	B) Lines 20–27 ("It was . . . books")
C) was an actor in more than two hundred plays, although only slightly more than twenty became popular productions.	C) Lines 27–34 ("Late . . . know")
D) would have been the most talented playwright of his day had he possessed more imagination and passion.	D) Lines 37–44 ("His style . . . contemporaries")

Don't worry about the question itself yet. Go straight to the best evidence lines.

- Choice (23A) says *In 1598 he became an actor, or, as Henslowe, who employed him, phrases it, "came and hired himself to me as a covenanted servant for two years." The date of his first published drama is 1601; that of his last published work, a "General History of Women," is 1657. As early as 1633 he represents himself as having had an "entire hand, or at least a main finger," in two hundred and twenty plays, of which only twenty-three were printed.* Does this evidence support any of the answer choices for question 22? Nope. So eliminate (23A) and move on.

- Choice (23B) says *It was said of him, by a contemporary, that he "not only acted every day, but also obliged himself to write a sheet every day for several years; but many of his plays being composed loosely in taverns, occasions them to be so mean." Besides his labors as a playwright, he worked as translator, versifier, and general maker of books.* Does this evidence support any of the answer choices for question 22? Choice (22B) looks possible, so draw a line physically connecting (23B) with (22B).

- Choice (23C) says *Late in life he conceived the design of writing the lives of all the poets of the world, including his contemporaries. Had this project been carried out, we should have known something about the external life of Shakespeare; for Heywood must have carried in his brain many of those facts which we of this age are most curious to know.* Does this evidence support any of the answer choices for question 22? Yes, it very strongly supports (22A), so draw a line physically connecting (23C) with (22A).

- Choice (23D) says *His style, indeed, is singularly simple, pure, clear, and straightforward; but it conveys the impression of a mind so diffused as almost to be characterless, and incapable of flashing its thoughts through the images of imaginative passion. He is more prosaic, closer to ordinary life and character, than his contemporaries.* Does this evidence support any of the answer choices for question 22? Nope. So eliminate (23D) and move on.

Look at your progress so far: (22C) and (22D) have no support from question 23, so go ahead and eliminate (22C) and (22D). No matter how good they may sound, they CANNOT be right if there is no evidence supporting them from the best evidence question.

Your work should look something like this at this point:

22. According to the information in the passage, the author most likely would agree that Heywood	23. Which choice provides the best evidence for the answer to the previous question?
A) could have contributed more to our knowledge of influential seventeenth-century writers than he actually did.	A) Lines 3–12 ("In 1598 . . . printed")
B) was more involved in professions other than playwriting than many authorities today believe.	B) Lines 20–27 ("It was . . . books")
C) was an actor in more than two hundred plays, although only slightly more than twenty became popular productions.	C) Lines 27–34 ("Late . . . know")
D) would have been the most talented playwright of his day had he possessed more imagination and passion.	D) Lines 37–44 ("His style . . . contemporaries")

Now you're down to a very nice 50/50 split. Go back to the question. Of the two pairs, which one best describes Heywood in a way that *the author would most likely agree with*? Your sense that (23C) strongly matched (22A) is a clue that this is what the author would most likely agree with, since it's something the author actually did say. The other pair was a weaker match, with a feeling of Could Be True. Eliminate (23B), eliminate (22B), choose the remaining answers (22A) and (23C), and get two points.

On the actual test, it would be too complicated for you to draw a full table like the one above, but all you need to do is create a column to the left of the best evidence answer choices for the answers to the previous question. Basically, it should look something like this:

Parallel POE

Since you can't draw a full table on the actual exam, try making notations as shown in question 22; that is, create a column to the left of the best evidence answer choices listing out the choices to the previous question.

There is a list of common question wording in the Chapter Summary on page 155. Use this list as you practice to help you identify the question types.

Q22   23. Which choice provides the best evidence for the answer to the previous question?

A   A) Lines 3–12 ("In 1598 . . . printed")

B   B) Lines 20–27 ("It was . . . books")

C   C) Lines 27–34 ("Late . . . know")

D   D) Lines 37–44 ("His style . . . contemporaries")

Best Evidence: Single Questions

You will also see some Best Evidence questions that are not paired with another question. When you see a single Best Evidence question, look at the lines given in each answer choice, and eliminate answers that don't provide evidence for the claim in the question. You will see an example of a single Best Evidence question in the next section.

SAMPLE PASSAGE AND QUESTIONS

Here is another example of a Reading passage and questions. We will use this passage to let you independently practice the Basic Approach on the WHAT questions you already know how to do (Detail, Infer, Vocabulary-in-Context, Best Evidence) and to model for you how to manage the WHY and HOW questions, as well as the Charts and Graphs questions and General questions.

Questions 19–28 are based on the following passage and supplementary material.

This passage is adapted from "Jumping Spiders Can Think Ahead, Plan Detours" by Michael Greshko, NG Image Collection. Published in 2016.

With brains the size of a sesame seed, jumping spiders may seem like mental lightweights. But a new study shows that many
Line species plan out intricate detours to reach their
5 prey—smarts usually associated with far bigger creatures. The arachnids, already well known for their colors and elaborate mating rituals, have sharp vision and an impressive awareness of three-dimensional space. "Their vision is more
10 on par with vertebrates," says Damian Elias of the University of California, Berkeley, who wasn't involved in the new research. "And that allows them to do things that are physically impossible for other animals that size."
15 Jumping spiders of the subfamily Spartaeinae (spar-TAY-in-ay) are particularly ambitious—they eat other spiders. Researchers suspect that preying on other predators requires extra intelligence and cunning. In the 1980s and
20 1990s, Robert Jackson of New Zealand's University of Canterbury demonstrated that *Portia fimbriata*, a member of this spider-snacking subfamily, methodically plans winding detours to sneak up on prey spiders. *Portia* can
25 even find hidden prey, suggesting that the predator can visualize its prey's location and a path to get there.

But Jackson, who received funding from National Geographic's Committee for Research
30 and Exploration, and his colleague Fiona Cross were sure that *Portia* wasn't alone in its forward thinking. "There's so much attention given to *Portia*," says Cross, "but there are these other [jumping] spiders: why not
35 them?" Demonstrating in the lab that other spider species also planned detours, however,

proved challenging: Other spiders ignored the experimental walkways that *Portia* used. So Jackson and Cross decided to take advantage of
40 jumping spiders' dislike of getting wet.

Their new setup consisted of a tower on a platform surrounded by moats. From atop the tower, a famished jumping spider could see two distant boxes: one containing juicy spider
45 fragments, the other containing unappetizing leaves. To reach the box containing the meal, the spider would have to crawl down the tower and onto the platform, which also had two pillars leading to separate suspended walkways—one
50 to the food, one to the leaves. But once the spider started its descent from the tower, the researchers emptied out the boxes, preventing it from getting visual reminders of the meal's location. In their lab at Kenya's International
55 Centre for Insect Physiology and Ecology, Cross and Jackson placed individuals from 14 different Spartaeinae species in this tortuous obstacle course. "We have to hide ourselves, so that the spider isn't distracted," says Cross.
60 "They're attracted to blinking."

It turned out that each species was overwhelmingly successful at finding its way to the box containing food—despite the fact that none of the subjects could see the food mid-
65 detour, according to the study, published Tuesday in the *Journal of the Experimental Analysis of Behavior*. What's more, spiders that chose the wrong path often paused, seemingly confused. "Their expectations for what they were going to
70 weren't met," says Cross. "It wasn't part of their plan."

The finding hammers home that, like *Portia*, many related jumping spiders must have an abstract sense of the food's location and a
75 working plan for how to navigate the walkways. "A lot of times, when papers are published about a particular organism, broad generalizations are made about the group," says Berkeley's Elias.

The study authors have "done a really good
80 job of showing [planning] in this very large
group." Researchers still have a long way to go
to understand how spiders think, but for now
they're left to wonder what's going on in those
tiny little heads.
85 "What they do just astounds me," says Cross.

Figure 1

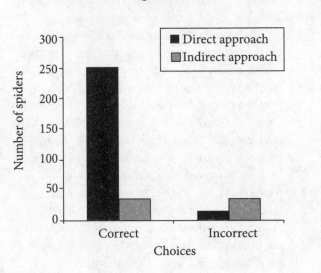

Figure 2

Species	Prey were in Box A		Prey were in Box B	
	Completed Walkway A	Completed Walkway B	Completed Walkway A	Completed Walkway B
Brettus adonis	6	0	0	5
Brettus albolimbatus	7	0	0	4
Cocalus gibbosus	5	0	0	5
Cyrba algerina	4	0	0	2
Cyrba ocellata	5	0	0	4
Cyrba simoni	4	0	1	4
Gelotia lanka	4	0	0	6
Meleon solitaria	6	0	0	6
Neobrettus nangalisagus	4	0	1	6
Portia africana	10	1	0	6
Portia albimana	3	0	0	4
Portia fimbriata	7	0	0	10
Portia labiata	10	1	0	9
Portia cf occidentalis	7	0	0	7
Portia schultzi	6	0	0	6

19

Over the course of the passage, the focus shifts from

A) a general discussion of animal behavior to specifics about a certain species.

B) an introduction of an unexpected characteristic to a discussion of an experiment testing that characteristic.

C) contradictory hypotheses to a discovery which resolved the conflict.

D) an overview of a certain animal to the specifics of that animal's eating habits.

20

Which choice best supports the claim that jumping spiders are more intelligent than their size would suggest?

A) Lines 1–6 ("With . . . creatures")

B) Lines 6–9 ("The . . . space")

C) Lines 15–17 ("Jumping . . . spiders")

D) Lines 35–37 ("Demonstrating . . . challenging")

21

As used in line 4, "intricate" most nearly means

A) complicated.

B) obscure.

C) unfathomable.

D) confused.

22

The primary purpose of the second paragraph (lines 15–27) is to

A) refute a controversial claim.

B) describe a complicated experiment.

C) provide a specific example.

D) prove a long-disputed hypothesis.

23

It can reasonably be inferred that, compared to other jumping spiders, the *Portia* spiders

A) don't mind getting wet.

B) are more aggressive.

C) have very small brains.

D) are more thoroughly researched.

24

Which choice is an underlying assumption of the experiment described in the passage?

A) If a jumping spider can simply see food, it will recognize it as food.

B) If a path is close to water, a jumping spider will avoid the path entirely.

C) If a jumping spider uses a walkway, then it must be in the *Portia* family.

D) If a jumping spider can't see its food, it will become confused.

25

Which choice provides the best evidence for the answer to the previous question?

A) Lines 37–38 ("Other . . . used")

B) Lines 42–46 ("From . . . leaves")

C) Lines 50–54 ("But once . . . location")

D) Lines 67–68 ("What's . . . confused")

26

As used in line 49, "suspended" most nearly means

A) hanging.

B) delayed.

C) discontinued.

D) attached.

27

Figure 2 best supports which claim from the passage?

A) Other spiders did not pay attention to the same walkways that *Portia* spiders used.

B) The *Portia* spider had a more accurate plan to get food than other species of jumping spider.

C) Each species of jumping spider was able to find its way to the box containing the food.

D) The spiders were distracted by the researchers' blinking.

28

Based on figure 1, the greatest number of spiders

A) made an incorrect choice with an indirect approach.

B) made an incorrect choice with a direct approach.

C) made a correct choice with an indirect approach.

D) made a correct choice with a direct approach.

Do you recognize the formats of questions 20, 21, 23, and 26? Question 20 is a single Best Evidence question. Question 21 and question 26 are Vocabulary-in-Context questions. Question 23 is an Inference question. Try answering those four questions on your own, using the strategies we've discussed. The answers can be found in Part IV.

That leaves us with a few other mysterious question types. In the following pages, we will demystify them for you.

PURPOSE QUESTIONS (*Why?*)

Take a look at this question, and think about how it's different from the WHAT questions we've been talking about.

22

The primary purpose of the second paragraph
(lines 15–27) is to

Notice that it's not asking you WHAT the second paragraph says. It is asking about the purpose. The purpose for something is the reason it is there. How would you talk about that? You would explain WHY it is there, right? Yes! So when you see questions with phrases like "what is the purpose" or "the author says/does X/Y/Z in order to," just translate them into questions starting with WHY.

So question 22 is really asking WHY the author included the second paragraph. Doesn't that feel easier to deal with than the way it was originally worded? We think so too.

Begin by carefully reading the second paragraph. It begins with a statement that jumping spiders *of the subfamily Spartaeinae* are *particularly ambitious* because they *eat other spiders.* The paragraph then goes on to explain that in order to do this, they must have *extra intelligence* and, in fact, researchers have done studies which show the spiders can *find hidden prey.* In this paragraph, the author tells the reader that this spider is unique and demonstrably intelligent. But remember, the question is asking WHY the author includes that information. If you look at the previous paragraph, you'll see that the author was discussing the unusual abilities of jumping spiders. The first paragraph discusses jumping spiders in general, and the second paragraph discusses one family of jumping spiders in particular. Let's compare that prediction with the answer choices.

    A) refute a controversial claim.

    B) describe a complicated experiment.

    C) provide a specific example.

    D) prove a long-disputed hypothesis.

The author did not include the second paragraph in order to *refute* or *prove* anything, nor to *describe a complicated experiment,* so eliminate (A), (B), and (D). Choice (C) is consistent with the prediction, so choose (C)!

STRUCTURE AND ARGUMENT QUESTIONS (*How?*)

The last time someone asked you about a film you just saw, did you answer "A character was introduced, a problem emerged, possible solutions were explored and rejected, and a resolution emerged from an unexpected alliance with a former antagonist"? Doubtful. But if so, the test-writers might have a job for you!

Take a look at this question, and think about how it's different from the WHAT and WHY questions we've been discussing.

Which choice is an underlying assumption of the experiment described in the passage?

Notice that this question is not asking WHAT the author says, nor is it asking WHY the author says something. Instead, it asks something about HOW an argument is constructed. Specifically, this question asks about an assumption in an experiment. By definition, an assumption is something that an author or researcher did not explicitly state.

As you can see in this example, the answers for some HOW questions may not come directly from the text, so you may not be able to predict exactly what the correct answer will say. However, the correct answer will still be supported by the text, and you can predict what the correct answer needs to *do*. The answer for question 24 needs to be an assumption of the experiment—in other words, the answer needs to state a belief the researchers held that affected the way they designed their experiment. Use Process of Elimination to eliminate answers that don't meet these criteria.

Notice that this is also the first question in a paired set, so you can use Parallel POE to answer questions 24 and 25.

Here are the answers to question 24.

A) If a spider can simply see food, it will recognize it as food.

B) If a path is close to water, a jumping spider will avoid the path entirely.

C) If a jumping spider uses a walkway, then it must be in the Portia family.

D) If a jumping spider can't see its food, it will become confused.

And here are the answers to question 25.

A) Lines 37–38 ("Other . . . used")

B) Lines 42–46 ("From . . . leaves")

C) Lines 50–54 ("But once . . . location")

D) Lines 67–68 ("What's . . . confused")

The lines for (25A) say that *other spiders ignored the walkways* Portia *used.* These lines might initially seem to support (24C), so draw a line connecting those two answers.

The lines for (25B) say that from the tower, *a famished jumping spider could see two boxes,* one containing *juicy spider fragments* and the other containing *unappetizing leaves.* These lines support (24A); although the passage does not directly state that the spider will see food and recognize it as such, the passage gives specific examples that still support that claim. Draw a line connecting these two answers.

The lines for (25C) state that once the spiders headed down the tower, the researchers emptied out the boxes. Although these lines might initially seem to support (24D), make sure you read carefully. While the spider certainly can't *see the food,* there is no evidence that it *will become confused.* Eliminate (25C).

The lines for (25D) say that spiders are *seemingly confused* when they *chose the wrong path.* Although we now have confused spiders, which goes with (24D), there's no indication that they can't see their food. Eliminate (25D).

Without support from Q25, (24B) and (24D) can both be eliminated. Now look back at your remaining two answer pairs. Choices (24A) and (25B) are solidly connected and supported by the passage. Choices (24C) and (25A) aren't so strongly connected. While the text says that other spiders ignored the walkways, the text doesn't support the idea that the researchers assumed that only *Portia* spiders use walkways. In fact, their subsequent experiment was designed to encourage other spider species to use the walkways. Eliminate (24C) and (25A).

The correct answers are (24A) and (25B).

CHARTS AND GRAPHS

Charts, graphs, and diagrams are no longer limited to the Math Test! You will now see a variety of graphics in the Reading Test and even in the Writing and Language Test! (More on the Writing and Language Test later.) The good news is that the graphics you'll be dealing with in the Reading Test are very straightforward and do not require any computations. All you need to do is make sure you can put your pencil on the place on the graphic that supports the correct answer. Let's take a look at an example.

Figure 2

Species	Prey were in Box A		Prey were in Box B	
	Completed Walkway A	Completed Walkway B	Completed Walkway A	Completed Walkway B
Brettus adonis	6	0	0	5
Brettus albolimbatus	7	0	0	4
Cocalus gibbosus	5	0	0	5
Cyrba algerina	4	0	0	2
Cyrba ocellata	5	0	0	4
Cyrba simoni	4	0	1	4
Gelotia lanka	4	0	0	6
Meleon solitaria	6	0	0	6
Neobrettus nangalisagus	4	0	1	6
Portia africana	10	1	0	6
Portia albimana	3	0	0	4
Portia fimbriata	7	0	0	10
Portia labiata	10	1	0	9
Portia cf occidentalis	7	0	0	7
Portia schultzi	6	0	0	6

Step 1: Read the graphic.

Carefully look the titles, labels, and units. In this figure, we have a list of spider species and which walkway each species chose when the prey were in either Box A or Box B.

Step 2: Read the question.

27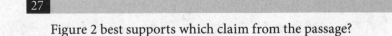

Figure 2 best supports which claim from the passage?

Since the question asks you which claim from the passage is best supported by the graph, your job will be to compare all four answer choices with information from the passage and information in the graph. It's often simplest to start by comparing the answers to the graph. Make sure you can put your pencil on the data point you're using to keep or eliminate certain answers.

Step 3: Read the answers.

> A) Other spiders did not pay attention to the same walkways that *Portia* spiders used.
>
> B) The *Portia* spider had a more accurate plan to get food than other species of jumping spider.
>
> C) Each species of jumping spider was able to find its way to the box containing the food.
>
> D) The spiders were distracted by the researchers' blinking.

Choice (A) says that other spiders *did not pay attention to the same walkways* that the *Portia* spiders used, but the table shows very clearly that they did use the same walkways. Eliminate (A).

Choice (B) says that the *Portia* spider had a *more accurate plan* to get to the food. There is nothing in the table that indicates whether one plan is more accurate than another, so eliminate (B).

Choice (C) is supported by the table: each species completed the walkway that corresponded with the box containing the prey multiple times. Keep (C).

Choice (D), while supported by the text of the passage, is irrelevant to the figure, so (D) can be eliminated.

The correct answer is (C).

Now, try question 28 on your own. The answer can be found in Part IV.

GENERAL QUESTIONS

For many of the Reading passages, the very first question will ask a general question about the passage as a whole. It might ask about the main idea or primary purpose of the passage, the narrative point of view, or the structure of the passage. In other words, General questions can be WHAT, WHY, or HOW questions.

Remember the Select a Question step? General questions are not good to do first because you haven't read the passage yet, but once you've answered most of the other questions, you have a good idea of the overall themes of the text.

Let's take a look at question 19.

Over the course of the passage, the focus shifts from

Because this question asks how the focus shifts *over the course of the passage,* there's no one place you can look. General questions don't have line references or lead words, so there's no way to use the text to predict an answer. It's okay, though: you've answered almost all of the questions about the passage, so you know what the main idea of the passage is. Not only that, but you also have a good sense of what the test-writers found most interesting about the passage. While having this knowledge does not always help, it sure can sometimes. If there are answer choices that have nothing to do with either the questions or the answers you've seen repeatedly, you can eliminate them and instead choose the one that is consistent with those questions and answers. For this question, consider what the passage begins with (how surprisingly awesome the jumping spiders are) and then how it shifts (to experiments about the jumping spiders). Eliminate anything that's inconsistent with that shift.

Let's take a look at the answer choices:

A) a general discussion of animal behavior to specifics about a certain species.

B) an introduction of an unexpected characteristic to a discussion of an experiment testing that characteristic.

C) contradictory hypotheses to a discovery which resolved the conflict.

D) an overview of a certain animal to the specifics of that animal's eating habits.

What can you eliminate?

The first half of (A) is immediately a problem. The passage begins with a discussion of the jumping spiders, not a *general discussion of animal behavior,* so eliminate (A).

The first half of (B) is consistent with the idea that the spiders are remarkable and the second half is consistent with the experiments described in the passage. Keep (B).

Choice (C) mentions *contradictory hypotheses.* Can you find any evidence in the text of hypotheses that contradict each other? No. Eliminate (C).

The first half of (D) is consistent with the beginning of the passage describing the spider. However, the passage goes on to describe experiments about the spiders' planning abilities, not their eating habits. Eliminate (D).

Since (B) is the only answer supported by the passage, that's the correct answer.

DUAL PASSAGES

One of your Science or History/Social Studies passages will be a set of dual passages. There will be two shorter passages about one topic. Although the two passages will be about the same topic, there will also be differences that you'll need to pay attention to. Rather than attempting to read and understand both passages at the same time, just follow the Basic Approach and focus on one passage at a time.

The questions for Passage 1 will come before the questions for Passage 2. The questions about both passages will follow the questions for Passage 2.

Two-Passage Questions

For questions that ask you to compare or contrast both passages, it's helpful to consider one passage at a time rather than trying to juggle both passages at the same time. First, find the answer for the first passage (or the second passage if that one is easier) and use POE to narrow down the answer choices. Then find the answer in the other passage and use POE to arrive at the correct answer. This will save time and keep you from confusing the two passages when you're evaluating the answer choices. Always keep in mind that the same POE criteria apply, no matter how two-passage questions are presented.

- If a question is about what is supported by both passages, make sure that you find specific support in both passages, and be wary of all the usual trap answers.

- If a question is about an issue on which the authors of the two passages disagree or on how the passages relate to one another, make sure you find support in each passage for the author's particular opinion.

- If the question asks how one author would respond to the other passage, find out what was said in that other passage, and then find out exactly what the author you are asked about said on that exact topic.

The bottom line is that if you are organized and remember your basic reading comprehension strategy, you'll see that two-passage questions are no harder than single-passage questions! In the following drill, you'll have a chance to try a set of dual passages. Answers and explanations can be found in Part IV.

Dual Passage Drill

Answers can be found in Part IV.

Questions 38–47 are based on the following passages.

The following are modified passages that explore the design and construction of drug delivery vehicles for biomedical applications.

Passage 1

The technology of drug delivery is one of the most important in the field of medicine and biomedical engineering. The more site-specific a delivery system is, the more effective the drug
Line
5 it is delivering will be; the more conservative a delivered drug dosage is, the less severe the side effects will be. This is especially true of different drugs used to predominantly treat infections and cancers. A new technology called electrostatic
10 processing, or electrospinning, accomplishes both of these goals.

Electrospinning creates biodegradable scaffolds composed of fibers ranging from nanometers to micrometers in diameter, an attribute that is
15 intrinsically difficult to obtain from other fiber-fabrication processes. The electrospinning process begins with a polymer solution at a prescribed charge and viscosity that is pumped through a spinneret. An electric field, powered by a high
20 voltage power supply, is applied to this spinneret so that a droplet is formed at the tip of the spinneret. This droplet morphs into the shape of a cone, in which the surface tension of the droplet is counterbalanced by the applied external
25 electrostatic forces. Once the applied voltage is strong enough to overcome the droplet's surface tension, a fibrous jet is emitted from the cone and captured on a grounded collecting plate. The distance between the spinneret and the collecting
30 plate is where any residual solvent in the ejected jet stream evaporates, resulting in a collection of non-woven submicron-sized fibers that, ultimately, form a highly porous scaffold. Drug delivery via these electrospun scaffolds affords ample
35 flexibility in creating an optimal delivery vehicle for therapeutic treatment.

The chemical properties of the materials utilized as base polymers determine how stable the electrospun scaffolds are and how well they
40 function. Both synthetic and natural materials can be used as base polymers. Between the two, natural polymers typically possess lower levels of toxicity, immunogenicity, and improved biocompatibility. In other words, natural polymers
45 have a greater ability to perform more effectively than synthetic polymers do in the treatment of human disease. Examples of a natural base commonly used as a base for electrospun fibers include collagen and elastin. Collagen is the most
50 prevalent protein in the extracellular matrix (ECM) of soft and hard tissues, and collagen types I, II, and III have all been utilized as the main component of electrospun scaffolds. Elastin has also been substantially utilized as a polymer
55 in electrospinning, especially for vascular tissue engineering. Beyond the inherent advantages that natural polymers possess, the combination of natural polymers can sometimes provide a greater benefit toward constructing an ideal electrospun
60 scaffold. For example, the combination of collagen and elastin in certain ratios has been demonstrated to produce ideally-sized fiber diameters. Thus, the potential to combine—or include—other natural polymers is tremendous
65 in attempting to engineer a drug delivery vehicle with optimal biodegradable properties.

Passage 2

Although it has historically been the case that natural polymers were favored in the construction of electrospun fibers for drug delivery systems,
70 there is a growing trend towards employing synthetic polymers. Synthetic polymers are used to enhance various characteristics of the drug delivery system goals. These characteristics include degradation time, mechanical properties, and cell
75 attachment affinities. Synthetic polymers are able to improve these characteristics as they are more easily tailored to a wider range of properties such as hydrophilicity and hydrophobicity—in other

words, the desired solubility of an electrospun
80 scaffold. Because synthetic polymers can be
created in laboratories, a nearly innumerable
number of possible products that are made from
synthetic polymers can be engineered to address
any particular clinical need. The most popular of
85 these are the most hydrophobic and biodegradable
polymers such as poly(glycolide) (PGA) and
poly(lactide).
    Despite the clear benefits of synthetic
polymers when compared with natural
90 polymers, it is of the utmost importance to not
limit scientific or medical pursuit by a purist
approach. The ability to blend the variety of
synthetic polymers with the strong biocompatible
properties of natural polymers may allow
95 biomedical engineers to more precisely fine-tune
the properties of electrospun scaffolds. It is this
wide-ranging flexibility of polymer compositions
that gives electrospun scaffolds such huge
promise in medical applications, causing the
100 huge spike of research done in this space in the
last several decades. With even more to discover,
it is both likely and lucky that this interest will
continue for some time.

38

The author mentions infections and cancers
(lines 8–9) in order to

A) provide an example of the types of diseases
that electrospun scaffolds have cured.

B) point out illnesses that still do not have
effective treatments.

C) illustrate types of medical conditions that
are more effectively treated by precisely
controlled internal drug delivery.

D) demonstrate the kind of vaccines
electrospinning technology will help to
develop.

39

In Passage 1, the reference to "nanometers to
micrometers" (lines 13–14) serves to

A) give a precise measurement of fibers used in
electrospinning.

B) further elaborate on the minuteness of
electrospun fibers.

C) relate the size of the fibers in electrospun
scaffolds to that of the cells of the human
body.

D) inform the reader of one of the qualities of
electrospun fibers absent in other similar
technological approaches.

40

As used in line 30, "residual" most nearly means

A) durable.

B) remaining.

C) steadfast.

D) inhabiting.

41

In discussing the nature of natural polymers, the
author of Passage 1 suggests that

A) they are more effective as an electrospun
scaffold base as they may be less harmful to
people than synthetic polymers.

B) they are not as effective as when blended with
synthetic polymers such as poly(glycolide)
and poly(lactide).

C) because they are natural materials that exist
in the human body, the body is unable to
reject them.

D) collagen and elastin are effective polymer
bases only when blended together.

42

In Passage 2, the connection between natural and synthetic polymers is best described in which of the following ways?

A) Researchers are increasingly using synthetic polymers more than the historically preferred natural polymers, while more attention is being paid to electrospun fiber research that combines the two types of polymers.

B) Because synthetic polymers can be created in laboratories, they are easier to work with than natural polymers.

C) Because of the importance of a purist approach, it is important to separate research conducted on differing types of base polymers.

D) Synthetic polymers are more hydrophobic when compared to natural polymers.

43

The second paragraph of Passage 2 primarily serves to

A) confirm the author's assertion that synthetic polymers are the most effective polymers for electrospinning.

B) support the purist approach to polymer research in order to preserve the impeccable methods of scientific and medical study.

C) assert that it is because there has been a huge spike in research on polymers that scientists have learned how flexible polymers are.

D) acknowledge that both types of polymers have positive attributes that, when combined, may lead to even more effective electrospun scaffolds.

44

From the information presented in Passage 2, it can be inferred that

A) history favors natural rather than synthetic designs.

B) it is the man-made nature of synthetic polymers that accounts for their flexibility.

C) the solubility of an electrospun scaffold depends more on its hydrophilicity than its hydrophobicity.

D) synthetic polymers degrade more quickly over time than natural polymers.

45

The authors of both passages would most likely agree with which of the following?

A) Hydrophilicity and hydrophobicity are important factors to consider when selecting a base polymer material.

B) Differing electric charges and viscosity will result in differing constructions of electrospun scaffolding.

C) The more exact the system of drug delivery is, the more beneficial it is likely to be.

D) A blended polymer base will be more effective than a non-blended one.

46

The passages differ in that Passage 1

A) does not discuss the possibility of using multiple materials for base polymers, while Passage 2 does.

B) provides information on electrospun scaffolding construction, while Passage 2 looks to the future of electrospun scaffolding research.

C) is concerned only with drug delivery systems to address cancers, while Passage 2 aims to treat all diseases.

D) advocates that the type of polymer base used for electrospun scaffolds is unimportant, while Passage 2 advocates that the type of polymer base is important.

47

What is the primary difference in the tones of Passages 1 and 2 with respect to their arguments regarding natural versus synthetic polymer bases?

A) Passage 1 is belligerent, while Passage 2 is enthusiastic.

B) Passage 1 biased, while Passage 2 is subjective.

C) Passage 1 is unequivocal, while Passage 2 is conciliatory.

D) Passage 1 is pessimistic, while Passage 2 is optimistic.

Summary

o The Reading Test on the PSAT makes up 50 percent of your Evidence-Based Reading and Writing score.

o Reading questions are *not* presented in order of difficulty, but they are in chronological order. Don't be afraid to skip a hard question, and don't worry if you can't answer every question.

o Use your POOD to pick up the points you can get, and don't forget LOTD on the rest!

o Reading is an open-book test! Use that to your advantage by focusing only on the text you need to get each point.

o Translate each question into a WHAT, WHY, or HOW question before you start reading the window.

o Use Line References, Lead Words, and the chronological order of the specific questions to help you find the answer in the passage. Always start reading a few lines above the Line Reference or the Lead Word(s) and read until you have the answer.

o Use the text to predict the answer to the question before you look at the answer choices.

o Use POE to eliminate answers that don't match your prediction.

o If you have more than one answer left after you eliminate the ones that don't match the prediction, compare the remaining answers to see if any of them:

   • are mostly right, slightly wrong
   • could be true
   • have the right answer to the wrong question
   • have the right words but the wrong meaning

o For Paired Sets, make sure you're following the right strategy.
   • Easy-to-Find Paired Questions simply require you to follow the Basic Approach, making sure you've underlined the evidence for your prediction in the text.
   • Harder-to-Find Paired Questions will be much more straightforward if you use Parallel POE to consider the "best evidence" in tandem with the previous question.

o   For Dual Passages, focus on one passage at a time. For questions that ask about both passages, be sure to find evidence in each passage.

o   Save Main Idea or General Questions until the end of the passage. POE will be much more efficient once you've completed all the other questions.

o   Don't get bogged down by hard or time-consuming questions! If you find yourself stuck or running short on time, use LOTD and move on!

	Common Question Wording
What Questions	according to the passage, based on the passage (Detail) the passage (or author) indicates (Detail) the passage (or author) implies/suggests (Infer/Imply/Suggest) it can reasonably be inferred (Infer/Imply/Suggest) the author would most likely agree (Infer/Imply/Suggest) the author's perspective, the author's point of view (Infer/Imply/Suggest) as used in line…most nearly means (Vocabulary-in-Context) provides the best evidence (Best Evidence) best supports (Best Evidence) the main idea, the main theme (General) summarizes (General)
Why Questions	the purpose in order to most likely to serves to the primary purpose (General)
How Questions	weaken strengthen structure of the passage (General) the main focus shifts (General)

Chapter 7
Introduction
to Writing and
Language Strategy

CAN YOU REALLY TEST WRITING ON A MULTIPLE-CHOICE TEST?

We'd say no, but the PSAT (and a heck of a lot of other tests) seems to think the answer is yes. To that end, the PSAT is giving you 35 minutes to answer 44 multiple-choice questions that ask about a variety of grammatical and stylistic topics. If you like to read and/or write, this test may frustrate you a bit because it may seem to boil writing down to a couple of dull rules. But as you will see, we will use the next few chapters to suggest a method that keeps things simple for pro- and anti-grammarians alike.

It is worth noting also that the breakdown of the test is exactly that of the SAT. While other sections of this test may provide slightly easier or shorter versions of what is to come on the real SAT, the Writing and Language Test is a carbon copy. Even the topics tested and the difficulty levels are likely to be the same.

WHERE DID ALL THE QUESTIONS GO?

One thing that can seem a little strange about the Writing and Language section of the PSAT is that many of the questions don't have, well, questions. Instead, many of the questions look something like this:

The history of standardized **1** testing although it may seem pretty dull, is in many ways a story about beliefs about how people learn and succeed.

1

A) NO CHANGE
B) testing, although it may seem pretty dull
C) testing, although it may seem, pretty dull,
D) testing, although it may seem pretty dull,

How are you supposed to pick an answer when there's no question?

Well, actually, what you'll find throughout this chapter and the next two is that the PSAT gives you a *lot* of information in this list of answer choices. (The answer is (D), by the way, but stick with us for a second here.)

Look at these pairs, and you'll see just what we mean. As you read through these pairs of answer choices, think about what each question is probably testing.

1. A) could of
   B) could have

2. A) tall, dark, and handsome
   B) tall, dark and handsome

3. A) let them in
   B) let Sister Susie and Brother John in

4. A) We arrived in Paris on a Sunday. Then we took the train to Nantes. Then we took the train to Bordeaux.
   B) We arrived in Paris on a Sunday. Then we took the train to Bordeaux. Then we took the train to Nantes.

If you were able to see the differences in these answer choices, you're already more than halfway there. Now, notice how the differences in these answers can reveal the question that is lurking in the heart of each list of answer choices.

1. The difference between the word "of" and "have" means that this question is asking *Is the correct form "could of" or "could have"?*

2. The difference between having a comma after the word "dark" and not having one there means that this question is asking *How many commas does this sentence need, and where do they belong?*

3. The difference between "them" and "Sister Susie and Brother John" means that this question is asking *Is "them" adequately specific, or do you need to refer to people by name?*

4. The difference in the order of these sentences asks *What order should the sentences be in?*

Therefore, what we have noticed in these pairs of answer choices is something that may seem fairly simple but which is essential to success on the PSAT.

THE ANSWER CHOICES ASK THE QUESTIONS

At some point, you've almost certainly had to do the English-class exercise called "peer editing." In this exercise, you are tasked with "editing" the work of one of your fellow students. But this can be really tough, because what exactly does it mean to "edit" an entire essay or paper when you aren't given any directions? It's *especially* tough when you start getting into the subtleties between whether things are *wrong* or whether they could merely be improved.

Look, for example, at these two sentences:

It was a beautiful day outside birds were singing cheerful songs.

It was a beautiful day outside; birds were singing cheerful songs.

You'd have to pick the second one in this case because the first has a grammatical error: it's a run-on sentence. Or for the non-grammarians out there, you have to break that thing up.

Now, look at these next two sentences:

> *The weather was just right, so I decided to play soccer.*

> *Just right was how I would describe the weather, so a decision of soccer-playing was made by me.*

In this case, the first sentence is obviously better than the second, but the second technically doesn't have any grammatical errors in it. The first may be *better*, but the second isn't exactly *wrong*.

What made each of these pairs of sentences relatively easy to deal with, though, was the fact that you could compare the sentences to one another. In doing so, you noted the differences between those sentences, and so you picked the *better* answer accordingly.

Let's see how this looks in a real PSAT situation.

In particular, the early history of standardized **2** tests that reveals some of the basic assumptions about what education was supposed to do.

2

A) NO CHANGE

B) tests they reveal

C) tests reveals

D) tests, which revealing

Here's How to Crack It

First, look at what's changing in the answer choices. The word *tests* remains the same in each, but what comes after it changes each time. This question, then, seems to be asking, *Which words will best link the two ideas in the sentence?*

Choices (A) and (D) make the sentence incomplete, so those should be eliminated. Choice (B) creates a run-on sentence, so that should also be eliminated. It looks like only (C) appropriately links the ideas without adding new errors.

Notice how that entire process started with asking *What's changing in the answer choices?* With that question, we figured out what was being tested, and we used POE to do the rest.

Let's try another.

In many ways, a civilization's self-image can be assessed through what that civilization expects 3 their citizens to know.

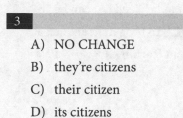

3

A) NO CHANGE

B) they're citizens

C) their citizen

D) its citizens

Here's How to Crack It

As always, start with what is changing in the answer choices. It looks like the main change is between the words *their*, *they're*, and *its* with a minor change between the words *citizen* and *citizens*. As such, this question seems to be asking, *What is the appropriate pronoun to use in this context, and just how many citizens are we talking about?*

Start wherever is easiest. In this case, we're talking about many *citizens*, not just one, so (C) can be eliminated. Now, let's work with the pronoun. What does it refer back to? In this sentence, it seems that the pronoun refers back to *civilization*, which is a singular noun (even though it describes a lot of people). Therefore, the only possible answer that could work is (D), which contains the singular pronoun "its."

LEARN FROM THE ANSWER CHOICES

Let's think about the previous question a bit more. If someone said to you *a civilization's self-image can be assessed through what that civilization expects their citizens to know*, you might not necessarily hear that as wrong. That's because the way we speak is often very different from the way we write. The PSAT is more concerned on this test with how we write and with the stricter set of rules that go along with writing.

As such, not only can the answer choices tell us what a particular question is testing, they can also reveal mistakes that we might not have otherwise seen (in the original sentence) or heard (in our heads). In the previous question, we might not have noted the mistake at all if we hadn't looked at what was changing in the answer choices.

Let's see another.

───────────────○───────────────

A good standardized test can be an effective way **4** to try a different tact at assessing student learning.

A) NO CHANGE
B) to try a different tack
C) for those trying a different tact
D) for those trying a different tack

Here's How to Crack It

First, as always, check what's changing in the answer choices. In this case, that step is especially important because you can't really hear the error. People misuse this idiom all the time because they so rarely see it written; each pair of answer choices sounds basically the same. The fact that they are not the same, that they *change*, tells us precisely what to pay attention to when we use POE.

Start the Process of Elimination. There's no good reason to add a bunch of extra words that don't make things any more precise, so eliminate (C) and (D). Then, if you're not sure, take a guess. The correct form of the saying here is (B).

Notice, though, that looking at the answer choices revealed the problem that you might not have otherwise been able to see or hear. Then, POE got you the rest of the way.

───────────────○───────────────

POE DOES THE BIG WORK

Once you have a sense of what the question is testing, POE can get you closer and closer to the answer. POE is especially helpful when you're dealing with sentences that have lots of issues, like this one:

───────────────○───────────────

It may seem that what you learn in school is too different from what you **5** are doing on the test. However, they would say that the underlying skills are the same.

5

A) NO CHANGE
B) do on the test, however, they'd
C) are doing on the test; however, the creators of the test would
D) do on the test; however, the creators of the test would

Here's How to Crack It

First, as always, check what's changing in the answer choices. In this case, there are three things changing: the difference between *do* and *are doing*, the difference between *they* and *the creators of the test*, and some differences in punctuation. While this may seem like a lot, this is actually a huge POE opportunity! Start with the one you find easiest, and work backward from there.

Because the semicolon is not commonly used, let's save the punctuation part for last. Hopefully we can get the right answer without having to deal with the punctuation at all. Let's start with the difference between *they* and *the creators of the test*. If we use the pronoun *they*, it's not entirely clear whom the sentence is talking about, so eliminate (A) and (B). Then, to choose between the last two, *do* is more concise and more consistent with the rest of the sentence than is *are doing*, which makes (D) better than (C). In this instance, we got to the correct answer without having to deal with all of the messiness in the question!

ALL OF THE QUESTIONS CAN'T BE WRONG ALL OF THE TIME

Now that our strategy is basically set, let's look at one more tough one.

[6] Your attitude toward these test creators may not be entirely sympathetic, but it might make you feel better to know that the tests were designed with you in mind.

6

A) NO CHANGE

B) You're attitude toward these test creators may not be entirely sympathetic,

C) Your attitude toward these test creators may not be sympathetically entire,

D) You're attitude toward these test creators may not be sympathetic or entire,

Here's How to Crack It

As always, check the answers first. In this case, here's what's changing: the answers are switching between *your* and *you're* and some weirdness with *entire* and *sympathetic*. Let's do the easy parts first!

First of all, we'll need the word *your*, because this is the attitude that belongs to *you*, thus eliminating (B) and (D). Then the choice is between *entirely sympathetic*, which is fine, and between *sympathetically entire*, which is really weird, so (C) is no good either. Choice (A) must be the one.

Remember, NO CHANGE is right sometimes! Some people pick it too much. Some people don't pick it enough, but if you've done the other steps in the process and have eliminated all the other choices, go ahead and pick (A)!

HOW TO ACE THE WRITING AND LANGUAGE SECTION: A STRATEGY

- Check what's changing in the answer choices.
- Figure out what the question is testing and let the differences reveal potential errors.
- Use Process of Elimination.
- If you haven't eliminated three answers, pick the shortest one that is most consistent with the rest of the sentence.

In the next few chapters, we'll get into some of the more technical issues in Writing and Language, but we'll be using this strategy throughout. Try the drill on the next page to get some of the basics down.

Writing and Language Drill 1

The purpose of this drill is to get a basic idea of what each question is testing from only the answer choices. Check your answers in Part IV.

1

A) NO CHANGE
B) singers' preferred songwriters
C) singer's preferred songwriter's
D) singers' preferred songwriters'

What's changing in the answer choices?

_____

What is this question testing?

_____

2

A) NO CHANGE
B) had
C) has
D) has had

What's changing in the answer choices?

_____

What is this question testing?

_____

3

A) NO CHANGE
B) Even though
C) If
D) Since

What's changing in the answer choices?

_____

What is this question testing?

_____

4

A) NO CHANGE
B) seem attractive for their
C) seems attractive for its
D) seems attractive for their

What's changing in the answer choices?

_____

What is this question testing?

_____

5

A) NO CHANGE
B) smooth, as in completely lumpless.
C) smooth, like talking not a single lump.
D) smooth.

What's changing in the answer choices?

_____

What is this question testing?

_____

Chapter 8
Punctuation

WAIT; THE PSAT WANTS ME TO KNOW HOW TO USE A SEMICOLON?

Kurt Vonnegut once wrote, "Here is a lesson in creative writing. First rule: Do not use semi-colons…All they do is show you've been to college." Unfortunately, the writers of the PSAT don't quite agree. They want you to know how to use the semicolon and a few other types of weird punctuation as well. In this chapter, we're going to talk about the varieties of punctuation that the PSAT wants you to know how to use. Learn these few simple rules, and you'll be all set on the punctuation questions.

First and foremost, remember how you can spot a question that's asking about punctuation. Start by asking,

> What's changing in the answer choices?

If you see punctuation marks—commas, periods, apostrophes, semicolons, colons—changing, then the question is testing punctuation. Then, as you work the question, make sure to ask the big question:

> Does this punctuation need to be here?

The particular punctuation mark you are using—no matter what it is—must have a specific role within the sentence. You wouldn't use a question mark without a question, would you? Nope! Well, all punctuation works that way, and in what follows, we'll give you some basic instances in which you would use some type of punctuation. Otherwise, let the words do their thing unobstructed!

COMPLETE AND INCOMPLETE IDEAS

In order to decide what type of punctuation is needed to connect ideas in a sentence, you must be able to identify whether the ideas being connected are complete or incomplete. A complete idea can stand on its own. It might be its own sentence, or it might be part of a longer sentence, but it's allowed to be by itself. Here are some examples.

> *The view is beautiful.*
> *Look at that sunset!*
> *How high is the summit?*
> *I gazed at the majestic mountains before me.*

As you can see, commands and questions can be complete ideas. However, they are rarely tested on the PSAT. Most complete ideas on the PSAT will be statements. In general, a complete idea must have a subject and a verb. Sometimes it needs more than that. Consider the following idea:

> *The tour guide told us we will need*

This idea has a subject (*tour guide*) and a verb (*told*), but it's missing the rest of the idea—what *we will need*. Therefore, this idea is incomplete. An incomplete idea could also be missing the subject, verb, or both, as in the examples below.

> *Bought hiking boots*
> *To get to the top of the mountain*
> *The people in our group*

In addition, some transition words and conjunctions can make an idea incomplete even when it has a subject and a verb. Consider the following statement.

> *We began to descend into the canyon*

The idea above is complete. It has a subject (*we*) and a verb (*began*). However, look what happens when we add some transition words.

> *Because we began to descend into the canyon*
> *When we began to descend into the canyon*
> *But we began to descend into the canyon*
> *As we began to descend into the canyon*

All of the ideas above are incomplete. Even though each has a subject and a verb, the transition word at the beginning makes each idea incomplete.

Now that we have established the difference between complete and incomplete ideas, let's take a look at the different types of punctuation that can connect two ideas.

STOP, GO, AND THE VERTICAL LINE TEST

Let's get the weird ones out of the way first. Everyone knows that a period ends a sentence, but even particularly nerdy grammarians can get lost when things get more complicated. Because of this confusion, we've come up with a basic chart that summarizes the different times you might use what the PSAT calls "end-of-sentence" and "middle-of-sentence" punctuation.

When you are linking ideas,

FANBOYS stands for **F**or, **A**nd, **N**or, **B**ut, **O**r, **Y**et, and **S**o.

STOP
- Period
- Semicolon
- Comma + FANBOYS
- Question mark
- Exclamation Mark

HALF-STOP
- Colon
- Long dash

GO
- Comma
- No punctuation

STOP punctuation can link *only* complete ideas.

HALF-STOP punctuation must be *preceded* by a complete idea.

GO punctuation can link anything *except* two complete ideas.

Let's see how these work. Here is a complete idea:

Samantha studied for the PSAT.

Notice that we've already used one form of STOP punctuation at the end of this sentence: a period.

Now, if we want to add a second complete idea, we'll keep the period.

Samantha studied for the PSAT. She ended up doing really well on the test.

In this case, the period is linking these two complete ideas. But the nice thing about STOP punctuation is that you can really use any of the punctuation in the list to do the same thing, so we could also say this:

> *Samantha studied for the PSAT; she ended up doing really well on the test.*

What the list of STOP punctuation shows us is that essentially, a period and a semicolon are the same thing. We could say the same for the use of a comma plus one of the FANBOYS.

> *Samantha studied for the PSAT, and she ended up doing really well on the test.*

You can also use HALF-STOP punctuation to separate two complete ideas, so you could say

> *Samantha studied for the PSAT: she ended up doing really well on the test.*

Or

> *Samantha studied for the PSAT— she ended up doing really well on the test.*

There's a subtle difference, however, between STOP and HALF-STOP punctuation: for STOP, both ideas have to be complete, but for HALF-STOP, only the first one does.

Let's see what this looks like. If we want to link a complete idea and an incomplete idea, we can use HALF-STOP punctuation as long as the complete idea is first. For example,

> *Samantha studied for the PSAT: all three sections of it.*

Or

> *Samantha studied for the PSAT: the silliest test in all the land.*

When you use HALF-STOP, there has to be a complete idea before the punctuation, so these examples wouldn't be correct:

> *Samantha studied for: the PSAT, the SAT, and every AP test in between.*

> *The PSAT—Samantha studied for it and was glad she did.*

When you are not linking two complete ideas, you can use GO punctuation. So you could say, for instance,

> *Having studied for the PSAT, Samantha was confident going into the test.*

Or

> *Samantha studied for the PSAT, all three sections of it.*

These are the three types of mid-sentence or end-of-sentence punctuation: STOP, HALF-STOP, and GO. You'll notice that there is a bit of overlap between the concepts, but the writers of the PSAT couldn't possibly make you get into the minutiae of choosing between, say, a period and a semicolon. If you can figure out which of the big three (STOP, HALF-STOP, and GO) categories you'll need, that's all you need to be able to do.

In the following exercise, choose the type of punctuation that will correctly work in the blank. Some questions have more than one answer! Check your answers on page 174.

	STOP	HALF-STOP	GO
The other day I went to the stadium _____ and bought a ticket.			
I had saved up all week _____ I couldn't think of anything better to spend the money on!			
Some of my favorite sports include _____ hockey, baseball, and tennis.			
There's always something _____ for me to see at the stadium.			
When I arrived _____ I was thrilled to see that I had bought great seats.			
Some people from my school were sitting next to me _____ we're all in the same math class.			
The game was exciting _____ a goal in the first five minutes!			
The crowd was extremely diverse _____ men, women, and children in the stands.			
I didn't want to go home _____ even though I had school the next day.			
You can be sure of one thing _____ I'll be back as soon as I can.			

	STOP	HALF-STOP	GO
The other day I went to the stadium _____ and bought a ticket.			X
I had saved up all week _____ I couldn't think of anything better to spend the money on!	X	X	
Some of my favorite sports include _____ hockey, baseball, and tennis.			X
There's always something _____ for me to see at the stadium.			X
When I arrived _____ I was thrilled to see that I had bought great seats.			X
Some people from my school were sitting next to me _____ we're all in the same math class.	X	X	
The game was exciting _____ a goal in the first five minutes!		X	X
The crowd was extremely diverse _____ men, women, and children in the stands.		X	
I didn't want to go home _____ even though I had school the next day.			X
You can be sure of one thing _____ I'll be back as soon as I can.	X	X	

Let's see what this will look like on the PSAT.

Noah took the PSAT way more seriously than many of his **1** friends he was almost certain he would get a National Merit honor of some kind.

1

A) NO CHANGE
B) friends, he was almost
C) friends he was almost,
D) friends; he was almost

Here's How to Crack It

As always, check what's changing in the answer choices. In this case, the words all stay the same. All that changes is the punctuation, and notice the types of punctuation that are changing: STOP and GO.

Now, when you see STOP punctuation changing in the answer choices, you can do a little something we like to call the Vertical Line Test.

Draw a line where you see the punctuation changing—in this case, between the words *friends* and *he*. Then, read up to the vertical line: *Noah took the PSAT way more seriously than many of his friends*. That's Complete. Now, read after the vertical line: *he was almost certain he'd get a National Merit honor of some kind.* That's also Complete.

By the time you're done, your page should look like this.

Complete   Complete

Noah took the PSAT way more seriously than many of his **1** friends | he was almost certain he would get a National Merit honor of some kind.

So let's think; we've got two complete ideas here. What kind of punctuation do we need? STOP or HALF-STOP. It looks like STOP is the only one available, so choose (D).

Let's try another.

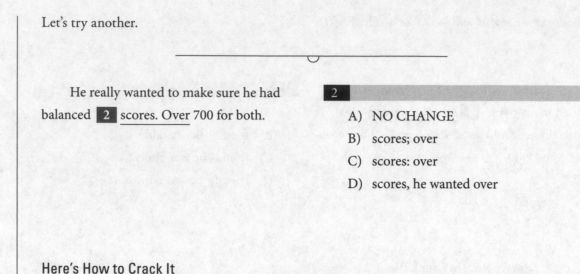

He really wanted to make sure he had balanced **2** scores. Over 700 for both.

2

A) NO CHANGE

B) scores; over

C) scores: over

D) scores, he wanted over

Here's How to Crack It

Check the answer choices. What's changing? It looks like the punctuation is changing, and some of that punctuation is STOP. Let's use the Vertical Line Test. Draw a vertical line where you see the punctuation: between *scores* and *over* in the underlined portion.

What's before the vertical line? *He really wanted to make sure he had balanced scores* is complete. Then, *over 700 for both* is not. Therefore, because we have one complete idea (the first) and one incomplete idea (the second), we can't use STOP punctuation, thus eliminating (A) and (B).

Now, what's different between the last two? Choice (C) contains HALF-STOP punctuation, which can work, so we'll keep that. Choice (D) adds some words, with which the second idea becomes *he wanted over 700 for both*, which is complete. That makes two complete ideas separated by a comma, but what do we need when we're separating two complete ideas? STOP punctuation! Eliminate (D)! Only (C) is left.

Let's see one more.

Every day after Noah got home from baseball **3** practice—he hit the books.

3

A) NO CHANGE

B) practice; he

C) practice, he,

D) practice, he

Here's How to Crack It

The punctuation is changing in the answer choices, and there's some STOP punctuation, so let's use the Vertical Line Test. Put the line between *practice* and *he*. The first idea, *Every day after Noah got home from baseball practice*, is incomplete, and the second idea, *he hit the books*, is complete. Therefore, we can't use STOP (which needs two complete ideas) or HALF-STOP (which needs a complete idea before the punctuation), thus eliminating (A) and (B). Then, because there is no good reason to put a comma after the word *he*, the best answer must be (D).

A SLIGHT PAUSE FOR COMMAS

Commas can be a little tricky. In the last question (#3), we got down to two answers, (C) and (D), after having completed the Vertical Line Test. But then, how do you decide whether to keep a comma in or not? It seems a little arbitrary to say that you use a comma "every time you want to pause," so let's make that thought a little more concrete.

If you can't cite a reason to use a comma, *don't use one*.

On the PSAT, there are only four reasons to use a comma:

- in STOP punctuation, with one of the FANBOYS
- in GO punctuation, to separate incomplete ideas from other ideas
- in a list of three or more things
- in a sentence containing unnecessary information

We've already seen the first two concepts, so let's look at the third and fourth.

Try this one.

His favorite classes were
[4] English, physics and history.

4

A) NO CHANGE

B) English, physics, and

C) English, physics, and,

D) English physics and

Here's How to Crack It

First, check what's changing in the answer choices. It looks like the commas in this list are changing. Because there's not any obvious STOP or HALF-STOP punctuation, the Vertical Line Test won't do us much good.

Then, it will help to know that that the PSAT wants a comma after every item in a series. Think of it this way. There's a potential misunderstanding in this sentence:

I went to the park with my parents, my cat Violet and my dog Stuart.

Without a comma, it sure sounds like this guy has some interesting parents. If there's no comma, how do we know that this sentence isn't supposed to say his parents are *my cat Violet and my dog Stuart*? The only way to remove the ambiguity would be to add a comma like this:

I went to the park with my parents, my cat Violet, and my dog Stuart.

Keep that in mind as we try to crack question 4. In this question, *English, physics, and history* form a list or series, so they should be set off from one another by commas, as they are in (B).

———————◯———————

Let's try another.

———————◯———————

5 Noah, it was clear to everyone, had a really good shot at being a National Merit finalist.

5

A) NO CHANGE
B) Noah it was clear to everyone
C) Noah, it was clear to everyone
D) Noah it was clear to everyone,

Here's How to Crack It

First, check what's changing in the answer choices. Just commas. And those commas seem to be circling around the words *it was clear to everyone*. When you have a few commas circling around a word, phrase, or clause like this, the question is usually testing necessary versus unnecessary information.

A good way to test whether the idea is necessary to the meaning of the sentence is to take it out. Read the original sentence again. Now read this one: *Noah had a really good shot at being a National Merit finalist.*

Is the sentence still complete? Yes. Has the meaning of the sentence changed? No, we just lost a little extra thing. Therefore, the idea is *unnecessary* to the meaning of the sentence and should be set off with commas, as it is in (A).

———————◯———————

Let's try a few more. Try to figure out whether the word or idea in italics is necessary to the meaning of the sentence.

1. The student *with the highest score* has a good chance at a National Merit scholarship.
2. Katie wants to go to Yale *which has a really good theater program.*
3. The team *that scored five touchdowns* won the game in a landslide.
4. The National Merit competition *which began in 1955* had over 1.25 million applicants in 2005.
5. Rising senior *Liam* is hoping to be one of the chosen few this year.

Answers are on page 182.

Let's put it all together in this question.

───────○───────

All his teachers **6** believed, he had a real shot, when he sat down to take the test.

6

A) NO CHANGE

B) believed, he had a real shot, when he sat down,

C) believed, he had a real shot when he sat, down,

D) believed he had a real shot when he sat down

Here's How to Crack It

Check what's changing in the answer choices. There are varying numbers of commas in varying places. Remember, the rule of thumb with commas is that if you can't cite a reason to use a comma, *don't use one.*

It looks like *he had a real shot* is being set off by commas. Let's see whether it's necessary or unnecessary information. Read the original sentence; then read the sentence again without that piece of information: *All his teachers believed when he sat down to take the test.* It looks like the sentence has changed meaning and is not really complete anymore. Therefore, that bit of information is necessary to the meaning of the sentence, so it doesn't need commas. Then, there are no good reasons to put commas around or in the word *down*.

In the end, there aren't reasons to put commas anywhere in this sentence. The best answer is (D). Sometimes the PSAT will test unnecessary punctuation explicitly, so make sure you have a good reason to use commas when you use them!

───────○───────

YOUR GOING TO BE TESTED ON APOSTROPHE'S (AND INTERNET SPELLING IS A TERRIBLE GUIDE!)

As with commas, apostrophes have only a very limited set of applications. Apostrophes are a little trickier, though, because you can't really hear them in speech, so people misuse them all the time. Think about the header of this section. The apostrophes are wrong there. Here's the correct way of punctuating it: *You're going to be tested on apostrophes.* Can you hear the difference? Neither can we.

Therefore, as with commas,

> If you can't cite a reason to use an apostrophe, *don't use one.*
>
> On the PSAT, there are only two reasons to use an apostrophe:
>
> - possessive nouns (NOT pronouns)
> - contractions

Here are some examples.

Some recognition from National Merit would help strengthen his **7** application's, especially for the high-end school's.

7

A) NO CHANGE

B) applications, especially for the high-end schools'.

C) application's, especially for the high-end schools.

D) applications, especially for the high-end schools.

Here's How to Crack It

Check what's changing in the answer choices. In this case, the words are all staying the same, but the apostrophes are changing. Remember: we don't want to use apostrophes at all if we can't cite a good reason to do so.

Does anything belong to *schools* or *applications*? No! Are they forming contractions like *school is* or *application is*? No! Therefore, there's no reason to use apostrophes, and the only possible answer is (D), which dispenses with the apostrophes altogether.

As in the previous question, there's no need for any punctuation, and in a question like this, the PSAT is testing whether you can spot unnecessary punctuation.

———————○———————

But sometimes the apostrophes will be necessary. Let's have a look at another.

———————○———————

8 It's not easy to get you're score high enough for National Merit.

8

A) NO CHANGE

B) Its not easy to get your

C) Its not easy to get you're

D) It's not easy to get your

Here's How to Crack It

Check what's changing in the answer choices. The main changes have to do with apostrophes, particularly on the words *its/it's* and *your/you're*.

The first word, *its/it's*, needs an apostrophe: it creates the contraction *it is*. Therefore, because this one needs an apostrophe, get rid of (B) and (C). As for the other, this word is possessive (as in, the *score* belonging to *you*). Remember that possessive *nouns* need an apostrophe, but possessive *pronouns* don't. Therefore, because *you* is a pronoun, this word should be spelled *your*, as it is in (D).

———————○———————

Phew! These apostrophes can get a little tricky, so let's try a few more. On these (as on many parts of the PSAT), you'll find that using your ear, sounding things out, doesn't really help all that much.

Circle the option that works. The big question is this: apostrophes or no apostrophes?

1. *Salims/Salim's* teacher said *hes/he's* allowed to miss next *Tuesdays/Tuesday's* exam.
2. *Its/It's* really not going to hurt my feelings if you don't want to go to *they're/their* party with me.
3. Whatever the *justification's/justifications* for *your/you're* attitude, *there/they're* is no reason to be so obnoxious about it.
4. *Were/We're* going to get back to you as soon as your *application's/applications* are processed.
5. *They're/Their they're/their* nachos, but they *wont/won't* share any unless *its/it's* absolutely necessary or we share *ours/our's*.

Answers are on page 182.

CONCLUSION

In sum, we've looked at all the punctuation you'd ever need on the PSAT. It's really not so much, and you probably knew a lot of it already. In general, checking what's changing in the answer choices can help reveal mistakes that you may not have heard, and POE can help you narrow those answers down.

Punctuation rules are easy to learn, as is the biggest rule of all about punctuation.

> Know why you are using punctuation, whether that punctuation is STOP, HALF-STOP, GO, commas, or apostrophes. If you can't cite reasons to use these punctuation marks, don't use them!

In the last few pages of this chapter, try out these skills on a drill.

Answers to Questions on Page 179:

1. NECESSARY to the meaning of the sentence (no commas). If you remove the italicized part, the sentence is not adequately specific.
2. UNNECESSARY to the meaning of the sentence (commas). If you remove the italicized part, the sentence is still complete and does not change meaning.
3. NECESSARY to the meaning of the sentence (no commas). If you remove the italicized part, the sentence is not adequately specific.
4. UNNECESSARY to the meaning of the sentence (commas). If you remove the italicized part, the sentence is still complete and does not change meaning.
5. NECESSARY to the meaning of the sentence (no commas). If you remove the italicized part, the sentence is no longer complete.

Answers to Questions on Page 181:

1. Salim's, he's, Tuesday's
2. It's, their
3. justifications, your, there
4. We're, applications
5. They're, their, won't, it's, ours

Writing and Language Drill 2

Time: 5–6 minutes. Check your answers in Part IV.

Born in the USSR

There is no question that the United States is a country of **1** immigrants, the original countries of those immigrants varies so much that it can be tough to know who has contributed what. Moreover, different groups have come at different **2** time's for they're different reason's. In the late 1980s and early **3** 1990s, for instance, those, from the former Soviet Union arrived in large numbers on American shores.

1

A) NO CHANGE
B) immigrants, and
C) immigrants and
D) immigrants. And

2

A) NO CHANGE
B) time's for their different reason's.
C) times for they're different reasons.
D) times for their different reasons.

3

A) NO CHANGE
B) 1990s, for instance those
C) 1990s, for instance, those
D) 1990s for instance those

This may seem a bit late, given that most of the USSR and USSR-affiliated empires fell around 1990 (starting with East Germany and   **4**   it's Berlin Wall in 1989) in fact the largest migrations of Soviets and ex-Soviets happened just *after* the Union had fallen. Indeed, whatever the shortcomings of the socialist republic, the real poverty,   **5**   depression and deprivation, began in earnest when the government was no longer tasked with providing basic necessities. As a result, while there had been a somewhat steady flow of immigration from the USSR since the   **6**   1970s, the largest numbers came to the United States in the early 1990s.

4

A) NO CHANGE
B) its Berlin Wall in 1989), in fact,
C) it's Berlin Wall in 1989). In fact,
D) its Berlin Wall in 1989); in fact,

5

A) NO CHANGE
B) depression, and deprivation
C) depression, and, deprivation
D) depression, and deprivation,

6

A) NO CHANGE
B) 1970s the
C) 1970s—the
D) 1970s. The

Whether we realize it or not, the contributions of these Russian expatriates are with us everywhere. The 7 co-founder, of Google, Sergey Brin, came to the United States from Moscow at the age of 6 in 1979. Singer-songwriter Regina Spektor moved at the age of 9 in 1989, the same year that historian Artemy Kalinovsky arrived with his 8 parents. These and other children of the Soviet Union continue to shape the American experience in all kinds of positive and enlightening ways.

7

A) NO CHANGE

B) co-founder of Google. Sergey Brin,

C) co-founder of Google, Sergey Brin,

D) co-founder, of Google, Sergey Brin

8

A) NO CHANGE

B) parents, today, these

C) parents. Today, these

D) parents today; these

In the same year and at the same age as Brin, a 9 writer, named David Bezmozgis, moved, with his family, from Riga, Latvia, then under Soviet control. While he has undoubtedly been one of the great success stories of Soviet immigration to North America (Canada in this case), he has found that success in detailing the difficult and often conflicting motivations that many people had for leaving the Soviet Union. While we have become comfortable believing that the Soviets came to North America looking for freedom, whatever that term may 10 mean. Bezmozgis shows that this was not always the case and that "freedom" could remain an elusive dream even for those who made the trip successfully. His first 11 novel *The Free World*, was published in 2011 to great critical acclaim.

As we think about the fact that ours is a nation of immigrants, we would be severely limited if we believed that people came from all over the world to assimilate to the American way of life. In fact, the peoples of the world may have become American, but they have done so while shaping and reshaping the meaning of that term in ever richer ways.

9

A) NO CHANGE

B) writer, named David Bezmozgis moved with his family,

C) writer named, David Bezmozgis, moved, with his family,

D) writer named David Bezmozgis moved with his family

10

A) NO CHANGE

B) mean:

C) mean,

D) mean;

11

A) NO CHANGE

B) novel:

C) novel—

D) novel,

Chapter 9
Words

THE WORDS CHANGE, BUT THE SONG REMAINS THE SAME

In the last chapter, we looked at what to do when the PSAT is testing punctuation. In this chapter, we're going to look at what to do when the PSAT is testing the parts of speech—mainly verbs, nouns, and pronouns.

Our basic strategy, however, has remained the same. As we saw in the previous two chapters, when faced with a PSAT Writing and Language question, you should always

> Check what's changing in the answer choices and use POE.

As you will notice, throughout this chapter, we talk a lot about certain parts of speech, but we don't really use a lot of grammar terms. That's because we find that on the PSAT, the best answers across a lot of different parts of speech can be summed up more succinctly with three basic terms: **consistency**, **precision**, and **concision**.

You don't need to know a ton of grammar if you can remember these three basic rules.

> **CONSISTENCY:** Correct answers are consistent with the rest of the sentence and the passage.
>
> **PRECISION:** Correct answers are as precise as possible.
>
> **CONCISION:** Barring other errors, correct answers are as concise as possible.

Let's look at some examples of each.

CONSISTENCY

The purveyors of the philosophy known as Pragmatism **1** is part of a long and complex movement.

1

A) NO CHANGE
B) has been
C) are
D) being

Here's How to Crack It

First, as always, check what's changing in the answer choices. In this case, the forms of the verb *to be* change. Therefore, because the verbs change, we know that the question is testing verbs.

When you see verbs changing in the answer choices, the first thing to check is the subject of the sentence. Is the verb consistent with the subject? In this case, it's not. The subject of this sentence is *purveyors*, which is plural. Therefore, (A) and (B) have to be eliminated, and (D) creates an incomplete idea. Only (C) can work in the context.

Thus, when you see verbs changing in the answer choices, check the subject first. Subjects and verbs need to be consistent with each other.

Let's have a look at another.

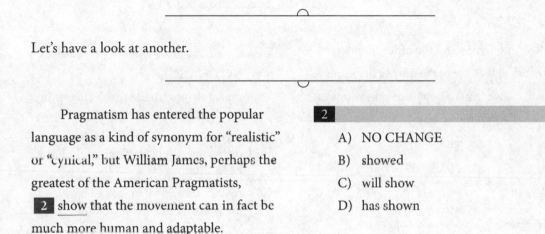

Pragmatism has entered the popular language as a kind of synonym for "realistic" or "cynical," but William James, perhaps the greatest of the American Pragmatists, **2** show that the movement can in fact be much more human and adaptable.

2

A) NO CHANGE

B) showed

C) will show

D) has shown

Here's How to Crack It

Check what's changing in the answer choices. The verbs are changing. Remember from the first question that whenever you see verbs changing, you want to make sure the verb is consistent with the subject. Because the subject of this part of the sentence is *William James,* a singular noun, you can eliminate (A), which isn't consistent.

Then, because all the others are consistent with the subject, make sure they are consistent with the other verbs. It looks like the other main verb in this sentence is *has been*, so the underlined verb should be in this form, as it is in (D). Choices (B) and (C) could work in some contexts, but not this one!

As you can see, verbs are all about consistency.

When you see verbs changing in the answer choices, make sure those verbs are:

- CONSISTENT with their subjects
- CONSISTENT with other verbs in the sentence and surrounding sentences

Let's try one that has a little bit of everything.

Reading James and the other theorists [3] reveal that as we make the big decisions in our lives, we think about those decisions in interestingly pragmatic ways.

[3]

A) NO CHANGE

B) reveal that we made the decisions in our lives, we have thought

C) reveals that as we make the big decisions in our lives, we could have been thinking

D) reveals that as we make the big decisions in our lives, we think

Here's How to Crack It

Check what's changing in the answer choices. It looks like lots of verbs!

Let's start with the first. See which one, *reveal* or *reveals*, is consistent with the subject. That subject is *Reading*, which is singular, thus eliminating (A) and (B).

Then, we have to choose between *think* and *could have been thinking*. Since both of these are consistent with the subject *we*, let's try to pick the one that is more consistent with other verbs. The only other verbs are *reveals* and *make*, both of which are in the present tense and don't use the odd *could have been* form. Therefore, if we have to choose between (C) and (D), (D) is definitely better.

Consistency applies across the test. Let's see another question in which the idea of Consistency might help us.

The early Pragmatists and  [4] their follower suggest that the big decisions in life should be measured by their possible outcomes alone.

4

A) NO CHANGE

B) they're followers suggest

C) their followers suggest

D) their follower suggests

Here's How to Crack It

Check the answer choices first. It looks like pretty much everything is changing here: *they're/their*, *followers/follower*, and *suggest/suggests*. Let's look at the ones we have done already.

We can't cite a good reason to use an apostrophe, so let's get rid of (B). Then, the verb changes, so let's check the subject. That subject is *The early Pragmatists and their follower/followers*, which is plural regardless of the word *follower* or *followers*. Keep the verb consistent with the plural subject and eliminate (D).

Then, we have to choose between *follower* and *followers*, two nouns. As with verbs, nouns are all about consistency. When you see nouns changing in the answer choices, make sure they are consistent with the other nouns in the sentence. In this case, we are talking about *The early Pragmatists*, all of them, who must have many *followers* as well, as (C) suggests.

Noun consistency can show up in other ways as well. Let's have a look the next question.

The logical processes of the Pragmatists are much different from [5] other schools of thought.

5

A) NO CHANGE

B) other school's

C) those of other schools

D) schools that are otherwise

Here's How to Crack It

Look at what's changing in the answer choices. It looks like the main change is between the nouns—*schools* and *those*. We saw in the last question that when nouns are changing in the answer choices, you want to make sure those nouns are consistent with other nouns in the sentence.

In this case, the nouns are being compared. *The logical processes of the Pragmatists* are being compared with the logical processes of people from other schools. Choices (A), (B), and (D) suggest that the *processes* are being compared with the *schools*, so both (B) and (D) are inconsistent. Only (C) is left.

———————————◯———————————

SAT calls this concept "faulty comparison," but you don't have to know that name. Instead, just remember that *nouns have to be consistent with other nouns*. When the answer choices show a change in nouns, look for the sentence's other nouns. They'll provide the clue!

———————————◯———————————

Pragmatism may be rooted in the German philosophers Immanuel Kant and Georg Friedrich Hegel, but it has found more popularity in Anglo-American communities than in **6** German or French ones.

6

A) NO CHANGE
B) German or French.
C) other ones.
D) European.

Here's How to Crack It

Check what's changing in the answer choices. There's a fairly significant change between *German or French* and *German or French ones*. As in the previous sentence, let's make sure this is consistent. The part of the sentence right before the underlined portion refers to *Anglo-American communities*, so we should make our part of the sentence consistent: *German or French communities*, not merely *German or French* or *European*, as in (B) and (D).

Then, we are down to (A) and (C). The difference here comes between the words *German or French* and *other*. While you do want to be concise when possible, you need to make sure first and foremost that we are being *precise*. Choice (A) is more precise than (C) in that it has a clearer relation to the *Anglo-American communities* with which it is being contrasted. Therefore, (A) is the best answer in that it is the most *consistent* with the rest of the sentence and the most *precise* of the remaining possible answers.

———————————◯———————————

7 However, the term 'Pragmatism' was first used by Americans—philosophers William James and Charles Sanders Peirce.

7

A) NO CHANGE

B) In fact,

C) Likewise,

D) Therefore,

Here's How to Crack It

Look to see what's changing in the answer choices: transition words. A transition connects the previous idea to the current sentence, so look back at the previous sentence (in question 6) to identify the relationship between the sentences. The previous sentence states that Pragmatism has German roots but *has found more popularity in Anglo-American communities*. This sentence states that the name of the philosophy *was first used by Americans*. This agrees with the previous idea that the field was popular in the United States, so the sentence needs a same-direction transition. Eliminate (A) because *however* is a contrasting transition, so it's not consistent.

The other answers are all same-direction transitions, so consider how consistent they are with the relationship between the sentences. Choice (B) works because *in fact* can be used to reinforce a previous statement, which is the relationship between these sentences. Choice (C) can be eliminated because *likewise* is used to provide another point or example that is similar to what was previously stated, but this sentence isn't a separate point—it's just agreeing with and adding on to the previous statement. Eliminate (D) because *therefore* comes before a conclusion, and this sentence doesn't draw a conclusion from previously stated evidence. Therefore, (see what we did there?) the correct answer is (B).

Consistency

- When the verbs are changing in the answer choices, make sure those verbs are consistent with their subjects and with other verbs.
- When the nouns are changing in the answer choices, make sure those nouns are consistent with the other nouns in the sentence and the paragraph.
- When transitions are changing in the answer choices, choose a transition that is consistent with the relationship between ideas before and after the underlined portion.

PRECISION

Consistency is probably the most important thing on the Writing and Language section of the PSAT, but precision is a close second. Once you've made sure that the underlined portion is consistent with the rest of the sentence, make sure that the underlined portion is as precise as possible. Perfect grammar is one thing, but it won't matter much if no one knows what the writer is talking about!

Let's hear that one more time.

> Once you are sure that a word or phrase is consistent with the non-underlined portion of the sentence, make that word or phrase as precise as you can.

Although purporting to be systems of universal truth, [8] most are bound to their countries of origin.

8

A) NO CHANGE

B) most of them

C) most from philosophy

D) most philosophical systems

Here's How to Crack It

Check what's changing in the answer choices. The changes could summed up with the question "*most* what?" We have four different options, so let's use our main guiding principles of consistency and precision.

Be as precise as possible. Choices (A) and (B) are very similar in that they say *most*, but they don't specify *what* that *most* refers to. Even though these are grammatically consistent with the rest of the sentence, they're not quite precise enough. Choice (C) is a little more precise, but it doesn't actually clarify what *most* refers to. With these answers out of the way, we can see that (D) is the best of the bunch because it is the only one that is sufficiently precise.

As this question shows, pronouns can be a bit of a challenge. They can appear in otherwise grammatically correct sentences. Still, precision is key when you're dealing with pronouns. Circle the potentially imprecise pronouns in each of the following sentences and rewrite each one.

1. Certain philosophers can be confusing, but it's still an important endeavor.
2. Each of us uses some of this philosophical logic in their everyday life.
3. Whether Anglo-American or Continental models, it can all tell us something important about how to live.

4. A philosopher's life cannot help but influence their work.
5. Self-help, psychology, economics are the cornerstones: it is each in a way part of the philosophical tradition.

Answers are on page 197.

Precision can show up in some other ways as well. Have a look at this question.

The Continental school's approach
9 has a tendency to problems to be far more abstract than the Anglo-American school's.

9

A) NO CHANGE

B) has a tendency to be far more abstract to problems

C) to problems has a tendency to be far more abstract

D) has a tendency to be to problems far more abstract

Here's How to Crack It

Check what's changing in the answer choices. This step is crucial here because there are no obvious grammatical errors, so the answer choices are essential to figuring out exactly what the question is asking you to do.

In the end, the only difference among the answer choices is that the phrase *to problems* is in different places. In the end, we will just need to put that phrase in the most precise place, hopefully right next to whatever it is modifying.

In this case, we can choose from among *approach*, *tendency*, *be*, and *abstract*. Which of these would have the most precise need for the phrase *to problems*? Because *problems* seem to have something to do with how those problems are solved, it would go best with *approach*, creating the phrase *approach to problems*, particularly because the other combinations don't make a lot of sense. What does it mean to be *abstract to problems*? Nothing! The best answer is (C).

Let's have a look at some more of these modifiers. Rewrite each sentence below so the modifier makes the *precise* sense that it should.

1. Given all its logical twists and turns, many people struggle with philosophy.
2. Readers in different times tend to gravitate toward different philosophers and places.
3. Once cracked, you can find incredible guidance and solace in philosophy.
4. I first learned about Pragmatism from a professor in college at 20.
5. Boring and uninteresting, Jack didn't care much for the work of William James.

Answers are on page 197.

CONCISION

When it comes to consistency and precision, you may find yourself sometimes choosing an answer that uses more words but makes the meaning more clear. This is fine—sometimes more words are needed. However, when the additional words don't make the meaning more precise, it's best to leave them out. For example, if you were to ask for directions, which answer would you rather receive?

Turn right at Main Street and walk four blocks.

Or

Since this street, Elm Street, is facing in a northerly direction, and your destination is due northeast, go east when you arrive at the intersection of Elm and Main. Going east will entail making a right turn in quite that easterly direction. After having made this turn and arrived on the perpendicular street…

The first one. Obviously.

And that's because concision is key when you want to communicate meaning. Really, as long as everything else is in order—as long as the grammar and punctuation are good to go—the best answer will almost always be the shortest.

Let's see an example.

I find Pragmatism to be one of the most **10** interesting and fascinating of the philosophical schools.

10
A) NO CHANGE
B) interesting
C) fascinatingly interesting
D) interestingly fascinating

Here's How to Crack It

Check what's changing in the answer choices. In this case, the word *interesting* appears in all the answer choices, and in some it is paired with the word *fascinating*. Typically, if you see a list of answer choices wherein one answer is short and the rest mean the same thing but are longer, the question is testing concision.

What, after all, is the difference between the words *interesting* and *fascinating*? There really isn't a very significant one, so there's no use in saying both of them, as in (A), or pairing them awkwardly, as in (C) and (D). In fact, the shortest answer, (B), does everything the other answers do, but it does so in the fewest words. Choice (B) is therefore the best answer.

Let's see one more.

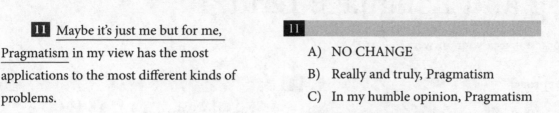

11 Maybe it's just me but for me, Pragmatism in my view has the most applications to the most different kinds of problems.

11

A) NO CHANGE
B) Really and truly, Pragmatism
C) In my humble opinion, Pragmatism
D) Pragmatism

Here's How to Crack It

As always, check what's changing in the answer choices. The changes could be summed up like this. There's a bunch of stuff before the word *Pragmatism*. Does any of that stuff contribute in a significant way to the sentence? No. Does the word *Pragmatism* alone help the sentence to fulfill its basic purpose? Yes. Therefore, the best answer is (D).

As we have seen in this chapter, when the PSAT is testing *words* (i.e., any time the words are changing in the answer choices), make sure that those words are

- **Consistent.** Verbs, nouns, pronouns, and transitions should agree within sentences and passages.
- **Precise.** The writing should communicate specific ideas and events.
- **Concise.** When everything else is correct, the shortest answer is the best.

Answers to Questions on Page 194:

1. *it* is the problem. *Certain philosophers can be confusing, but the pursuit of philosophical knowledge can still be an important endeavor.*
2. *their* is the problem. *Each of us uses some of this philosophical logical in his or her everyday life.*
3. *it* is the problem. Take it out! *Anglo-American and Continental models can all tell us something important about how to live.*
4. *their* is the problem. *A philosopher's life cannot help but influence that philosopher's work.*
5. *it* is the problem. *Self-help, psychology, economics are the cornerstones: each of these is part of the philosophical tradition.*

Answers to Questions on Page 195:

1. Many people struggle with philosophy given all its logical twists and turns.
2. Readers in different times and places tend to gravitate toward different philosophers.
3. Once cracked, philosophy can provide incredible guidance and solace.
4. I first learned about Pragmatism from a college professor when I was 20 years old.
5. Jack didn't care much for the work of William James, which he found boring and uninteresting.

Writing and Language Drill 3

Time: 7–8 minutes. Check your answers in Part IV.

A Pragmatic Approach

William James's *Pragmatism* (1907) has been called the **1** greatest and best book of American philosophy. The array of lectures that would become *Pragmatism* **2** encompass James's adaptation of the great Pragmatists—such as Charles Peirce—and adds a uniquely human element to the philosophical movement. **3** His work in psychology and religion laid the foundation for how theoretical work intersects with the concrete work of living.

In a way, pragmatism turns the philosophical endeavor on its head and **4** attacked the importance of its big questions. Philosophy is traditionally concerned with the big questions: What is the meaning of life? Are there many worlds like this one or only this one? What if none of us exist? Pragmatism is concerned with these questions as well, but it is equally concerned with another question: So what? Pragmatism is concerned, with what difference a particular truth means in the world **5** with *practice*.

1

A) NO CHANGE
B) best and truly greatest
C) greatly best
D) greatest

2

A) NO CHANGE
B) encompasses
C) do encompass
D) are encompassing

3

A) NO CHANGE
B) James's
C) Their
D) Some

4

A) NO CHANGE
B) has been attacking
C) attacks
D) could be said to attack

5

If the punctuation were adjusted accordingly, the best placement for the underlined portion would be

A) where it is now.
B) after the word *Pragmatism*.
C) after the word *concerned*.
D) after the word *truth*.

Let's consider a basic example. Say you are stressed about an upcoming math test. You're afraid you might not get the grade you want, and the fear of it [6] keeps you up at night. Rather than asking, "Will you do well on this test?", the Pragmatists will want to know instead "What difference does it make whether you do well or poorly on the test?" If your answer is, "Well, no difference, I guess," then you've got [7] one. If your answer is, "I won't be able to get an A in the class!" then you've got another and a whole other series of questions. By constantly asking "So what?", the pragmatic approach helps to situate problems in their practice and their consequences rather than [8] abstracting.

6

A) NO CHANGE

B) keeping you up

C) awakens

D) kept you up

7

A) NO CHANGE

B) something.

C) one approach.

D) approaching.

8

A) NO CHANGE

B) abstractly.

C) in their abstraction.

D) by a process of abstraction.

The approach is especially interesting for life's big questions. One of James's particular favorites was, "Is life fated or free?" In other words, do we make our own choices, or are our lives completely predetermined? Well, for James, the question is an interesting but fundamentally irrelevant one. **9** Whether there is a cosmic order to our lives or not, we still have to live them responsibly, so it doesn't **10** differ whether our lives are "fated or free," because the distinction won't create practical differences.

These are two relatively simple examples of the pragmatic method in action, but give it a try yourself. Next time something is really stressing you out, ask the simple question: What difference does it make if that does happen? You may find that the real consequences are what help you to see through the problem, establish a plan, or **11** forgot about the issue entirely.

9

The writer is considering deleting the phrase *but fundamentally irrelevant*. Should the phrase be kept or deleted?

A) Kept, because it shows James's sense of humor as displayed in his writings.

B) Kept, because it sets up the subject of the remainder of the paragraph.

C) Deleted, because it dismisses the importance of Pragmatism as a movement.

D) Deleted, because the paragraph as a whole is focused on relevant subjects.

10

A) NO CHANGE

B) concern us or anyone else

C) count

D) make a significant difference

11

A) NO CHANGE

B) forget about them

C) forget about the issue

D) forget about the issues

Chapter 10
Questions

AND THEN THE PSAT WAS LIKE, "HEY, CAN I ASK YOU A QUESTION?"

In the previous two chapters, we saw most of the concepts that the PSAT will test on the Writing and Language portion of the exam. In this chapter, we're not going to learn a lot of new stuff in the way of grammar. Instead, we'll look at some of the questions that the PSAT asks.

As we've seen, a lot of the questions on the Writing and Language Test aren't technically questions at all. They're just lists of answer choices, and you start the process of answering them by asking a question of your own: "What's changing in the answer choices?" Because you need to move quickly through this test, you may fall into the habit of not checking for questions. Even when you do read the questions, you may read them hastily or vaguely. Well, we are here to tell you that neither of these approaches will work.

> The most important thing about Writing and Language questions is that you *notice* those questions and then *answer* those questions.

This may seem like just about the most obvious advice you've ever been given, but you'd be surprised how much less precise your brain is when you're working quickly.

Here's an example. Do these next 10 questions as quickly as you can.

1. $2 + 1 =$
2. $1 + 2 =$
3. $3 + 1 =$
4. $3 + 2 \neq$
5. $1 + 2 =$
6. $2 - 1 <$
7. $2 \pm 2 =$
8. $3 + 1 =$
9. $3 + 2 =$
10. $3 + 3 \neq$

Now check your answers.

1. 3

2. 3

3. 4

4. Anything but 5

5. 3

6. Any number greater than 1 (but not 1!)

7. 0 or 4

8. 4

9. 5

10. Anything but 6

Now, it's very possible that you got at least one of those questions wrong. What happened? It's not that the questions are hard. In fact, the questions are about as easy as can be. So why did you get some of them wrong? You were probably moving too quickly to notice that the signs changed a few times.

This is a lot like the Writing and Language section. You might miss some of the easiest points on the whole test by not reading carefully enough.

As you will see throughout this chapter, most of the questions will test concepts with which you are already familiar.

WORDS AND PUNCTUATION…AGAIN?

Many of the concepts we saw in the Punctuation and Words chapters show up explicitly with questions. Let's take a look at an example.

It is **1** super obvious that the film industry has largely eclipsed the once-booming theater business in the United States: once the silver screen came along, audiences were more interested in the new medium.

1

Which choice best preserves the overall tone of the passage?

A) NO CHANGE

B) a no-brainer

C) unbelievably clear

D) well-known

Here's How to Crack It

First and foremost, it's important to notice the question. We're looking for an answer that *best preserves the overall tone of the passage*. In the Words chapter, we saw that one of the key ideas to keep in mind on the Writing and Language is consistency. This question is simply asking you to choose an answer that is consistent with the passage. Sometimes the PSAT will explicitly ask you to pick a word that is consistent with the passage's style and tone, as in the question above, and in other cases you may simply see answer choices like these but no question. Either way, the key is consistency!

Choices (A) and (B) are overly casual, so they aren't consistent with the passage's tone. Never pick an answer with slang words such as *cool, super, chill,* or *awesome*—unless the word is used in a non-slang context (for instance, weather could be described as *cool*, but describing an idea as *cool* is too casual for the PSAT). Choice (C) is overly dramatic. There isn't any evidence that the statement is so clear as to be *unbelievable*. On these questions, you may also see answers that are too strong or too dramatic to be consistent with the passage's tone—most, if not all, PSAT passages will take a somewhat formal, academic tone with little to no excited or dramatic language. Only (D) is consistent with the passage's tone, so it's the correct answer.

As you can see, some Writing and Language questions that ask a question are just another way of testing something you already know how to do. Let's see another.

The wonder that a beautiful film can inspire would seem to be unsurpassable. [2] Specifically, by 1920, half of all Americans visited a movie theater each week.

2

Which choice provides the most logical transition from the previous sentence to the sentence that follows?

A) Live theater performances cannot provide the digital special effects audiences have come to expect from movies.

B) Once films were introduced in the early 1900s, people of all ages flocked to theaters to view the novel and exciting images.

C) Today, plays and musicals are making a comeback, especially as movie theaters have become more expensive.

D) Early films did not include sound, but audiences were thrilled by the moving images.

Here's How to Crack It

First, notice what the question is asking for: a *logical transition* between the sentences. This is a great example of the importance of reading the question. You might like some of the answer choices, but that's not enough—the correct answer must do what the question is asking and connect the ideas. When we discussed transitions in the previous chapter, we considered the relationship between sentences. These questions are no different. Can we go ahead and answer this question as soon as we see the box with the number? No! We need to know what the next sentence is about before we can figure out which option would be most consistent with that new idea. Read the sentence after the boxed number if you haven't already.

The first sentence explains the *beauty* and *wonder* of films. The following sentence uses the word *specifically* and provides a detail about the size of the movie-going audience in 1920. This suggests that the sentence in between needs to provide a less specific statement about how frequently people were viewing movies in the past, and it should connect back to how beautiful and wondrous the films were. Eliminate (A) and (C) because they don't relate to history at all. Keep (B) because it provides a less specific statement on the popularity of films in the past and connects back to the *wonder* or excitement mentioned in the previous sentence. Choice (D) mentions history and *thrilling* images, but it does not provide a less specific statement about film attendance that the second sentence would then elaborate on, so (D) does not provide a consistent and precise transition between the sentences. The correct answer is (B).

For transition questions, the answer should move smoothly from the topic of one sentence or paragraph into the topic of the next sentence or paragraph. Make sure you read enough to know what those topics are. Similarly, you may see questions asking you what sentence would best introduce or conclude a paragraph. In the same way, you'll need to read the entire paragraph and consider its main idea before tackling one of these questions.

Questions like #2 are why...

The most important thing about Writing and Language questions is that you notice that a question is being asked and answer that particular question.

Let's look at another that deals with some of the topics we've seen earlier.

What many have forgotten, however, is that the theater remains a vibrant medium. The vibrancy of the medium comes partly from the particular intimacy of the connection between actors and audience. **3**

3

Which of the following gives the best way to combine these two sentences?

A) What many have forgotten, however, is that the theater remains a vibrant medium; the vibrancy of the medium comes partly from the particular intimacy of the connection between actors and audience.

B) What many have forgotten, however, is that the theater remains a vibrant medium, particularly given the intimacy of the connection between actors and audience.

C) A lot of people forget, however, about the vibrancy of theater as a medium when they don't think about how intimate the connection is between the actors in the theater and the audience in the seats.

D) Many have forgotten, however, that the theater remains a vibrant medium, and the intimacy of the connection between actors and audience creates this vibrancy.

Here's How to Crack It

The question asks us to combine the two sentences. Now that we have covered punctuation rules, consistency, precision, and concision, you have all the tools you need to answer this type of question. Questions on combining sentences require you to choose an option that uses correct punctuation and isn't overly wordy. A great strategy for these questions is to start with the shortest option. In this case, that's (B). Choice (B) doesn't seem to have any punctuation or grammar errors, so keep it, but check the other options just in case.

Choices (A) and (D) both repeat the words *vibrant* and *vibrancy*, which makes them unnecessarily wordy. Choice (C) uses the word *forget* and the phrase *when they don't think about*, which is repetitive. Choice (B) is concise and clear, so it is the correct answer.

For these questions, the shortest answer is often the correct one—but not always. Start with the shortest option, but still consider the other choices. Remember that sometimes more words are necessary in order to make the meaning precise.

PRECISION QUESTIONS

Not all questions will just be applications of punctuation and parts of speech. Some questions will ask you to do more specific things. Remember the three terms we kept repeating in the Words chapter: Consistency, Precision, and Concision. We'll start with the Precision-related questions. Even in those where Precision is not asked about directly, or when it is mixed with Consistency or Concision, remember this:

> Answer the question in the most precise way possible. Read literally!

Let's try one.

In fact, the history of the theater in the United States provides as riveting a story as the greatest stage drama. **4**

4

The writer is considering deleting the phrase *of the theater in the United States* from the preceding sentence. Should this phrase be kept or deleted?

A) Kept, because removing it would remove a crucial piece of information from this part of the sentence.

B) Kept, because it stirs the reader's national sentiments and might generate extra interest in the story.

C) Deleted, because it wrongly implies that stage plays are not interesting on their own terms.

D) Deleted, because it gives information that has no bearing on this particular essay.

Here's How to Crack It

This question asks whether we should keep or delete the phrase *of the theater in the United States*. Without that phrase, the sentence reads: *In fact, the history provides as riveting a story as the greatest stage drama*. Because nothing in this sentence or any of the previous ones specifies what this *history* might be, keep the phrase. You want to be as precise as possible!

And, as (A) says, you want to keep the phrase because it is crucial to clarifying precisely what *the question* is. Choice (B) is a little too grandiose and vague a reason to keep the phrase. Choice (A) is therefore the best answer.

Let's try another.

The history of the theater in the United States is part of Revolutionary history. [5] The early provisional government banned all theaters during the War for Independence.

5

At this point, the writer is considering adding the following true statement:

> William Shakespeare was a British playwright, but his stature extends to all parts of the English-speaking world.

Should the writer make this addition here?

A) Yes, because it names an important figure in theatrical history.

B) Yes, because it shows that theater can bring nations together rather than drive them apart.

C) No, because it does not contribute in a significant way to the discussion of the history of the theater in the United States.

D) No, because other playwrights have had a large impact in the United States as well.

Here's How to Crack It

The proposed sentence does contain an interesting bit of information, but that piece of information has no clear place either in these few sentences or in the passage as a whole. Therefore, it should not be added, thus eliminating (A) and (B).

Then, because it does not play a significant role in the passage, the sentence should not be added for the reason stated in (C). While (D) may be true in a way, it does not reflect anything clearly relating to the role the sentence might play in the passage as a whole. Read literally, and answer as literally and precisely as you can.

CONSISTENCY QUESTIONS

Just as questions should be answered as *precisely* as possible, they should also be answered with information that is *consistent* with what's in the passage.

When answering consistency questions, keep this general rule in mind:

> Writing and Language passages should be judged on what they *do* say, not on what they *could* say. When dealing with Style, Tone, and Focus, make sure to work with the words and phrases the passage has already used.

Let's look at two questions that deal with the idea of consistency.

---

[1] The status of the theater was especially controversial in the Pre-Revolutionary Era. [2] These writings may have even influenced Shakespeare himself. [3] In particularly religious places, like Boston, the theater **6** has become a popular and respected profession in the twentieth century. [4] In Philadelphia, too, theater could have only a marginal influence over and above religious protests. [5] It was really in the southern colonies, especially around Virginia, that the real English love of the theater came through. [6] In fact, John Smith's writings of his trip to this early colony are full of imagery from the theater. **7**

6

Which of the following choices would best complete the idea presented in this sentence?

A) NO CHANGE

B) was thought to encourage unrighteous behavior in the audience and the actors.

C) may have hosted one of the first performances of the temperance play *The Drunkard*.

D) could be a pleasant way to spend a Sunday afternoon after church.

7

The best placement for sentence 2 would be

A) where it is now.

B) before sentence 1.

C) after sentence 5.

D) after sentence 6.

Here's How to Crack Them

Let's look at question 6 first. In this case, the question tells us exactly what to look for: something that would *complete the idea* in the sentence, an idea about how religious places were less likely to allow the theater. Choices (A) and (C) may be true, but they don't have anything to do with religion. Choice (D) addresses religion, but not in the way that the rest of the sentence or surrounding ideas do. Only (B) discusses religion in an appropriate way by noting how religious authorities saw the theater as promoting *unrighteous* behavior.

As for question 7, we need to find some very literal way to make sentence 2 consistent with the rest of the paragraph. Look for words and phrases that will link sentence 2 to other sentences. Remember, it's not what the passage *could* say; it's what the passage *does* say. Sentence 2, we should note, starts with *These writings*, thus clearly referring to writings that have been mentioned before it. As such, sentence 2 belongs definitively after sentence 6, which discusses the *writings* of John Smith. This is (D).

───────○───────

As we have seen, these questions are not difficult, but they do require very specific actions on your part. Make sure you read the questions carefully and that you answer those questions as precisely and consistently as you can.

The same goes for charts and graphs on the Writing and Language Test. Don't let the strangeness of the charts throw you off! Just read the graphs with as much precision as you can and choose the most precise answers possible.

Let's have a look at one.

───────○───────

For all the interest of its history, however, the theater has seen a remarkable decline in popularity. A recent study showed that in 2002 just 17.1%, 12.3%, and 3.2% of adults had seen a performance of an opera, a musical, or a non-musical play within the previous year. **8**

8

The writer wants the information in the passage to correspond as closely as possible with the information in the chart. Given that goal and assuming that the rest of the previous sentence would remain unchanged, in which sequence should the three cultural activities be listed?

A) NO CHANGE

B) Opera, non-musical, musical

C) Non-musical, musical, opera

D) Musical, non-musical, opera

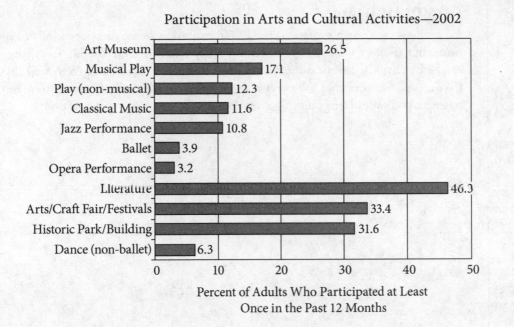

Participation in Arts and Cultural Activities—2002

Percent of Adults Who Participated at Least
Once in the Past 12 Months

Here's How to Crack It

This question is asking for what agrees with the graph. From what we have seen, these questions are usually pretty straightforward. You don't have to do anything overly complex with the graphs, and that is certainly the case here.

There are three activities: opera, non-musical plays, and musical plays. Notice how the numbers are listed in the passage and match each of these numbers with the graph. The graph shows "Musical Play" at 17.1%, "Play (non-musical)" at 12.3%, and "Opera Performance" at 3.2%. This should therefore be the order in which the activities are listed, as in (D).

In general, graphs on the PSAT Reading and Writing and Language Tests are very straightforward, and the fundamental question they ask is this: "Can you read a graph?" These are easy points as long as you read the graphs carefully and use POE.

Take a Breather
You've made it through the entire Writing and Language section! Next up is Math, so feel free to take a break before diving in. Grab a snack, relax with a book, go for a walk—anything that will help you refresh before reviewing more content. Remember that study breaks can make you more productive, so don't deprive yourself of some needed relaxation time.

CONCLUSION

As we have seen in this chapter, the PSAT can ask a lot of different kinds of questions, but the test won't throw anything really crazy at you. The biggest things to remember, aside from the punctuation rules, are *PRECISION* and *CONSISTENCY*. If you pick answers that are precise and consistent with other information in the passage, you should be good to go. Just make sure to answer the question!

Writing and Language Drill 4

Time: 10 minutes. Check your answers in Part IV.

Screen Time Woes

[1] In the 1980s and 1990s, cultural critics had begun to express concern that Americans watched too much television. The numbers varied, but it was widely touted that Americans spent anywhere from three to five hours a day in front of the tube. [2] Whether this was true, it certainly did present a startling finding, especially to those who were interested in promoting other media and activities.

1

Which of the following choices would best introduce the essay by identifying a way that a historical period understood a particular medium?

A) NO CHANGE

B) If you don't own a TV today, it's not considered that weird anymore.

C) It's very possible that the only thing you listen to on the radio is music.

D) The old cathode-ray-tube TVs are relics of the past by this point.

2

The writer is considering deleting the phrase *in front of the tube* and ending the sentence with a period after the word *day*. Should the phrase be kept or deleted?

A) Kept, because the meaning of the sentence is unclear without the phrase.

B) Kept, because it shows what the viewers of television find so compelling.

C) Deleted, because it does not clarify whether the number was closer to three or five.

D) Deleted, because this kind of slangy language should be avoided at all costs.

3 All the while, TV is as good now as it has ever been in its 60-year history. Political theorists warned that too much time in front of the television would dampen people's political awareness. Nutrition activists feared that such a sedentary activity would spur an obesity epidemic. **4** Movie-theater owners cautioned that the lower-quality television could destroy the high-end film industry. Lovers of literature fretted that people no longer had the time or attention span to read the great works.

3

Which of the following choices would offer the most effective introduction to this paragraph?

A) NO CHANGE

B) Concerns about the increase in television-watching came from all corners.

C) The first televised presidential debate came during the 1960 election.

D) The technology of new TVs has improved by leaps and bounds even in the last ten years.

4

At this point, the author is considering adding the following true statement:

A 2015 study showed that over two-thirds of American adults are overweight or obese.

Should the writer make this addition here?

A) Yes, because the essay as a whole has very little hard statistical data like this.

B) Yes, because the obesity rate shows that TV was truly a destructive medium.

C) No, because the mention of these statistics is cruel to those who are overweight.

D) No, because the essay as a whole is focused on a different subject.

5 These criticisms are particularly apt because television has been proven to have negative effects on children's attention spans. Movies were controversial in the 1920s. The National Association of Librarians wrote a report in the **6** 1940s. In this report, radio was excoriated for distracting children from life's real pursuits. The criticisms went even further back. The printing press, even early in its history as mainly a printer of Bibles, was thought to give religious messages to too many who couldn't properly **7** get the messages. Even newspapers, now a mainstay of the serious American consumer, were once considered politically subversive.

5

Which choice provides the most effective introduction to the paragraph?

A) NO CHANGE

B) While each of these criticisms certainly has its merits, each was in a way following in a long path of conservative skepticism at new media developments.

C) Unlike television, other forms of media were readily accepted when they were introduced, with little criticism from experts.

D) Criticism of television is rare today because this form of media has become so commonplace that few remember life before it.

6

Which choice most effectively combines the sentences at the underlined portion?

A) 1940s; in this report,

B) 1940s, and in this report,

C) 1940s, in which

D) 1940s that gave information in which

7

Which choice is most consistent with the style and tone of the passage?

A) NO CHANGE

B) dig

C) take in a lot of

D) understand

Therefore, in today's world, where the Internet seems to be the new medium of choice, we should not be so quick to criticize it in these terms. Still, as a recent survey has shown, American consumers spend more time online than they have on any other media platform in the last five years. ■8 Spending more time on the Internet as of 2012, ■9 American consumers in 2013 spent an average of over 5 hours a day on the Internet.

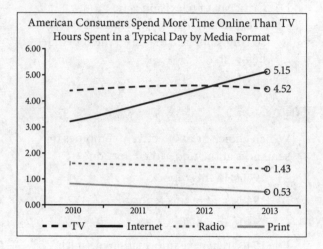

American Consumers Spend More Time Online Than TV
Hours Spent in a Typical Day by Media Format

8

The writer is considering replacing the word *spend* in the preceding sentence with the phrase *pay out*. Should the writer make the change or keep the sentence as it is?

A) Make the change, because the words *pay out* are more relatable to readers.

B) Make the change, because the words *pay out* provide a more direct indication of the action of the sentence.

C) Keep the sentence as it is, because the words *pay out* change the meaning in a way inconsistent with the passage as a whole.

D) Keep the sentence as it is, because the word *spend* hides the fact that the use of media platforms varies widely by socioeconomic status.

9

Which of the following gives information consistent with the graph?

A) NO CHANGE

B) the world's consumers in 2013 spent an average of over 3 hours a day on the Internet.

C) American consumers only a year earlier spent an average of as few as 2 hours a day on the Internet.

D) American consumers decided that the Internet was a better place to watch shows than was the television.

Is this increase in Internet usage a troubling change? Well, history would seem to say that it's not. **10** After all, the Internet has the advantage of being significantly more active than all those other media. In short, effective use of the Internet requires your participation in a way that TV does not. Even so, upwards of six hours a day is a tremendous amount. There must at least be some kind of change, even if it's not necessarily for the worse. **11** Some of the criticisms historically associated with television are frequently applied to Internet usage.

10

At this point, the writer wants to insert an idea that will support the idea given in the previous sentence. Which of the following true statements would offer that support?

A) The rate of literacy remains at an all-time high, despite the introduction of the radio in the 1930s.

B) The number of creative-writing majors may soon eclipse the number of English majors, which will lead to an odd imbalance.

C) Then-candidate Richard Nixon looked really bad on TV in 1960, and how else would people have known his big scandal was coming?

D) The printing press, the newspapers, the radio, and even the television have all been integrated effectively into American culture.

11

The writer wants to end the paragraph with a future-oriented statement that reinforces the main idea of the passage. Which choice best accomplishes this goal?

A) NO CHANGE

B) Some researchers have suggested that human bodies will eventually exhibit physical changes as a result of all of this time spent viewing screens.

C) Rather than simply reacting negatively to a new form of media, society will need to look closely at the long-term risks and benefits associated with significant time spent online.

D) Some people actually experience Internet addiction and spend almost all of their waking hours online.

Chapter 11
Math Basics

Although we'll show you which mathematical concepts are most important to know for the PSAT, this book relies on your knowledge of basic math concepts. If you're a little rusty, this chapter is for you. Read on for a review of the math basics you'll need to know before you continue.

HOW TO CONQUER PSAT MATH

So what do you need to do? There are three important steps:

1. **Know the basic content.** Obviously you do need to know the basics of arithmetic, algebra, and geometry. We'll cover what you need to know in this chapter.
2. **Learn some PSAT-specific problem-solving skills.** Since these basic concepts appear in ways you're probably not used to from math class, you need to prepare yourself with a set of test-specific problem-solving skills designed to help you solve PSAT Math problems. We'll cover the most important ones in the next chapter.
3. **Have a sound overall testing strategy.** This means knowing what to do with difficult questions or when calculator use is not allowed, and having a plan to pace yourself to get the maximum number of points in the time allotted. Be sure to read carefully the material in Chapter 3 to make sure you're using the strategy that will get you the greatest number of points in the time you have.

(PERSONAL) ORDER OF DIFFICULTY

The Math sections on the PSAT are Sections 3 and 4. Section 3 contains 13 multiple-choice questions and 4 grid-in questions. Section 4 contains 27 multiple-choice questions and 4 grid-in questions. Within each question type, there is a loose order of difficulty, with most of the questions being of medium difficulty. (This means that the first few multiple-choice and first few grid-in questions are likely to be rated as easy, and the last few multiple-choice and last two grid-ins are typically considered the most difficult.) More important than any order of difficulty is your own Personal Order of Difficulty. Though the last questions of each type in a section are likely to be the hardest, use your own personal strengths and weaknesses to decide which questions to do and which to skip.

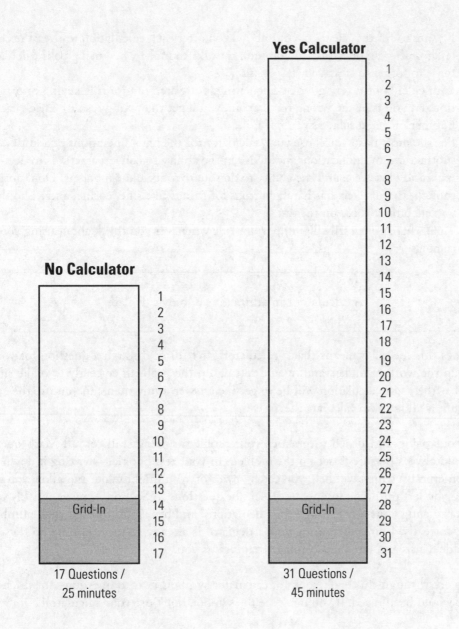

No Calculator

1
2
3
4
5
6
7
8
9
10
11
12
13
Grid-In   14
15
16
17

17 Questions /
25 minutes

Yes Calculator

1
2
3
4
5
6
7
8
9
10
11
12
13
14
15
16
17
18
19
20
21
22
23
24
25
26
27
Grid-In   28
29
30
31

31 Questions /
45 minutes

USING YOUR CALCULATOR

You are allowed to use a calculator on Section 4 of the PSAT, and you should definitely do so. You can use any graphing, scientific, or plain old four-function calculator, **provided that it doesn't have a keyboard.**

There are a few simple rules to remember when dealing with your calculator:

1. Use the calculator you're most comfortable with. You definitely don't want to be trying to find the right button on test day. Ideally, you should be practicing with the same calculator you'll use on test day.
2. Change or charge your batteries the week before the test. If they run out during the test, there's nothing you can do about it.

Not sure whether your calculator is acceptable? Check College Board's website for a list of approved calculators.

3.   Be sure to hit the "clear" or "on/off" button after each calculation to reset the calculator after an operation. A common mistake to make when using your calculator is to forget to clear your last result.

4.   Your calculator is very good at calculating, but watch out for mis-keying information. (If you type the wrong numbers in, you'll get the wrong result.) Check each number on the display as you key it in.

5.   For the most part, you'll use your calculator for the basic operations of addition, subtraction, multiplication, and division; the ability to convert fractions to decimals and vice versa; and the ability to do square roots and exponents. Don't forget, though, that it likely has handy buttons for things like sine, cosine, and *i*, should you encounter those on the test.

6.   Then, there's one really big, important rule whenever you think about using your calculator:

> A calculator can't think; it can only calculate.

What does this mean? It means that a calculator can't think through a question for you. You have to do the work of understanding and setting up the problem correctly to make sure you know what the right calculation will be to get the answer. Only then can you use the calculator, when it is allowed, to calculate the answer.

So use your paper and pencil to practice your problem-solving skills on all Math questions. You should always be sure to set up the problem in your test booklet—writing it down is still the best method—which will help you catch any errors you might make and allow you to pick up where you left off if you lose focus. Then, for questions in Section 4, move quickly to your calculator to chug your way through the calculations, and be careful to enter each number and operator correctly. Remember, using your calculator is already saving you time on these questions—don't rush and lose the advantage that it gives you.

As you work through this book, look for calculator symbols next to questions on which calculator use would be allowed. If you don't see the symbol, don't use your calculator!

Drill 1

DEFINITIONS

One of the reasons that good math students often don't get the credit they deserve on the PSAT is that they've forgotten one or more of these definitions—or they read too fast and skip over these "little" words. Be sure you know them cold and watch out for them!

Match the words with their definitions, and then come up with some examples. Answers can be found in Part IV.

1. integers

2. positive numbers

3. negative numbers

4. even numbers

5. odd numbers

6. factors

7. multiples

8. prime numbers

9. distinct

10. digit

a. numbers that a certain number can be divided by, leaving no remainder
    Examples: _____

b. integers that cannot be divided evenly by 2
    Examples: _____

c. numbers that have no fractional or decimal parts
    Examples: _____

d. numbers that are greater than zero
    Examples: _____

e. having a different value
    Examples: _____

f. integers that can be divided by 2 evenly (with no remainder)
    Examples: _____

g. numbers that are less than zero
    Examples: _____

h. numbers that have exactly two distinct factors: themselves and 1
    Examples: _____

i. numbers that can be divided by a certain number with no remainder
    Examples: _____

j. a figure from 0 through 9 that is used as a placeholder
    Examples: _____

11. consecutive numbers

12. divisible

13. remainder

14. sum

15. product

16. difference

17. quotient

18. absolute value

k. the result of addition
    Examples: _____

l. a whole number left over after division
    Examples: _____

m. the result of subtraction
    Examples:_____

n. can be divided with no remainder
    Examples: _____

o. a number's distance from zero; always a
    positive value
    Examples: _____

p. numbers in a row
    Examples: _____

q. the result of division
    Examples: _____

r. the result of multiplication
    Examples: _____

EXPONENTS AND SQUARE ROOTS

Exponents are just a shorthand for multiplication. Instead of writing $3 \times 3 \times 3 \times 3$, you can write 3^4. Thus, you can handle exponents by expanding them out if necessary.

$$y^2 \times y^3 = y \times y \times y \times y \times y = y^5$$

$$\frac{y^4}{y^2} = \frac{y \times y \times y \times y}{y \times y} = \frac{\cancel{y} \times \cancel{y} \times y \times y}{\cancel{y} \times \cancel{y}} = y \times y = y^2$$

$$y^{(2)3} = (y \times y)^3 = (y \times y)\,(y \times y)\,(y \times y) = y^6$$

However, you can also multiply and divide exponents that have the same base using a shortcut called MADSPM. MADSPM also helps you remember how to deal with raising exponents to another power. Let's see the breakdown:

- **MA** means when you see a MULTIPLICATION sign between like bases, ADD the exponents.
  So $y^2 \times y^3 = y^{2+3} = y^5$.
- **DS** means when you see a DIVISION sign (or fraction), SUBTRACT the exponents. So $\dfrac{y^5}{y^2} = y^{5-2} = y^3$.

- **PM** means when you see a base with an exponent raised to a POWER, MULTIPLY the exponents. So $(y^2)^3 = y^{2 \times 3} = y^6$. (This is really easy to confuse with multiplication, so watch out!)

Be careful, because the rules of MADSPM don't work for addition and subtraction. For example, $3^2 + 3^5$ does NOT equal 3^7. (Crunch it on your calculator if you want to prove it.)

Here are some additional rules to remember about exponents:

- Anything to the zero power equals 1: $3^0 = 1$. Mathematicians argue about whether 0^0 is 1 or is undefined, but that won't come up on the PSAT.
- Anything to the first power equals itself: $3^1 = 3$.
- 1 to any power equals 1: $1^{3876} = 1$.
- A **negative exponent** means to take the reciprocal of what would be the result as if the negative weren't there: $2^{-2} = \dfrac{1}{2^2} = \dfrac{1}{4}$.
- A **fractional exponent** has two parts (like any other fraction): the numerator is the power the base is raised to, and the denominator is the root of the base. For example, $8^{2/3} = \sqrt[3]{8^2} = \sqrt[3]{64} = 4$.

> **Warning**
> The rules for multiplying and dividing exponents do not apply to addition or subtraction:
> $2^2 + 2^3 = 12$
> $(2 \times 2) + (2 \times 2 \times 2) = 12$
> It does not equal 2^5 or 32.

Remember that in calculating the value of a root, you're looking for what number multiplied by itself results in the number under the radical. In the above example, $\sqrt[3]{64} = 4$ because $4 \times 4 \times 4 = 64$.

When you see the square root sign, that means to take the positive root only. So, $\sqrt{9} = 3$, but not -3.

Square roots work just like exponents: You can *always* multiply and divide roots, but you can add and subtract only with the *same* root.

Multiplication and Division:

$$\sqrt{8} \times \sqrt{2} = \sqrt{8 \times 2} = \sqrt{16} = 4$$

$$\sqrt{\frac{1}{4}} = \frac{\sqrt{1}}{\sqrt{4}} = \frac{1}{2}$$

$$\sqrt{300} = \sqrt{100 \times 3} = \sqrt{100} \times \sqrt{3} = 10\sqrt{3}$$

Addition and Subtraction:

$$2\sqrt{2} + 3\sqrt{2} = 5\sqrt{2}$$

$$4\sqrt{3} - \sqrt{3} = 3\sqrt{3}$$

$2\sqrt{3} + 3\sqrt{2}$ *Cannot be added without a calculator since the terms do not have the same root.*

Drill 2

Answers can be found in Part IV.

a. $3^3 \times 3^2 =$ _____

b. $\dfrac{3^3}{3^2} =$ _____

c. $\left(3^3\right)^2 =$ _____

d. $x^6 \times x^2 =$ _____

e. $\dfrac{x^6}{x^2} =$ _____

f. $\left(x^6\right)^2 =$ _____

g. $\sqrt{8} =$ _____

h. $\sqrt[3]{-64} =$ _____

i. $\sqrt{12} + 5\sqrt{3} =$ _____

j. $\sqrt{y^3} =$ _____

k. $\sqrt[3]{-y^3} =$ _____

l. $\sqrt{x^2 y} + 5x\sqrt{y} =$ _____

3

If $3^4 = 9^x$, what is the value of x ?

A) 2

B) 3

C) 4

D) 5

6

$$\sqrt{m^2 + 39} = 8$$

In the equation above, what is a possible value of m ?

A) 3

B) 4

C) 5

D) 6

5

If $\left(3^x\right)^3 = 3^{15}$, what is the value of x ?

A) 3

B) 5

C) 7

D) 9

8

If $x^y x^6 = x^{54}$ and $\left(x^3\right)^z = x^9$, what is the value of $y + z$?

A) 11

B) 12

C) 48

D) 51

7

If $\sqrt{s} - 3 = 9$, which of the following is a possible value of s ?

A) 12

B) 36

C) 81

D) 144

8

Which of the following is equivalent to the expression

$x^6 y^{-3} z^{\frac{1}{2}}$?

A) $\dfrac{x^6 \sqrt{z}}{3y}$

B) $\dfrac{x^6 \sqrt{2z}}{y^3}$

C) $\dfrac{6x \sqrt{z}}{y^3}$

D) $\dfrac{x^6 \sqrt{z}}{y^3}$

9

Which of the following expressions is equivalent to $\sqrt[4]{81b^3c}$?

A) $3b^{\frac{3}{4}}c^{\frac{1}{4}}$

B) $3b^3c$

C) $20.25b^{\frac{3}{4}}c^{\frac{1}{4}}$

D) $20.25b^3c$

12

The function $f(x) = k^{0.3x}$, where k is a constant, can also be expressed as $f(x) = k^{\frac{Bx}{9}}$ for what value of B ?

A) 2.7

B) 9.3

C) 27

D) 30

10

If $x^{\frac{5}{2}} = 8x$, which of the following could be the value of x ?

A) 2

B) 4

C) 6

D) 8

11

Which of the following expressions is equivalent to

$\left(3m^2n^{-3}\right)^{\frac{2}{3}}$?

A) $2m^{\frac{4}{3}}n^{-2}$

B) $\sqrt[3]{9}m^{\frac{4}{3}}n^{-2}$

C) $3m^{\frac{4}{3}}n^{-2}$

D) $3m^4n^{-6}$

16

$$b\sqrt[3]{64a^{\frac{b}{2}}} = \left(4\sqrt{3a}\right)^2$$

Which of the following values of b makes the equation above true?

A) 4

B) 6

C) 8

D) 12

23

Which of the following shows the expression $\dfrac{9 \cdot 8^y}{5 \cdot 16^{y+\frac{1}{2}}}$ in the form of $A \cdot (B)^y$?

A) $\dfrac{9}{20} \cdot \left(\dfrac{1}{2}\right)^y$

B) $\dfrac{9}{10} \cdot (1)^{\frac{y}{2}}$

C) $\dfrac{9}{5} \cdot \left(\dfrac{1}{2}\right)^{\frac{y}{2}}$

D) $\dfrac{9}{5} \cdot \left(\dfrac{1}{2}\right)^y$

EQUATIONS AND INEQUALITIES

An **equation** is a statement that contains an equals sign, such as $3x + 5 = 17$.

To solve an equation, you must get the variable x alone on one side of the equals sign and everything else on the other side.

The first step is to put all of the variables on one side of the equation and all of the numbers on the other side, using addition and subtraction. As long as you perform the same operation on both sides of the equals sign, you aren't changing the value of the variable.

Then you can divide both sides of the equation by the *coefficient*, which is the number in front of the variable. If that number is a fraction, you can multiply everything by its reciprocal.

For example,

$$
\begin{array}{rl}
3x + 5 = 17 & \\
\underline{-5 \quad -5} & \text{Subtract 5 from each side.} \\
3x = 12 & \\
\underline{\div 3 \quad \div 3} & \text{Divide each side by 3.} \\
x = 4 &
\end{array}
$$

Always remember the rule of equations.

> Whatever you do to one side of the equation, you must also do to the other side.

The example above was fairly simple. The PSAT may test this idea with more complex equations and formulas, though. Just keep trying to isolate the variable in question by undoing the operations that have been done to it. Here's an example.

14

Logging companies can use Doyle's Log Rule to estimate the amount of usable lumber, in board feet B, that can be milled from logs. The rule is defined as $B = L\left(\dfrac{d-4}{4}\right)^2$, where d is the diameter inside the bark measured in inches at the small end of the log and L is the log length measured in feet. Which of the following gives the value of d, in terms of B and L?

A) $d = \dfrac{1}{4}\left(\sqrt{\dfrac{B}{L}} + 16\right)$

B) $d = 4\left(\sqrt{BL} + 1\right)$

C) $d = 4\left(\sqrt{\dfrac{B}{L}} - 1\right)$

D) $d = 4\left(\sqrt{\dfrac{B}{L}} + 1\right)$

Here's How to Crack It

The question asks for an equation that gives the value of d in terms of the other variables. To isolate d, start with the L on the outside of the parentheses on the right. Divide both sides by L to get $\dfrac{B}{L} = \left(\dfrac{d-4}{4}\right)^2$. Now undo the power of 2 outside the parentheses. Take the square root of both sides of the equation to get $\sqrt{\dfrac{B}{L}} = \dfrac{d-4}{4}$. Multiply both sides by 4 to get $4\sqrt{\dfrac{B}{L}} = d - 4$. Add 4 to both sides to get $4\sqrt{\dfrac{B}{L}} + 4 = d$. Factor out the 4 to get $4\left(\sqrt{\dfrac{B}{L}} + 1\right) = d$. The correct answer is (D).

An **inequality** is any statement with one of these signs:

> <   (less than)
> \>   (greater than)
> ≤   (less than or equal to)
> ≥   (greater than or equal to)

You can solve inequalities in the same way you solve equations, with one exception: whenever you multiply or divide an inequality by a negative value, you must change the direction of the sign: < becomes >, and ≤ becomes ≥.

For example,

$$
\begin{array}{rl}
3x + 5 \ >\ 17 & \\
\underline{-5 \quad\ -5} & \text{Subtract 5 from each side.} \\
3x \quad\ >\ 12 & \\
\underline{\div 3 \qquad \div 3} & \text{Divide each side by 3.} \\
x \quad\ >\ 4 &
\end{array}
$$

In this case, we didn't multiply or divide by a negative value, so the direction of the sign didn't change. However, if we were to divide by a negative value, we would need to change the direction of the sign.

$$
\begin{array}{rl}
-4x + 3\ >\ 15 & \\
\underline{-3 \quad\ -3} & \text{Subtract 3 from each side.} \\
-4x \quad\ >\ 12 & \\
\underline{\div -4 \qquad \div -4} & \text{Divide each side by } -4. \\
x \quad\ <\ -3 &
\end{array}
$$

Now let's look at how the PSAT may make things more complicated with a question about a range of values.

6

Which of the following is equivalent to $-12 \leq 3b + 3 \leq 18$?

A) $-5 \leq b \leq 5$

B) $-5 \leq b \leq 6$

C) $-4 \leq b \leq 6$

D) $3 \leq b \leq 5$

Here's How to Crack It

The question asks for an inequality that is equivalent to the one given. Like many questions on the PSAT, this question will be difficult if you try to do it all at once. Instead, break it down into Bite-Sized Pieces. Start with just part of the inequality, $-12 \leq 3b + 3$. Remember that you can solve inequalities just like equations—provided that if you multiply or divide by a negative value, you swap the direction of the inequality sign. To solve this part of the inequality, though, you just need to subtract 3 from each side (giving you $-15 \leq 3b$) and then divide each side by 3, which leaves you with $-5 \leq b$. Now you can eliminate any choices that you know won't work: (C) and (D) don't have $-5 \leq b$ in them. Now take the other part of the inequality: $3b + 3 \leq 18$. If you subtract 3 from each side and then divide by 3, you get $b \leq 5$. Now you can cross off (B), and you're left with (A).

SOLVING RATIONAL EQUATIONS

Since you are not always allowed to use your calculator on the PSAT, there will be some instances in which you will need to solve an equation algebraically. Even on the sections in which calculator use is permitted, you may find it faster and more effective to use your mathematical skills to efficiently answer a question. Another way the College Board may make your calculator less effective is by asking you to solve for an expression. A lot of the time, algebraic manipulation will be the means by which you can solve that problem.

Here is an example.

5

Which of the following is equivalent to $\dfrac{f}{f-2} - \dfrac{5}{f+3}$?

A) $\dfrac{f-5}{2f+1}$

B) $\dfrac{-5f}{f^2-6}$

C) $\dfrac{f^2 - 2f + 10}{f^2 + f - 6}$

D) $\dfrac{f^2 + 8f - 10}{f^2 + f - 6}$

Here's How to Crack It

The question asks for an expression that is equivalent to the given one. In order to be able to add these fractions, you need a common denominator. Multiply both the top and the bottom of the left fraction by $(f + 3)$ and multiply both the top and bottom of the right fraction by $(f–2)$. The expression becomes $\dfrac{f(f + 3)}{(f - 2)(f + 3)} - \dfrac{5(f - 2)}{(f + 3)(f - 2)}$ or $\dfrac{f^2 + 3f}{f^2 + f - 6} - \dfrac{5f - 10}{f^2 + f - 6}$.

Now the numerators can be combined over the common denominator and you get $\dfrac{f^2 + 3f - 5f + 10}{f^2 + f - 6} = \dfrac{f^2 - 2f + 10}{f^2 + f - 6}$, which is (C).

EXTRANEOUS SOLUTIONS

Sometimes solving a rational or radical expression makes funny things happen. Let's look at an example.

$$\frac{1}{z + 2} + \frac{1}{z - 2} = \frac{4}{(z + 2)(z - 2)}$$

Given the equation above, what is the value of z?

To add the fractions on the left side, you need a common denominator. Multiply the numerator and the denominator of the first fraction by $(z - 2)$ and the numerator and denominator of the second fraction by $(z + 2)$. Now the fractions can be added together.

The equation becomes

$$\frac{(z - 2) + (z + 2)}{(z + 2)(z - 2)} = \frac{4}{(z + 2)(z - 2)}$$

Since the denominators are equal, the numerators are equal. This gives you

$$(z - 2) + (z + 2) = 4$$

When you simplify the left side, you get $2z = 4$, so $z = 2$. Sounds great, right? However, you need to plug this solution back into the original equation to make sure that it works. You get

$$\frac{1}{2 + 2} + \frac{1}{2 - 2} = \frac{4}{(2 + 2)(2 - 2)}$$

Once simplified, two of the three denominators become zero. That is not allowed, so the solution you found isn't really a solution at all. It is referred to as an "extraneous solution." That term refers to any answer you get to an algebraic equation that results in a false statement when plugged back in to the original equation.

Here's how it might look on the PSAT.

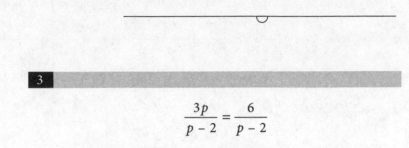

3

$$\frac{3p}{p-2} = \frac{6}{p-2}$$

Which of the following is a true statement about the equation above?

A) There are no solutions to the equation.

B) The solution is $p = 2$.

C) The solution is $p = 3$.

D) There are infinitely many solutions to the equation.

Here's How to Crack It

The question asks for a true statement based on an equation. When given two fraction sets equal to one another, you often have to cross-multiply to solve. In this case, though, the fractions have the same denominator. This tells you that their numerators are equal. Therefore, $3p = 6$, so $p = 2$, right? But what if you put that value back into the denominators? They become 0, which can't happen. Therefore, 2 is an extraneous solution and the answer is (A).

An answer like (D) would occur if literally any value for a variable would make the equation true, such as would be the case in $x + 3 = x + 3$.

ABSOLUTE VALUES

Absolute value is just a measure of the distance between a number and 0. Since distances are always positive, the absolute value of a number is also always positive. The absolute value of a number is written as $|x|$.

When solving for the value of a variable inside the absolute value bars, it is important to remember that variable could be either positive or negative. For example, if $|x| = 2$, then $x = 2$ or $x = -2$ since both 2 and –2 are a distance of 2 from 0.

Here's an example.

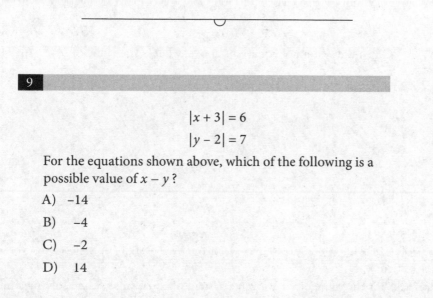

9

$$|x + 3| = 6$$
$$|y - 2| = 7$$

For the equations shown above, which of the following is a possible value of $x - y$?

A) –14

B) –4

C) –2

D) 14

Here's How to Crack It

The question asks for a possible value of $x - y$ given a system of equations. To solve the first equation, set $x + 3 = 6$ and set $x + 3 = -6$. If $x + 3 = -6$, then the absolute value would still be 6. So, x can be either 3 or –9. Now, do the same thing to solve for y. Either $y = 9$ or $y = -5$.

To get the credited answer, you need to try the different combinations. One combination is $x = -9$ and $y = -5$. So, $x - y = -9 - (-5) = -4$, which is (B).

SIMULTANEOUS EQUATIONS

Simultaneous equations occur when you have two equations at the same time. Occasionally, all you have to do is stack the equations and then add or subtract them, so try that first. Sometimes, it won't get you exactly what you want, but it will get you close to it.

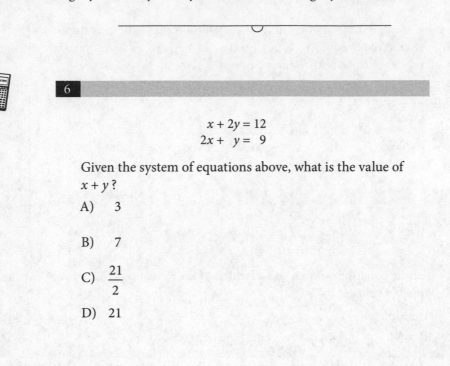

6

$$x + 2y = 12$$
$$2x + y = 9$$

Given the system of equations above, what is the value of $x + y$?

A) 3

B) 7

C) $\dfrac{21}{2}$

D) 21

Here's How to Crack It

The question asks for the value of $x + y$ given a system of equations. When solving simultaneous equations, you can sometimes get what you need by adding the equations together. Even getting closer to $x + y$, such as getting a multiple of that expression, would be useful.

Let's see what happens when you add the equations:

$$
\begin{array}{r}
x + 2y = 12 \\
+\ 2x + y = \ 9 \\
\hline
3x + 3y = 21
\end{array}
$$

Now all you need to do is divide both sides of the equation by 3 to get the expression you're being asked for, $x + y$, and you end up with the answer, 7. The correct answer is (B).

That was pretty simple, but simultaneous equations on the PSAT can be tougher. Let's look at a really challenging one.

27

Two competing fast food restaurants sell both hamburgers and orders of French fries at the same prices. Burger Planet's lunchtime sales can be modeled as $40h + 70f = \$260.00$, where h is the cost of a hamburger and f is the cost of an order of French fries. If Slider Heaven sells 80 hamburgers and 60 orders of French fries over the same period and outsells Burger Planet by $100, what is the total cost of three hamburgers and three orders of French fries at either establishment?

A) $5.00

B) $9.00

C) $11.00

D) $15.00

Here's How to Crack It

The question asks for the total cost of three hamburgers and three orders of fries at either restaurant. The sales equation at Burger Planet is given in the question. Create an equation for Slider Heaven's lunchtime sales so you can solve the two equations. Slider Heaven's sales can be modeled as $80h + 60f = 260 + 100 = 360$. Adding these equations together or subtracting one from the other won't give you the 3 burgers and 3 fries that you want. Instead, you need to create a common coefficient for one of the variables and then add or subtract the two equations from each other to get rid of that variable. In this case, multiply the Burger Planet equation by -2 to get $-80h - 140f = -520$. Place the two equations on top of each other and add:

$$\begin{array}{r} -80h - 140f = -520 \\ +80h + 60f = 360 \\ \hline -80f = -160 \end{array}$$

Divide both sides by -80 to get $f = 2$. Plug 2 into the Burger Planet equation to get $40h + 70(2) = 260$. Solve for h to get $40h + 140 = 260$, or $40h = 120$, so $h = 3$. Therefore, the total cost of 3 hamburgers and 3 orders of French fries is $3(3) + 3(2) = 9 + 6 = 15$. The correct answer is (D).

WRITING YOUR OWN EQUATIONS

For the most part, we've been looking at solving equations given to you in questions. That last question, though, required you to create one of your own. The PSAT Math sections are testing not only your math skills but also, and possibly even more important to your score improvement, your reading skills. It is imperative that you read the questions carefully and translate the words in the question into mathematical symbols.

ENGLISH	MATH EQUIVALENTS
is, are, were, did, does, costs	=
what (or any unknown value)	*any variable (x, y, k, b)*
more, sum	+
less, difference	−
of, times, product	× *(multiply)*
ratio, quotient, out of, per	÷ *(divide)*

Sometimes you'll be asked to take a word problem and create equations or inequalities from that information. Usually they will not ask you to solve these equations/inequalities, so if you are able to locate and translate the information in the question, you have a good shot at getting the correct answer. Always start with the most straightforward piece of information. What is the most straightforward piece of information? Well, that's up to you to decide. Consider the following question.

3

Elom joined a gym that charges a monthly fee of $35. A one-time enrollment fee of $40 is charged when he joins. Which of the following represents the total amount of fees that Elom has paid to his gym after m months, in dollars?

A) $35m + 40$

B) $35 + 40m$

C) $35m - 40$

D) $(35 + 40)m$

Here's How to Crack It

The question asks for an equation to represent a situation. Read the question carefully and translate the information. The question states that there is a monthly fee of $35 and that the variable m represents the number of months. Therefore, the correct answer should include $35m$, so you can eliminate (B). The one-time enrollment fee of $40 has nothing to do with the number of months, so the 40 should be by itself. Eliminate (D), which multiplies the 40 by m. The fee should be added on, so the correct answer is (A).

Now let's look at harder one. The following question has a lot more words and more than one inequality in each answer choice. This makes it even more important to translate one piece at a time and eliminate after each step.

5

Kai has two different after-school jobs, one at a bookstore and one at a grocery store. He can only work a total of 10 hours each week due to his heavy homework load. When he works at the bookstore, he earns $10 per hour, and when he works at the grocery store, he earns $13 per hour. He never earns less than $100 in a week, and he always works more hours at the bookstore because he can get free coffee from the café. Solving which of the following systems of inequalities yields the number of hours at the bookstore, b, and the number of hours at the grocery store, g, that Kai can work in one week?

A) $\begin{cases} b - g \le 10 \\ b < g \\ 10b + 13g > 100 \end{cases}$

B) $\begin{cases} b + g \le 10 \\ b > g \\ 10b + 13g \ge 100 \end{cases}$

C) $\begin{cases} b + g \le 10 \\ b > g \\ 13b + 10g \ge 100 \end{cases}$

D) $\begin{cases} bg \le 10 \\ b > g \\ 10b + 10g \ge 100 \end{cases}$

Here's How to Crack It

The question asks for a system of inequalities that represents a situation. Start with a straightforward piece of information to translate. If you start with the fact that Kai works more hours at the bookstore than at the grocery store, you can translate that into $b > g$. This would eliminate (A). If you start with the fact that Kai works no more than 10 hours each week, you can translate that into $b + g \le 10$. This would eliminate (D). Now, to decide between (B) and (C), compare the answers and see what the differences are. Choice (B) has a coefficient of 10 in front of the variable b. Check the question to see if 10 should be associated with b. Since b is the number of hours Kai works at the bookstore, and he earns $10 per hour there, the correct answer should have $10b$, not $13b$. Eliminate (C) and choose (B).

Drill 3

Answers can be found in Part IV.

3

If a certain number is 3 more than 7 times itself, what is the number?

A) −3

B) $-\dfrac{3}{2}$

C) $-\dfrac{1}{2}$

D) $-\dfrac{3}{8}$

2

If $\dfrac{7}{x+4} = \dfrac{x+3}{y}$, then which of the following represents an equivalent equation for y, in terms of x ?

A) $y = \dfrac{7(x+3)}{x+4}$

B) $y = \dfrac{x^2 + 7x + 12}{7}$

C) $y = \dfrac{x+3}{7(x+4)}$

D) $y = \dfrac{7}{x^2 + 7x + 12}$

5

Ann is writing a book that will include up to 98 recipes. She currently has 32 main dish recipes and 18 dessert recipes. If r represents the number of additional recipes that Ann could include in her book, which of the following inequalities represents all possible values of r ?

A) $r - 50 \geq 98$

B) $r - 50 \leq 98$

C) $98 - (32 + 18) - r \leq 0$

D) $98 - (32 + 18) - r \geq 0$

4

If $\dfrac{3a}{4b} = \dfrac{5c}{6d}$, then which of the following is equal to bc ?

A) $\dfrac{a}{2d}$

B) $\dfrac{5a}{8d}$

C) $\dfrac{9ad}{10}$

D) $18ad$

28

A fitness tracking watch collects data on how many miles a user walks per day. The data is collected from 12:00 A.M. each morning until 12:00 A.M. the following day, and resets each day at midnight. After one month of use, Debbie reviews her data in the fitness tracker. She discovers that her average daily miles walked are equal to one-hundredth of the square of the number of hours in one day. How many miles does Debbie walk in one day, on average, rounded to the nearest mile?

7

$$\frac{2(p-2)+2(3-p)}{p-2} = \frac{2(3p-6)+3(6-2p)}{p-2}$$

Which of the following is a true statement about the equation above?

A) There are no solutions to the equation.

B) The solution is $p = 2$.

C) The solution is $p = 3$.

D) There are infinitely many solutions to the equation.

8

A ski resort is renting skis for $30 and snowboards for $20 over a weekend. On Friday, 40 skis and snowboards were rented, and the resort collected $1,100 in rental fees. On Saturday, 55 skis and snowboards were rented and the resort collected $1,400 in rental fees. On Sunday, the resort rented 85 skis and snowboards and collected $2,100 rental fees. Solving which of the following system of equations yields the number of skis, s, and the number of snowboards, b, that were rented over the three-day weekend?

A) $s + b = 50$
$30s + 20b = 180$

B) $s + b = 180$
$30s + 20b = 460$

C) $s + b = 180$
$30s + 20b = 4,600$

D) $s + b = 4,600$
$30s + 20b = 180$

12

$$\frac{m+9}{3} + 2 = \frac{m-2}{7} + 3$$

In the equation above, what is the value of m ?

A) −17

B) −12

C) 5

D) 10

9

$$-4(h + 5) = -3(2 - h) + 14$$

In the equation above, what is the value of h ?

A) −18

B) −4

C) $\dfrac{18}{7}$

D) 18

23

A group of students sells different types of cookies at a bake sale to raise funds for a school trip. When the students sell two snickerdoodle cookies, s, and seven cinnamon cookies, c, they raise $14.00. When the students sell eight snickerdoodle cookies and three cinnamon cookies, they raise $17.50. Assuming the price per cookie does not change, which of the following equations represents a sale the students could make during the fundraiser?

A) $2s + 3c = \$8.00$

B) $4s + 6c = \$16.25$

C) $6s + 5c = \$17.36$

D) $8s + 7c - \$24.50$

13

$$10(3x + a) - a(4x + 2) = 2a(x + 4)$$

If the equation above has infinitely many solutions for x, what is the value of a ?

A) 5

B) 4

C) 3

D) 1

25

Laura has a recipe for cake that calls for both eggs and cups of flour. Laura can purchase five eggs and four cups of flour for $5.50 and nine eggs and eight cups of flour for $10.50. Based on these costs, what is the cost of the ten eggs that Laura will need for her recipe?

A) $5.00

B) $5.50

C) $7.50

D) $10.50

THE COORDINATE PLANE

You will definitely see some questions on the coordinate plane, or *xy*-plane, on the PSAT. Let's start by covering the basics here. You'll see more advanced concepts in the Advanced Math chapter. So let's just review:

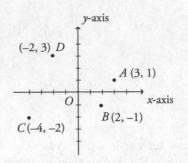

The *x*-axis is the horizontal axis, and the *y*-axis is the vertical axis. Points are given on the coordinate plane with the *x*-coordinate first. Positive *x*-values go to the right, and negative ones go to the left; positive *y*-values go up, and negative ones go down. So point *A* (3, 1) is 3 points to the right on the *x*-axis and 1 point up from the *y*-axis. Point *B* (2, –1) is 2 points to the right on the *x*-axis and 1 point down from the *y*-axis.

Slope is a measure of the steepness of a line on the coordinate plane. On most slope questions, you need to recognize only whether the slope is positive, negative, or zero. A line that goes up and to the right has positive slope; a line that goes down and to the right has negative slope, and a flat line has zero slope. In the figure below, ℓ_1 has positive slope, ℓ_2 has zero slope, and ℓ_3 has negative slope.

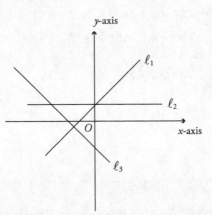

If you do need to calculate the slope, and the graph is drawn for you, here's how: slope = $\frac{y_2 - y_1}{x_2 - x_1}$. The *slope* of a line is equal to $\frac{rise}{run}$. To find the slope, take any two points on the line and count off or calculate the distance you need to get from one of these points to the other.

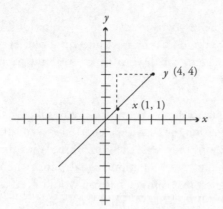

In the graph above, to get from point x to point y, we count up (rise) 3 units, and count over (run) 3 units. Therefore, the slope is $\dfrac{rise}{run} = \dfrac{3}{3} = 1$. Always remember to check whether the slope is positive or negative when you use $= \dfrac{rise}{run}$.

If you're not given a figure and you can't draw one easily using the points given, you can find the slope by plugging the coordinates you know into the slope formula. Just remember to plug the numbers into the formula carefully!

Knowing how to find the slope is useful for solving questions about perpendicular and parallel lines. **Perpendicular lines** have slopes that are negative reciprocals of one another. **Parallel lines** have the same slope and no solutions. You may also be given two equations that have infinitely many solutions.

Take a look at an example.

———————————————◯———————————————

20

$$gx - hy = 78$$

$$4x + 3y = 13$$

In the system of equations above, g and h are constants. If the system has infinitely many solutions, what is the value of gh ?

A) −432

B)   −6

C)   6

D)   432

To Infinity…and Beyond!
When given two equations with infinitely many solutions, find a way to make them equal. The equations represent the same line.

Here's How to Crack It

The question asks for the value of *gh* given a system of equations. This question may have you scratching your head and moving on to the next question, but let's explore what you can do to solve this before you decide it's not worth your time. You may be surprised by how easy it is to solve a problem like this.

When they say that these equations have infinitely many solutions, what they are really saying is that these are the same equation, or that one equation is a multiple of the other equation. In other words, these two equations represent the same line. With that in mind, try to determine what needs to be done to make these equations equal. Since the right side of the equation is dealing with only a number, first determine what you would need to do to make 13 equal to 78.

In this case, you need to multiply 13 by 6. Since we are working with equations, we need to do the same thing to both sides of the equation in order for the equation to remain equal.

$$6(4x + 3y) = 6 \times 13$$
$$24x + 18y = 78$$

Since both equations are now equal to 78, you can set them equal to each other, giving you this equation:

$$24x + 18y = gx - hy$$

You may know that when you have equations with the same variables on each side the coefficients on those variables must be equal, so you can deduce that $g = 24$ and $h = -18$. (Be cautious when you evaluate this equation. The test-writers are being sneaky by using addition in one equation and subtraction in another.) Therefore, *gh* equals $(24)(-18) = -432$. Choice (A) is correct.

The equation of a line can take multiple forms. One is known as the **standard form**, and we saw it in question 20. In this form, $Ax + By = C$, the slope is $-\dfrac{A}{B}$ and the *y*-intercept is $\dfrac{C}{B}$.

Knowing these shortcuts can help you avoid having to convert a line equation into the more common form known as the **slope-intercept form**. A slope-intercept equation takes the form $y = mx + b$, where *m* is the slope and *b* is the *y*-intercept.

Let's look at a question for which the slope-intercept form is useful.

5

If c is a constant less than 0, which of the following could be the graph of $y = c(x + y)$ in the xy-plane?

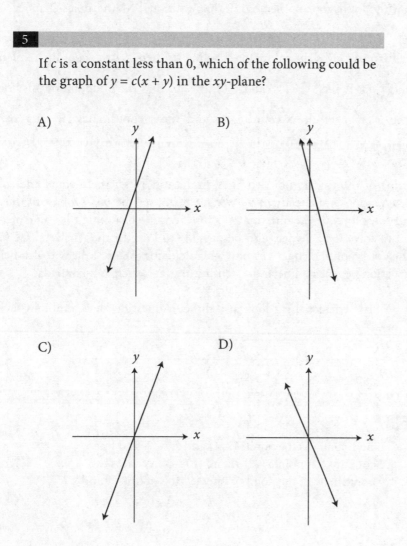

A)

B)

C)

D)

Here's How to Crack It

The question asks for the graph of the equation of a line. No points are labeled on the graphs in the answers, and the equation of the line has a mysterious c in it. If you knew the slope or y-intercept of the equation, you could use Process of Elimination. To see what is going on with this question, make up a value for c that is less than 0. Let's say that $c = -2$, in which case $y = -2(x + y)$. Distribute the -2 to get $y = -2x - 2y$. Rewrite the equation so that it is in the slope-intercept form, $y = mx + b$, to get $3y = -2x$ or $y = -\dfrac{2}{3}x$. Therefore, the slope is $-\dfrac{2}{3}$ and the y-intercept is 0. In fact, no matter what value you picked for c, if c is a constant less than 0, the slope will be negative, and the y-intercept will be 0. Eliminate (A) and (C) since both of these lines have positive slopes. Eliminate (B) because the y-intercept is not 0. The correct answer is (D).

The **distance formula** looks quite complicated. The easiest way to solve the distance between two points is to connect them and form a triangle. Then use the Pythagorean Theorem. Many times, the triangle formed is one of the common Pythagorean triples (3-4-5 or 5-12-13). We'll talk more about the Pythagorean Theorem in the Additional Math Topics chapter.

The **midpoint formula** gives the midpoint of a line segment on the coordinate plane. For example, the line ST has points $S(x_1, y_1)$ and $T(x_2, y_2)$. To find the midpoint of this line segment, simply find the average of the x-coordinates and the y-coordinates. In our example, the midpoint would be $\left(\dfrac{x_1 + x_2}{2}, \dfrac{y_1 + y_2}{2} \right)$.

To find the **point of intersection** of two lines, find a way to set them equal and solve for the variable. If the equations are already in $y = mx + b$ form, set the $mx + b$ part of the two equations equal and solve for x. If the question asks for the value of y, plug the value of x back into either equation to solve for y. It may also be possible to Plug In the Answers (see Chapter 12 for more on this) or graph the equations on your calculator. These skills will also help find the points of intersection between a line and a non-linear graph such as a parabola.

Sometimes, it's a little trickier. Let's look at a difficult question that combines several of the previous concepts.

---○---

24

Line 1 contains the points (2, 1) and (1, –2), and line 2 contains the points (–2, 9) and (10, –3). What is the y-coordinate of the point of intersection of lines 1 and 2 ?

A) –1

B) 3

C) 4

D) 7

Here's How to Crack It

The question asks for the y-coordinate of a point of intersection. To answer this question, first you need to find the equations of the two lines in order to set the equations equal to each other and find the value of x. Given two points on a line, you can find the slope using $\dfrac{y_2 - y_1}{x_2 - x_1}$. Therefore, the slope of line 1 can be calculated as $\dfrac{-2 - 1}{1 - 2} = \dfrac{-3}{-1} = 3$. Plug this and the coordinates of the easier point, (2, 1), into $y = mx + b$ to find the value of b. The equation for line 1 becomes

$1 = 3(2) + b$. Solve for b to find that the value is –5, so line 1 is $y = 3x - 5$. The slope of line 2 can be calculated as $\dfrac{-3 - 9}{10 - (-2)} = \dfrac{-12}{12} = -1$. Find the value of b: $9 = -1(-2) + b$, so $b = 7$. The equation for line 2 is $y = -x + 7$. Set the two equations equal to each other to get $3x - 5 = -x + 7$. Solve for x to get $4x - 5 = 7$ or $4x = 12$, so $x = 3$. Finally, plug x into one of the equations to solve for y. Plug x into the equation $y = -x + 7$, to get $y = -3 + 7 = 4$. Therefore, the correct answer is 4, which is (C).

Drill 4

Answers can be found in Part IV.

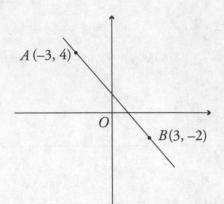

a. How many units do you count up (rise) to get from point *B* to point *A*?
_____

b. How many units must you count over (run) to get from point *A* to point *B*?
_____

c. What is the slope of the line above? _____

(Remember, the line is going down to the right, so it must have a negative slope.)

d. What would be the slope of a line parallel to *AB*? _____

e. What would be the slope of a line perpendicular to *AB*? _____

f. What is the distance from point *A* to point *B*? _____

g. What is the midpoint of line segment *AB*? _____

2

If $y = 6x + 3$ and $y = cx + 3$ are the equations of perpendicular lines, then what is the value of c ?

A) -6

B) $-\dfrac{1}{6}$

C) $\dfrac{1}{6}$

D) 6

6

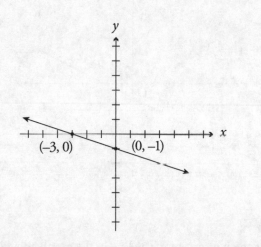

Line l is shown in the graph above. If line m is parallel to line l, which of the following could be the equation of line m ?

A) $y = -3x - 1$

B) $y = -\dfrac{1}{3}x + 2$

C) $y = \dfrac{1}{3}x - 3$

D) $y = 3x + 2$

3

What is the *y*-intercept of the line with equation
$2x + 3y = 12$?

A) 4

B) 3

C) 2

D) $\frac{1}{4}$

12

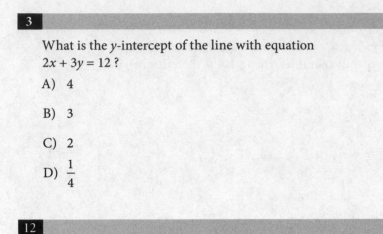

What is the *x*-intercept of the line in the graph above?

A) −1

B) 0

C) 1

D) 2

7

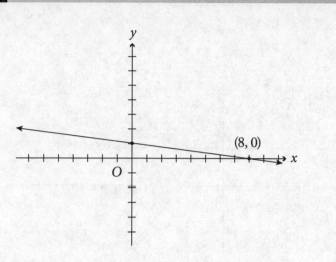

Which of the following could be the equation of the line in the graph above?

A) $2y - x = -8$

B) $4y + x = -8$

C) $8y - 3x = 8$

D) $8y + x = 8$

14

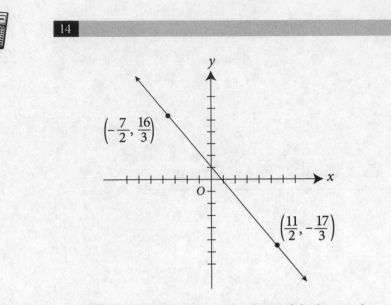

Which of the following is the slope of the line in the graph above?

A) $-\dfrac{11}{6}$

B) $-\dfrac{11}{9}$

C) $-\dfrac{9}{8}$

D) $-\dfrac{9}{11}$

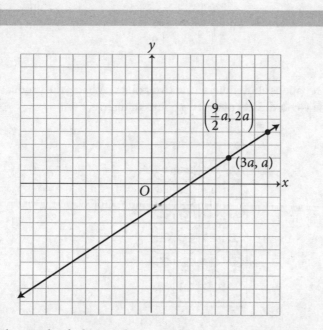

The graph of a line is shown in the xy-plane above. It contains the points $(3a, a)$ and $\left(\dfrac{9}{2}a, 2a\right)$, where a is a positive constant. Which of the following could be the equation of this line?

A) $y = \dfrac{2}{3}x - 2$

B) $y = \dfrac{2}{3}x + 2$

C) $y = \dfrac{4}{3}x - 2$

D) $y = \dfrac{3}{2}x - 2$

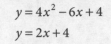

$$y = 4x^2 - 6x + 4$$
$$y = 2x + 4$$

The equations above intersect at two points. What is the product of the y-coordinates of the two points of intersection?

CHARTS AND GRAPHS

Another basic math skill you will need for the PSAT is the ability to read charts and graphs. The PSAT includes charts, graphs, and tables throughout the test (not just in the Math sections) to present data for students to analyze. The test-writers believe this better reflects what students learn in school and need to understand in the real world. The situations will typically include real-life applications, such as finance and business situations, social science issues, and science.

Since you'll be seeing graphics throughout the test, let's look at the types you may encounter and the skills you'll need to be familiar with when you work with charts and graphs.

The Scatterplot

A scatterplot is a graph with distinct data points, each representing one piece of information. On the scatterplot below, each dot represents the number of televisions sold at a certain price point.

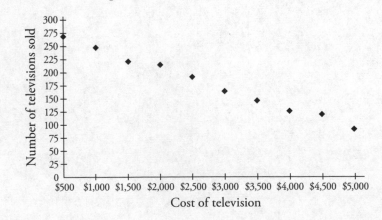

Here's How to Read It

To find the cost of a television when 225 televisions are sold, start at 225 on the vertical axis and draw a horizontal line to the right until you hit a data point. Use the edge of your answer sheet as a straightedge if you have trouble drawing your own straight lines. Once you hit a point, draw a straight line down from it to the horizontal axis and read the number the line hits, which should be $1,500. To determine the number of televisions sold when they cost a certain amount, reverse the steps—start at the bottom, draw up until you hit a point, and then move left until you intersect the vertical axis.

A question may ask you to draw a "line of best fit" on a scatterplot diagram. This is the line that best represents the data. You can use the edge of your answer sheet as a ruler to help you draw a line that goes through most of the data.

The Line Graph

A line graph is similar to a scatterplot in that it shows different data points that relate the two variables. The difference with a line graph, though, is that the points have been connected to create a continuous line.

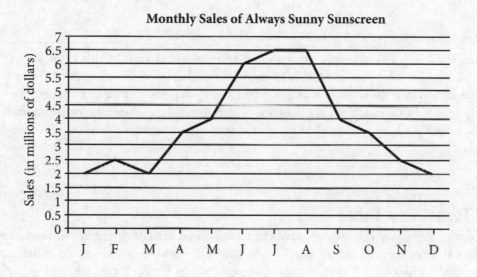

Monthly Sales of Always Sunny Sunscreen

Here's How to Read It

Reading a line graph is very similar to reading a scatterplot. Start at the axis that represents the data given, and draw a straight line up or to the right until you intersect the graph line. Then move left or down until you hit the other axis. For example, in February, indicated by an F on the horizontal axis, Always Sunny Sunscreen had 2.5 million in sales. Make sure to notice the units on each axis. If February sales were only $2.50, rather than $2.5 million, then this company wouldn't be doing very well!

The Bar Graph (or Histogram)

Instead of showing a variety of different data points, a bar graph will show how many items belong to a particular category. If the variable at the bottom is given in ranges, instead of distinct items, the graph is called a histogram, but you read it the same way.

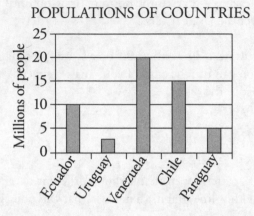

POPULATIONS OF COUNTRIES

Here's How to Read It

The height of each bar corresponds to a value on the vertical axis. In this case, the bar above Chile hits the line that intersects with 15 on the vertical axis, so there are 15 million people in Chile. Again, watch the units to make sure you know what the numbers on the axes represent. On this graph, horizontal lines are drawn at 5-unit intervals, making the graph easier to read. If these lines do not appear on a bar graph, use your answer sheet to determine the height of a given bar.

The Two-Way Table

A two-way table is another way to represent data without actually graphing it. Instead of having the variables represented on the vertical and horizontal axes, the data will be arranged in rows and columns. The top row will give the headings for each column, and the left-most column will give the headings for each row. The numbers in each box indicate the data for the category represented by the row and the column the box is in.

	Computer Production	
	Morning Shift	**Afternoon Shift**
Monday	200	375
Tuesday	245	330
Wednesday	255	340
Thursday	250	315
Friday	225	360

Here's How to Read It

If you wanted to see the number of computers produced on Tuesday morning, you could start in the Morning Shift column and look down until you found the number in the row that says "Tuesday," or you could start in the row for Tuesday and look to the right until you found the Morning Shift column. Either way, the result is 245. Some tables will give you totals in the bottom row and/or the right-most column, but sometimes you will need to find the totals yourself by adding up all the numbers in each row or in each column. More complicated tables will have more categories listed in rows and/or columns, or the tables may even contain extraneous information.

THE BOX PLOT

A box plot shows data broken into quartiles, as follows:

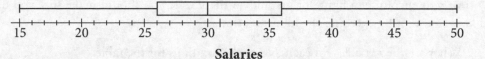

Salaries

Here's How to Read It

Here is what all the parts of the box plot represent.

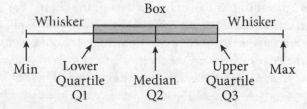

The line in the middle of the box shows the median value of the data, which is 30 in the example above. The "whiskers," which give this figure the alternate name "box-and-whisker plot," represent the highest value on the list with the end of the whisker on the right and the lowest value with the end of the whisker on the left. Thus, the minimum value of this data set is 15, and the maximum is 50. Then the data between the median and these minimum and maximum values is broken into two equal parts on each side, creating four "quartiles." The value halfway between the minimum and the median is the Q1 value on the left side of the box, at about 26, and the value halfway between the maximum and the median is the Q3 value on the right side of the box, at about 36.

The Stem-and-Leaf Plot

A stem-and-leaf plot shows data according to a common first digit.

$$
\begin{array}{c|ccccccc}
2 & 0 & 1 & 7 \\
3 & 2 & 2 & 4 \\
4 & 0 & 1 & 5 & 7 & 7 & 8 \\
5 & 1 & 1 & 4 & 5 & 5 & 7 & 9 \\
6 & 2 & 5 & 8 & 8 & 9 \\
7 & 0
\end{array}
$$

A book club took a survey of the age, in years, of its members. The data is shown in the stem-and-leaf plot above.

Here's How to Read It

The numbers on the left of the vertical line are the initial digit of each age, and the numbers to the left of the vertical line are the following digits corresponding to the given first digit. This means that the ages of the members of the book club are 20, 21, 27, 32, 32, 34, etc. Questions using stem-and-leaf plots often ask for things like the range of the data, the median of the data, or the probability of selecting a certain number. We will look at all those statistical measures in the Math Techniques chapter.

From a stem-and-leaf plot or a box plot, you can determine the median and range of the set of data. It is also impossible to calculate the mode and mean from a stem-and-leaf plot and the interquartile range from a box plot.

Figure Facts

Every time you encounter a figure or graphic on the PSAT, you should make sure you understand how to read it by checking the following things:

- What are the variables for each axis or the headings for the table?
- What units are used for each variable?
- Are there any key pieces of information (numbers, for example) in the legend of the chart that you should note?
- What type of relationship is shown by the data in the chart? For instance, if the chart includes curves that show an upward slope, then the graph shows a *positive association*, while curves that show a downward slope show a *negative association*.
- You can use the edge of your answer sheet as a ruler to help you make sure you are locating the correct data in the graph or to draw a line of best fit if necessary.

GRIDS-INS: THE BASICS

You will see 8 questions on the PSAT that ask you to bubble in a numerical answer on a grid, rather than answer a multiple-choice question. These Grid-In questions are arranged in a loose order of difficulty, meaning they start easier and get progressively harder, and can be solved according to the methods outlined for the multiple-choice questions on the test. The last two grid-ins in Section 4 are usually a paired set, but each question can be answered separately. Don't worry that there are no answer choices—your approach is the same.

Keep Left
No matter how many digits in your answer, always start gridding in the leftmost column. That way, you'll avoid omitting digits and losing points.

The only difficulty with grid-ins is getting used to the way in which you are asked to answer the question. For each question, you'll have a grid like the following:

We recommend that you write the answer on top of the grid to help you bubble, but it's important to know that the scoring machine reads only the bubbles. *If you bubble incorrectly, the computer will consider the answer to be incorrect.*

Here are the basic rules of gridding:

1. If your answer uses fewer than four boxes, you can grid it anywhere you like. To avoid confusion, we suggest that you start at the leftmost box. For example,

2. You can grid your answer as either a fraction or a decimal, *if* the fraction will fit.

    You can grid an answer of .5 as either .5 or $\frac{1}{2}$.

or

Relax

If your answer is a fraction and it fits in the grid (fraction bar included), don't reduce it. Why bother? You won't get an extra point for doing so. However, if your fraction doesn't fit, reduce it or turn it into a decimal on your calculator.

3. You do not need to reduce your fractions *if* the fraction will fit.

If your answer is $\frac{2}{4}$, you can grid it as $\frac{2}{4}$, $\frac{1}{2}$, or .5.

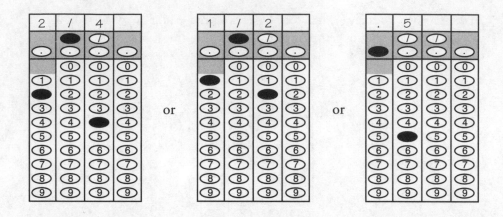

4. If you have a decimal that will not fit in the spaces provided, you *must grid as many places as will fit*.

If your answer is $\frac{2}{3}$, you can grid it as $\frac{2}{3}$, .666, or .667, but .66 or 0.66 are *not* acceptable.

You do *not* need to round your numbers, so we suggest that you don't. There's no reason to give yourself a chance to make a mistake if you don't have to.

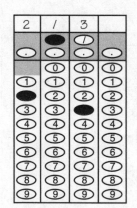 or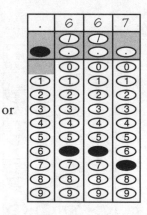

5. You cannot grid mixed numbers. Convert all mixed numbers to ordinary fractions.

    If your answer is $2\frac{1}{2}$, you must convert it to $\frac{5}{2}$ or 2.5; otherwise the computer

    will read your 2 1/2 as 21/2.

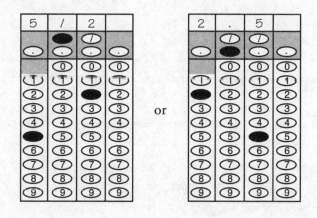

or

Don't Mix
Never grid in a mixed number. Change it into an improper fraction or decimal. To convert mixed fractions into improper fractions, all you have to do is multiply the denominator with the whole number in front of the fraction, then add that product to the numerator, and finally put that number over the denominator you started with.

6. You can't grid π, square roots, variables, or negative numbers, so if you get an answer with one of those terms, you've made a mistake. Reread the final questions and check your work.

Drill 5

Answers can be found in Part IV.

28

Estimated Numbers of Cell Phone Users by Type
(in millions)

	Prepaid users	Contracted users	Total
2008	45	225	270
2012	75	250	325
Total	120	475	595

If a cell phone user is selected at random in 2008, what is the probability that user is a contracted user?

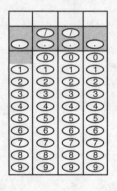

14

If $5x^2 = 125$, what could be the value of $5x^3$?

15

$$z = 5 - 5[5z - 2(1 - z)]$$

In the equation above, what is the value of z ?

29

If $5 - \sqrt{z} = \sqrt{z - 5}$, what is the value of z ?

16

If $3a + 2b = 37$ and $7a + 4b = 85$, what is the value of $b^2 + 6b - 10$?

30

Linh travels from his home in Canada, where temperature is measured in degrees Celsius, to Houston, where temperature is measured in degrees Fahrenheit. The weather channel forecasts the high temperature in Houston for the next 2 days as 95 degrees and 86 degrees Fahrenheit, respectively. He wants to convert these temperatures from Fahrenheit to Celsius. To do so, he subtracts 32 from the degrees in Fahrenheit for each day and multiplies the difference by $\frac{5}{9}$. How many degrees higher is the predicted temperature for the first day than the predicted temperature for the second day, in degrees Celsius?

31

Mathew and Moriah purchased a tandem bicycle for $540. If the amount Moriah paid was $30 less than twice the amount Mathew paid, how much, in dollars, did Moriah pay? (Disregard the dollar sign when gridding in your answer.)

17

Kimberly is an apiologist studying the sugar content of different sugar-water solutions to determine which is preferred by her hive of honeybees. After trying Solution 1, which has a sugar content of 25%, and Solution 2, which has a sugar content of 10%, she decides to make a new solution. She mixes 50 ounces of Solution 1 with some quantity of Solution 2 to make Solution 3, which has a sugar content of 15%. How many ounces of Solution 2 did Kimberly use to make Solution 3 ?

Summary

o The Math sections are arranged in a loose Order of Difficulty, which can make it easier to spot the less difficult questions. However, remember that the test-writers' idea of "easier" questions is not necessarily the same as your idea. Let your Personal Order of Difficulty be your guide.

o Write in your test booklet to set up problems, and then use your calculator (when allowed) to figure out solutions. And remember to type carefully—your calculator won't check for mistakes.

o Review basic definitions again before the test to make sure you don't get stuck on the "little words."

o When you have to manipulate exponents, remember your MADSPM rules.

o To solve equations for a variable, isolate the variable. Make sure you perform the same operations on both sides of the equation.

o Inequalities can be worked just like equations until you have to multiply or divide by a negative number. Then you need to flip the inequality sign.

o When adding or subtracting rational expressions, get a common denominator. When given two rational expressions set equal to each other, cross-multiply and solve the resulting equation.

o When solving radical and rational equations, be on the lookout for extraneous solutions. They are answers you get that don't work when plugged back into the original equation.

o The absolute value of a number is the positive distance from zero, or practically, making the thing inside the | | sign positive. Everything inside the | | is equal to the positive and the negative value of the expression to which it is equal. Also remember that | | work like ( ); you need to complete all the operations inside the | | before you can make the value positive.

o To solve simultaneous equations, simply add or subtract the equations. If you don't have the answer, look for multiples of your solutions. When the simultaneous equation question asks for a single variable and addition and subtraction don't work, try to make something disappear. Multiply the equations by a constant to make the coefficient(s) of the variable(s) you want go to zero when the equations are added or subtracted.

o   When writing a system of equations, start with the most straightforward piece of information.

o   You can also use the equations in the answer choices to help you narrow down the possibilities for your equations. Eliminate any answers in which an equation doesn't match a piece of information in the question.

o   Parallel lines have the same slope and no solutions. If two lines have the same slope and infinitely many solutions, they are actually the same line. Perpendicular lines have slopes that are negative reciprocals of each other.

o   Rather than worrying about the distance formula, connect the two points and make the resulting line the hypotenuse of a right triangle. Then you can use the Pythagorean Theorem to find the distance.

o   The coordinates of the midpoint of a line segment with endpoints (x_1, y_1) and (x_2, y_2) will be $\left(\dfrac{x_1 + x_2}{2}, \dfrac{y_1 + y_2}{2}\right)$.

o   When you encounter charts, carefully check the chart for information you should note, and remember that you can use your answer sheet as a ruler to help you locate information or to draw a line of best fit.

o   When doing grid-in questions, be sure to keep to the left, and don't bother reducing fractions if they fit in the allotted spaces.

Chapter 12
Math Techniques

In the previous chapter, we mentioned that one of the keys to doing well on the PSAT is to have a set of test-specific problem-solving skills. This chapter discusses some powerful strategies, which—though you may not use them in school—are specifically designed to get you points on the PSAT. Learn them well!

PLUGGING IN

One of the most powerful problem-solving skills on the PSAT is a technique we call Plugging In. Plugging In will turn nasty algebra questions into simple arithmetic and help you through the particularly twisted problems that you'll often see on the PSAT. There are several varieties of Plugging In, each suited to a different kind of question.

Plugging In Your Own Numbers

The problem with doing algebra is that it's just too easy to make a mistake.

> Whenever you see a question with variables in the answer choices, use Plugging In.

Start by picking a number for the variable in the question (or for more than one variable, if necessary), solve the problem using your number, and then see which answer choice gives you the correct answer.

Take a look at the following question.

When to Plug In
- phrases like "in terms of" or "equivalent form" in the question
- variables in the question and/or answer choices

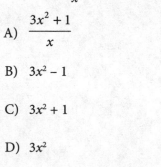

13

If $2x + x + \dfrac{1}{x} = y$, what is the value of $xy - 1$, in terms of x ?

A) $\dfrac{3x^2 + 1}{x}$

B) $3x^2 - 1$

C) $3x^2 + 1$

D) $3x^2$

Here's How to Crack It

The question asks for the value of $xy - 1$ in terms of x. Let's try to avoid the algebra by plugging in. First, start by choosing a value for one of the variables. Here, all the action is happening to the x, so choose a value for x. Make $x = 2$. Next, work the question in Bite-Sized Pieces until you've come up with a numerical answer for the question. If $x = 2$, then the equation becomes

$2(2) + 2 + \dfrac{1}{2} = y$. Multiply; then add on the left side: $4 + 2 + \dfrac{1}{2} = y$; $\dfrac{13}{2} = y$. Note the question

doesn't want the value of y, but rather $xy - 1$. Because $x = 2$ and $y = \dfrac{13}{2}$, $xy - 1 = (2)\left(\dfrac{13}{2}\right) - 1 =$

$13 - 1 = 12$. This is the target number; circle it.

Now that you have a target number, work your answer choices using Process of Elimination. Make $x = 2$ in each answer choice and eliminate any choice that doesn't equal your target number of 12:

A) $\dfrac{3(2)^2 + 1}{2} = \dfrac{13}{2}$ 　　　Not 12; eliminate!

B) $3(2)^2 - 1 = 11$ 　　　Not 12; eliminate!

C) $3(2)^2 + 1 = 13$ 　　　Not 12; eliminate!

D) $3(2)^2 = 12$ 　　　Is 12; keep!

Only (D) matches your target number, so it must be the answer!

As you can see, Plugging In can turn messy algebra questions into more straightforward arithmetic questions. This technique is especially powerful when the PSAT asks you to find the equivalent form of an expression.

16

The expression $x^2 + 4x - 4$ is written in the equivalent form $N^2 - 8$. What is the value of N?

A) $x^2 + 4x - 4$

B) $x^2 + 4x + 4$

C) $x - 2$

D) $x + 2$

Plugging In: Quick Reference
- When you see *in terms of* or *equivalent form* and there are variables in the answer choices, you can Plug In.
- Pick your own number for an unknown in the question.
- Do the necessary math to find the answer you're shooting for, which is the target number. Circle the target number.
- Use POE to eliminate every answer that doesn't match the target number.

Here's How to Crack It

The question asks for the value of N given two equivalent expressions. The variable x is all over the place, so assign a value for x. Try $x = 2$. Next, work the problem in Bite-Sized Pieces. The first expression becomes $2^2 + 4(2) - 4 = 4 + 8 - 4 = 8$. The question then states that this is "written in the equivalent form" of $N^2 - 8$. If these expressions are equivalent, then $N^2 - 8$ must also equal 8. So set it equal to 8 and solve for N: $N^2 - 8 = 8$; $N^2 = 16$; $N = \pm 4$. The question is asking for N, so you're looking for any answer that equals either -4 or 4 (because there are two possible values). These are your target numbers; circle them. Make $x = 2$ in each answer choice and eliminate any option that doesn't match one of the target numbers:

A) $2^2 + 4(2) - 4 = 4 + 8 - 4 = 8$ Not -4 or 4; eliminate!

B) $2^2 + 4(2) + 4 = 4 + 8 + 4 = 16$ Not -4 or 4; eliminate!

C) $2 - 2 = 0$ Not -4 or 4; eliminate!

D) $2 + 2 = 4$ Yes!

The answer is (D).

———————◯———————

Plugging In is such a great technique because it turns hard algebra questions into medium and sometimes even easy arithmetic questions. Remember this when you're thinking of your POOD and looking for questions to do among the hard ones; if you see variables in the answers, there's a good chance it's one to try.

Don't worry too much about what numbers you choose to plug in; just plug in easy numbers (small numbers like 2, 5, or 10 or numbers that make the arithmetic easy, like 100 if you're looking for a percent). Also, be sure your numbers fit the conditions of the questions (for example, if they say $x \leq 11$, don't plug in 12).

What If There's No Variable?

Sometimes you'll see a question that doesn't contain an x, y, or z, but which contains a hidden variable. If your answers are percents or fractional parts of some unknown quantity (total number of marbles in a jar, total miles to travel in a trip), try Plugging In.

Take a look at this question.

27

A neighborhood is comprised of square blocks, as shown above. Genna launches a drone from point A. The drone flies directly to point B, as shown by the dotted line. Genna then walks from point A to point B by following the streets by the shortest route possible. By approximately what percent was the distance Genna walked greater than the distance the drone flew?

A)   25%

B)   34%

C)   75%

D)   134%

Here's How to Crack It

The question asks for a comparison of the distance Genna walked to the distance the drone flew. No actual values are given, but the question deals with a relationship between numbers, so pick a number for the unknown value. Plug in for the size of the blocks. Assume each block is 1 unit by 1 unit. Genna must travel 4 blocks east and 2 blocks north, so she must travel 6 units total. (Note that it doesn't matter whether she goes north then east, east then north, or a zigzag pattern from A to B; the shortest path will always be 6 units.)

To find the distance the drone travels, make a right triangle with legs 4 units (the distance east) and 2 units (the distance north). Find the hypotenuse (which is the direct distance from A to B) using the Pythagorean Theorem. The Pythagorean Theorem is $a^2 + b^2 = c^2$, where c is the hypotenuse. Therefore, $4^2 + 2^2 = c^2$; $16 + 4 = c^2$; $20 = c^2$; $\sqrt{20} = c$.

> We'll cover the Pythagorean Theorem in more detail in Chapter 14.

To find the percent difference, use the formula $\dfrac{difference}{original} \times 100$. Because you want percent greater, the original is the smaller value (in this case $\sqrt{20}$): $\dfrac{6 - \sqrt{20}}{\sqrt{20}} \times 100 \approx 34.16$, which is closest to (B).

Try another one.

16

Ratio of Students in a Club

	Male	Female	Total
Junior	0.18	0.27	0.45
Senior	0.24	0.31	0.55
Total	0.42	0.58	1.00

The two-way table above shows the ratio of males and females and juniors and seniors in a particular club. If a male is chosen at random, what is the probability that he will be a junior?

A) $\dfrac{9}{50}$

B) $\dfrac{3}{7}$

C) $\dfrac{27}{58}$

D) $\dfrac{3}{4}$

We'll cover probability in more detail later in this chapter.

Here's How to Crack It

The question asks for the probability that a male chosen at random will be a junior. The total ratio of students is 1.00, so plug in for the total number of students. Make the number of students 100. To find the number of students in each category, you only need to multiply each number in the table by 100. This gives you the following:

	Male	Female	Total
Junior	18	27	45
Senior	24	31	55
Total	42	58	100

You're asked to find the probability of choosing a junior if you choose from the males. Probability is $\dfrac{number\ of\ outcomes\ you\ want}{number\ of\ possible\ outcomes}$. There are 18 male juniors and 42 total males, making the probability of choosing a junior from the males $\dfrac{18}{42}$, which reduces to $\dfrac{3}{7}$. This matches (B).

Drill 1

Answers can be found in Part IV.

5

David acquired a data plan for his smart phone. Every month he pays a flat rate of $25 and an additional $0.05 for every megabyte he goes over his monthly limit. Which of the following represents David's monthly data bill when he goes over his limit by m megabytes?

A) $25 + 1.05m$

B) $25 + 0.05m$

C) $0.05(25 + m)$

D) $1.05(25 + m)$

4

If $a = \dfrac{b}{c^2}$ and $c \neq 0$, what is the value of $\dfrac{1}{b^2}$?

A) ac^2

B) a^2c^4

C) $\dfrac{1}{ac^2}$

D) $\dfrac{1}{a^2c^4}$

11

Luciano measured the amount of water that evaporated over a period of time from a container holding w ounces of water, where w is greater than 12. By the end of the first day, the cup had lost 2 ounces of water. By the end of the 7th day, the cup had lost an additional 8 ounces of water. By the end of the 11th day, the cup had lost half of the water that remained after the 7th day. Which of the following represents the remaining amount of water, in ounces, in Luciano's container at the end of the 11th day?

A) $\dfrac{w-2}{8}$

B) $\dfrac{w-2}{2} - 10$

C) $\dfrac{1}{2}w - 10$

D) $\dfrac{w-10}{2}$

7

If $p \neq 0$, what is the value of $\dfrac{\frac{1}{8}}{2p}$?

A) $\dfrac{1}{16p}$

B) $\dfrac{p}{4}$

C) $\dfrac{4}{p}$

D) $4p$

9

A certain standardized test has 50 questions. A student receives 1 point for each correct answer and loses $\dfrac{1}{4}$ of a point for each incorrect answer. Which of the following equations best models the net score, S, in points, for a student who completes all 50 questions and answers c of the questions correctly?

A) $S = 50 - 0.25c$

B) $S = 50 - 0.75c$

C) $S = c - 0.25(50 - c)$

D) $S = c - 0.75(50 - c)$

18

Jodi has x dollars in her bank account. She withdraws $\dfrac{1}{6}$ of the money in her account to pay her rent and another $\dfrac{1}{6}$ of the money in her account to make her car payment. Jodi then deposits her paycheck of y dollars into her account. A week later, she withdraws $\dfrac{1}{2}$ of the money in her account to spend on a new set of knives. In terms of x, how many dollars are left in Jodi's account?

A) $\dfrac{(4x - 3y)}{6}$

B) $\dfrac{(3x - 5y)}{6}$

C) $\dfrac{(3x - y)}{6}$

D) $\dfrac{(2x + 3y)}{6}$

12

$$2\left|4y - 5\right| < 24$$

What is the sum of all the integer solutions to the inequality above?

A)   7

B)   9

C)   10

D)   14

29

15% of the members of the incoming freshmen class at a certain university are left-handed, and the remaining members are right-handed. 65% of the same incoming freshmen class are female, and the rest are male. If $\frac{2}{3}$ of the left-handed students are male, then what percent of the female class is right-handed, to the nearest tenth of a percent? (Disregard the percent sign when gridding your answers. For example, if the answer is 43.2%, grid in 43.2.)

PLUGGING IN THE ANSWERS (PITA)

You can also plug in when the answer provided to a question is an actual value, such as 2, 4, 10, or 20. Why would you want to do a lot of complicated algebra to solve a question, when the answer is right there on the page? All you have to do is figure out *which* choice it is.

How can you tell which is the correct answer? Try every choice *until you find the one that works*. Even if this means you have to try all four choices, PITA is still a fast and reliable means of getting the right answer.

If you work strategically, however, you almost never need to try all four answers. If the question asks for either the greatest or the least answer, start there. Otherwise, start with one of the middle answer choices. If that answer works, you're done. If the answer you started with was too big, try a smaller answer. If the answer you started with was too small, try a bigger answer. You can almost always find the answer in two or three tries this way. Let's try PITA on the following question.

4

If the average (arithmetic mean) of 8 and x is equal to the average of 5, 9, and x, what is the value of x ?

A) 1

B) 2

C) 4

D) 8

PITA = Plugging In the Answers
Don't try to solve problems like this by writing equations and solving for x or y. Plugging In the Answers lets you use arithmetic instead of algebra, so you're less likely to make errors.

Here's How to Crack It

The question asks for the value of x based on an average. Rather than doing complicated algebra, try out the answers. Let's start with (C) and plug in 4 for x. The question now reads:

> If the average (arithmetic mean) of 8 and 4 is equal to the average of 5, 9, and 4 . . .

Does this work? The average of 8 and 4 is 6, and the average of 5, 9, and 4 is also 6. Therefore, (C) is the answer.

Neat, huh? Of course, the first answer you choose won't always be the correct one. Let's try one more.

10

If $(x - 2)^2 = 2x - 1$, which of the following is a possible value of x ?

A) 1

B) 2

C) 3

D) 6

Here's How to Crack It

The question asks for the value of x, and there are numbers in the answer choices. Try plugging in the answers any time the question asks for a specific value like this. If we try plugging in (C), 3, for x, the equation becomes $1 = 5$, which is false. So (C) can't be right. If you're not sure which way to go next, just pick a direction. It won't take very long to figure out the correct answer. If we try plugging in (B), 2, for x, the equation becomes $0 = 3$, which is false. If we try plugging in (A), 1, for x, the equation becomes $1 = 1$, which is true. There's no need to try other answers because there are no variables in the answers; only one answer choice can work. So the answer is (A).

Drill 2

Answers can be found in Part IV.

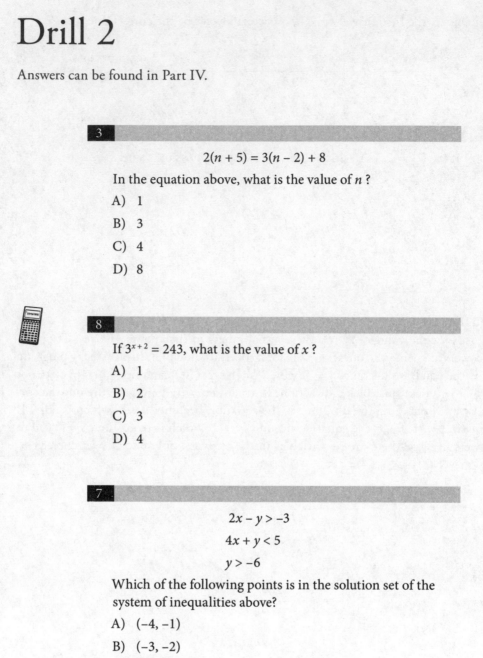

3

$$2(n + 5) = 3(n - 2) + 8$$

In the equation above, what is the value of n ?

A) 1

B) 3

C) 4

D) 8

8

If $3^{x+2} = 243$, what is the value of x ?

A) 1

B) 2

C) 3

D) 4

7

$$2x - y > -3$$

$$4x + y < 5$$

$$y > -6$$

Which of the following points is in the solution set of the system of inequalities above?

A) $(-4, -1)$

B) $(-3, -2)$

C) $(-1, -1)$

D) $(3, -5)$

10

If $\dfrac{24x}{4} + \dfrac{1}{x} = 5$, what is the value of x ?

A) $-\dfrac{1}{6}$

B) $\dfrac{1}{6}$

C) $\dfrac{1}{4}$

D) $\dfrac{1}{2}$

20

$$-\dfrac{5}{7} - \dfrac{11}{7}u = -v$$
$$2v = 7 + 5u$$

Based on the system of equations above, what is the value of v ?

A) -4

B) -3

C) -1

D) 0

25

An alloy needs to contain between 10 and 15% of titanium. Which of the following inequalities represents the amount in kilograms, x, of a 20% titanium alloy that should be mixed with a 5% titanium alloy to produce 10 kilograms of an alloy with the acceptable percentage of titanium?

A) $1.33 \le x \le 1.67$

B) $2.25 \le x \le 3.25$

C) $3.33 \le x \le 6.67$

D) $7.25 \le x \le 9.75$

DATA ANALYSIS

In the calculator-allowed Math section (Section 4), there will be questions that will ask you to work with concepts such as averages, percentages, and unit conversions. Luckily, The Princeton Review has you covered! The rest of this chapter will give you techniques and strategies to help you tackle these questions.

Averages and $T = AN$

You probably remember the average formula from math class, which says **Average** (arithmetic mean) $= \dfrac{\text{total}}{\text{\# of things}}$. However, the PSAT rarely will ask you to take a simple average. Of the three parts of an average problem—the average, the total, and the number of things—you're usually given the average and the number of things, and you'll need to use the total to answer the question. If you multiply both sides of the average formula by the number of things, you get (average) × (# of things) = total. You can remember this as $T = AN$. Plug the information into the formula and solve.

Let's try this example.

> 9
>
> The average (arithmetic mean) of 3 numbers is 22 and the smallest of these numbers is 2. If the remaining two numbers are equal, what are their values?
>
> A) 22
>
> B) 32
>
> C) 40
>
> D) 64

Total
When calculating averages, always find the total. It's the one piece of information that PSAT loves to withhold.

Here's How to Crack It

The question gives the value of one number and the average of all three numbers and asks for the value of the two remaining numbers. Use $T = AN$. The average is 22, and there are 3 numbers. Therefore, $T = (22)(3)$, so $T = 66$. If the smallest number is 2, the remaining two numbers equal $66 - 2 = 64$. Finally, the remaining two numbers are equal, so divide: $64 \div 2 = 32$. The answer is (B).

Try one more.

8

Caroline scored 85, 88, and 89 on three of her four history tests. If her average (arithmetic mean) score for all four tests was 90, what did she score on her fourth test?

A) 90

B) 93

C) 96

D) 98

Here's How to Crack It

The question asks for the score Caroline received on her fourth test. Let's start with what we know: we know that the average of all four of her tests was 90. Putting these into the formula $T = AN$ gives us $T = (90)(4)$, which means the total is 360. Since three of these tests have a sum of 85 + 88 + 89, or 262, we know that the score on the fourth test must be equal to 360 − 262, or 98. This makes the answer (D).

Median and Mode

Another two terms that are often tested along with average are median and mode.

The **median** of a group of numbers is the number in the middle, just as the "median" is the large divider in the middle of a road. To find the median, here's what you do:

- First, put the elements in the group in numerical order from lowest to highest.
- If the number of elements in your group is *odd*, find the number in the middle. That's the median.
- If you have an *even* number of elements in the group, find the two numbers in the middle and calculate their average (arithmetic mean).

Try this on the following question.

> **Finding a Median**
> To find the median of a set containing an even number of items, take the average of the two middle numbers after putting the numbers in order.

○

3

If the 5 students in Ms. Jaffray's math class scored 91, 83, 84, 90, and 85 on their final exams, what is the median score for her class on the final exam?

A) 84

B) 85

C) 86

D) 88

Here's How to Crack It

First, let's place these numbers in order from lowest to highest: 83, 84, 85, 90, 91. There are an odd number of elements in the group, and the number in the middle is 85, so the median of this group is 85 and the answer is (B).

○

The **mode** of a group of numbers is the number that appears the most. (Remember: *mode* sounds like *most*.) To find the mode of a group of numbers, simply see which element appears the greatest number of times.

○

28

Score on Final Paper	Frequency
85	4
86	2
87	6
88	3
89	4
90	7
91	11
92	6
93	5
94	2

An English professor graded the final papers of the
50 students in her Honors courses and recorded the
information in the frequency table above. For this data, how
much greater is the mode than the median?

Here's How to Crack It

The question asks for the difference between the mode and the median of a list of data. On a
frequency table, the mode is easy to see—it is the data with the greatest number in the Frequency column. On this table, the greatest number in that column is 11, and it is associated
with the score of 91. Therefore, the mode is 91. The median is a little more difficult to find. You
don't want to take the time to list out all 50 scores, but the median will be the average of the
25th and 26th scores. If you can find those, you are all set. Start at the top of the chart and add
up the numbers in the Frequency column till you get to 25. The first three scores, 85–87, account for 4 + 2 + 6 = 12 of the students. The scores of 88 and 89 account for another 3 + 4 = 7
students, so now we are up to the 19th student on the list. The next 7 students received a score
of 90, so the 25th and 26th scores are both 90. The average of 90 and 90 is 90, so the median is
90. The difference between the mode and the median is 91 – 90 = 1. This is the correct answer.

Range

Another measure of the spread of data is range. The **range** of a list of numbers is the difference
between the greatest number on the list and the least number on the list. For the list 4, 5, 5, 6,
7, 8, 9, 10, 20, the greatest number is 20 and the least is 4, so the range is 20 – 4 = 16.

Let's look at a question.

25

| 184 | 176 | 181 | 157 | 168 |
| 154 | 148 | 165 | 190 | 162 |

A group of patients is recruited for a clinical trial. Their heights, recorded in centimeters, are listed in the table above. Two more patients are recruited to the study. After these patients join, the range of the heights is 42 cm. Which of the following could NOT be the heights of the two new patients?

A) 154 cm and 186 cm

B) 146 cm and 179 cm

C) 150 cm and 188 cm

D) 148 cm and 185 cm

Here's How to Crack It

The question asks for the values that cannot be the heights of two new patients given information about the range of the data. To determine the current range, take the difference of the greatest and least values: 190 − 148 = 42 cm. If the range is to remain 42 cm, then the new patients' heights cannot be greater than 190 cm or less than 148 cm tall. Choice (B) violates this restriction. Because the question wants what could NOT be the heights of the new patients, the answer is (B).

PROBABILITY

Probability refers to the chance that an event will happen, and it is given as a percent or a fractional value between 0 and 1, inclusive. A probability of 0 means that the event will never happen; a probability of 1 means that it is certain to happen.

$$\text{Probability} = \frac{\text{number of outcomes you want}}{\text{number of possible outcomes}}$$

For instance, if you have a die with faces numbered 1 to 6, what is the chance of rolling a 2? There is one face with the number 2 on it, out of 6 total faces. Therefore, the probability of rolling a 2 is $\frac{1}{6}$.

What is the chance of rolling an even number on one roll of this die? There are 3 faces of the die with an even number (the sides numbered 2, 4, and 6) out of a total of 6 faces. Therefore, the probability of rolling an even number is $\frac{3}{6}$, or $\frac{1}{2}$.

Let's look at how this concept will be tested on the PSAT.

18

A survey was conducted among a randomly chosen sample of full-time salaried workers about satisfaction in their current jobs. The table below shows a summary of the survey results.

Reported Job Satisfaction by Education Level (in thousands)

Highest Level of Education	Satisfied	Not Satisfied	No Response	Total
High School Diploma	17,880	12,053	2,575	32,508
Bachelor's Degree	24,236	8,496	3,442	36,174
Master's Degree	17,605	5,324	1,861	24,790
Doctoral Degree	12,210	2,081	972	15,263
Total	71,931	27,954	8,850	108,735

All persons who have earned a Master's or Doctoral degree must have previously earned a Bachelor's degree. What is the probability that a full-time salaried worker does NOT have a Bachelor's degree?

A) 29.9%

B) 33.3%

C) 36.8%

D) 66.7%

Here's How to Crack It

The question asks for the probability that a full-time worker does not have a Bachelor's degree.

If everyone with a Master's or Doctoral degree has a Bachelor's degree, then the only people who do NOT have a Bachelor's degree are those whose highest level of education is a High School Diploma. Find the probability of choosing someone with a High School Diploma out of the total: $\frac{32,508}{108,735} = 0.299 = 29.9\%$, which is (A).

———————————○———————————

Rates

Rate is a concept related to averages. Cars travel at an average speed. Work gets done at an average rate. Because the ideas are similar, you can use Distance = Speed × Time ($D = ST$) or Work = Rate × Time ($W = RT$) to tackle these problems.

Of course, you might use the simple definitions of speed or rate to answer some questions.

Problem: If a fisherman can tie 9 flies for fly fishing in an hour and a half, how long does it take him to tie one fly, in minutes?

Solution: First, convert the hour and a half to 90 minutes so your units are consistent. Since Work = Rate × Time, the definition of rate is **Rate** = $\frac{\text{Work}}{\text{Time}}$. Divide 9 by 90 to get the rate, $\frac{9}{90} = \frac{1}{10}$, or one fly every 10 minutes.

Let's look at an example of a PSAT rate question.

———————————○———————————

28

Sally, Abdul, and Juanita have volunteered to stuff a certain number of envelopes for a local charity. Working by herself, Sally could stuff all the envelopes in exactly 3 hours. Working by himself, Abdul could stuff all the envelopes in exactly 4 hours. Working by herself, Juanita could stuff all the envelopes in exactly 6 hours. If Sally, Abdul, and Juanita work together at these rates to stuff all the envelopes, what fraction of the envelopes will be stuffed by Juanita?

Here's How to Crack It

The question asks for the fraction of the envelopes Juanita will stuff when she works together with two others, all at different rates. Since the question doesn't tell you how many envelopes to stuff, this is a great question to plug in on. Because Sally takes 3 hours, Abdul takes 4 hours, and Juanita takes 6 hours, you want to choose a multiple of all those numbers. Make the total number of envelopes to stuff 120. Next, use the definition of rate to find each person's rate. Sally stuffs 120 envelopes in 3 hours, so her rate is $\frac{120 \text{ envelopes}}{3 \text{ hours}} = 40$ envelopes per hour. Similarly, Abdul's rate is $\frac{120 \text{ envelopes}}{4 \text{ hours}} = 30$ envelopes per hour, and Juanita's rate is $\frac{120 \text{ envelopes}}{6 \text{ hours}} = 20$ envelopes per hour.

If all three people work together, their total rate will be 40 + 30 + 20 = 90 envelopes/hour. During that hour Juanita will stuff 20 envelopes, meaning she does $\frac{20}{90}$, or $\frac{2}{9}$, of the job.

PERCENTS

Percent just means "divided by 100." So 20 percent = $\frac{20}{100} = \frac{1}{5}$, or .2.

Likewise, 400 percent = $\frac{400}{100} = \frac{4}{1} = 4$.

Any percent question can be translated into algebra—just use the following rules:

Percent	÷ 100
Of	×
What	x (or any variable)
Is, Are, Equals	=

Take a look at some examples of phrases you might have to translate on the PSAT:

8 percent of 10		$0.08 \times 10 = 0.8$
10 percent of 80		$0.1 \times 80 = 8$
5 is what percent of 80?	becomes	$5 = \dfrac{x}{100} \times 80$
5 is 80 percent of what number?		$5 = \dfrac{80}{100} x$
What percent of 5 is 80?		$\dfrac{x}{100} \times 5 = 80$

Percent Increase/Decrease

Percent Increase or *Percent Decrease* = $\dfrac{difference}{original} \times 100$

For example, if an $80 item is reduced to $60 during a sale, the percent decrease is the change in price ($80 − $60 = $20) divided by the original amount ($80), which gives us .25. Multiply by 100 to get 25 percent.

Try a question.

26

Estimated Numbers of Cell Phone Users by Type
(in millions)

	Prepaid users	Contracted users	Totals
2008	45	225	270
2012	75	250	325
Total	120	475	595

By how much greater was the percent increase in prepaid users from 2008 to 2012 than the percent increase in contracted users over the same period, to the nearest percent?

A)   6%

B)   10%

C)   30%

D)   56%

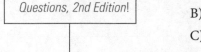

Looking for More Practice?
Check out our *550+ PSAT Practice Questions, 2nd Edition!*

Here's How to Crack It

The question asks for a comparison of the percent increase in prepaid users over time to the percent increase in contracted users over time. First, find the percent increase in each group.

Remember that percent increase is $\dfrac{difference}{original} \times 100$. For prepaid users, the equation would

be $\dfrac{75-45}{45} \times 100 = 66\dfrac{2}{3}\%$. Contracted users: $\dfrac{250-225}{225} \times 100 = 11\dfrac{1}{9}\%$. Finally, subtract:

$66\dfrac{2}{3} - 11\dfrac{1}{9} = 55\dfrac{5}{9}\%$, which is closest to (D).

GROWTH AND DECAY

Another aspect of percent questions may relate to things that increase or decrease by a certain percent over time. This is known as "growth and decay." Real-world examples include population growth, radioactive decay, and credit payments, to name a few. While Plugging In can help on these, it is also useful to know the growth and decay formula.

> When the growth or decay rate is a percent of the total population:
>
> $$\textit{final amount} = \textit{original amount } (1 \pm \textit{rate})^{\textit{number of changes}}$$

Let's see how this formula can make quick work of an otherwise tedious question.

14

The population of Bethesda, Maryland is currently 61,000 and is growing at a rate of 2.5% every three months. If Bethesda's population, P, is a function of time in years, t, then which of the following functions represents the town's population growth?

A) $P(t) = 61,000(1.025)^t$

B) $P(t) = 61,000(1.1)^t$

C) $P(t) = 61,000(1.025)^{4t}$

D) $P(t) = 61,000(1.1)^{3t}$

Here's How to Crack It

The question asks for a function to represent population growth over time. Carefully translate the information in the question in Bite-Sized Pieces. Because the rate of growth is 2.5%, you need to add 0.025 (2.5% in decimal form) to 1 within the parenthesis. This would be 1 + 0.025 = 1.025. Eliminate (B) and (D) because they do not have this piece. The only difference between (A) and (C) is the exponent, which represents the number of changes. Here, t is in years, but the population increases every 3 months, which is 4 times a year. This means you want 4 changes when $t = 1$; this gives you (C) as your answer.

RATIOS AND PROPORTIONS

Some questions in the calculator-allowed Math section (Section 4) will ask about ratios and proportions. With the strategies that you'll learn on the next few pages, you'll be well prepared to tackle these concepts on the PSAT.

Ratios

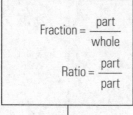

$$\text{Fraction} = \frac{\text{part}}{\text{whole}}$$

$$\text{Ratio} = \frac{\text{part}}{\text{part}}$$

Ratios are about relationships between numbers. Whereas a fraction is a relationship between a part and a whole, a ratio is about the relationship between parts. So, for example, if there were 3 boys and 7 girls in a room, the fraction of boys in the room would be $\frac{3}{10}$. But the ratio of boys to girls would be 3:7 or $\frac{3}{7}$. Notice that if you add up the parts, you get the whole: 7 + 3 = 10. That's important for PSAT ratio questions, and you'll see why in a moment.

Gridding In

A ratio is usually expressed as 2:3 or 2 to 3, but if you need to grid a ratio, grid it as $\frac{2}{3}$.

Ratio questions usually aren't difficult to identify. The question will tell you that there is a "ratio" of one thing to another, such as a 2:3 ratio of boys to girls in a club. Often, the PSAT will ask you to compare different ratios or to find the greatest or least ratio. To do so, divide the first part of the ratio by the second and compare the resulting values.

Try this one.

5

The ice cream flavor preferences of a randomly selected group of young Americans aged 3–18 are represented in the table below. Survey participants were asked to choose their favorite flavor among the following five: Vanilla, Chocolate, Mint Chocolate Chip, Cookies and Cream, and Coffee.

Reported favorite ice cream flavor by age group

Age	Vanilla	Chocolate	Mint Chocolate Chip	Cookies and Cream	Coffee
3–6	8,534	7,835	6,135	4,526	254
7–10	9,250	10,936	4,019	7,530	497
11–15	5,093	7,591	9,495	1,076	760
16–18	11,024	7,345	2,026	4,620	1,062

According to the data in the table above, the ratio of the most- to least-favorite flavors among the 7–10 age group is approximately how many times greater than the ratio of the most- to least-favorite flavors among the 11–15 age group?

A) 1.8

B) 3.4

C) 4.2

D) 6.7

Here's How to Crack It

The question asks for a comparison of two ratios based on the data in the table. First, you need to find the ratio of the most- to least-favorite flavor for each of the two age groups in question. For the 7–10 age group, the most favorite flavor is chocolate, with 10,936 votes, and the least favorite is coffee, with 497 votes. The ratio is thus $\frac{10,936}{497} = 22.0$. For the 11–15 age group, the most favorite flavor is mint chocolate chip, with 9,495 votes, and the least favorite flavor is coffee, with 760 votes. The ratio is thus $\frac{9,495}{760} = 12.5$. To find out how many times greater the first ratio is, divide these numbers: $\frac{22.0}{12.5} = 1.8$, which is (A).

Direct Variation

Direct variations or proportions occur when two variables increase together or decrease together. These questions generally ask you to make a conversion (such as from ounces to pounds) or to compare two sets of information and find a missing piece. For example, a proportion question may ask you to figure out the amount of time it will take to travel 300 miles at a rate of 50 miles per hour.

> To solve proportion problems, just set up two equal fractions. One will have all the information you know, and the other will have a missing piece that you're trying to figure out.

$$\frac{50 \text{ miles}}{1 \text{ hour}} = \frac{300 \text{ miles}}{x \text{ hours}}$$

Be sure to label the parts of your proportion so you'll know you have the right information in the right place; the same units should be in the numerator on both sides of the equals sign and the same units should be in the denominator on both sides of the equals sign. Notice how using a setup like this helps us keep track of the information we have and to find the information we're looking for, so we can use Bite-Sized Pieces to work through the question.

Now we can cross-multiply and then solve for x: $50x = 300$, so $x = 6$ hours.

> $$\frac{x_1}{y_1} = \frac{x_2}{y_2}$$

Let's try the following question.

2

John receives $2.50 for every 4 pounds of berries he picks. How much money will he receive if he picks 90 pounds of berries?

A) $36.00

B) $42.25

C) $48.50

D) $56.25

Here's How to Crack It

The question gives a relationship between two variables and asks for a value based on that relationship. To solve this, set up a proportion.

$$\frac{\$2.50}{4\,\text{pounds}} = \frac{x}{90\,\text{pounds}}$$

Now we can cross-multiply: $4x = 2.50 \times 90$, so $4x = 225$, and $x = 56.25$. The answer is (D).

Occasionally, you may see a question that tells you there are two equal ratios. For example, if a question says that the ratio of 24 to 0.6 is equal to the ratio of 12 to y, you can solve for y by setting up a proportion. A proportion, after all, is really just two ratios set equal to each other.

$$\frac{24}{0.6} = \frac{12}{y}$$

Then you can cross-multiply and solve to get 0.3 for your answer.

Inverse Variation

Inverse variation is simply the opposite of direct variation, or proportion. In a proportion, when one variable increases, the other variable also increases. With inverse variation, when one variable increases, the other variable decreases, or vice versa. These types of questions are generally clearly labeled and all you have to do is apply the inverse variation formula:

$$x_1 y_1 = x_2 y_2$$

Once you memorize the formula, applying it will become second nature to you.

Now try this one.

_____◯_____

18

On a particular test, the percentage of people answering a question with the same response is inversely proportional to the number of the question. If 80% of test takers answered the 8th question correctly, then approximately what percentage of test takers gave the correct response to the 30th question?

A)   3%

B)   13%

C)   18%

D)   21%

Here's How to Crack It

The question asks for the percentage of test-takers that correctly answered the 30th question. The question tells us that the numbers are inversely proportional, so we need to figure out what to put into the formula. The first piece of information is that 80 percent of the people answered the 8th question correctly; we need to know the percent of people who answered the 30th question correctly. Let's make x the percent and y the question number. Your equation should look like this:

$$(80)(8) = (x_2)(30)$$

When you solve the equation, you should end up with $\frac{640}{30}$ or $21\frac{1}{3}$, which is (D) (remember, when the question says "approximately," you'll probably have to round up or down).

_____◯_____

Drill 3

Remember, answers to these drill questions can be found in Part IV!

a.   If a student scores 70, 90, 95, and 105, what is the average (arithmetic mean) for these tests? _____

b.   If a student has an average (arithmetic mean) score of 80 on 4 tests, what is the total of the scores received on those tests? _____

c.   If a student has an average of 60 on tests, with a total of 360, how many tests has the student taken? _____

d.   If the average of 2, 8, and x is 6, what is the value of x? _____

2, 3, 3, 4, 6, 8, 10, 12

e.   What is the median of the group of numbers above? _____

f.   What is the mode of the group of numbers above? _____

g.   What is the range of the group of numbers above? _____

h.   What percent of 5 is 6? _____

i.   60 percent of 90 is the same as 50 percent of what number? _____

j.   Jenny's salary increased from $30,000 to $33,000. By what percent did her salary increase? _____

k.   In 1980, factory X produced 18,600 pieces. In 1981, factory X produced only 16,000 pieces. By approximately what percent did production decrease from 1980 to 1981? _____

The amount of money in a savings account after m months is modeled by the function $f(m) = 1,000(1.01)^m$.

l.   What was the original amount in the bank account? _____

m.   By what percent does the amount in the account increase each month? _____

n.   In a certain bag of marbles, the ratio of red marbles to green marbles is 7:5. If the bag contains 96 marbles, how many green marbles are in the bag? _____

o.   One hogshead is equal to 64 gallons. How many hogsheads are equal to 96 gallons? _____

p.   The pressure and volume of a gas are inversely related. If the gas is at 10 kPa at 2 liters, then what is the pressure when the gas is at 4 liters? _____

2

If 10 pecks are equivalent to 2.5 bushels, then 4 bushels are equivalent to how many pecks?

A)   4

B)   10

C)   12.5

D)   16

28

Estimated Numbers of Cell Phone Users by Type
(in millions)

	Prepaid users	Contracted users	Total
2008	45	225	270
2012	75	250	325
Total	120	475	595

If a cell phone user is selected at random in 2008, what is the probability that user is a contracted user?

12

A forest fire is burning an area of forest that is 10 square miles. An air squad is able to reduce the size of the fire by 7% every 12 hours. If $F(t)$ is the area being burned by the fire, which expression for $F(t)$ represents the area of forest still on fire after t hours?

A) $10 - (0.93)^{12t}$

B) $10 \times (1 - 0.07)^{\frac{t}{12}}$

C) $10 - 93^{12t}$

D) 0.93^{10-12t}

15

A student took five tests. He scored an average (arithmetic mean) of 80 on the first three tests and an average of 90 on the other two. Which of the following must be true?

   I. The student scored more than 85 on at least one test.

  II. The average (arithmetic mean) score for all five tests is less than 85.

 III. The student scored less than 80 on at least two tests.

A) I only

B) II only

C) I and II

D) II and III

19

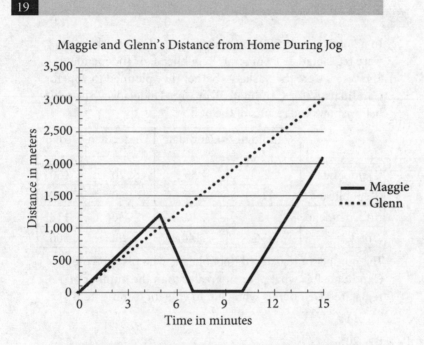

Maggie and Glenn's Distance from Home During Jog

Maggie and Glenn both leave from the same house to go for a jog along a trail. Shortly after leaving, Maggie realizes she forgot her iPhone and returns home to find it before heading back out onto the same trail. The graph above shows how far each of them is from home for the first fifteen minutes of their jogs. Excluding the time she spends at home, which of the following is closest to Maggie's average speed, in meters per second, during the portion of her jog shown?

A)   2.3

B)   5

C)   6.3

D) 140

29

Marcia can type 18 pages per hour, and David can type 14 pages per hour. If they work together, how many minutes will it take them to type 24 pages?

·	⊘	⊘	/
·	·	·	·
	⓪	⓪	⓪
①	①	①	①
②	②	②	②
③	③	③	③
④	④	④	④
⑤	⑤	⑤	⑤
⑥	⑥	⑥	⑥
⑦	⑦	⑦	⑦
⑧	⑧	⑧	⑧
⑨	⑨	⑨	⑨

22

In a political poll, 500 voters were first asked whether they were registered as Democrat, Republican, or Independent. The voters were then asked whether they planned to vote for Candidate A, for Candidate B, or were Undecided. The table below shows the results of the poll.

	Candidate A	Candidate B	Undecided	Total
Democrat	24	56	70	150
Republican	117	70	50	237
Independent	15	18	80	113
Total	156	144	200	500

The number of registered Republicans who plan to vote for Candidate B is what percent greater than the number of registered Democrats who plan to vote for Candidate B ?

A) 14%

B) 20%

C) 25%

D) 28%

25

The college that Everett attends in Chicago is exactly 200 miles from his parents' home. When his parents come to visit him at school, they drive at an average speed of 45 miles per hour for maximum safety. When Everett drives home for winter break, his average speed is x% greater than the average speed at which his parents drive when they make the trip. Which of the following represents the time Everett saves on the 200-mile trip compared with his parents' average time, in hours?

A) $\dfrac{-2x}{45\left(1+\dfrac{x}{100}\right)}$

B) $\dfrac{2x}{45\left(1-\dfrac{x}{100}\right)}$

C) $\dfrac{2x}{45\left(1+\dfrac{x}{100}\right)}$

D) $\dfrac{45\left(\dfrac{x}{100}\right)}{200\left(1+\dfrac{x}{100}\right)}$

27

A survey company gathered data regarding people's transportation habits in four major U.S. cities. The survey asked participants in each of these cities to indicate whether they regularly used a personal vehicle, public transportation, or neither to commute. Participants were not limited to one response and could check both personal vehicle and public transportation. The results are shown below.

	Personal Vehicle	Public Transportation	Neither	Total Responses
Washington, D.C.	5,687	3,134	1,232	8,505
New York	2,476	5,738	1,459	7,789
Boston	5,281	3,504	1,025	7,556
San Francisco	4,122	4,629	1,192	7,934

Which one of the following statements is supported by the data shown above?

A) Approximately 20% more people checked both personal vehicle and public transportation in Boston than in New York.

B) Washington, D.C. has the highest proportion of people that regularly use both public transportation and a personal vehicle.

C) The number of people that reported regularly using public transportation in New York is approximately 230% more than the number that reported regularly using a personal vehicle.

D) The ratio of personal vehicle use to public transportation use was lowest in San Francisco.

Summary

o The test is full of opportunities to use arithmetic instead of algebra—just look for your chances to use Plugging In and Plugging In the Answers (PITA).

o If a question has *in terms of* or variables in the answer choices, it's a Plugging In question. Plug in your own number, do the math, find the target number, and use POE to get down to one correct answer.

o If a question doesn't have variables but asks for a fraction or a percent of an unknown number, you can also plug in. Just substitute your own number for the unknown and take the rest of the question step by step.

o If a question has an unknown and asks for a specific amount, making you feel like you have to write an equation, try PITA instead.

o When a question asks about an average or arithmetic mean, use $T = AN$, plug in the values given in the question, and solve for what you need.

o The median is the middle value in a list of consecutive numbers. If there is an even number of elements, the median is the average of the two middle values.

o The mode is the most commonly occurring value in a list of numbers.

o The range is the difference between the greatest and least values in a list of numbers.

o Probability is a fractional value between 0 and 1 (inclusive), and it is equal to the number of outcomes the question is asking for divided by the total number of possible outcomes. It can also be expressed as a percent.

o Rates are closely related to averages. Use $D = RT$ or $W = RT$ just like you use $T = AN$. Remember that the PSAT likes to make you find the totals (distance or work in rate questions).

o Percent simply means "per 100." Many percent questions can be tackled by translating English to math.

- Percent increase or decrease is $\dfrac{difference}{original} \times 100$.

- Growth and decay are given by the formula $final\ amount = original\ amount(1 \pm rate)^{number\ of\ changes}$.

- Set up ratios like fractions. Take care to put the first term of the ratio in the numerator and the second term in the denominator.

- Sometimes you'll need to treat ratios like fractions or decimals. Use your calculator to turn the numbers into the easiest form to work the question.

- Direct variation or proportion means as one value goes up, the other goes up. The formula is $\dfrac{x_1}{y_1} = \dfrac{x_2}{y_2}$.

- Inverse variation means as one value goes up, the other goes down. The formula is $x_1 y_1 = x_2 y_2$.

Chapter 13
Advanced Math

There will be 14 questions on the PSAT that test what College Board calls "Passport to Advanced Math." This category includes topics such as functions and quadratics. If you've learned these topics already in school, great! You'll have a step up on the PSAT. If not, fear not—this chapter will give you the foundation needed for tackling these questions on the PSAT. You will also find information on how to tackle Meaning in Context questions and questions that determine the Analysis in Science score.

FUNCTIONS

In the Math Basics chapter, we looked at some concepts related to the *xy*-plane. Here, we will look at some more complicated topics involving functions and graphs. The functions on the PSAT mostly look like this:

$$f(x) = x^2 + 6x + 24$$

> **Just Follow the Instructions**
> Functions are like recipes. Each one is just a set of directions for you to follow. The College Board provides the ingredients and you work your magic.

Most questions of this type will give you a specific value to plug in for *x* and then ask you to find the value of the function. Each function is just a set of instructions that tells you what to do to *x*—or the number you plug in for *x*—in order to find the corresponding value for *f(x)* (a fancy name for *y*). Just plug your information into that equation and follow the instructions.

Let's try an easy one.

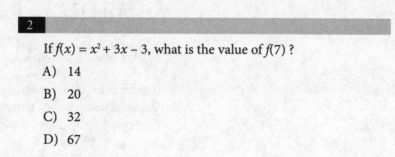

2

If $f(x) = x^2 + 3x - 3$, what is the value of $f(7)$?

A) 14

B) 20

C) 32

D) 67

Here's How to Crack It

The question asks for the value of $f(7)$ given the definition of $f(x)$. Function questions are just trying to see if you can follow the directions, so follow them! The instructions, in this case, are in the equation. So plug 7 into the equation and it should look like this: $f(7) = (7)^2 + 3(7) - 3$. Do the math and $f(7) = 67$. Therefore, the answer is (D).

Sometimes you'll get more complicated questions. As long as you know that when you put in *x*, your function will spit out another number, you'll be fine. Try this next one.

20

Let the function g be defined by $g(x) = 5x + 2$. If $\sqrt{g\left(\dfrac{a}{2}\right)} = 6$,

what is the value of a?

A) $\dfrac{1}{\sqrt{6}}$

B) $\dfrac{1}{\sqrt{2}}$

C) $\dfrac{34}{5}$

D) $\dfrac{68}{5}$

Here's How to Crack It

The question asks for the value of a given the definition of $g(x)$. This may look complicated, but

just follow the directions. You know that $g(x) = 5x + 2$. You also know that $\sqrt{g\left(\dfrac{a}{2}\right)} = 6$. First,

get rid of the square root by squaring both sides. Now you have $g\left(\dfrac{a}{2}\right) = 36$. Usually there's an

x inside the parentheses. Treat this the same. This statement says that g of some number equals

36. We also know that g of some number is the same as $5x + 2$. So $5x + 2 = 36$. Simplify and

you get $\dfrac{34}{5}$. Careful, you're not done. You now know that $\dfrac{a}{2} = \dfrac{34}{5}$, so $a = \dfrac{68}{5}$, or (D).

Another way the PSAT can make functions more complicated is to give you two functions to deal with together. If you approach these questions one piece at a time, they will be easier to handle.

Here's an example.

───────────────○───────────────

| 15 |

If $f(x) = -x + \dfrac{1}{x}$ and $g(x) = x^2 - 7$, what is the value of $f(g(-2))$?

Here's How to Crack It

The question asks for the value of $f(g(-2))$ given the definitions of $f(x)$ and $g(x)$. With compound functions like this one, start from the inside and work your way out. Plug -2 into the g function to get $g(-2) = (-2)^2 - 7 = 4 - 7 = -3$. Plug this value into the f function to get $f(-3) = -(-3) + \dfrac{1}{-3} = 3 - \dfrac{1}{3} = 2\dfrac{2}{3}$. You can't grid in mixed fractions, so convert it to an improper fraction $\dfrac{8}{3}$ or the decimal 2.66 or 2.67. Any of these would be acceptable answers.

───────────────○───────────────

Sometimes the PSAT will use a word problem to describe a function, and then ask you to "build a function" that describes that real-world situation.

Try one of those.

6

A scientist noted that the rate of growth of a tree which he had been observing is directly proportional to time. The scientist first measured the height of the tree to be 20 feet; two years later, the tree was 21 feet tall. If the tree continues to grow at a constant rate, which of the following represents the height of the tree in feet, y, as a function of time, x, in years since the scientist's first measurement?

A) $y(x) = 0.5x + 20$

B) $y(x) = 21x + 20$

C) $y(x) = x + 20$

D) $y(x) = 20x + 21$

Here's How to Crack It

The question asks for the function that represents the height of the tree over time. Instead of trying to write your own equation, use the ones in the answer choices. According to the question, 2 years after the first measurement, the tree was 21 feet tall. Therefore, when $x = 2$, $y(x) = 21$. Plug these points into the answers to see which answer works. Choice (A) becomes $21 = 0.5(2) + 20$. Solve the right side of the equation to get $21 = 1 + 20$, or $21 = 21$. The correct answer is (A).

Roots of a Function

You may also be asked about the roots of a function. These are the solutions for x that you get when you solve the function or the places where the graph of the function crosses the x-axis. Here's how this concept may be tested on the PSAT.

The graph of the function f in the xy-plane contains the points $(-3, 0)$, $(0, -2)$, and $(4, 0)$. Which of the following is a factor of function f?

A) $x - 2$

B) $x + 2$

C) $x + 3$

D) $x + 4$

Here's How to Crack It

The question asks for a factor of a function given points on the graph of the function. The factors are used to find the roots of a function, which are also known as the x-intercepts. At the x-intercept, $y = 0$. Therefore, the point $(0, -2)$ is not a root, so that point cannot be used to determine the factors of the function. You can eliminate (A) and (B) because they include 2. According to the question, one of the x-intercepts is at $(-3, 0)$. This means that one solution to the function can be found by $x + 3 = 0$, and one of the factors of the function is $x + 3$. The other factor would be $(x - 4)$, but that's not a choice. The correct answer is (C).

Drill 1

Answers can be found in Part IV.

3

Which of the following equivalent forms of the equation $x^2 + 8x + 15 = 0$ would be the most useful for finding the x-intercepts of the equation?

A) $x(x) + 8(x) + 15 - 0$

B) $x^2 + 3x + 5x + 15 = 0$

C) $(x + 3)(x + 5) = 0$

D) $x^2 + 8x + 4 + 11 = 0$

4

Monster Truck Inc. leases a new truck for a down payment of \$3,200 plus monthly payments of \$380 per month for 36 months. Which of the following functions, f, represents the total amount paid, in dollars, after m months, where $0 \le m \le 36$?

A) $f(m) = 380 + 3{,}200m$

B) $f(m) = 3{,}200 + 36m$

C) $f(m) = 3{,}200 + 380m$

D) $f(m) - 10{,}480 - 380m$

15

If $f(x) = x^2 - x + 4$, a is non-negative, and $f(a) = 10$, what is the value of a ?

9

The number of bonus points, $B(p)$, that a credit card holder receives is given by the function $B(p) = ap + 7$, where p represents the number of purchases made and a is a constant. If the number of purchases is increased by 4, the number of bonus points increases by 25. What is the value of a ?

A)   4

B)   4.5

C)   6.25

D)   11

21

If $f(x) = x^{-\frac{2}{3}}$, what is the value of $\dfrac{f(8)}{f(3)}$?

A) $\dfrac{4}{\sqrt[3]{9}}$

B) $\dfrac{8}{3}$

C) $\sqrt{\dfrac{512}{27}}$

D) $\dfrac{\sqrt[3]{9}}{4}$

23

The temperature, T, in degrees Celsius on a winter day can be written as a function of x, the time in hours since midnight (12:00 A.M.), as shown below.

$$T(x) = -\frac{1}{10}x^2 + \frac{24}{10}x - \frac{44}{10}$$

If $100 = x^2 - 24x + 144$ is an equivalent form of the equation when $T(x) = 0$, which of the following gives a time on that day when the temperature was 0°C ?

A)   6 P.M.

B)   10 P.M.

C)   3 A.M.

D)   9 A.M.

x	−1	j	5
$f(x)$	2	j	−6

The table above shows selected values for the linear function $f(x)$. What is the value of j ?

A) $-\dfrac{1}{6}$

B) $\dfrac{2}{7}$

C) $\dfrac{5}{7}$

D) $\dfrac{7}{6}$

Questions 30 and 31 refer to the following information.

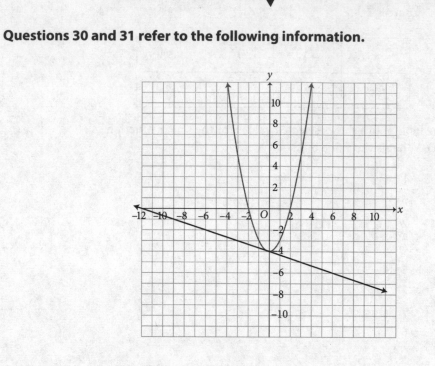

In the above graph, parabola $f(x)$ is represented by the equation $f(x) = x^2 - 4$ and line $g(x)$ is represented by the equation $g(x) = -\dfrac{1}{3}x - 4$. Line $g(x)$ intersects parabola $f(x)$ at point $(0, -4)$.

30

For $x = 12$, how much greater is the value of $f(x)$ than $g(x)$?

31

A new line, $h(x)$, is added to the graph. The line $h(x)$ is perpendicular to line $g(x)$, intersecting with line $g(x)$ at the point $(-12, 0)$. What is the x-coordinate of the point where line $h(x)$ will intersect parabola $f(x)$ in Quadrant I ?

QUADRATIC EQUATIONS

Ah, quadratics. You're likely to see several questions on the PSAT that require you to expand, factor, or solve quadratics. You may even need to find the vertex of a parabola or the points of intersection of a quadratic and a line. So let's review, starting with the basics.

Expanding

Most often you'll be asked to expand an expression simply by multiplying it out. When working with an expression of the form $(x + 3)(x + 4)$, multiply it out using the following rule:

FOIL = First Outer Inner Last

Start with the *first* figure in each set of parentheses: $x \times x = x^2$.

Now do the two *outer* figures: $x \times 4 = 4x$.

Next, the two *inner* figures: $3 \times x = 3x$.

Finally, the *last* figure in each set of parentheses: $3 \times 4 = 12$.

Add them all together, and we get $x^2 + 4x + 3x + 12$, or $x^2 + 7x + 12$.

Factoring

If you ever see an expression of the form $x^2 + 7x + 12$ on the PSAT, there is a good chance that factoring it will be the key to cracking it.

The key to factoring is figuring out what pair of numbers will multiply to give you the constant term (12, in this case) and add up to the coefficient of the x term (7, in this question).

Let's try an example:

$$x^2 + 7x + 12$$

Step 1: Draw two sets of parentheses next to each other and fill an x into the left side of each. That's what gives us our x^2 term.

$$(x \quad)(x \quad)$$

Step 2: 12 can be factored a number of ways: 1×12, 2×6, or 3×4. Which of these adds up to 7? 3 and 4, so place a 3 on the right side of one parenthesis and a 4 in the other.

$$(x \quad 3)(x \quad 4)$$

Step 3: Now we need to figure out what the correct signs should be. They should both be positive in this case, because that will sum to 7 and multiply to 12, so fill plus signs into each parenthesis.

$$(x + 3)(x + 4)$$

If you want to double-check your work, try expanding out $(x + 3)(x + 4)$ using FOIL and you'll get the original expression.

Now try the following question.

8

Travis determines that the average speed of his kayak traveling down the river when he is not paddling can be calculated using the formula $4r^2 - 40r + 100$, where r represents the strength of the river's current in feet per second. Which of the following expressions would be an equivalent formula that Travis could use to determine his kayak's speed?

A) $(2r + 10)^2$

B) $(2r + 10)(2r - 10)$

C) $4(r + 5)^2$

D) $4(r - 5)^2$

Here's How to Crack It

The question asks for an equivalent formula that can be used to determine Travis's speed. To compare the equation in the question with the answer choices, you need to either factor the equation in the question or expand out the answer choices. The first option is probably faster. Start by factoring a 4 out of the entire equation to get $4(r^2 - 10r + 25)$. Now, determine what two numbers can be added to get -10 and multiplied to get 25. In this case, it's -5 and -5. The equation becomes $4(r - 5)(r - 5)$ or $4(r - 5)^2$, which is (D).

Don't forget that you can also plug in on a question like the last one. Let's look at one in which Plugging In makes a strange question much more manageable.

8

If the expression $x + 2(x - 4)$ is multiplied by R to form the expression $3x^2 - 5x - 8$, then which of the following is equivalent to R ?

A) $x + 1$

B) $x + 2$

C) $x + 3$

D) $x + 4$

Here's How to Crack It

The question asks for an expression that is equivalent to R. Whenever the question and the answers include variables, see if you can plug in. If $x = 2$, the first expression becomes $2 + 2(2 - 4) = 2 + 2(-2) = 2 + (-4) = -2$, and the second expression becomes $3(2^2) - 5(2) - 8 = 3(4) - 10 - 8 = 12 - 10 - 8 = -6$. To find R, set up the following equation: $-2R = -6$. Solve for R to get $R = 3$. Plug 2 in for x in the equations to see which answer equals the target number of 3. Choice (A) becomes $2 + 1 = 3$. Keep (A), but check the remaining answers just in case. Choice (B) becomes $2 + 2 = 4$, (C) becomes $2 + 3 = 5$, and (D) becomes $2 + 4 = 6$. Eliminate (B), (C), and (D). The correct answer is (A).

Solving Quadratic Equations

Sometimes you'll want to factor to solve an equation. In this case, there will be two possible values for x, called the roots of the equation. To solve for x, use the following steps:

Step 1: Make sure that the equation is set equal to zero.
Step 2: Factor the equation.

Step 3: Set each parenthetical expression equal to zero. So if you have $(x + 2)(x - 7) = 0$, you get $(x + 2) = 0$ and $(x - 7) = 0$. When you solve for each, you get $x = -2$ and $x = 7$. Therefore, -2 and 7 are the solutions or roots of the equation.

Try the following question.

4

If $b^2 + 2b - 8 = 0$, and $b < 0$, what is the value of b ?

A) -6

B) -4

C) -2

D) 0

Here's How to Crack It

The question asks for the value of b in a quadratic equation. Begin by using Process of Elimination. Since the question states that $b < 0$, eliminate (D). Now follow the steps:

1. The equation is already set equal to zero.
2. You can now factor the left side of the equation to get $(b + 4)(b - 2) = 0$.
3. When you set each parenthetical expression equal to zero, you get $b = -4$ and $b = 2$. Since $b < 0$, the answer is (B).

An alternative approach to this question is to plug in the answers. For (A), plug $b = -6$ into the equation to get $(-6)^2 + 2(-6) - 8 = 0$. Solve the left side of the equation to get $36 - 12 - 8 = 0$, or $16 = 0$. Since this statement is not true, eliminate (A). For (B), plug $b = -4$ into the equation to get $(-4)^2 + 2(-4) - 8 = 0$. Solve the left side of the equation to get $16 - 8 - 8 = 0$, or $0 = 0$. Since this statement is true, the correct answer is (B).

Sometimes, solving will get a little trickier. When quadratics do not factor easily and there are no answer choices to plug in, you can use the quadratic formula to solve.

The values of x for a quadratic equation in the form $y = ax^2 + bx + c$ are

$$x = \frac{-b \pm \sqrt{b^2 - 4ac}}{2a}$$

Let's try one.

29

If $y = x^2 - 4x + 3.75$, what is one possible value of x ?

Here's How to Crack It

The question asks for the value of x in a quadratic equation. This one is not easy to factor, so try the quadratic formula. In the given equation, $a = 1$, $b = -4$, and $c = 3.75$. Therefore,

$$x = \frac{-(-4) \pm \sqrt{(-4)^2 - 4(1)(3.75)}}{2(1)} = \frac{4 \pm \sqrt{16 - 15}}{2} = \frac{4 \pm 1}{2}$$

So x equals $\frac{5}{2}$ (or 2.5) and $\frac{3}{2}$ (or 1.5). Any of these 4 options could be entered into the grid.

You may have noticed that this is a calculator question. Another option for this one would be to graph the equation on your calculator to determine the x-intercepts, which are the roots, or solutions, to the equation.

Other Quadratic Questions

Sometimes, quadratic equations will be tested with word problems or charts. Let's look at these types of questions.

29

An Olympic shot-putter throws a heavy spherical object that follows a parabolic trajectory. The equation describing the trajectory of the shot-putter's throw is $y = -0.04x^2 + 2.02x + 5.5$, where y represents the height of the object in feet and x represents the horizontal distance in feet traveled by the object. What is the original height of the object (in feet) immediately before it leaves the shot-putter's hand?

Here's How to Crack It

The question asks for the original height of an object based on an equation for the object's trajectory. According to the question, x represents the horizontal distance in feet traveled by the object, and y represents the height. Before the shot-putter throws the object, $x = 0$. Plug 0 into the equation and solve for y. The equation becomes $y = -0.04(0^2) + 2.02(0) + 5.5 = 0 + 0 + 5.5 = 5.5$. The correct answer is 5.5.

Now look at an example of a chart-based quadratic question.

14

Trajectory of a Dolphin's Jump

Horizontal Distance (feet)	Vertical Height (feet)
0	0
1	2.7
2	4.8
3	6.3
4	7.2
5	7.5
6	7.2
7	6.3
8	4.8
9	2.7
10	0

The table above shows the horizontal distance and vertical height, both in feet, of a typical dolphin jumping out of the water (a height of 0 represents the surface of the water). If d represents the horizontal distance and h represents the vertical height, which of the following equations would best represent the trajectory of the dolphin's jump?

A) $h = -0.3d^2 + 3d$

B) $h = -0.4d^2 + 4d$

C) $h = -0.5d^2 + 5d$

D) $h = -0.6d^2 + 6d$

Here's How to Crack It

The question asks for an equation to model the trajectory of a dolphin's jump based on a table of values. This is a similar task to "building a function" that we discussed earlier in this chapter. You should plug values from the table into the equations in the answer choices to see which equation works. According to the table, when $d = 1$, $h = 2.7$. Plug these values into (A) to get $2.7 = -0.3(1^2) + 3(1)$. Solve the right side of the equation to get $2.7 = -0.3 + 3$ or $2.7 = 2.7$. Keep (A), but check the remaining answers just in case. Choice (B) becomes $2.7 = -0.4(1^2) + 4(1)$. Solve the right side of the equation to get $2.7 = -0.4 + 4$ or $2.7 = 3.6$. This is not true, so eliminate (B). Choice (C) becomes $2.7 = -0.5(1^2) + 5(1)$. Solve the right side of the equation to get $2.7 = -0.5 + 5$ or $2.7 = 4.5$. Eliminate (C). Choice (D) becomes $2.7 = -0.6(1^2) + 6(1)$. Solve the right side of the equation to get $2.7 = -0.6 + 6$ or $2.7 = 5.4$. Eliminate (D). The correct answer is (A).

Forms of Quadratics

When graphed in the xy-plane, quadratics form a parabola. The PSAT will ask questions using three different forms of the equation for a parabola.

> The **standard form** of a parabola equation is as follows:
>
> $$y = ax^2 + bx + c$$

In the standard form of a parabola, the value of a tells whether a parabola opens upwards or downwards (if a is positive, the parabola opens upwards, and if a is negative, the parabola opens downwards).

> The **factored form** of a parabola equation is as follows:
>
> $$y = a(x - s)(x - t)$$
>
> In the factored form, s and t are the x-intercepts.

We discussed factoring quadratics a few pages back. The result of factoring a parabolic equation is the factored form.

> The **vertex form** of a parabola equation is as follows:
>
> $$y = a(x - h)^2 + k$$
>
> In the vertex form, the point (h, k) is the vertex of the parabola.

Simply knowing what the vertex form looks like may help you answer a question, like the following example.

6

Which of the following equations has its vertex at (−4, 3) ?

A) $y = (x - 4)^2 + 3$

B) $y = (x + 4)^2 + 3$

C) $y = (x - 3)^2 + 4$

D) $y = (x + 3)^2 - 4$

Here's How to Crack It

The question asks for a quadratic equation that has a given vertex. If you know the vertex form, you can create the correct equation for the parabola. Be careful with the signs, though, as the signs are all changing in the answer choices. In the vertex (−4, 3), −4 is h and 3 is k. The correct answer should end in + 3, so eliminate (C) and (D). For the $(x - h)^2$ part of the equation, it becomes $(x - (-4))^2$, or $(x + 4)^2$, so the correct answer is (B).

Knowing the form makes Process of Elimination a quick way to answer these, but if you forget the form, you can always plug in the given point to see which equation is true.

The vertex form is great for answering questions about the minimum or maximum value a parabolic function will reach or the x-value that results in that minimum or maximum y-value. So another good thing to know is the method for turning a quadratic in the standard form into the vertex form. Here are the steps to do that.

To convert a parabola equation in the standard form to the vertex form, complete the square.

1. Make $y = 0$, and move any constants over to the left side of the equation.
2. Take half of the coefficient on the x-term, square it, and add it to both sides of the equation.
3. Convert the x-terms and the number on the right to square form: $(x - h)^2$.
4. Move the constant on the left back over to the right and set it equal to y again.

Say you were given the equation $y = x^2 - 4x - 12$. You would make it $0 = x^2 - 4x - 12$, and then $12 = x^2 - 4x$. You'd add 4 to both sides to get $16 = x^2 - 4x + 4$, and then convert the right side to the square form to get $16 = (x - 2)^2$. Finally, you'd move the 16 back over and set it equal to y to get $y = (x - 2)^2 - 16$.

Drill 2

Answers can be found in Part IV.

3

In his physics class, Yigit determined that the height in feet (h) of a projectile t seconds after being launched can be expressed using the function $h(t) = -5t^2 + 20t + 45$. Which of the following values of t would be most helpful in finding the initial height of the projectile?

A) $t = 0$

B) $t = 1$

C) $t = 2$

D) $t = 3$

4

If $12 - (t + 2)^2 = 3$, which of the following could be the value of t ?

A) -9

B) -5

C) 5

D) 7

6

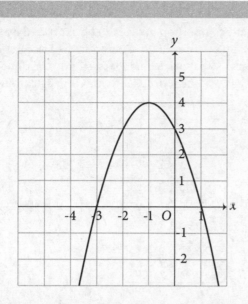

Which of the following equations is shown in the graph above?

A) $y = -(x - 3)(x + 1)$

B) $y = -(x + 3)(x - 1)$

C) $y = -(x + 3)(x + 4)$

D) $y = -(x - 1)(x + 4)$

9

Aubri determines that her score in a particular video game can be calculated using the formula $x^4 - y^4$, where x represents the number of treasures she discovers, and y represents the number of hidden traps she falls into. Which of the following expressions would be a suitable equivalent for Aubri's score calculation formula?

A) $(x + y)(x - y)(x^2 + y^2)$

B) $(x + y)^2(x^2 + y^2)$

C) $(x - y)^2(x^2 + y^2)$

D) $(x + y)(x - y)(x^2 - y^2)$

10

Which of the following equations has a vertex of $(-5, 2)$?

A) $y = (x + 5)^2 - 2$

B) $y = (x - 5)^2 - 2$

C) $y = 2(x + 5)^2 + 2$

D) $y = 2(x - 5)^2 + 2$

14

The profit that a donut shop makes can be expressed by the equation $P = -4(x - 3)^2 + 2,000$, where x is the price per donut sold (in dollars). What price, in dollars, should the donut shop charge its customers in order to maximize its profit?

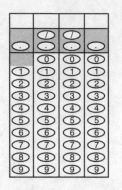

23

In the equation $x^2 + 24x + c = (x + 9)(x + p)$, c and p are constants. If the equation is true for all values of x, what is the value of c?

A)   33

B)   135

C)   144

D)   216

26

The stream of water that shoots out of a public fountain in Central Park takes the form of a parabola. The water shoots from a spout that is 8 feet above the ground and reaches a maximum height of 39.25 feet. If y represents the height of the water and x represents the time (in seconds), which of the following equations could describe the trajectory of the stream of water?

A) $y = -x^2 + 15$

B) $y = -5x^2 + 25x + 8$

C) $y = 2x^2 + 32x + 8$

D) $y = 8x + 39.25$

ANALYSIS IN SCIENCE

If some of the questions you've seen so far are reminding you of science class, you're not crazy. One of the cross-test scores the PSAT aims to measure is called Analysis in Science. This means that questions on science-based ideas will show up in Reading and Writing passages and also in Math questions.

One way this concept will be tested is through word problems. Many of the strategies we've already discussed, such as translating or Plugging In, will help you to answer these questions, regardless of the scientific context.

Here's an example.

29

The electric potential of a point charge Q is given by the equation $V = \dfrac{kQ}{r}$, where V is the charge in volts or Joules per Coulomb, Q is the charge in Coulombs, r is the distance from the charge in meters, and k is a constant equal to 9.0×10^9 Nm^2/C^2. If a point charge has an electric potential of 225 volts at a distance of 1 meter from the charge, what is the charge in nanocoulombs? (Note: 1 Coulomb = 10^9 nanocoulombs.)

Here's How to Crack It

The question asks for the charge in nanocoulombs for a given electric potential and distance. Start by identifying the values of all of the variables given. According to the question, $r = 1$, $k = 9.0 \times 10^9$, and $V = 225$ coulombs. The question asks for the charge in nanocoulombs, so multiply 225 by 10^9 and you find that $V = 225 \times 10^9$. Plug these values into the equation to get $225 \times 10^9 = \dfrac{(9.0 \times 10^9)Q}{1}$. Solve for Q by dividing both sides by 9.0×10^9 to get $\dfrac{225 \times 10^9}{9.0 \times 10^9} = Q$, or $\dfrac{225}{9.0} = Q$. So $25 = Q$, and that's your answer.

Sometimes, you will be asked science questions based on a chart or graph. In those cases, carefully look up the numbers in question, do the required calculations, and eliminate answers that aren't true.

Let's look at one.

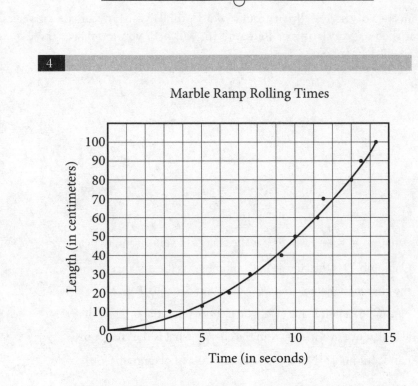

4

Marble Ramp Rolling Times

A student is rolling a marble down ramps of varying lengths. The scatterplot above shows the time, in seconds, it takes the marble to roll down each ramp. Based on the curve of best fit to the data represented, which of the following is the closest to the expected length of a ramp if a marble takes 12 seconds to roll down?

A) 61

B) 72

C) 79

D) 84

Here's How to Crack It

The question asks for the expected length of a ramp given a certain roll time based on the graph. Roll time is shown on the horizontal axis of the graph, given in seconds. Look for the mark indicating 12 seconds on this axis; then draw a vertical line from that mark to the curve of best fit. Once you hit it, draw a horizontal line over to the vertical axis. It should hit between 60 and 80 centimeters, right around 70. This makes (B) the credited response, since it is slightly closer to the mark for 70. Draw your lines carefully, using your answer sheet as a straightedge if necessary, since three of these answer choices are between 60 and 80.

You may also be asked to graph the data presented in a table. Your knowledge of graphing in the *xy*-plane should help you with most of those. If anything gets too tricky, consider skipping it and spending your time on something else.

The last science-based question type you may see doesn't involve charts, graphs, or equations. In fact, these don't even look much like math questions at all. They will have a lot of words to describe a scientific situation and ask about the conclusion that can be drawn. Just use a lot of Process of Elimination and a little knowledge of what makes a good experiment, and you should be fine.

Try this one.

15

A psychologist wants to know whether there is a relationship between increased water consumption and exam scores. He obtains survey responses from a random sample of 3,500 20-year-old college students in the United States and finds a strong positive correlation between increased water consumption and test scores. Which of the following conclusions is well-supported by the data?

A) There is a positive association between increased water consumption and test scores for 20-year-olds in the United States.

B) There is a positive association between increased water consumption and test scores for adults in the United States.

C) High test scores are caused by increased water consumption for 20-year-olds in the United States.

D) High test scores are caused by increased water consumption for adults in the United States.

Here's How to Crack It

The question asks for the conclusion that is well-supported by the data of a survey. Consider each answer choice one at a time and use Process of Elimination. Choice (A) merely restates what the evidence says, which makes it a safe conclusion, so keep it. Choice (B) is similar but shifts from "20-year-old college students" to "adults." This is a less safe conclusion than (A), because it generalizes from a more particular group, so eliminate (B). Choices (C) and (D) both introduce the idea of causation. This is a problem—no information was given about cause. Maybe people who tend to score higher on tests are also smart enough to drink more water, or maybe there is another factor causing both high test scores and increased water consumption. Eliminate (C) and (D) and choose (A).

MEANING IN CONTEXT

Some questions, instead of asking you to come up with an equation, just want you to recognize what a part of the equation stands for. It sounds like a simple enough task, but when you look at the equation, they have made it really hard to see what is going on. For this reason, Meaning in Context questions are a great opportunity to plug in real numbers and start to see how the equation really works!

First things first, though, you want to think about your POOD. Does this question fit into your pacing goals? It might take a bit of legwork to get an answer, and you may need that time to go collect points on easier, quicker questions.

If this question does fit into your pacing plan, you should read carefully, label everything you can in the equation, and POE to get rid of any answer choices that are clearly on the wrong track. Then, it's time to plug some of your own numbers in to see what is going on in there.

Here's an example.

7

$$n = 1{,}273 - 4p$$

The equation above was used by the cafeteria in a large public high school to model the relationship between the number of slices of pizza, n, sold daily and the price of a slice of pizza, p, in dollars. What does the number 4 represent in this equation?

A) For every \$4 the price of pizza decreases, the cafeteria sells 1 more slice of pizza.

B) For every dollar the price of pizza decreases, the cafeteria sells 4 more slices of pizza.

C) For every \$4 the price of pizza increases, the cafeteria sells 1 more slice of pizza.

D) For every dollar the price of pizza increases, the cafeteria sells 4 more slices of pizza.

Here's How to Crack It

The question asks what the number 4 represents in an equation modeling a certain situation. First, read the question very carefully, and use your pencil to label the variables. You know that p is the price of pizza, and n is the number of slices, so you can add that information to the equation. If you can, eliminate answer choices that don't make sense. But what if you can't eliminate anything, or you can eliminate only an answer choice or two?

Even with everything labeled, this equation is difficult to decode, so it's time to plug in! Try a few of your own numbers in the equation, and you will get a much better understanding of what is happening.

Let's try it out with $p = 2$. When you put 2 in for p, $n = 1{,}273 - 4(2)$ or 1,265.

So, when $p = 2$, $n = 1{,}265$. In other words, at \$2 a slice, the cafeteria sells 1,265 slices.

When $p = 3$, $n = 1{,}261$, so at \$3 a slice, the cafeteria sells 1,261 slices.

When $p = 4$, $n = 1{,}257$, so at \$4 a slice, the cafeteria sells 1,257 slices.

So now, let's use POE. First of all, is the cafeteria selling more pizza as the price goes up? No, as the price of pizza goes up, the cafeteria sells fewer slices of pizza. That means you can eliminate (C) and (D).

Choice (A) says that for every \$4 the price goes down, the cafeteria sells 1 more slice of pizza. Does your plugging in back that up? No. The cafeteria sells 8 more slices of pizza when the price drops from \$4 to \$2, so (A) is no good.

Now, let's take a look at (B). Does the cafeteria sell 4 more slices of pizza for every dollar the price drops? Yes! Choice (B) is the correct answer.

Here are the steps for using Plugging In to solve Meaning in Context questions:

Meaning In Context

1. Read the question carefully. Make sure you know which part of the equation you are being asked to identify.

2. Use your pencil to label the parts of the equation you can identify.

3. Eliminate any answer choices that clearly describe the wrong part of the equation, or go against what you have labeled.

4. Plug in! Use your own numbers to start seeing what is happening in the equation.

5. Use POE again, using the information you learned from plugging in real numbers, until you can get it down to one answer choice. Or, get it down to as few choices as you can, and guess.

Let's look at a slightly different one now.

10

$$7x + y = 133$$

Jeffrey has set a monthly budget for purchasing frozen blended mocha drinks from his local SpendBucks coffee shop. The equation above can be used to model the amount of his budget, y, in dollars, that remains after buying coffee for x days in a month. What does it mean that (19, 0) is a solution to this equation?

A) Jeffrey starts the month with a budget of $19.

B) Jeffrey spends $19 on coffee every day.

C) It takes 19 days for Jeffrey to drink 133 cups of coffee.

D) It takes 19 days for Jeffrey to run out of money in his budget for purchasing coffee.

Here's How to Crack It

The question asks for the meaning of a given solution to an equation modeling a situation. Start by labeling the x and the y in the equation to keep track of what they stand for. Use your pencil to write "days" above the x and "budget" above the y. So 7 × days + budget = 133. Hmm, still not very clear, is it? One way to approach this is to plug in the point (19, 0). If x = days = 19 when y = budget = 0, then Jeffrey will have no budget left after 19 days. This matches (D).

If you have trouble seeing this, you can use the answer choices to help you plug in. If (A) is true, the budget at the start of the month, when days = 0, is $19. Plug these values into the equation to see if it is true. Is 7 × 0 + 19 = 133? Not at all, so eliminate (A). If (B) is true, Jeffrey drinks a lot of coffee! Let's try some numbers and see if it works. For x = 1, the equation becomes 7(1) + y = 133 or y = 126, and for x = 2, it is 7(2) + y = 133 or y = 119. The difference in y, the budget remaining, is 126 − 119 = 7, so that's not $19 per day. Eliminate (B), so only (C) and (D) remain. These both have 19 for the number of days, and the point (19, 0) would indicate that 19 is the x value, or days. If you saw that right away—great! That would allow you to skip right to testing (C) and (D).

For (C), you can plug in 19 for days in the equation to get 7 × 19 + budget = 133, or budget = 0. Does that tell you how many cups of coffee Jeffrey drank? You have no information about the cost of a single cup of coffee, so the answer can't be (C). It does tell you, however, that after 19 days, Jeffrey has no budget left, so (D) is not only the one remaining answer, but it is also the correct one!

Drill 3

Answers can be found in Part IV.

3

An oceanographer is trying to determine the concentration profile of dissolved oxygen in the ocean at depths lower than 10 meters. He determines that the dissolved oxygen concentration is 0.0022 g/L at a depth of 15 meters, and it is 0.00125 g/L at a depth of 20 meters. If $C(d)$ is the concentration of dissolved oxygen at d meters, which of the follow equations best describes the profile below 10 meters?

A) $C(d) = \dfrac{1}{2} - \dfrac{1}{d^2}$

B) $C(d) = \dfrac{1}{100d}$

C) $C(d) = \dfrac{1}{d}$

D) $C(d) = \dfrac{1}{2d^2}$

6

A shipping company pays a driver a fixed fee for each delivery, and deducts a separate fee daily for the use of the company's delivery truck. The driver's net pay in dollars, P, for one day is given by the equation $P = 8d - 40$, where d is the number of deliveries made in one day. What does the number 40 most likely represent?

A) The amount, in dollars, that the company deducts for use of the delivery truck

B) The amount, in dollars, that the driver is paid for each delivery

C) The average number of deliveries per hour made by the driver

D) The total number of deliveries made per day by the driver

9

At a buffet restaurant, students pay $5 per meal and non-students pay $7. The total revenue, R, in dollars, earned per day by the restaurant is given by the equation $R = 5s + 7n$, where s is the number of student customers and n is the number of non-student customers. Which of the following represents the total number of customers on a given day?

A) $s - n$

B) $s + n$

C) sn

D) $\dfrac{s}{n}$

7

$$T(t) = \Delta T^{(-kt)}$$

The simple cooling of an object can be represented by the equation above, where T is temperature in degrees Celsius, k is a rate constant, and t is time. What might the quantity ΔT represent?

A) Temperature at a certain time

B) The difference between the initial temperature of the object and the temperature of its surroundings

C) A conversion from Celsius to Fahrenheit

D) A constant factor that is dependent on the object

10

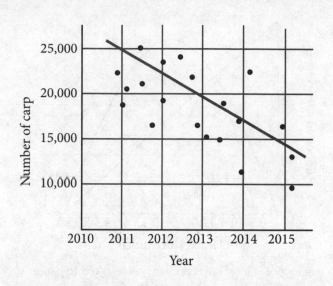

Between 2010 and 2015, researchers tracked populations of Crucian carp in the Ohio River. The graph above displays population sizes as counted by the researchers. According to the line of best fit, what is the approximate average yearly decrease in the number of Crucian carp?

A)   1

B)   2.5

C) 1,200

D) 2,500

8

A group of students decided to have a car wash to raise funds for the school. The students charged the same rate to wash each car, and they paid for cleaning supplies out of the proceeds. If the net amount, $N(c)$, in dollars, raised from washing c cars is given by the function $N(c) = 8c - 0.40c$, which of the following can be deduced from the function?

A) The students paid a total of $8 for cleaning supplies.

B) The students paid a total of $40 for cleaning supplies.

C) The students paid $0.40 per car for cleaning supplies.

D) The students paid $8 per car for cleaning supplies.

12

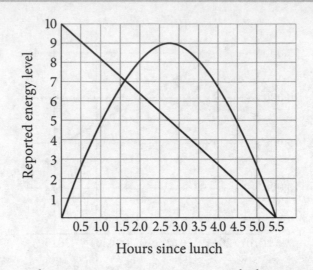

Hours since lunch

Two employees at a certain company were asked to gauge their energy levels on a scale of 1 to 10 after eating lunch at noon. The results were averaged and plotted as illustrated in the above figure. Which of the following statements is most consistent with the given data?

A) Both employees experienced the same fluctuation in energy during the afternoon hours.

B) Both employees were drowsy after eating big lunches.

C) One of the employees consumed energy-boosting foods and drinks and became less energetic throughout the afternoon.

D) One of the employees consumed foods that resulted in her feeling more energetic throughout the day.

11

Delphine is studying the growth of bacteria in a petri dish. She grows 100 colonies of bacteria in dishes at varying temperatures to find the optimal temperature for bacteria growth. The temperature of the 10 colonies with the most rapid growth is used to determine the optimal temperature range, which Delphine finds to be from 30° to 37°C, inclusive. Which of the following inequalities represents the optimal temperature range, t, for bacteria growth?

A) $|t + 7| \le 37$

B) $|t - 3.5| \le 33.5$

C) $|t - 30| \le 7$

D) $|t - 33.5| \le 3.5$

13

The sum, S, of a set of n consecutive integers is given by the equation $S = \left(\dfrac{a+k}{2}\right)n$. What does $a + k$ represent?

A) The sum of the two least integers

B) The sum of the least and greatest integers

C) The sum of the two middle integers

D) The sum of the two greatest integers

23

If interest deposits are made monthly into an account with a beginning balance of \$250, supposing no withdrawals are made from the account, the balance B of an account with an annual interest rate of 5% after t years can be computed using the equation below.

$$B = 250\left(1 + \frac{0.05}{12}\right)^{12t}$$

Which of the following describes what the quantity $\dfrac{0.05}{12}$ represents in the equation?

A) The amount of money deposited into an account with balance B during a given month

B) The amount of money in an account with balance B after a monthly interest deposit is made

C) The percentage of the starting balance B added during a monthly interest deposit

D) The number of months over which interest payments will be made in a year

Summary

- Given a function, you put an x value in and get an $f(x)$ or y value out.

- Look for ways to use Plugging In and PITA on function questions.

- For questions about the graphs of functions, remember that $f(x) = y$.

- If the graph contains a labeled point or the question gives you a point, plug it into the equations in the answers and eliminate any that aren't true.

- To find a point of intersection, set the equations equal, plug a given point into both equations to see if it works, or graph the equations on your calculator when it is allowed.

- When solving quadratic equations, you may need to FOIL or factor to get the equation into the easiest form for the question task.

- The standard form of a quadratic equation is $ax^2 + bx + c = 0$. The factored form is $y = a(x - s)(x - t)$, where s and t are the x-intercepts.

- To solve for the roots of a quadratic equation, set it equal to zero by moving all the terms to the left side of the equation, or use the quadratic formula:

$$x = \frac{-b \pm \sqrt{b^2 - 4ac}}{2a}$$

- The vertex form of a parabola equation is $y = a(x - h)^2 + k$, where (h, k) is the vertex. To get a parabola in the standard form into vertex form, complete the square.

- Plugging In can also be used on Meaning In Context questions. If a question asks you to identify a part of an equation, plug your own amounts into the equation so you can start to see what is going on.

o   Analysis in Science questions may seem weird, but they can usually be handled with the same strategies as those used for other math questions. Plug in or translate, read the chart or text carefully, and always use Process of Elimination to get rid of answers that don't match the data or don't make sense.

o   If you come across a hard Meaning in Context question or Science question, see if you can eliminate anything and make a guess. If not, find another question to do!

Chapter 14
Additional Math Topics

The PSAT has a clever name for the rest of the math concepts tested—Additional Topics. Well, maybe it's not that clever. It consists of some geometry concepts and possibly a question about imaginary numbers. While there are many geometry ideas that could be tested, these Additional Topics will really make up only a small fraction of the PSAT. Spend time on this chapter only after you have mastered the topics and techniques in the previous three chapters.

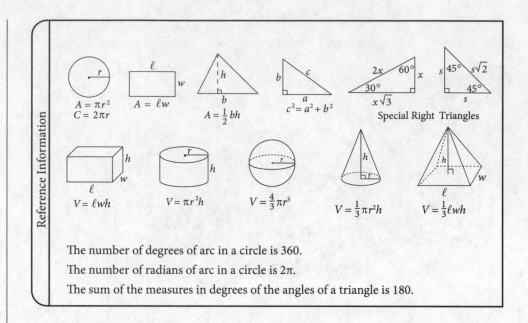

The number of degrees of arc in a circle is 360.

The number of radians of arc in a circle is 2π.

The sum of the measures in degrees of the angles of a triangle is 180.

GEOMETRY

Lines and Angles

Common sense might tell you what a line is, but for this test you are going to have to learn the particulars of a line, a ray, and a line segment.

A **line** continues on in each direction forever. You need only two points to form a line, but that line does not end at those points. A straight line has 180 degrees on each side.

A **ray** is a line with one distinct endpoint. Again, you need only two points to designate a ray, but one of those points is where it stops—it continues on forever in the other direction. A ray has 180 degrees as well.

A **line segment** is a line with two distinct endpoints. It requires two points, and it is the length from one point to the other. A line segment has 180 degrees.

Whenever you have angles on a line, remember *the rule of 180*: The angles on any line must add up to 180. These angles are called *supplementary angles*. In the figure below, what is the value of x? We know that $2x + x$ must add up to 180, so we know that $3x = 180$. This makes $x = 60$.

$2x°$ $x°$

Note: Figure not drawn to scale.

If two lines cross each other, they make *vertical angles*—that is, angles opposite each other when two lines intersect. These angles will always have the same measure. In the figure below, z and x are vertical angles, and y and the 130° angle are vertical angles. Also, we know that z must equal 50, since $130 + z$ must equal 180. We know that y is 130, since it is across from the angle 130. We also know that x is 50, since it is across from z.

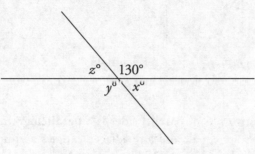

Any time you have two parallel lines and a line that crosses them, you have two kinds of angles: big angles and small angles. All of the big angles have the same measure, and all of the small angles have the same measure. In the following figure, angles a, d, e, and h all have the same measure; angles b, c, f, and g also all have the same measure. The sum of the measure of any big angle plus any small angle equals 180 degrees.

Four-Sided Figures

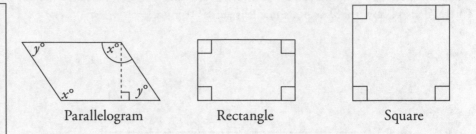

Parallelogram   Rectangle   Square

A figure with two sets of parallel sides is a **parallelogram**. In a parallelogram, the opposite angles are equal, and any adjacent angles add up to 180 degrees. (In the left-hand figure above, $x + y = 180$ degrees.) Opposite sides are also equal. The sum of all angles of a parallelogram is 360 degrees.

If all of the angles are also right angles, then the figure is a **rectangle**. And if all of the sides are the same length, then the figure is a **square**.

The *area* of a square, rectangle, or parallelogram is *length × width*. (In the parallelogram above, the length is shown by the dotted line.)

The *perimeter* of any figure is the sum of the lengths of its sides. A trapezoid with sides of 6, 8, 10, and 8 has a perimeter of 32.

Drill 1

Answers can be found in Part IV.

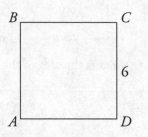

a. What is the area of square *ABCD* above? _____

b. What is the perimeter of square *ABCD* above? _____

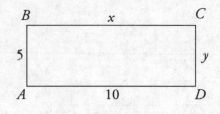

c. If *ABCD* is a rectangle, $x =$ _____ $y =$ _____

d. What is the perimeter of rectangle *ABCD* above? _____

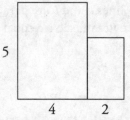

e. If the above figure is composed of two rectangles, what is the perimeter of the figure?

_____

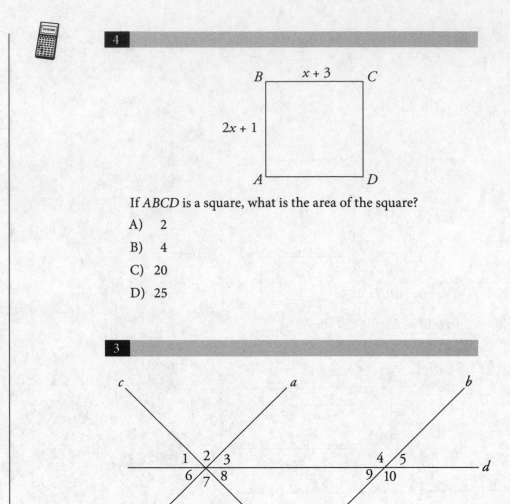

4

If $ABCD$ is a square, what is the area of the square?

A) 2

B) 4

C) 20

D) 25

3

In the figure above, lines a and b are parallel. Which of the following pairs of angles must have equal degree measures?

    I.   1 and 5

    II.   2 and 7

    III.   3 and 9

A) I only

B) II only

C) III only

D) II and III only

28

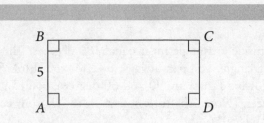

The diagonal of rectangle *ABCD* is 13 inches long. What is the area of rectangle *ABCD* ?

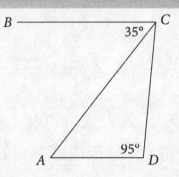

9

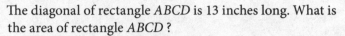

In the figure above, $\overline{BC} \parallel \overline{AD}$. What is the measure of ∠*ACD* ?

A) 35

B) 40

C) 50

D) 55

TRIANGLES

The sum of the angles inside a triangle must equal 180 degrees. This means that if you know two of the angles in a triangle, you can always solve for the third. Since you know that two of the angles in the following figure are 90 and 60 degrees, you can solve for the third angle, which must be 30 degrees. (Note: The little square in the bottom corner of the triangle indicates a right angle, which is 90°.)

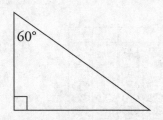

An **isosceles triangle** has two sides that are equal. Angles that are opposite equal sides must be equal. The figure below is an isosceles triangle. Since $AB = BC$, you know that angles x and y are equal. And since their sum must be 150 degrees (to make a total of 180 degrees when you add the last angle), they each must be 75 degrees.

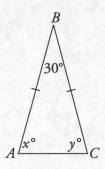

The **area** of a triangle is $\frac{1}{2}$ *base × height*. Note that the height is always perpendicular to the base.

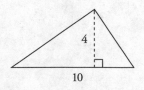   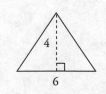

$$\text{Area} = \frac{1}{2} \times 10 \times 4 = 20 \qquad \text{Area} = \frac{1}{2} \times 6 \times 4 = 12$$

An **equilateral triangle** has all three sides equal and all of its angles equal to 60 degrees.

Here's a typical example of a PSAT question on triangles.

5

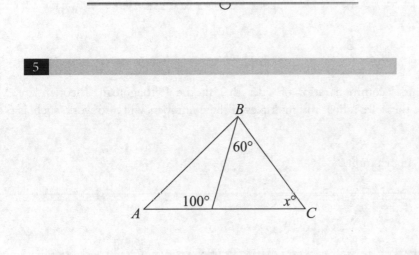

In triangle *ABC* above, what is the value of *x* ?

A) 30

B) 40

C) 50

D) 60

Here's How to Crack It

The question asks for the value of *x*, which is an angle measure in a triangle. We know that the angle adjacent to the 100° angle must equal 80° since we know that a straight line is 180°. Fill it in on your diagram. Now, since we know that the sum of the angles contained in a triangle must equal 180°, we know that 80 + 60 + *x* = 180, so *x* = 40. That's (B).

Being Aggressive on Geometry Questions

The most important problem-solving technique for tackling PSAT geometry is to learn to be aggressive. This means, whenever you have a diagram, ask yourself *What else do I know?* Write everything you can think of on your booklet. You may not see right away why it's important, but write it down anyway. Chances are good that you will be making progress toward the answer, without even knowing it.

The PSAT is also fond of disguising familiar figures within more complex shapes by extending lines, overlapping figures, or combining several basic shapes. So be on the lookout for the basic figures hidden in complicated shapes.

The Pythagorean Theorem

Whenever you have a right triangle, you can use the Pythagorean Theorem. The theorem says that the sum of the squares of the legs of the triangle (the sides that form the right angle) will equal the square of the hypotenuse (the side opposite the right angle).

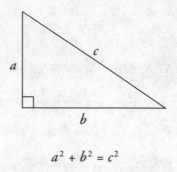

$$a^2 + b^2 = c^2$$

Two of the most common ratios of sides that fit the Pythagorean Theorem are 3-4-5 and 5-12-13. Since these are ratios, any multiples of these numbers will also work, such as 6-8-10 and 30-40-50.

Try the following example.

14

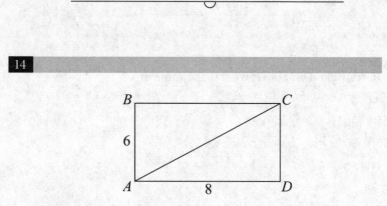

If *ABCD* is a rectangle, what is the perimeter of triangle *ABC*?

Here's How to Crack It

The question asks for the perimeter of triangle *ABC* based on the figure. We can use the Pythagorean Theorem to figure out the length of the diagonal of the rectangle—since it has sides 6 and 8, its diagonal must be 10. (If you remembered that this is one of those well-known Pythagorean triples, you didn't actually have to do the calculations.) Therefore, the perimeter of the triangle is 6 + 8 + 10, or 24.

○

Special Right Triangles

There are two specific right triangles, the properties of which may play a role in some harder PSAT math questions. They are the right triangles with angles 45°-45°-90° and 30°-60°-90°. These triangles appear at the front of each Math section, so you don't have to memorize them.

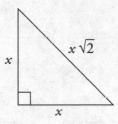

An isosceles right triangle has angles that measure 45, 45, and 90 degrees. Whenever you have a 45°-45°-90° triangle with sides of *x*, the hypotenuse will always be $x\sqrt{2}$. This means that if one of the legs of the triangle measures 3, then the hypotenuse will be $3\sqrt{2}$.

This right triangle is important because it is half of a square. Understanding the 45°-45°-90° triangle will allow you to easily find the diagonal of a square from its side, or find the side of a square from its diagonal.

Here's an example.

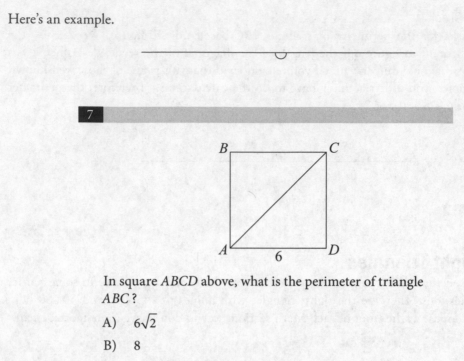

7

In square *ABCD* above, what is the perimeter of triangle *ABC*?

A) $6\sqrt{2}$

B) 8

C) $12 + \sqrt{2}$

D) $12 + 6\sqrt{2}$

Here's How to Crack It

The question asks for the perimeter of triangle *ABC* based on the figure. This question looks like a question about a square, and it certainly is in part, but it's really more about the two triangles formed by the diagonal.

In this square, we know that each of the triangles formed by the diagonal $\overline{AC}$ is a 45°-45°-90° right triangle. Since the square has a side of 6, using the 45°-45°-90° right triangle rule, each of the sides is 6 and the diagonal is $6\sqrt{2}$. Therefore, the perimeter of the triangle is $6 + 6 + 6\sqrt{2}$, or $12 + 6\sqrt{2}$ and the answer is (D).

The other important right triangle to understand is the 30°-60°-90° right triangle.

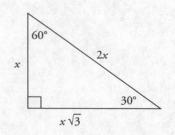

A 30°-60°-90° triangle with a short side of x will have a hypotenuse of $2x$ and a middle side of $x\sqrt{3}$. If the smallest side (the x side) of the triangle is 5, then the sides measure 5, $5\sqrt{3}$, and 10. This triangle is important because it is half of an equilateral triangle, and it allows us to find the height of an equilateral triangle, which is what we'll need to find the area of an equilateral triangle.

Try the following.

13

Triangle *ABC* above is equilateral, with sides of length 4.
What is its area?

A) 3

B) $4\sqrt{2}$

C) $4\sqrt{3}$

D) 8

> **Triangle Tip**
> An easy way to figure out the height of an equilateral triangle is to take half of its side and multiply it by the square root of 3.

Here's How to Crack It

The question asks for the area of an equilateral triangle with a given side length. To find the area of the triangle, we need to know the base and the height. The question tells you that the base $\overline{AC}$ is 4; now we need to find the height, which is *perpendicular* to the base. You can create the height by drawing a line from angle *B* straight down to the base. Now you have two 30°-60°-90° triangles, and you can use the rules of 30°-60°-90° triangles to figure out the height. Half of the base would be 2, and that's the side across from the 30° angle, so you would multiply it by $\sqrt{3}$ to get the height.

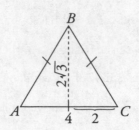

Now we know that the base is 4 and the height is $2\sqrt{3}$, so when we plug those numbers into the formula for area of a triangle, we get $A = \dfrac{1}{2} \times 4 \times 2\sqrt{3}$, which equals $4\sqrt{3}$. Thus, (C) is the correct answer.

SOHCAHTOA

Trigonometry will likely appear on your PSAT. But fear not! Many trigonometry questions you will see mostly require you to know the basic definitions of the three main trigonometric functions. SOHCAHTOA is a way to remember the three functions:

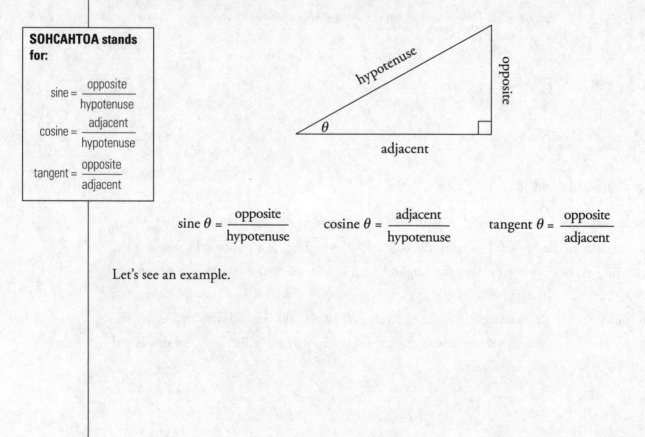

SOHCAHTOA stands for:

$$\text{sine} = \frac{\text{opposite}}{\text{hypotenuse}}$$

$$\text{cosine} = \frac{\text{adjacent}}{\text{hypotenuse}}$$

$$\text{tangent} = \frac{\text{opposite}}{\text{adjacent}}$$

$$\text{sine } \theta = \frac{\text{opposite}}{\text{hypotenuse}} \qquad \text{cosine } \theta = \frac{\text{adjacent}}{\text{hypotenuse}} \qquad \text{tangent } \theta = \frac{\text{opposite}}{\text{adjacent}}$$

Let's see an example.

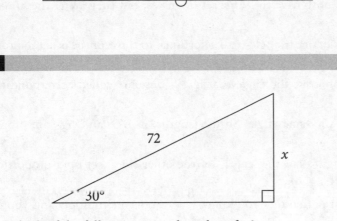

11

Which of the following gives the value of x ?

A) $72 \sin 30°$

B) $\dfrac{72}{\sin 30°}$

C) $72 \cos 30°$

D) $72 \tan 30°$

Here's How to Crack It

The question asks for the value of x, which is a leg on a right triangle. You know the hypotenuse of the triangle, and you want to find the side opposite the 30° angle. SOHCAHTOA tells you that sine is $\dfrac{\text{opposite}}{\text{hypotenuse}}$, so you want sine. You can eliminate (C) and (D), which do not contain sine. Next, set up the equation using the definition of sine: $\sin 30° = \dfrac{x}{72}$. To solve for x, multiply both sides by 72 and you get $72 \sin 30° = x$. This matches (A).

Similar Triangles

Similar triangles have the same shape, but they are not necessarily the same size. Having the same shape means that the angles of the triangles are identical and that the corresponding sides have the same ratio. Look at the following two similar triangles:

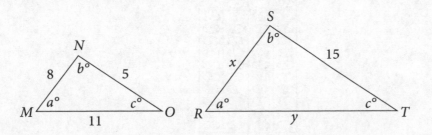

These two triangles both have the same set of angles, but they aren't the same size. Whenever this is true, the sides of one triangle are proportional to those of the other. Notice that sides $\overline{NO}$ and $\overline{ST}$ are both opposite the angle that is $a°$. These are called corresponding sides, because they correspond to the same angle. So the lengths of $\overline{NO}$ and $\overline{ST}$ are proportional to each other. In order to figure out the lengths of the other sides, set up a proportion: $\dfrac{MN}{RS} = \dfrac{NO}{ST}$. Now fill in the information that you know: $\dfrac{8}{x} = \dfrac{5}{15}$. Cross-multiply and you find that $x = 24$. You could also figure out the length of y: $\dfrac{NO}{ST} = \dfrac{MO}{RT}$. So, $\dfrac{5}{15} = \dfrac{11}{y}$, and $y = 33$. Whenever you have to deal with sides of similar triangles, just set up a proportion.

Give it a try.

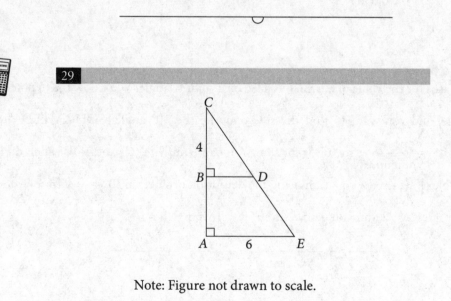

29

Note: Figure not drawn to scale.

If the area of triangle *ACE* is 18, what is the area of triangle *BCD*?

Here's How to Crack It

The question asks for the area of triangle *BCD*. The formula to find the area of a triangle is $A = \frac{1}{2}bh$. Plugging in the area and base of triangle *ACE* as given in the question and the figure gives you the equation $18 = \frac{1}{2}(6)h$. Simplify the fraction and you will get $18 = 3h$. Divide both sides by 3 and you can see that the height of triangle *ACE* is 6. Because triangle *ACE* and triangle *BCD* have the same angle measures, they are similar. Therefore, you should create a proportion to find the length of $\overline{BD}$. The proportion should look like this: $\frac{4}{x} = \frac{6}{6}$, if *x* represents the length of $\overline{BD}$. Simplify your fractions and cross-multiply to see that $x = 4$. Plug the base and height of triangle *BCD* into the area formula: $A = \frac{1}{2}(4)(4)$. Simplify the equation and you will see that the area of triangle *BCD* is 8.

Drill 2

Answers can be found in Part IV.

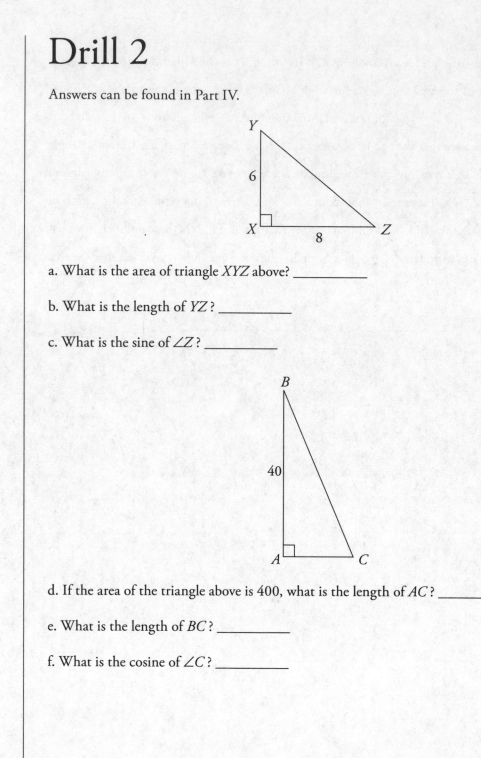

a. What is the area of triangle *XYZ* above? _____

b. What is the length of *YZ*? _____

c. What is the sine of ∠*Z*? _____

d. If the area of the triangle above is 400, what is the length of *AC*? _____

e. What is the length of *BC*? _____

f. What is the cosine of ∠*C*? _____

28

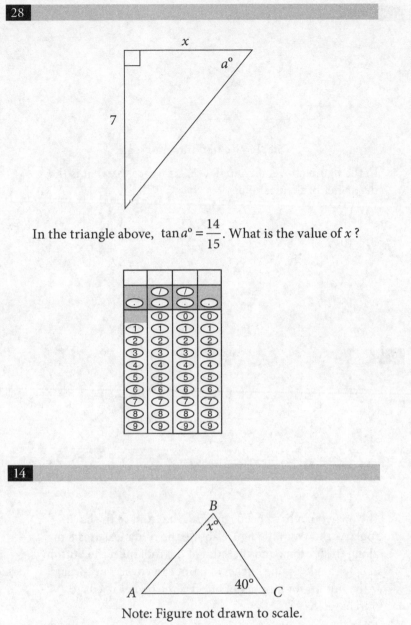

In the triangle above, $\tan a° = \dfrac{14}{15}$. What is the value of x ?

14

Note: Figure not drawn to scale.

In triangle ABC above, if $AB = BC$, what is the value of x ?

(Disregard the degree symbol when gridding your answer.)

8

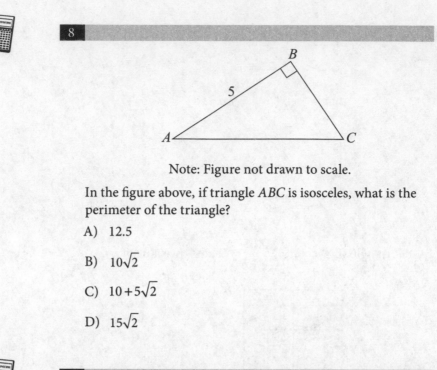

Note: Figure not drawn to scale.

In the figure above, if triangle *ABC* is isosceles, what is the perimeter of the triangle?

A) 12.5

B) $10\sqrt{2}$

C) $10+5\sqrt{2}$

D) $15\sqrt{2}$

9

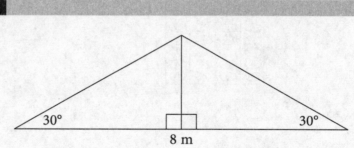

The owner of a barn needs to paint the front of the barn's roof. As shown in the figure above, the roof measures 8 m along the bottom, and the sides of the roof meet the bottom at a 30° angle. If one bucket of paint can cover 5 m², what is the minimum number of buckets the owner needs to purchase?

A) 1

B) 2

C) 3

D) 4

10

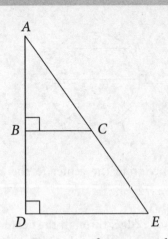

Note: Figure not drawn to scale.

In the figure above, if $AB = 5$, $AC = 13$, and $DE = 24$, what is the value of BD ?

A) 12

B) 10

C) 8

D) 5

13

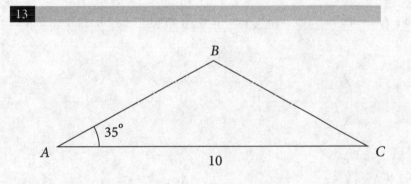

In the triangle above, $AB = BC$. Which of the following accurately expresses the perimeter of the triangle?

A) $10 + 10 \sin 55°$

B) $10 + 10 \cos 35°$

C) $10 + \dfrac{10}{\sin 55°}$

D) $25 \tan 35°$

CIRCLES

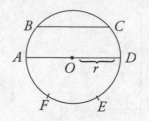

The **radius** of a circle is the distance from the center to the edge of the circle. In the figure above, $\overline{OD}$ is a radius. So is $\overline{OA}$.

The **diameter** is the distance from one edge, through the center, to the other edge of the circle. The diameter will always be twice the measure of the radius and will always be the longest line you can draw through a circle. In the figure above, $\overline{AD}$ is a diameter.

A **chord** is any line drawn from one point on the edge of the circle to the other. In the figure above, $\overline{BC}$ is a chord. A diameter is the longest chord in a circle.

An **arc** is any section of the circumference (the edge) of the circle. $\overset{\frown}{EF}$ is an arc in the figure above.

The **circumference** is the distance around the outside edge of the circle. The circumference of a circle with radius r is $2\pi r$. A circle with radius of 5 has a circumference of 10π.

The **area** of a circle with radius r is πr^2. A circle with a radius of 5 has an area of 25π.

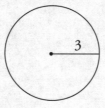

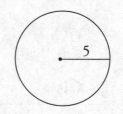

Area = 9π

Area = 25π

Circumference = 6π

Circumference = 10π

Quick Review
- An interior angle is an angle formed by two radii.
- A sector is the portion of the circle between the two radii.

Proportionality in a Circle

Here's another rule that plays a role in more advanced circle questions.

Arc measure is proportional to interior angle measure,
which is proportional to sector area.

This means that whatever fraction of the total degree measure is made up by the interior angle, the arc described by that angle is the same fraction of the circumference, and the pie piece created has the same fraction of the area.

Take a look at the figure below.

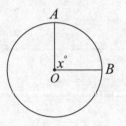

If angle x is equal to 90 degrees, which is one-quarter of 360 degrees, then arc $\overparen{AB}$ is equal to one-quarter of the circumference of the circle and the area of the sector of the circle enclosed by radii $\overline{OA}$ and $\overline{OB}$ is equal to one-quarter of the area of the circle.

To see how this works, try the following question.

6

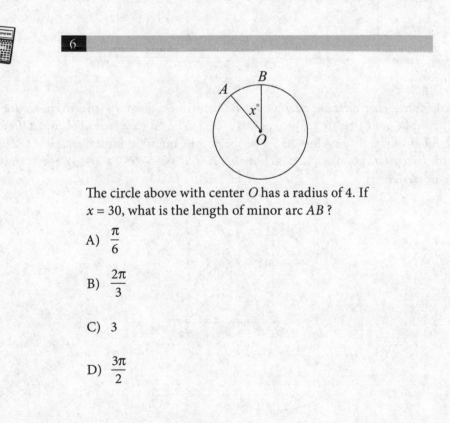

The circle above with center O has a radius of 4. If $x = 30$, what is the length of minor arc AB ?

A) $\dfrac{\pi}{6}$

B) $\dfrac{2\pi}{3}$

C) 3

D) $\dfrac{3\pi}{2}$

Here's How to Crack It

The question asks for the length of minor arc AB. Since the interior angle x is equal to 30°, which is $\frac{1}{12}$ of 360°, we know that minor arc AB will be equal to $\frac{1}{12}$ of the circumference of the circle. Since the circle has radius 4, its circumference will be 8π. Therefore, arc AB will measure $\frac{1}{12} \times 8\pi$, or $\frac{2\pi}{3}$, (B).

11

Points A and B lie on a circle with center O such that the measure of $\angle OAB$ is 45°. If the area of the circle is 64π, what is the perimeter of $\triangle AOB$?

A) $8 + 8\sqrt{2}$

B) $16 + 8\sqrt{2}$

C) $16 + 16\sqrt{2}$

D) $32 + 16\sqrt{2}$

Here's How to Crack It

The question asks for the perimeter of triangle AOB. This time a diagram isn't given, so drawing the circle should be your first step. Since points A and B lie on the circle, $\overline{OA}$ and $\overline{OB}$ are both radii and equal in length, making $\triangle AOB$ isosceles. The question indicates that $\angle OAB$ is 45°, which means that $\angle OBA$ is also 45°, which makes $\triangle AOB$ a 45°-45°-90° triangle (remember those special right triangles?).

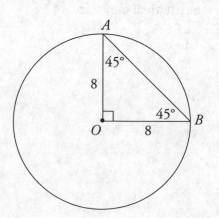

Given the circle's area of 64π, the radii of the circle (which are the legs of the isosceles right triangle) are 8 and the hypotenuse is $8\sqrt{2}$, making the perimeter $8 + 8 + 8\sqrt{2}$, or $16 + 8\sqrt{2}$, which is (B).

───────○───────

Tangents to a Circle

A tangent is a line that touches the edge of a circle at exactly one point. A radius drawn to the point of tangency forms a 90-degree angle with the tangent line. This comes up occasionally on hard questions, so take a look at the example below. As you work through this question, if you're thinking that you'd never know how to do it yourself, there's still a valuable lesson here, and it's that this question is not in your POOD, so you should look instead for a plug-in or something you're more familiar with.

───────○───────

27

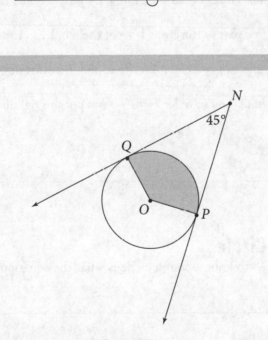

In the figure above, $\overline{NP}$ and $\overline{NQ}$ are tangent to the circle with center O at points P and Q, respectively. If the area of the shaded region is 24 π, what is the circumference of the circle?

A) 8π

B) 12π

C) 16π

D) 40π

Here's How to Crack It

The question asks for the circumference of the circle. The key is remembering that any line or line segment drawn tangent to a circle is perpendicular to a radius drawn from the center of the circle to that tangent point; this means both $\angle OQN$ and $\angle OPN$ equal 90°. With $\angle QNP$ given as 45°, that leaves the central $\angle QOP$ of quadrilateral $QNPO$. Since all quadrilaterals contain 360° and the three angles mentioned so far account for 90 + 90 + 45 = 225°, that remaining angle must be 360 − 225 = 135°. As all circles contain 360° of arc, this means the shaded area represents $\frac{135}{360}$, or $\frac{3}{8}$, of the area of the entire circle.

Remember, we want to write down the formulas for quantities the question talks about, so that's $A = \pi r^2$ and $C = 2\pi r$. So far we don't have anything we can put directly into a formula, so what do we know? We're told that the area of the shaded sector is 24π, so we can use that to figure out the area of the whole circle, because we know it's proportional to the central angle. In fact, we've figured out that this part of the circle is $\frac{3}{8}$ of the whole, so the proportion looks like this: $\frac{3}{8} = \frac{24\pi}{x}$. Cross-multiply to get $3x = 192\pi$, then divide both sides by 3 to get $x = 64\pi$. Now we can use the first formula and solve for $r = 8$. We can put this right into the second formula and get $C = 16\pi$, so the answer is (C).

The Equation of a Circle

One last thing you may need to know about a circle is what the equation of a circle in the xy-plane looks like.

The equation of a circle is as follows:

$$(x - h)^2 + (y - k)^2 = r^2$$

In the circle equation, the center of the circle is the point (h, k), and the radius of the circle is r.

Let's look at one.

13

What is the equation of a circle with center (2, 4) that passes through the point (−6, −2) ?

A) $(x + 2)^2 + (y + 4)^2 = 100$

B) $(x + 2)^2 + (y + 4)^2 = \sqrt{20}$

C) $(x - 2)^2 + (y - 4)^2 = 100$

D) $(x - 2)^2 + (y - 4)^2 = \sqrt{20}$

Here's How to Crack It

The question asks for the equation of a circle with a given center and containing a certain point. Take the given center and put it into the circle equation above. Plugging in $h = 2$ and $k = 4$, you get $(x - 2)^2 + (y - 4)^2 = r^2$. In the circle equation, x and y are the coordinates of a point on the circle. Plugging in the point (−6, −2), you get $(-6 - 2)^2 + (-2 - 4)^2 = r^2$, which simplifies to $(-8)^2 + (-6)^2 = r^2$, or $64 + 36 = r^2$. This means $r^2 = 100$, so the equation is $(x - 2)^2 + (y - 4)^2 = 100$. The correct answer is (C).

There is a chance that you might see a circle equation that is not in the form shown above. If this happens, you will need to complete the square to get the given equation into the proper form. Just follow the steps listed for completing the square in the Quadratic Equations section of the previous chapter. The only difference is that you'll have to do it twice—for the x-terms and for the y-terms. You may decide, however, that such a question is not worth your time. In that case, move on to something else!

Drill 3

Answers can be found in Part IV.

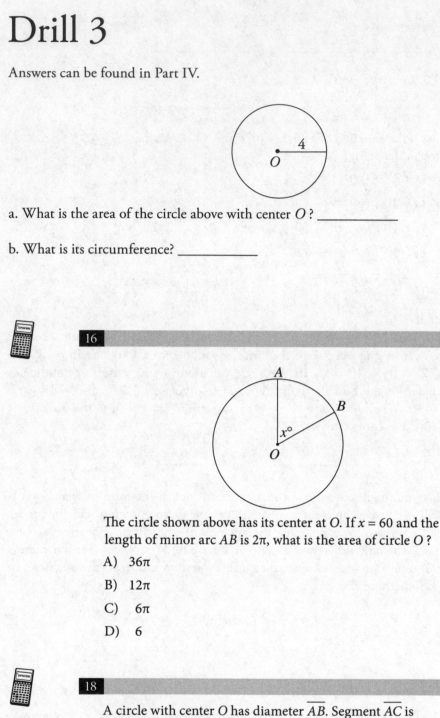

a. What is the area of the circle above with center O? _____

b. What is its circumference? _____

16

The circle shown above has its center at O. If $x = 60$ and the length of minor arc AB is 2π, what is the area of circle O?

A) 36π

B) 12π

C) 6π

D) 6

18

A circle with center O has diameter $\overline{AB}$. Segment $\overline{AC}$ is tangent to the circle at point A and has a length of 5. If the area of the circle is 36π, what is the perimeter of triangle ABC?

A) 15

B) 25

C) 30

D) 60

12

What is the center of a circle with equation
$x^2 + y^2 - 2x + 8y + 8 = 0$?

A) $(-1, 4)$

B) $(1, -4)$

C) $(-2, 8)$

D) $(2, -8)$

29

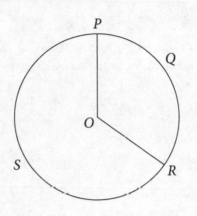

Note: Figure not drawn to scale.

Major arc PSR is $\dfrac{4}{3}$ the length of minor arc PQR. The length of major arc PSR is 6π units. What is the radius of the circle?

VOLUME

Volume questions on the PSAT can seem intimidating at times. The PSAT sometimes gives you questions featuring unusual shapes such as pyramids and spheres. Luckily, at the beginning of the Math sections (and the beginning of this chapter), you're given a reference information box with all the formulas you will ever need for volume questions on the PSAT.

Let's look at an example.

15

A sphere has a volume of 36π. What is the surface area of the sphere? (The surface area of a sphere is given by the formula $A = 4\pi r^2$.)

A) 3π

B) 9π

C) 27π

D) 36π

Here's How to Crack It

The question asks for the surface area of a sphere with a given volume. Start by writing down the formula for the volume of a sphere from the beginning of the chapter: $V = \dfrac{4}{3}\pi r^3$. Put what you know into the equation: $36\pi = \dfrac{4}{3}\pi r^3$. From this you can solve for r. Divide both sides by π to get $36 = \dfrac{4}{3}r^3$. Multiply both sides by 3 to clear the fraction: $36(3) = 4r^3$. Note that we left 36 as 36 because the next step is to divide both sides by 4, and 36 divided by 4 is 9, so $9(3) = r^3$ or $27 = r^3$. Take the cube root of both sides to get $r = 3$. Now that you have the radius, use the formula provided to find the surface area: $A = 4\pi(3)^2$, which comes out to 36π, (D).

PLUGGING IN ON GEOMETRY

You can also use Plugging In on geometry questions, just as you can for algebra. Any time that you have variables in the answer choices or hidden variables, use Plugging In! As long as you follow all the rules of geometry while you solve, you'll get the answer.

Take a look at this question.

8

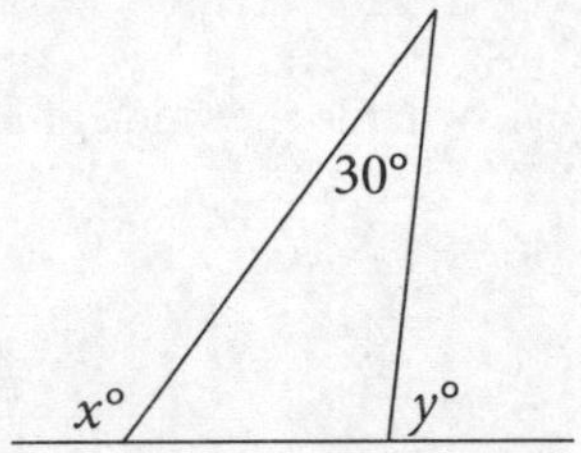

In the figure above, what is the value of $x + y$?

A) 140

B) 180

C) 190

D) 210

Here's How to Crack It

The question asks for the value of $x + y$, which are two angle measures on a figure. You could answer this question using algebra, but why? You can plug in whatever numbers you want for the other angles inside the triangle—as long as you make sure that all the angles in the triangle add up to 180°. So plug in 60 and 90 for the other angles inside that triangle. Now you can solve for x and y: if the angle next to x is 60°, then x will be equal to 120. If the angle next to y is equal to 90°, then y will be equal to 90. This makes the sum $x + y$ equal to 120 + 90, or 210. No matter what numbers we pick for the angles inside the triangle, we'll always get the same answer, (D).

Drill 4

Try to use Plugging In on the following questions. Answers can be found in Part IV.

3

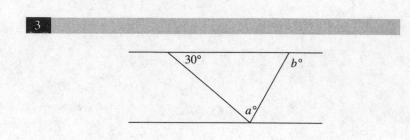

In the figure above, what is the value of *b*, in terms of *a* ?

A) 30 − *a*

B) 30 + *a*

C) 60 + *a*

D) 80 − *a*

7

Cone *A* and Cone *B* are both right circular cones with the same height. If the radius of Cone *A* is $\frac{3}{4}$ of the radius of Cone *B*, which of the following is the ratio of the volume of Cone *A* to the volume of Cone *B* ?

A) 27:64

B) 9:16

C) 3:4

D) 4:3

5

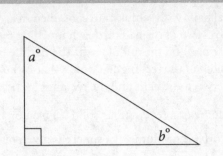

If $\sin a° = x$, then $\cos b° =$

A) x

B) $1 - x$

C) $\dfrac{1}{x}$

D) $x - 1$

22

In the figure above, O is the center of the circle, the radius of the circle is x, and the length of minor arc PQ is $\dfrac{\pi x}{18}$. What is the area of sector POQ ?

A) $\dfrac{\pi x^2}{36}$

B) $\dfrac{\pi x^2}{18}$

C) $\dfrac{\pi x^2}{9}$

D) $\dfrac{\pi x^2}{3}$

26

Three spherical balls with radius *r* are contained in a rectangular box. Two of the balls are each touching 5 sides of the rectangular box and the middle ball. The middle ball also touches four sides of the rectangular box. What is the volume of the space between the balls and the rectangular box?

(Note: The volume of a rectangular solid is given by the equation $V = lwh$. The volume of a sphere is given by the equation $V = \frac{4}{3}\pi r^3$.)

A) $r^3(3 - 4\pi)$

B) $4r^2(14 - \pi)$

C) $4r^3(6 - \pi)$

D) $12r^2(r - \pi)$

29

A rectangular box is half as long as it is wide and one-third as wide as it is tall. If the volume of the box is 96, then what is its surface area? (Note: The formula for the volume of a rectangular solid is $V = lwh$.)

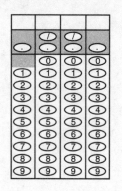

IMAGINARY AND COMPLEX NUMBERS

So far you have been working with real numbers, which are any numbers that you can place on a number line. The PSAT may ask you to do mathematical operations with imaginary or complex numbers.

An **imaginary number**, very simply, is the square root of a negative number. Since there is no way to have a real number that is the square root of a negative number, mathematicians needed to come up with a way to represent this concept when writing equations. They use an italicized lowercase "I" to do that: $i = \sqrt{-1}$, and the PSAT will likely tell you that in any question involving imaginary numbers.

A **complex number** is one that has a real component and an imaginary component connected by addition or subtraction. $8 + 7i$ and $3 - 4i$ are two examples of complex numbers.

You may be tested on complex numbers in a variety of ways. You may be asked to add or subtract the complex numbers. When you are completing these operations, you can treat i as a variable. Just combine the like terms in these expressions and then simplify. (Don't forget to distribute the subtraction sign.)

Here is an example.

7

If $i = \sqrt{-1}$, which of the following is equivalent to $(4 + 3i) - (2 - 2i)$?

A) 3

B) $2 + i$

C) $6 + i$

D) $2 + 5i$

Here's How to Crack It

The question asks for an expression equivalent to one containing complex numbers. Start by distributing the negative sign: $(4 + 3i) - (2 - 2i) = 4 + 3i - 2 + 2i$. Be careful with the negative signs, which are often the trickiest part of imaginary number questions. The real parts are 4 and $- 2$, which can be added together to get 2. The imaginary parts are $3i$ and $2i$. These can also be added together to get $5i$. Note you cannot combine real parts and imaginary parts in a complex number, so the answer is simply (D).

The PSAT may also ask you to multiply complex numbers. Again, you can treat i as a variable as you work through the multiplication as if you were multiplying binominals. In other words, use FOIL to work through the question. The only difference is that you substitute -1 for i^2.

Let's look at one.

10

If $i^2 = -1$ and $a = (i + 6)$, which of the following is the result of squaring a ?

A) $36i$

B) $i + 36$

C) $12i + 35$

D) $12i + 36$

Here's How to Crack It

The question asks for the result of squaring a. The question states that $a = (i + 6)$, so the square of a must be $(i + 6)^2$. Expand the squared term using FOIL and you get $i^2 + 6i + 6i + 36$. Combine like terms to get $i^2 + 12i + 36$. Since $i^2 = -1$, you can simplify further to $(-1) + 12i + 36$, or $12i + 35$, which is (C).

Note that this question would appear in the calculator-allowed section. Your calculator has a handy i button, so feel free to use it when allowed if things get tricky.

Summary

o   Be sure to review your basic geometry rules before the test; often, questions hinge on knowing that vertical angles are equal or that the sum of the angles in a quadrilateral is 360°.

o   On all geometry questions, draw figures out and aggressively fill in everything you know.

o   When two parallel lines are cut by a third line, the small angles are equal, the big angles are equal, and the sum of a big angle and a small angle is 180°.

o   The perimeter of a rectangle is the sum of the lengths of its sides. The area of a rectangle is *length × width*.

o   The perimeter of a triangle is the sum of the lengths of its sides. The area of a triangle is 1/2 *base × height*.

o   Knowing the Pythagorean Theorem, common Pythagorean triples (such as 3-4-5 and 5-12-13), and special right triangles (45°-45°-90° and 30°-60°-90°) will help you figure out angles and lengths in a right triangle.

o   For trigonometry questions, remember SOHCAHTOA:

-   sine $= \dfrac{opposite}{hypotenuse}$

-   cosine $= \dfrac{adjacent}{hypotenuse}$

-   tangent $= \dfrac{opposite}{adjacent}$

o   Similar triangles have the same angles and their side lengths are proportional.

o   The circumference of a circle is $2\pi r$. The area of a circle is πr^2.

o   Circles that show an interior angle (an angle that extends from the center of the circle) have proportionality. The interior angle over the whole degree measure (360°) equals the same fraction as the arc enclosed by that angle over the circumference. Likewise, both of these fractions are equal to the area of the segment over the entire area of the circle.

o   When you see a line that is "tangent to" a circle, remember two things:
- The line touches the circle at exactly one point.
- The radius of the circle that intersects the tangent line is perpendicular (90°) to that tangent line.

o   The formulas to compute the volumes of many three-dimensional figures are supplied in the instructions at the front of both Math sections.

o   When plugging in on geometry questions, remember to use your knowledge of basic geometry rules; e.g., there are still 180° in a triangle when you're using Plugging In.

o   The imaginary number $i = \sqrt{-1}$. When doing algebra with i, treat it as a variable, unless you are able to substitute −1 for i^2 when appropriate.

Part IV
Drill Answers
and Explanations

CHAPTER 6

Dual-Passage Drill (page 150)

38. **C**   The question asks why the author *mentions infections and cancers*. Use the given line reference to find the window. Lines 3–9 state, *The more site-specific a delivery system is, the more effective the drug it is delivering will be…This is especially true of different drugs used to predominantly treat infections and cancers*. Eliminate answers that don't match the prediction. Choice (A) is a Right Words, Wrong Meaning answer; the passage discusses treating these types of illnesses, but not curing them, so eliminate (A). Choice (B) is contradicted by the passage; the paragraph refers to drugs used to *treat infections and cancers*, so eliminate (B). Choice (C) matches the prediction: the phrase *precisely controlled internal drug delivery* matches *The more site-specific a delivery system is*, so keep (C). Choice (D) is a Mostly Right, Slightly Wrong trap answer because it references *vaccines*, rather than treatments. Eliminate (D). The correct answer is (C).

39. **D**   The question asks the purpose of the reference to *nanometers to micrometers* in Passage 1. Use the given line reference to find the window. Lines 12–16 state, *Electrospinning creates biodegradable scaffolds composed of fibers ranging from nanometers to micrometers in diameter, an attribute that is intrinsically difficult to obtain from other fiber-fabrication processes*. Eliminate answers that don't match this prediction. Choice (A) is a Mostly Right, Slightly Wrong trap answer: the text gives a range of measurements, not a *precise* one, so eliminate (A). Eliminate (B) because the passage is describing the sizes of the fibers for the first time, not *further elaborating* on their size. Eliminate (C) because the size of *cells of the human body* is not mentioned in the window. Choice (D) matches the prediction: the range of diameters is one of the *qualities of electrospun fibers* and the phrase *absent in other similar technological approaches* in the answer matches *is intrinsically difficult to obtain from other fiber-fabrication processes*. The correct answer is (D).

40. **B**   The question asks what the word *residual* means in line 30. Go back to the text, find the word *residual*, and underline it. Carefully read the surrounding text to determine another word that would fit in its place, based on the context of the passage. This paragraph describes the *electrospinning process*, and lines 27–31 say that *a fibrous jet is emitted from the cone and captured on a grounded collecting plate*, however, *any residual solvent in the ejected jet stream evaporates*. Since *residual* refers to the solvent that evaporates, as opposed to what is captured on the collecting plate, it must mean something like "left over." *Durable* means "long-lasting," which does not match "left over," so eliminate (A). *Remaining* matches "left over," so keep (B). Neither *steadfast* nor *inhabiting* matches "left over," so eliminate (C) and (D). The correct answer is (B).

41. **A**   The question asks what the author of Passage 1 suggests about *natural polymers*. Look for the lead words *natural polymers* to find the window in Passage 1. Lines 40–47 indicate that *natural polymers typically possess lower levels of toxicity, immunogenicity, and improved biocompatibility* compared with synthetic polymers, and therefore *natural polymers…perform more effectively than synthetic polymers do*

in the treatment of human disease. Eliminate answers that don't match this prediction. Choice (A) says that natural polymers are *more effective* than synthetic polymers, and that natural polymers *may be less harmful to people*, which matches *possess lower levels of toxicity*. Keep (A). Eliminate (B) because Passage 1 does not discuss blending natural polymers with synthetic polymers (that's discussed in Passage 2). Eliminate (C) because the passage does not state that the body is *unable to reject* natural polymers. Choice (D) is a Mostly Right, Slightly Wrong trap answer—while the passage states that *collagen and elastin* are effective *when blended together*, it does not say they are effective *only* when they are combined. Eliminate (D). The correct answer is (A).

42. **A** The question asks for a description of *the connection between natural and synthetic polymers* in Passage 2. Since this is a general question, it should be answered after the specific questions. Lines 67–71 state, *Although it has historically been the case that natural polymers were favored in the construction of electrospun fibers for drug delivery systems, there is a growing trend towards employing synthetic polymers.* The second paragraph discusses *the ability to blend the variety of synthetic polymers with…natural polymers* and says there has been a *huge spike of research* related to *polymer compositions*. Choice (A) matches both the increasing use of *synthetic polymers* over *natural polymers* and the growing *research that combines the two types of polymers*. Keep (A). Choice (B) is a Mostly Right, Slightly Wrong trap answer: lines 80–81 state that *synthetic polymers can be created in laboratories*, but the passage does not say that synthetic polymers are *easier to work with than natural polymers*. Eliminate (B). Eliminate (C) because it contradicts the passage—lines 90–92 say that *it is of the utmost importance to not limit scientific or medical pursuit by a purist approach*. Choice (D) is a Right Words, Wrong Meaning trap answer: lines 75–78 state that synthetic polymers *are more easily tailored to a wider range of properties*, including *hydrophobicity*, but the passage does not state that synthetic polymers are *more hydrophobic* than natural polymers. Eliminate (D). The correct answer is (A).

43. **D** The question asks for the purpose of the *second paragraph of Passage 2*. Read the second paragraph. The paragraph indicates that while synthetic polymers have *clear benefits* compared with natural polymers, the *ability to blend…synthetic polymers with…natural polymers* is what makes *electrospun scaffolds* a promising technology with *even more to discover*. Eliminate answers that don't match this prediction. Eliminate (A) because it does not include *the ability to blend* synthetic polymers with natural polymers. Choice (B) is a Right Words, Wrong Meaning trap answer: *the purist approach* is mentioned, but the paragraph opposes it, saying it is important not to *limit scientific or medical pursuit by a purist approach*. Eliminate (B). Choice (C) is also a Right Words, Wrong Meaning trap: the paragraph says that the *flexibility of polymer compositions* caused *a huge spike in research*, but (C) says that the scientists learned *how flexible polymers are* as a result of *a huge spike in research*. Eliminate (C). Choice (D) matches the prediction because it says that *both types of polymers…when combined* may be even *more effective*. The correct answer is (D).

44. **B** The question asks for an inference based on the information in Passage 2. Because there are no line references or lead words, do this question after the specific questions and use Process of Elimination. Choice (A) is a Right Words, Wrong Meaning trap answer: lines 67–71 state, *Although it has historically been the case that natural polymers were favored…there is a growing trend toward using synthetic polymers;*

it does not say that *history favors natural rather than synthetic designs*. Eliminate (A). Lines 80–84 state, *Because synthetic polymers can be created in laboratories...[they] can be engineered to address any particular clinical need*. These lines support the statement in (B) that it is *the man-made nature of synthetic polymers that accounts for their flexibility*, so keep (B). Choice (C) is a Right Words, Wrong Meaning trap answer: lines 77–80 mention both the *hydrophilicity* and *hydrophobicity* in relation to the *solubility* of a polymer, but the passage does not indicate that one has more effect on solubility than the other. Eliminate (C). Lines 71–74 state, *Synthetic polymers are used to enhance various characteristics of the drug delivery system goals* including *degradation time*. This does not mean that synthetic polymers *degrade more quickly* than natural polymers, so eliminate (D). The correct answer is (B).

45. **C**   The question asks for a statement that the *authors of both passages* would *agree with*. Consider one passage at a time. *Hydrophilicity* and *hydrophobicity* are not mentioned in Passage 1, so eliminate (A). Choice (B) is a Could Be True trap answer; while it may seem logical, there is no direct support for it in Passage 1, so eliminate (B). Choice (C) matches lines 3–5, which state, *The more site-specific a delivery system is, the more effective the drug it is delivering will be*. Keep (C). Choice (D) is a Mostly Right, Slightly Wrong trap answer: lines 57–59 state that combining natural polymers *can sometimes provide a greater benefit*, but (D) makes a stronger claim: *a blended polymer base will be more effective than a non-blended one*. Eliminate (D). Alternatively, (B) and (D) could be eliminated based on Passage 2. Choice (C) is supported by Passage 2: lines 92–96 suggest that *biomedical engineers* aim to *more precisely fine-tune the properties of electrospun scaffolds*. The correct answer is (C).

46. **B**   The question asks for a difference between the passages. Consider one passage at a time. Lines 56–64 discuss *the combination of natural polymers* such as *collagen and elastin*. Therefore, Passage 1 does *discuss the possibility of using multiple materials for base polymers*, so eliminate (A). Lines 12–36 describe the process by which *[e]lectrospinning creates biodegradable scaffolds*. Therefore, Passage 1 *provides information on electrospun scaffolding construction*; keep (B). Lines 8–9 mention treating both *infections and cancers*. Passage 1 is not concerned *only with drug delivery systems to address cancers*, so eliminate (C). Alternatively, (C) could be eliminated based on Passage 2. Lines 44–47 state that *natural polymers have a greater ability to perform more effectively than synthetic polymers do in the treatment of human disease*, contradicting the idea that *the type of polymer base used for electrospun scaffolds is unimportant*. Eliminate (D). Choice (B) is supported by Passage 2: lines 99–103 say that a *spike of research* about *electrospun scaffolds* is likely to *continue for some time*. Therefore, Passage 2 *looks to the future of electrospun scaffolding research*. The correct answer is (B).

47. **C**   The question asks for *a primary difference* between the tones of the passages *with respect to their arguments regarding natural versus synthetic polymer bases*. Consider one passage at a time. Eliminate (A) because the tone of Passage 1 is not *belligerent*, which means "combative." Eliminate (B) because *biased* and *subjective* do not convey a *difference*. Lines 44–47 state that *natural polymers have a greater ability to perform more effectively than synthetic polymers do in the treatment of human disease*. This statement is *unequivocal*, which means "leaving no doubt," so keep (C). Eliminate (D) because Passage 1 is not *pessimistic*; lines 63–66 express hope about *the potential...to engineer a drug delivery vehicle with optimal biodegradable properties*. Choice (C) is supported by Passage 2: in lines 88–92, the author strikes a *conciliatory* tone (meaning "intended to reconcile"). Although the author argues for the *clear benefits* of

synthetic polymers over *natural* ones, the author also urges against limiting *scientific or medical pursuit* by abandoning natural polymers completely. The correct answer is (C).

CHAPTER 7

Writing and Language Drill 1 (page 165)

1. Apostrophes; apostrophes and where they go

2. Verbs; verb tense and number

3. Words; transition words (direction)

4. Seem/Seems and their/its; verb number and pronoun number

5. Number of words; conciseness

CHAPTER 8

Writing and Language Drill 2 (page 183)

1. **B** Punctuation changes in the answer choices, so this question tests STOP, HALF-STOP, and GO punctuation. Use the Vertical Line Test and identify the ideas as complete or incomplete. Draw the vertical line between the words *immigrants* and *the*. The first part of the sentence, *There is no question that the United States is a country of immigrants*, is a complete idea. The second part, *the original countries of those immigrants varies so much that it can be tough to know who has contributed what*, is a complete idea. To connect two complete ideas, STOP or HALF-STOP punctuation is needed. Eliminate (A) and (C) because both commas and no punctuation are GO punctuation. Keep (B) because a comma + FANBOYS (*and*) is STOP punctuation. Eliminate (D) because STOP punctuation requires either a period by itself or a comma + FANBOYS, not a period + FANBOYS. The correct answer is (B).

2. **D** Apostrophes change in the answer choices, so the question tests apostrophe usage. When used with a noun, on the PSAT, an apostrophe indicates possession. In this sentence, there are two nouns with apostrophes: *time* and *reason*. Nothing belongs to either time or reason, so no apostrophes are needed. Eliminate (A) and (B) because both use apostrophes with *time* and *reason*. When used with a pronoun, an apostrophe indicates a contraction. In this sentence, the *different reasons* belong to the *different groups*, so the correct pronoun must show possession. Eliminate (C) because *they're* is a contraction of "they are," which is not necessary in this sentence. Choice (D) correctly uses the possessive pronoun *their*. The correct answer is (D).

3. **C**   Commas change in the answer choices, so this question tests the four ways to use a comma. The phrase *for instance* is unnecessary information, so it should have commas both before and after it. Choice (C) appropriately places commas both before and after the unnecessary phrase. Eliminate (B) because it lacks a comma after the phrase, and eliminate (D) because it lacks a comma before the phrase. There is no need for a comma after *those*, so eliminate (A). The correct answer is (C).

4. **D**   Punctuation changes in the answer choices, so this question tests STOP, HALF-STOP, and GO punctuation. Use the Vertical Line Test and identify the ideas as complete or incomplete. Draw the vertical line between the words *1989* and *in*. The first part of the sentence, *This may seem a bit late, given that most of the USSR and USSR-affiliated empires fell around 1990 (starting with East Germany and its Berlin Wall in 1989)*, is a complete idea. The second part, *in fact the largest migrations of Soviets and ex-Soviets happened just after the Union had fallen*, is a complete idea. To connect two complete ideas, STOP or HALF-STOP punctuation is needed. Eliminate (A) and (B) because both no punctuation and commas are GO punctuation. To choose between (C) and (D), look to the underlined pronoun, *it's*. When used with a pronoun, an apostrophe indicates a contraction. In this sentence, the *Berlin Wall* belongs to *East Germany*, so the pronoun must indicate possession. Eliminate (C), because *it's* means "it is," which is not necessary in this sentence. Choice (D) correctly uses the possessive pronoun *its*. The correct answer is (D).

5. **B**   Commas change in the answer choices, so this question tests the four ways to use a comma. The sentence contains a list of three things: 1) *poverty*, 2) *depression*, and 3) *deprivation*. There should be a comma after each item in the list before the word *and*. Eliminate (A) because it does not have a comma after *depression*. Keep (B) because it has a comma after each item in the list. Eliminate (C) because there should not be a comma after the word *and*. Eliminate (D) because there is no reason to use a comma after the list of three things. The correct answer is (B).

6. **A**   Punctuation changes in the answer choices, so this question tests STOP, HALF-STOP, and GO punctuation. Use the Vertical Line Test and identify the ideas as complete or incomplete. Draw the vertical line between the words *1970s* and *the*. The first part of the sentence, *As a result, while there had been a somewhat steady flow of immigration from the USSR since the 1970s*, is an incomplete idea. The second part, *the largest numbers came to the United States in the early 1990s*, is a complete idea. To connect an incomplete idea to a complete idea, GO punctuation is needed. Eliminate (C) because a long dash is HALF-STOP punctuation. Eliminate (D) because a period is STOP punctuation. To choose between (A) and (B), consider the four ways to use a comma. The sentence makes sense without the phrase *while there had been a somewhat steady flow of immigration from the USSR since the 1970s*, so treat this like unnecessary information, which should have commas both before and after it. Eliminate (B) because it lacks a comma after the phrase. The correct answer is (A).

7. **C**   Commas change in the answer choices, so this question tests the four ways to use a comma. The phrase *of Google* is necessary information, so it should not be surrounded by commas. However, *Sergey Brin* is unnecessary information in this sentence, so it should have commas both before and after it. Therefore, the correct answer must have no comma before *of Google*, but commas before and after *Sergey Brin*. Eliminate (A) and (D) because they use a comma before *of Google*. Eliminate (B) because the first phrase of the sentence,

The co-founder of Google, is an incomplete idea and cannot end with STOP punctuation. Choice (C) appropriately places commas both before and after the unnecessary phrase. The correct answer is (C).

8. **C** Punctuation changes in the answer choices, so this question tests STOP, HALF-STOP, and GO punctuation. Use the Vertical Line Test and identify the ideas as complete or incomplete. However, first determine whether the word *today* is necessary, since it occurs in three of the choices. The last sentence of the paragraph discusses how a specific group of people *continue to shape the American experience.* The word *today* indicates that the actions of this group are happening in the present day, which makes the final idea more precise. Eliminate (A), which does not include the word *today.* Now draw the vertical line between the words *parents* and *today.* The first part of the sentence, *Singer-songwriter Regina Spektor moved at the age of 9 in 1989, the same year that historian Artemy Kalinovsky arrived with his parents,* is a complete idea. The second part, *today, these and other children of the Soviet Union continue to shape the American experience in all kinds of positive and enlightening ways,* is a complete idea. To connect two complete ideas, STOP or HALF-STOP punctuation is needed. Eliminate (B) and (D) because both commas and no punctuation are GO punctuation. The correct answer is (C).

9. **D** Commas change in the answer choices, so this question tests the four ways to use a comma. Commas change in multiple places, so start from the beginning of the underlined portion. There should not be a comma after *writer,* since *named David Bezmozgis* is necessary to make the phrase *a writer* more precise; eliminate (A) and (B). There is no need for a comma between *named* and *David Bezmozgis,* so eliminate (C). The correct answer is (D).

10. **C** Punctuation changes in the answer choices, so this question tests STOP, HALF-STOP, and GO punctuation. Use the Vertical Line Test and identify the ideas as complete or incomplete. Draw the vertical line between the words *mean* and *Bezmozgis.* The first part of the sentence, *While we have become comfortable believing that the Soviets came to North America looking for freedom, whatever that term may mean,* is an incomplete idea. The second part, *Bezmozgis shows that this was not always the case and that "freedom" could remain an elusive dream even for those who made the trip successfully,* is a complete idea. To connect an incomplete idea to a complete idea, GO punctuation is needed. Eliminate (A) and (D) because both periods and semicolons are STOP punctuation. Eliminate (B) because a colon is HALF-STOP punctuation. Keep (C) because a comma is GO punctuation, and (C) appropriately places commas both before and after the unnecessary phrase *whatever that term may mean.* The correct answer is (C).

11. **D** Punctuation changes in the answer choices, so this question tests STOP, HALF-STOP, and GO punctuation. Use the Vertical Line Test and identify the ideas as complete or incomplete. Draw the vertical line between the words *novel* and *The.* The first part of the sentence, *His first novel The Free World,* is an incomplete idea. The second part, *was published in 2011 to great critical acclaim,* is also an incomplete idea. To connect two incomplete ideas, GO punctuation is needed. Eliminate (B) and (C) because both colons and long dashes are HALF-STOP punctuation. Compare (A) and (D), since both no punctuation and commas are GO punctuation. The phrase *The Free World* is unnecessary information, so it should have commas both before and after it. Eliminate (A) because it lacks a comma before the phrase. Choice (D) appropriately places commas both before and after the unnecessary phrase. The correct answer is (D).

CHAPTER 9

Writing and Language Drill 3 (page 198)

1. **D**   The length of the phrase after *called the* changes in the answer choices, so this question tests precision and concision. The words *greatest* and *best* mean the same thing in this context, so it is redundant to use both; eliminate (A) and (B). Eliminate (C) because *greatly* means "considerably," which doesn't make sense when paired with *best*. Choice (D) is concise and makes the meaning of the sentence precise. The correct answer is (D).

2. **B**   Verbs change in the answer choices, so this question tests consistency of verbs. A verb must be consistent in number with its subject. Locate the subject of the verb: the *array*. Notice that *of lectures that would become Pragmatism* is a phrase describing the *array*, so the subject cannot be found in that describing phrase. Furthermore, the sentence contains another verb, *adds*, that is singular. This can be tested by substituting the pronouns "it" and "they." The correct phrase is "it adds," not "they adds," so *adds* is singular because it goes with "it." Because *array* and *adds* are singular, the verb must also be singular to be consistent. Eliminate (A), (C), and (D) because they are all plural. Only (B), *encompasses*, is singular. The correct answer is (B).

3. **B**   Pronouns and nouns change in the answer choices, so this question tests precision. A pronoun can only be used if it is clear what the pronoun refers to. The pronoun *His* could refer to *William James* or to *Charles Peirce*, so the pronoun is not precise; eliminate (A). Eliminate (C) because the paragraph only discusses the work of *William James*, one person, so a plural pronoun is incorrect. The word before *work in psychology* needs to show whose *work* it was, and the word *some* does not indicate a particular person, so eliminate (D). Choice (B) is the most precise choice because it provides a specific noun (*James*). The correct answer is (B).

4. **C**   Verbs change in the answer choices, so this question tests consistency of verbs. A verb must be consistent with its subject and with the other verbs in the sentence. The subject of the verb is *pragmatism*, which is singular. To be consistent, the underlined verb must also be singular. The other verb in the sentence is *turns*, which is in the present tense. To be consistent, the underlined verb must also be in the present tense. Eliminate (A) and (B) because they are not in the present tense. Eliminate (D) because the phrase *could be said to* is not concise. The correct answer is (C).

5. **C**   Note the question! The question asks where the underlined portion should be placed, so it tests consistency of ideas. The underlined portion must be consistent with the ideas that come both before and after it. The beginning of the sentence currently says *Pragmatism is concerned* and then is followed by a comma, indicating that the next phrase is a separate idea. This doesn't make sense because an idea (*pragmatism*) can't be concerned. The word *with* needs to follow *concerned*, because the phrase *concerned with* means "focused on," and an idea can be focused on something. Thus, the phrase must follow *concerned* in order for the sentence to provide a precise meaning. The correct answer is (C).

6. **A** Verbs change in the answer choices, so this question tests consistency of verbs. A verb must be consistent with its subject and with the other verbs in the sentence. The other verb in the sentence is *want*, which is in the present tense. Eliminate (B) and (D) because they are not in the present tense. Eliminate (C) because *awakens* indicates *fear* waking up at night, which doesn't make sense. The correct answer is (A).

7. **C** Nouns and pronouns change in the answer choices, so this question tests precision. The underlined word or phrase must refer to something owned by the reader, as the underlined portion follows the phrase *you've got*. Therefore, it must be a noun or pronoun. Eliminate (D) because *approaching* is a verb. Choices (A), (B), and (C) all contain nouns or pronouns that could work in context. Choices (A) and (B) provide pronouns. These pronouns do not make it clear what *you've got*, so eliminate (A) and (B). Choice (C) provides a noun to indicate what *you've got*, so it is precise. The correct answer is (C).

8. **C** The length of the phrase after *rather than* changes in the answer choices. There is a comparison in the sentence, so this question tests consistency. When two things are compared, they should be consistent with each other. The first item in the comparison is *in their practice and their consequences*. Eliminate (A), (B), and (D) because they do not match the structure of *in their* followed by a noun. Keep (C) because it appropriately compares *abstraction* to *practice* using the same phrase structure. The correct answer is (C).

9. **B** Note the question! The question asks whether a phrase should be deleted, so it tests consistency. If the content of the phrase is not consistent with the ideas surrounding it, then it should be deleted. The paragraph discusses James's approach to one of *life's big questions*. It ends by saying that the answer to the question doesn't matter, *because the distinction won't create practical differences*. The underlined portion describes the question as *fundamentally irrelevant*, meaning that it does not matter to James. This matches the idea that the answer to one of *life's big questions* doesn't matter to James, so it is consistent with ideas in the text; the phrase should not be deleted. Eliminate (C) and (D). Eliminate (A) because the underlined portion does not describe *James's sense of humor*. Keep (B) because it accurately states that the underlined portion *sets up the subject of the remainder of the paragraph*. The correct answer is (B).

10. **D** Vocabulary changes in the answer choices, so this question tests precision of word choice. Look for a word with a definition that is consistent with the other ideas in the sentence. The sentence says that people have to live *responsibly*, regardless of *whether our lives are "fated or free,"* so the correct answer should mean something like "doesn't matter." The phrase *doesn't differ* means "isn't different," which does not match "doesn't matter." Eliminate (A). Choice (B) could have two possible meanings—*doesn't concern us* could mean either "doesn't relate to us" or "doesn't worry us." Neither matches with "doesn't matter," so eliminate (B). The phrase *doesn't count* means "is not legitimate," which does not mean the same thing as "doesn't matter," so eliminate (C). The phrase *doesn't make a significant difference* does match with "doesn't matter," so keep (D). The correct answer is (D).

11. **C** Verbs change in the answer choices. The underlined portion is part of a list in the sentence, so this question tests consistency. All items in a list must be phrased the same way to be consistent with one another. The first two items in the lists are verb phrases—*see through the problem* and *establish a plan*—so the third item must also be a verb phrase that is consistent in form and tense. Eliminate (A) because the verb *forgot* is in the past tense instead of the present tense. Eliminate (B) because each item in the list ends with a noun, not a pronoun. Each noun in the list is singular, so the underlined noun must also be singular; eliminate (D) because *issues* is plural. The correct answer is (C).

CHAPTER 10

Writing and Language Drill 4 (page 213)

1. **A** Note the question! The question asks which choice *would best introduce the essay,* so it tests consistency of ideas. Look for an answer choice that is consistent with the purpose stated in the question. The paragraph states that *Americans spent anywhere from three to five hours a day in front of the tube.* Look for an answer choice that is consistent with the discussion of American television-watching habits and identifies *a way that a historical period understood a particular medium.* Eliminate (C) because it does not discuss television. Keep (A) because it states that people in the *1980s and 1990s* (a historical period) expressed *concern that Americans watched too much television* (a medium). Eliminate (B) because a *historical period* is a defined length of time that happened in the past, not *today.* Eliminate (D) because it does not describe how anyone *understood* the *medium* of television in the past. The correct answer is (A).

2. **A** Note the question! The question asks whether a phrase should be deleted, so it tests consistency. If the content of the phrase is not consistent with the ideas surrounding it, then it should be deleted. Determine the function of the phrase in the sentence. The sentence states that *Americans spent* multiple *hours a day in front of the tube.* The phrase *in front of the tube* explains what *Americans spent* multiple *hours a day* doing, so it is necessary to the meaning of the sentence and should be kept. Eliminate (C) and (D). Keep (A) because it accurately states that *the sentence is unclear without the phrase.* Eliminate (B) because the phrase does not state *what the viewers of television find so compelling.* The correct answer is (A).

3. **B** Note the question! The question asks which choice *would offer the most effective introduction to the paragraph,* so it tests consistency of ideas. Determine the subject of the paragraph and find the answer that is consistent with that idea. This paragraph gives examples of different groups that were unhappy about the increase in television-viewing. Eliminate (A) because the current quality of TV is not relevant to the idea of unhappiness. Keep (B) because the *concerns about the increase* are consistent with information in the paragraph. Eliminate (C) because *the first televised presidential debate* is not relevant to the negativity described in the paragraph. Eliminate (D) because improvements in *the technology of new TVs* are not relevant to the subject of this paragraph. The correct answer is (B).

4. **D** Note the question! The question asks whether a sentence should be added, so it tests consistency. If the content of the new sentence is consistent with the ideas surrounding it, then it should be added. The paragraph discusses historical arguments that were made to protest *too much time in front of the television.* The new sentence gives a statistic about how many *American adults are overweight or obese,* so it is not consistent with the ideas in the text. Therefore, the new sentence is not consistent with the ideas in the text and should not be added. Eliminate (A) and (B). Eliminate (C) because whether *the mention of these statistics is cruel* is not relevant to the paragraph. Keep (D) because it accurately states that the *essay as a whole is focused on a different subject.* The correct answer is (D).

5. **B** Note the question! The question asks for the *most effective introduction*, so start by reading the entire paragraph to identify its main idea. The paragraph lists several forms of media (movies, the radio, the printing press, and newspapers) and the *criticisms* people had for them when they were introduced. To be consistent, the answer must introduce this idea. Eliminate (A) because it discusses a specific harm of *television* instead of introducing the idea of historical criticisms to new forms of media. Keep (B) because the phrase *long path of conservative skepticism at new media developments* introduces the idea that people were *skeptical* or critical of *new* forms of media throughout history. Eliminate (C) because it directly contradicts the main idea of the paragraph. Eliminate (D) because it discusses criticisms *today* instead of those throughout history. The correct answer is (B).

6. **C** Note the question! The question asks for the *most effective* way to combine the sentences, so it is testing concision and precision. Start with the shortest option, (C). Choice (C) makes the meaning of the sentence clear and is concise, so keep it. Eliminate (A) and (B) because they unnecessarily repeat the word *report*. Eliminate (D) because it is overly wordy compared to (C). The correct answer is (C).

7. **D** Note the question! The question asks for the choice that is *most consistent with the style and tone of the passage*, so it's testing consistency. Choices (A) and (B) are overly casual—the passage has a formal, academic tone, and neither "getting" nor "digging" an idea is consistent with that tone. Eliminate (A) and (B). Choice (C) is also overly casual through the use of the phrase *a lot of*, so eliminate (C). Choice (D) is appropriate for the tone of the passage. The correct answer is (D).

8. **C** Note the question! The question asks whether the word *spend* should be replaced with the words *pay out*, so it tests consistency. If *pay out* is more consistent with the sentence and surrounding paragraph than *spend*, then the change should be made. Since both choices are verbs, look to other verbs in the paragraph for consistency. The phrase is *spend more time* in the original sentence. Since it is discussing how people use time, the word *spend* is appropriate. The phrase *pay out more time* does not work because it suggests money, which is not the intended meaning of the sentence. Eliminate (A) and (B). Keep (C) because it accurately states that the meaning given by *pay out* is *inconsistent with the passage*. Eliminate (D) because *socioeconomic status* is not relevant to the paragraph. The correct answer is (C).

9. **A** Note the question! The question asks which choice *gives information consistent with the graph*, so it tests consistency. Read the labels on the graph carefully, and look for an answer that is consistent with the information given in the graph. The graph shows that *American consumers in 2013* spent 5.15 hours a day *on the Internet*, which supports (A). Choice (B) is not consistent with the figure, since the graph only shows American consumers, not *the world's consumers* so eliminate (B). Choice (C) is not consistent with the figure since American consumers did not have *an average of as few as 2 hours a day on the Internet* for any year shown. Choice (D) is not consistent with the figure since the graph does not indicate whether people were watching *shows* on the Internet or not. The correct answer is (A).

10. **D** Note the question! The question asks for the statement that would *support the idea given in the previous sentence*, so it tests consistency. Eliminate answers that are inconsistent with the purpose stated in the question. The previous sentence says that *history would say that* [the change] is not *troubling*. The change refers to an *increase in Internet usage*. Therefore, the correct answer must support the idea that increased

Internet time may not be a bad thing, according to history. Eliminate (A) because *the rate of literacy* is too specific—time spent reading is only one idea mentioned as a potential harm of new technology. Eliminate (B) because the *odd imbalance* does not support the idea that the change is not troubling. Eliminate (C) because the example is too specific for the content of this paragraph. Keep (D) because *The printing press, the newspapers, the radio, and even the television* are all examples of things that, like the Internet, were subject to criticism but proved to be eventually *integrated effectively into American culture*. The correct answer is (D).

11.   **C**   Note the question! The question asks for a choice that is *a future-oriented statement that reinforces the main idea of the passage*, so it's testing consistency. First consider the main idea of the passage. The author discusses early criticisms of television, then explains that other forms of media faced similar criticisms when they were introduced, and then states that the Internet should not be quickly criticized. Finally, the author notes that people spend *tremendous* amounts of time on the Internet and states that *There must at least be some kind of change* that this Internet usage is causing. Check the answers to see whether they are *future-oriented* and *reinforce the main idea of the passage*. Choice (A) has some relationship to the passage's *main idea*, but it is focused on the present, not the *future*, so eliminate (A). Choice (B) mentions the future, but the idea of *physical changes* to the human body isn't related to the passage's *main idea*, so eliminate (B). Keep (C) because it describes what people *will need* to do in the future, and it references the main idea by drawing a contrast between *simply reacting negatively to a new form of media* and weighing its *risks and benefits*. Eliminate (D) because it doesn't mention anything related to the *future*, and it lacks a strong relationship to the passage's *main idea*. The correct answer is (C).

CHAPTER 11

Drill 1 (page 223)

1.   **c**   Examples: –7, 0, 1, 8

2.   **d**   Examples: .5, 2, 118

3.   **g**   Examples: –.5, –2, –118

4.   **f**   Examples: –4, 0, 10

5.   **b**   Examples: –5, 1, 17

6.   **a**   Examples: *Factors* of 12 are 1, 2, 3, 4, 6, and 12. Factors of 10 are 1, 2, 5, and 10.

7.   **i**   Examples: *Multiples* of 12 include –24, –12, 0, 12, 24, and so on. Multiples of 10 include –20, –10, 0, 10, 20, 30, and so on.

8. **h** Examples: 2, 3, 5, 7, 11, and so on. There are no negative *prime numbers*, and 1 is not prime.

9. **e** Examples: 3 and 4 are *distinct* numbers. –2 and 2 are also distinct.

10. **j** Examples: In the number 274, 2 is the *digit* in the hundreds place, 7 is the digit in the tens place, and 4 is the digit in the ones place.

11. **p** Examples: –1, 0, 1, and 2 are *consecutive* numbers. Be careful—sometimes you will be asked for *consecutive even* or *consecutive odd* numbers, in which case you would use just the odds or evens in a consecutive list of numbers.

12. **n** Examples: 6 is *divisible* by 2 and 3, but not by 4 or 5.

13. **l** Examples: When you divide 26 by 8, you get 3 with a *remainder* of 2 (2 is left over). When you divide 14 by 5, you get 2 with a remainder of 4 (4 is left over).

14. **k** Examples: When you add 2 and 3, you get a *sum* of 5. When you add –4 and 1, you get a sum of –3.

15. **r** Examples: When you multiply 2 and 3, you get a *product* of 6. When you multiply –4 and 1, you get a product of –4.

16. **m** Examples: When you subtract 2 from 3, you get a *difference* of 1. When you subtract –4 from 1, you get a difference of 5.

17. **q** Examples: When you divide 2 by 3, you get a quotient of $\frac{2}{3}$. When you divide –4 by 1, you get a quotient of –4.

18. **o** Examples: The absolute value of –3 is 3. The absolute value of 41 is 41.

Drill 2 (page 227)

a. 3^5
b. 3^1
c. 3^6
d. x^8
e. x^4
f. x^{12}
g. $2\sqrt{2}$
h. -4
i. $7\sqrt{3}$
j. $y\sqrt{y}$
k. $-y$
l. $6x\sqrt{y}$

3. **A** The question asks for the value of a variable in an equation involving exponents. When given equivalent exponent terms with different bases, rewrite the exponent terms using the same base. Rewrite 3^4 as $3 \times 3 \times 3 \times 3 = 9 \times 9$. Therefore, $3^4 = 9^2$ and $x = 2$. An alternative solution is to calculate $3^4 = 81$. If $3^4 = 9^x$, then $81 = 9^x$, and $x = 2$. The correct answer is (A).

6. **C** The question asks for the value of a variable. Solve for m. To begin to isolate m, square both sides of the equation to get $m^2 + 39 = 64$. Subtract 39 from both sides of the equation to get $m^2 = 25$. Take the square root of both sides to get $m = 5$. Therefore, one possible value for m is 5. The correct answer is (C).

5. **B** The question asks for the value of a variable in an equation involving exponents. When dealing with questions about exponents, remember the MADSPM rules. The PM part of the acronym indicates that raising a base with an exponent to another Power means to Multiply the exponents. By the MADSPM rules, $(3^x)^3 = 3^{3x}$. If $3^{3x} = 3^{15}$, then $3x = 15$. Divide both sides by 3 to get $x = 5$. The correct answer is (B).

8. **D** The question asks for the value of an expression based on two equations involving exponents. When dealing with questions about exponents, remember the MADSPM rules. Take the two equations separately. The MA part of the MADSPM acronym indicates that Multiplying matching bases means to Add the exponents. If $x^y \times x^6 = x^{54}$, then $x^{y+6} = x^{54}$. Therefore, $y + 6 = 54$. Subtract 6 from both sides to get $y = 48$. The PM part of the MADSPM acronym indicates that raising a base with an exponent to another Power means to Multiply the exponents. If $(x^3)^z = x^9$, then $x^{3z} = x^9$. Therefore, $3z = 9$. Divide both sides by 3 to get $z = 3$. Now you know that $y = 48$ and $z = 3$, so $y + z = 51$. The correct answer is (D).

7. **D** The question asks for a possible value of a variable. Solve for s. To begin to isolate s, add 3 to both sides to get $\sqrt{s} = 12$. Square both sides of the equation to get $s = 144$. The correct answer is (D).

8. **D** The question asks for an equivalent form of an expression. When dealing with a question about negative and fractional exponents, remember the exponent rules. Since x^6 doesn't change form, eliminate (C). A negative exponent means to take the reciprocal of what would be the result if the negative weren't there. Therefore, y^{-3} can be rewritten as $\frac{1}{y^3}$, so eliminate (A). In a fractional exponent, the numerator is the power the base is raised to and the denominator is the root of the base. Therefore, $z^{\frac{1}{2}}$ can be rewritten as $\sqrt{z}$, so eliminate (B). The correct answer is (D).

9. **A** The question asks for an equivalent form of an expression. Notice the fractional exponents in the answer choices; when dealing with a question about fractional exponents, remember the exponent rules. Start with applying the root to the coefficient 81. Use your calculator to find $\sqrt[4]{81} = 3$. Eliminate (C) and (D) because these answer choices include the wrong coefficient. Next, apply the root to the b^3 term. In a fractional exponent, the numerator is the power the base is raised to and the denominator is the root of the base. Therefore, $\sqrt[4]{b^3} = b^{\frac{3}{4}}$. Eliminate (B) because this answer choice includes b^3 instead. Similarly, $\sqrt[4]{c} = c^{\frac{1}{4}}$, and (B) can be eliminated because it includes c instead. The correct answer is (A).

12. **A** The question asks for the value of a constant and refers to two functions that are equal to each other. Solve for B. Since the question states that the two functions are equivalent, set them equal to one another. Since $k^{0.3x} = k^{\frac{Bx}{9}}$, $0.3x = \frac{Bx}{9}$. To begin to isolate B, multiply both sides by 9 to get $2.7x = Bx$. Divide both sides by x to get $2.7 = B$. The correct answer is (A).

10. **B** The question asks for the value of a variable in an equation involving a fractional exponent. When dealing with a question about fractional exponents, remember the exponent rules: in a fractional exponent, the numerator is the power the base is raised to and the denominator is the root of the base. Therefore, $x^{\frac{5}{2}}$ can be written as $\sqrt[2]{x^5}$, so $\sqrt[2]{x^5} = 8x$. Solve for x. To begin to isolate x, square both sides of the equation to get $x^5 = 64x^2$. Divide by x^2 on each side. Remember the MADSPM rules: the DS part of the MADSPM acronym indicates that Dividing matching bases means to Subtract the exponents. So, $\frac{x^5}{x^2} = x^3$, and $x^3 = 64$. Take the cube root of both sides to get $x = 4$. The correct answer is (B).

11. **B** The question asks for an equivalent form of an expression. When dealing with a question about fractional exponents, remember the exponent rules. In a fractional exponent, the numerator is the power the base is raised to and the denominator is the root of the base. Start with applying the fractional exponent to the coefficient of 3. Therefore, $3^{\frac{2}{3}} = \sqrt[3]{3^2}$, or $\sqrt[3]{9}$. Eliminate (A), (C), and (D) because they do not include the correct coefficient. Simplifying the m and n terms confirms this. Remember the MADSPM rules: the MA part of the MADSPM acronym indicates that Multiplying matching bases means to Add the exponents. Therefore, $(m^2)^{\frac{2}{3}} = m^{\frac{4}{3}}$. Similarly, $(n^{-3})^{\frac{2}{3}} = n^{-2}$. The correct answer is (B).

16. **D** The question asks for the value of a variable in an equation that includes fractional exponents. Simplify this equation one piece at a time and solve for b. Start with the left side. Take the cube root of 64 and rewrite: $b\sqrt[3]{64a^{\frac{b}{2}}} = 4b\sqrt[3]{a^{\frac{b}{2}}}$. Taking the cube root is the same as raising an expression to the $\frac{1}{3}$ power, so continue simplifying the left side: $4b\sqrt[3]{a^{\frac{b}{2}}} = 4b(a^{\frac{b}{2}})^{\frac{1}{3}}$. Use the MADSPM rules to multiply the exponents: $4b(a^{\frac{b}{2}})^{\frac{1}{3}} = 4b\left(a^{\frac{b}{6}}\right)$. Now that the left side is simplified, start simplifying the right side. Be careful as you square each term in the parentheses: $\left(4\sqrt{3}\,a\right)^2 = 4^2 \times \left(\sqrt{3}\right)^2 \times a^2$. Continue simplifying the right side of the equation to get $16 \times 3 \times a^2 = 48a^2$. At this point, $4b\left(a^{\frac{b}{6}}\right) = 48a^2$. When dealing with exponents, equal terms that have the same bases also have equal exponents, so set the terms with base a equal to each other to solve for the value of b: $a^{\frac{b}{6}} = a^2$. Solve for b by setting the exponents equal to each other: $\frac{b}{6} = 2$. Multiply both sides by 6 to get $b = 12$. An alternative final step is to set 48 equal to $4b$ and get $b = 12$. The correct answer is (D).

23. **A** The question asks for an expression rewritten in another form. When dealing with questions about exponents, remember the MADSPM rules. The MA part of the MADSPM acronym indicates that Multiplying matching bases means to Add the exponents. Therefore, $16^{y+\frac{1}{2}} = 16^y \times 16^{\frac{1}{2}}$ and the fraction is equivalent to $\dfrac{9 \times 8^y}{5 \times 16^y \times 16^{\frac{1}{2}}}$. Taking a number to the $\dfrac{1}{2}$ power is the same as taking the square root of the number. Therefore, $\dfrac{9 \times 8^y}{5 \times 16^y \times 16^{\frac{1}{2}}} = \dfrac{9 \times 8^y}{5 \times 16^y \times 4}$. In order to cancel the terms with y exponents, a common base is needed. Rewrite 16^y as $(2 \times 8)^y$ or $2^y 8^y$. Reduce the fraction to get $\dfrac{9}{5 \times 2^y \times 4}$. Simplify the denominator to get $\dfrac{9}{20 \times 2^y}$. Separate the fraction to get $\dfrac{9}{20 \times 2^y} = \dfrac{9}{20} \times \dfrac{1}{2^y}$. Only (A) includes the correct fractions. The correct answer is (A).

Drill 3 (page 242)

3. **C** The question asks for a certain number that works for the given information. Translate the English into math in order to write an equation. In math terms, "is" means equals, "more" is addition, and "times" is multiplication. The equation becomes $x = 3 + 7x$. Solve the equation for x. Subtract $7x$ from both sides to get $-6x = 3$. Divide both sides by -6 to get $x = \dfrac{3}{-6}$. Reduce to get $-\dfrac{1}{2}$. The correct answer is (C).

2. **B** The question asks for an equivalent equation for y. To find the equivalent equation, isolate y on one side of the equation. Start by cross-multiplying to get $7y = (x + 3)(x + 4)$. Use FOIL on the right side to get $7y = x^2 + 7x + 12$. Divide both sides by 7 to get $y = \dfrac{x^2 + 7x + 12}{7}$. The correct answer is (B).

5. **D** The question asks for an inequality that represents all values of r. Translate the question in Bite-Sized Pieces, and use Process of Elimination. The total number of recipes Ann will include in her book is the sum of 32 main dish recipes, 18 dessert recipes, and r additional recipes. The book will include up to 98 recipes, meaning the greatest possible number of recipes in the book is 98. This information can be written as the inequality $32 + 18 + r \le 98$. Subtract 32 and 18 from both sides to get $r \le 48$. Isolate r in the answer choices to find the one that matches $r \le 48$. For (A), add 50 to both sides to get $r \ge 148$. Eliminate (A). For (B), add 50 to both sides to get $r \le 148$. Eliminate (B). For (C), add r to both sides to get $98 - (32 + 18) \le r$, which becomes $48 \le r$. Eliminate (C). For (D), add r to both sides to get $98 - (32 + 18) \ge r$, which becomes $48 \ge r$. The correct answer is (D).

4. **C** The question asks for what is equivalent to bc. To solve, isolate bc on one side of the equation. Start by cross-multiplying to get $18ad = 20bc$. Divide both sides by 20 to get $bc = \dfrac{18ad}{20}$. Reduce the fraction to get $\dfrac{9ad}{10}$. The correct answer is (C).

28. **6** The question asks how many miles Debbie walks in one day. Translate the English into math, and solve to find Debbie's average daily miles. Her average daily miles (m) equal one-hundredth of the square of the number of hours in one day (24). In equation form, $m = \frac{1}{100}(24^2) = \frac{24^2}{100}$. Solve for m to find $m = 5.76$. Round to the nearest mile to get 6 miles. The correct answer is 6.

7. **A** The question asks for a true statement about the equation. Solve the equation to find the true statement. Since the denominator of both equations is $p - 2$, set both numerators equal to each other to get $2(p - 2) + 2(3 - p) = 2(3p - 6) + 3(6 - 2p)$. Distribute the numbers in front of the parentheses to get $2p - 4 + 6 - 2p = 6p - 12 + 18 - 6p$. Combine like terms to get $2 = 6$. Since this statement is false and the variables were eliminated, the equation has no solutions. The correct answer is (A).

8. **C** The question asks for a system of equations that can be solved to find the number of skis and the number of snowboards rented over the three-day weekend. Use Bite-Sized Pieces and translate the given information into equations. Start with the number of skis and snowboards. The number of skis and snowboards rented on Friday was 40, on Saturday was 55, and on Sunday was 85. The total number of skis and snowboards rented for the weekend is 180. In equation form, $s + b = 180$. Eliminate (A) and (D), which both contain the incorrect equation for the number of skis and snowboards rented. Next write an equation for the amount of money collected in rental fees. Skis are rented for $30 and snowboards are rented for $20. The rental fees collected were $1,100 on Friday, $1,400 on Saturday, and $2,100 on Sunday. The total amount of fees collected was $4,600. In equation form $30s + 20b = 4,600$. Eliminate (B), which contains the incorrect equation for rental fees collected. The correct answer is (C).

12. **B** The question asks for the value of m. Isolate m on one side of the equation. To start, multiply the whole equation by 21 to eliminate the fractions. $21\left(\frac{m+9}{3} + 2\right) - 21\left(\frac{m-2}{7} + 3\right)$ becomes $7(m + 9) + 42 - 3(m - 2) + 63$. Distribute to get $7m + 63 + 42 = 3m - 6 + 63$. Combine like terms to get $7m + 105 = 3m + 57$. Subtract $3m$ and 105 from both sides to get $4m = -48$. Divide both sides by 4 to get $m = -12$. The correct answer is (B).

9. **B** The question asks for the value of h. Isolate h on one side of the equation. Start by distributing the numbers in front of the parentheses to get $-4h - 20 = -6 + 3h + 14$. Combine like terms on the right side to get $-4h - 20 = 3h + 8$. Add $4h$ to both sides to get $-20 = 7h + 8$. Subtract 8 from both sides to get $-28 = 7h$. Divide both sides by 7 to get $h = -4$. The correct answer is (B).

23. **C** The question asks which equation represents a sale the students could make during the fundraiser. Translate the English into math to create a system of equations, and then solve the equations to find the prices for snickerdoodle and cinnamon cookies. The first sale described can be written as $2s + 7c = 14.00$. The second sale described can be written as $8s + 3c = 17.50$. Multiply the first equation by -4 to get $-8s - 28c = -56.00$, stack the equations, and add.

$$
\begin{array}{r}
-8s - 28c = -56.00 \\
\underline{+8s + 3c = 17.50} \\
-25c = -38.50
\end{array}
$$

Divide both sides by –25 to get $c = 1.54$. Plug in the value for c into the original first equation to get $2s + 7(1.54) = 14.00$. Subtract $7(1.54)$ from both sides, and divide by 2 to get $s = 1.61$. Plug the values for s and c into the answer choices to find an equation that works. $2(1.61) + 3(1.54)$ does not equal 8, so eliminate (A). $4(1.61) + 6(1.54)$ does not equal 16.25, so eliminate (B). $6(1.61) + 5(1.54)$ does equal 17.36. The correct answer is (C).

13.   **A**   The question asks for the value of a. Since the equation has infinitely many solutions for x, any value of x can be used to find the value of a. Plug in an easy number for x. If $x = 1$, the equation becomes $10(3(1) + a) - a(4(1) + 2) = 2a(1 + 4)$. Distribute the numbers before the parentheses to get $30 + 10a - 4a - 2a = 2a + 8a$. Combine like terms to get $30 + 4a = 10a$. Subtract $4a$ from both sides to get $30 = 6a$. Divide both sides by 6 to get $a = 5$. The correct answer is (A).

25.   **A**   The question asks for the cost of ten eggs. Translate the English into math to create a system of equations, and then solve the equations to find the price of eggs. The first purchase can be written as $5e + 4f = 5.50$. The second purchase can be written as $9e + 8f = 10.50$. Multiply the first equation by –2 to get $-10e - 8f = -11.00$, stack the equations, and add.

$$-10e + 8f = -11.00$$
$$\underline{9e + 8f = 10.50}$$
$$-e = -0.50$$

Therefore, $e = 0.50$. Multiply 0.50 by 10 to find the price of 10 eggs, which is $5.00. The correct answer is (A).

Drill 4 (page 252)

a.   6
b.   6
c.   –1
d.   –1
e.   1
f. $6\sqrt{2}$
g.   (0, 1)

2.   **B**   The question asks for the value of a constant in one of the two given equations. The slope-intercept form of the equation of a line is $y = mx + b$, where m is the slope and b is the y-intercept. So, the slope of the line given by the first equation is 6. The question states that the two equations are of perpendicular lines. To find the slope of a perpendicular lines, which have slopes that are negative reciprocals of each other. The equation of the second line is also in slope-intercept form, so c is the slope. Take the negative reciprocal of 6 to find that $c = -\dfrac{1}{6}$. The correct answer is (B).

6.   **B**   The question asks for the equation of a line that is parallel to a line shown in a graph. Parallel lines have equal slopes. Therefore, because the line in the graph has a negative slope, the correct answer will also have a negative slope. Eliminate (C) and (D) right away because they have positive slopes. Now find

the exact slope of the line shown, and compare it with the remaining answers to see which line equation has the same slope. The slope of a line is determined by the equation $\frac{y_2-y_1}{x_2-x_1}$. Calculate the slope of the line shown to get $\frac{-1-0}{0-3}=-\frac{1}{3}$. The answers are all in the slope-intercept form of an equation, $y = mx + b$, where m = slope. Only (B) has a slope of $-\frac{1}{3}$. The correct answer is (B).

3. **A** The question asks for the y-intercept of a line with a given equation. The slope-intercept form of the equation of a line is $y = mx + b$, where m is the slope and b is the y-intercept. Manipulate this equation to solve for y. Subtract $2x$ from both sides of the equation to get $3y = -2x + 12$, and then divide both sides by 3 to get $y = -\frac{2}{3}x + 4$. Therefore, the y-intercept is 4. The correct answer is (A).

12. **D** The question asks for the x-intercept of the line shown in the graph. The x-intercept of a line is the point where the line crosses the x-axis. The line in the graph has a positive x-intercept, so eliminate (A) and (B). To find the x-intercept, first find the slope of the line and then use one of the points given to determine the value of x. The slope of a line is determined by the equation $\frac{y_2-y_1}{x_2-x_1}$. The slope of the line shown is $\frac{-4-(-2)}{-6-(-2)}=\frac{-2}{-4}$. Continue to simplify the expression to find a slope of $\frac{1}{2}$. At the x-intercept, $y = 0$, so the coordinates for the x-intercept are $(x, 0)$. To find x, plug points $(x, 0)$ and $(-2, -2)$ into the slope equation and solve for x: $\frac{-2-0}{-2-x}=\frac{1}{2}$, so $\frac{-2}{-2-x}=\frac{1}{2}$. Cross-multiply to get $-2 - x = -4$, or $-x = -2$. Therefore, $x = 2$. The correct answer is (D).

7. **D** The question asks for an equation that represents a graph. To find the best equation, compare features of the graph to the answer choices. In the line shown, the point at which the line crosses the y-axis is 1, so the y-intercept is 1. Use the two points on the line, $(0, 1)$ and $(8, 0)$, to calculate the slope: $\frac{y_2-y_1}{x_2-x_1}=\frac{(0-1)}{(8-0)}=-\frac{1}{8}$. The correct answer must be the equation of a line with a slope of $-\frac{1}{8}$ and a y-intercept of 1. Rewrite the answers in the slope-intercept form of the equation, $y = mx + b$, where m is the slope of the line and b is the y-intercept. In (A), the equation becomes $2y = x - 8$, or $y = \frac{1}{2}x - 4$. The slope of this line is $\frac{1}{2}$, and the y-intercept is -4, so eliminate (A). In (B), the equation becomes $4y = -x - 8$, or $y = -\frac{1}{4}x - 2$. The slope of this line is $-\frac{1}{4}$, and the y-intercept is -2, so eliminate (B). In (C), the equation becomes $8y = 3x + 8$, or $y = \frac{3}{8}x + 1$. The slope of this line is $\frac{3}{8}$, and the y-intercept is 1, so eliminate (C). In (D), the equation becomes $8y = -x + 8$, or $y = -\frac{1}{8}x + 1$. The slope of this line is $-\frac{1}{8}$, and the y-intercept is 1, which is the same as the slope and y-intercept of the line shown in the graph. The correct answer is (D).

14. **B** The question asks for the slope of a line shown in a graph. Use the two points on the line, $\left(-\frac{7}{2}, \frac{16}{3}\right)$ and $\left(\frac{11}{2}, -\frac{17}{3}\right)$, to calculate the slope: $\frac{y_2 - y_1}{x_2 - x_1} = \frac{-\frac{17}{3} - \frac{16}{3}}{\frac{11}{2} - \left(-\frac{7}{2}\right)} = \frac{-\frac{33}{3}}{\frac{18}{2}}$. Continue simplifying to get $-\frac{33}{3} \times \frac{2}{18} = -\frac{66}{54} = -\frac{11}{9}$. The correct answer is (B).

15. **A** The question asks for an equation that represents a graph. To find the best equation, compare features of the graph to the answer choices. In the line shown, the point at which the line crosses the y-axis is –2, so the y-intercept is –2. The answers are all in the slope-intercept form, $y = mx + b$, where m is the slope and b is the y-intercept. Eliminate (B) which has a y-intercept of 2. Next, calculate the slope of the line with two points on the line. The given points are all in terms of a, so that variable will cancel out when the points are put into the slop formula: $\frac{y_2 - y_1}{x_2 - x_1}$. The slope becomes $\frac{2a - a}{\frac{9}{2}a - 3a} = \frac{a}{\frac{9}{2}a - \frac{6}{2}a} = \frac{a}{\frac{3}{2}a}$. Cancel the a in the numerator with the a in the denominator, then multiply the numerator and denominator by 2 to get rid of the fraction in the denominator. The resulting slope is $\frac{2}{\frac{3}{2}(2)} = \frac{2}{3}$. Eliminate (C) and (D) because they do not have this slope. The correct answer is (A).

17. **32** The question asks for the product of the y-coordinates of the two points of intersection of a system of equations. Since both equations are set equal to the same value, set the right sides of the two equations equal to each other and solve for x. This gives $4x^2 - 6x + 4 = 2x + 4$. Subtract $2x$ and 4 from both sides to set the equation equal to 0, so the equation becomes $4x^2 - 8x = 0$. Divide both sides of the equation by 4 to get $x^2 - 2x = 0$. Factor x out of the equation to get $x(x - 2) = 0$. Therefore, the two possible values for x are $x = 0$ and $x = 2$. Plug both of these values into the second equation to find the corresponding y-values. If $x = 0$, then $y = 2(0) + 4 = 4$. If $x = 2$, then $y = 2(2) + 4 = 8$. The two points of intersection are (0, 4) and (2, 8). Therefore, the product of the two possible values of y is $4 \times 8 = 32$. The correct answer is 32.

Drill 5 (page 266)

28. $\frac{5}{6}$ The question asks for the probability that a cell phone user selected at random in 2008 is a contracted user. Probability is defined as $\frac{number\ of\ outcomes\ you\ want}{number\ of\ possible\ of\ outcomes}$. Read the table carefully to find the numbers for the top and bottom of the fraction. The number of contracted users in 2008 is 225. The total number of users in 2008 is 270. The probability is $\frac{225}{270}$, which reduces to $\frac{5}{6}$. The correct answer is $\frac{5}{6}$.

14. **625**   The question asks for the value of $5x^3$. Use the given equation $5x^2 = 125$ to find the value of x. Divide both sides of the equation by 5 to get $x^2 = 25$. Take the square root of both sides to get $x = 5$. Plug $x = 5$ into $5x^3$ to get $5(5^3)$. This equals $5(125)$ or 625. The correct answer is 625.

15. $\dfrac{5}{12}$ The question asks for the value of z. Isolate z on one side of the equation. Follow order of operations, and start with the innermost parentheses. Distribute the number in front of the parentheses to get $z = 5 - 5[5z - 2 + 2z]$. Combine like terms in the brackets to get $z = 5 - 5[7z - 2]$. Distribute the number in front of the brackets to get $z = 5 - 35z + 10$. Combine like terms to get $z = 15 - 35z$. Add $35z$ to both sides to get $36z = 15$. Divide both sides by 36 to get $z = \dfrac{15}{36}$. Since that doesn't fit in the box, reduce the fraction to get $\dfrac{5}{12}$. The correct answer is $\dfrac{5}{12}$.

29. **9**   The question asks for the value of z. Isolate z on one side of the equation. Start by squaring both sides of the equation to get $(5 - \sqrt{z})(5 - \sqrt{z}) = z - 5$. Use FOIL on the left side to get $25 - 5\sqrt{z} - 5\sqrt{z} + z = z - 5$. Combine like terms to get $25 - 10\sqrt{z} + z = z - 5$. Subtract z and 25 from both sides to get $-10\sqrt{z} = -30$. Divide both sides by -10 to get $\sqrt{z} = 3$. Square both sides to get $z = 9$. The correct answer is 9.

16. **6**   The question asks for the value of the expression $b^2 + 6b - 10$. Solve the system of equations to find the value of b. Multiply the first equation by -2 to get $-6a - 4b = -74$, stack the equations, and add:

$$7u + 4b = 85$$
$$\underline{-6a + 4b = -74}$$
$$a \qquad\quad = 11$$

Plug in 11 for a in the original first equation to get $3(11) + 2b = 37$ and then $33 + 2b = 37$. Subtract 33 from both sides to get $2b = 4$. Divide both sides by 2 to get $b = 2$. Plug $b = 2$ into the expression to get $2^2 + 6(2) - 10 = 4 + 12 - 10 = 6$. The correct answer is 6.

30. **5**   The question asks for the difference in temperature between the first and second day in Celsius. Start by converting the temperatures from Fahrenheit into Celsius. To convert to Celsius, subtract 32 and then multiply by $\dfrac{5}{9}$. The first temperature is $(95 - 32)\dfrac{5}{9} = 35$. The second temperature is $(86 - 32)\dfrac{5}{9} = 30$. The difference in temperature is $35 - 30 = 5$. The correct answer is 5.

31. **350**   The question asks for how much Moriah paid. Translate English into math to find how much Moriah paid. Moriah, m_1, and Mathew, m_2, paid a total of \$540. In equation form, $m_1 + m_2 = 540$. The amount Moriah paid was \$30 less than twice the amount Mathew paid. In equation form, $m_1 = 2m_2 - 30$. Plug the second equation into the first to get $2m_2 - 30 + m_2 = 540$. Combine like terms to get $3m_2 - 30 = 540$. Add 30 to both sides to get $3m_2 = 570$. Divide both sides by 3 to get $m_2 = 190$. \$190 is the amount Mathew paid. Moriah paid \$540 − \$190 = \$350. The correct answer is 350.

17. **100**   The question asks for the number of ounces of Solution 2 used to make Solution 3. Use Bite-Sized Pieces to write an equation. Solution 3 is composed of 50 ounces of Solution 1 and x ounces of Solution 2. Solution 1 has a sugar content of 25%, and Solution 2 has a sugar content of 10%. Apply those sugar contents to the amounts of Solution 1 and Solution 2 in Solution 3 to get $0.25(50) + 0.10x$. Solution

3 has a sugar content of 15%; since Solution 3 is made up of 50 ounces of Solution 1 and x ounces of Solution 2, the expression $0.15(50 + x)$ represents Solution 3. Set the two expressions equal to each other to solve for x. $0.25(50) + 0.10x = 0.15(50 + x)$. Distribute the numbers in front of the parentheses to get $12.5 + 0.10x = 7.5 + 0.15x$. Subtract 7.5 from both sides to get $5 + 0.10x = 0.15x$. Subtract $0.10x$ from both sides to get $5 = 0.05x$. Divide both sides by 0.05 to get $x = 100$. The correct answer is 100.

CHAPTER 12

Drill 1 (page 279)

5. **B** The question asks for an expression that models a specific situation. There are variables in the answer choices, so plug in. Make $m = 10$. If David goes over his limit by 10 megabytes, then David pays $25 + \$0.05(10) = \$25.50$. This is the target value; circle it. Now plug $m = 10$ into the answer choices to see which one matches the target value. Choice (A) becomes $25 + 1.05(10) = \$35.50$. This does not match the target, so eliminate (A). Choice (B) becomes $25 + 0.05(10) = \$25.50$. Keep (B), but check the remaining answers just in case. Choice (C) becomes $0.05(25 + 10) = \$1.75$. Eliminate (C). Choice (D) becomes $1.05(25 + 10) = \$36.75$. Eliminate (D). The correct answer is (B).

4. **D** The question asks for the value of an expression. There are variables in the answer choices, so plug in. Pick numbers for a, b, and c such that $a = \dfrac{b}{c^2}$; $1 = \dfrac{4}{2^2}$, so make $a = 1$, $b = 4$, and $c = 2$. Now, $\dfrac{1}{b^2} = \dfrac{1}{4^2} = \dfrac{1}{16}$. This is the target value; circle it. Now plug $a = 1$ and $c = 2$ into the answer choices to see which one matches the target value. Choice (A) becomes $(1)(2)^2 = (1)(4)$. This becomes 4, which does not match the target, so eliminate (A). Choice (B) becomes $(1)^2(2)^4 = (1)(16)$. This becomes 16, so eliminate (B). Choice (C) becomes $\dfrac{1}{(1)(2)^2} = \dfrac{1}{(1)(4)}$. This becomes $\dfrac{1}{4}$, so eliminate (C). Choice (D) becomes $\dfrac{1}{(1)^2(2)^4} = \dfrac{1}{(1)(16)}$. This becomes $\dfrac{1}{16}$, which matches the target. The correct answer is (D).

11. **D** The question asks for an expression that models a specific situation. There are variables in the answer choices, so plug in. Note that $w > 12$. Make $w = 20$. Now work the question in Bite-Sized Pieces. By the end of the first day, Luciano's cup has $20 - 2 = 18$ ounces. At the end of 7 days, Luciano's cup has $18 - 8 = 10$ ounces. Half of the remaining water is 5 ounces, so after 11 days, Luciano's cup would hold $10 - 5 = 5$ ounces. This is the target value; circle it. Now plug $w = 20$ into the answer choices to see which one matches the target value. Choice (A) becomes $\dfrac{20 - 2}{8} = \dfrac{18}{8}$. This does not match the target,

so eliminate (A). Choice (B) becomes $\dfrac{20-2}{2} - 10 = \dfrac{18}{2} - 10$. Continue simplifying to get $9 - 10 = -1$.

Eliminate (B). Choice (C) becomes $\dfrac{1}{2}(20) - 10 = 10 - 10$. This equals 0, so eliminate (C). Choice (D)

becomes $\dfrac{20-10}{2} = \dfrac{10}{2}$. This equals 5, which matches the target. The correct answer is (D).

7. **A** The question asks for the value of an expression. There are variables in the answer choices, so plug in.

Make $p = 2$. The expression becomes $\dfrac{\frac{1}{8}}{2(2)} = \dfrac{\frac{1}{8}}{4}$. Continue simplifying to get $\dfrac{1}{8} \times \dfrac{1}{4} = \dfrac{1}{32}$. This is the

target value; circle it. Now plug $p = 2$ into the answer choices to see which one matches the target value.

Choice (A) becomes $\dfrac{1}{16(2)} = \dfrac{1}{32}$. This matches the target value, so keep (A), but check the remaining

answers just in case. Choice (B) becomes $\dfrac{2}{4} = \dfrac{1}{2}$. This does not match the target, so eliminate (B). Choice

(C) becomes $\dfrac{4}{2} = 2$. Eliminate (C). Choice (D) becomes $4(2) = 8$. Eliminate (D). The correct answer is (A).

9. **C** The question asks for an equation that models a specific situation. There are variables in the answer choices, so plug in. The variable c appears on the more complicated side of the equations in the answers, so plug in a value for c, which is the number of correct answers. The total number of questions is 50, so c must be less than 50. Make $c = 46$. Now work the question in Bite-Sized Pieces. The student got 46 questions correct and 4 questions wrong. The student earned 1 point for each of the 46 correct answers and lost $\dfrac{1}{4}$ point for each of the 4 incorrect answers. The student's score would be $(1)(46) - \dfrac{1}{4}(4) = 46 - 1$. Subtract $46 - 1 = 45$. This is the target answer; circle it. Now plug $c = 46$ into the answer choices to see which one matches the target value. Choice (A) becomes $S = 50 - 0.25(46) = 50 - 11.5$. This becomes 38.5, which does not match the target, so eliminate (A). Choice (B) becomes $S = 50 - 0.75(46) = 50 - 34.5$. This becomes 15.5, so eliminate (B). Choice (C) becomes $S = 46 - 0.25(50 - 46) = 46 - 0.25(4)$. Continue simplifying to get $46 - 1 = 45$. This matches the target. Keep (C), but check (D) just in case. Choice (D) becomes $S = 46 - 0.75(50 - 46) = 46 - 0.75(4)$. Continue simplifying to get $46 - 3 = 43$. Eliminate (D). The correct answer is (C).

18. **D** The question asks for a value in terms of a variable. There are variables in the answer choices, and the question includes the phrase *in terms of*, so plug in. The problem involves taking $\dfrac{1}{6}$ of the amount in the account, so choose a number for x that is divisible by 6. Make $x = 18$. Now work the question in Bite-Sized Pieces. $\dfrac{1}{6}$ of the \$18 in the account is $18 \times \dfrac{1}{6} = 3$. That means Jodi withdraws \$3 and has $\$18 - \$3 = \$15$ remaining. Then she withdraws another \$3 and has $\$15 - \$3 = \$12$ remaining. Next, Jodi deposits y

dollars into her account. Make $y = \$8$. Jodi has $\$12 + \$8 = \$20$. Last, Jodi withdraws half the money in her account, so she withdraws $\$10$ and has $\$20 - \$10 = \$10$ left in her account. This is the target; circle it. Plug $x = 18$ and $y = 8$ into the answer choices to see which one matches the target value. Choice (A) becomes $\frac{4(18) - 3(8)}{6} = \frac{72 - 24}{6}$. Continue simplifying the expression to get $\frac{48}{6} = 8$. This does not match the target, so eliminate (A). Choice (B) becomes $\frac{3(18) - 5(8)}{6} = \frac{54 - 40}{6}$. Continue simplifying to get $\frac{14}{6} = \frac{7}{3}$. Eliminate (B). Choice (C) becomes $\frac{3(18) - (8)}{6} = \frac{54 - 8}{6}$. Continue simplifying to get $\frac{46}{6} = \frac{23}{3}$. Eliminate (C). Choice (D) becomes $\frac{2(18) + 3(8)}{6} = \frac{36 + 24}{6}$. Continue simplifying to get $\frac{60}{6} = 10$. This matches the target. The correct answer is (D).

12. **B** The question asks for the sum of the integer solutions to an inequality that includes an absolute value. Inequalities with an absolute value can be tough to set up: there are two parts, and it's not always easy to remember how to deal with the negative values. Instead, try plugging in some integers. Make $y = 0$. The inequality becomes $2\,|0(4) - 5| < 24$, which becomes $2\,|0 - 5| < 24$. Continue following the order of operations to get $2\,|{-5}| < 24$, or $2(5) < 24$. It is true that $10 < 24$, so 0 is one of the solutions. Now plug in $y = 1$, which results in $2\,|4-5| < 24$, or $2(1) < 24$. That's true, too, so 1 is one of the solutions. Keep going: plugging in $y = 2$ results in $2(3) < 24$, $y = 3$ results in $2(7) < 24$, and $y = 4$ results in $2(9) < 24$. All of these are true, but plugging in $y = 5$ results in $2(15) < 24$, which isn't true. So 4 is the greatest integer solution. Now, try plugging in negative integers. If $y = -1$, the inequality is $2(9) < 24$, which is true, but if $y = -2$, the inequality is $2(13) < 24$, which is not true. Therefore, -1 is the smallest integer solution. The integers that satisfy the inequality are -1, 0, 1, 2, 3, and 4, and their sum is 9. The correct answer is (B).

29. **92.3** The question asks for a percent. The question does not say how many students are in the freshman class, so that is a hidden variable. When a question asks for a percent of an unknown quantity, plug in. Because the question is about percentages, make the total number of students 100. That means that there are 15 left-handed students and 85 right-handed students in the class. There are also 65 female students and 35 male students. If $\frac{2}{3}$ of the left-handed students are male, then there are $\frac{2}{3} \times 15 = 10$ male left-handed students. This leaves $15 - 10 = 5$ female left-handed students. If 5 of the 65 female students are left-handed, then the other 60 female students are right-handed. To find the percentage of female students who are right-handed, divide: $60 \div 65 = 0.923$. Remember to multiply a decimal by 100 to get the equivalent percentage, which is 92.3%. The correct answer is 92.3.

Drill 2 (page 284)

3. **D** The question asks for the value of the variable n in the given equation. Since the question asks for a specific value and the answers contain numbers in increasing order, plug in the answers. Begin by labeling the answers as n and starting with (B), 3. Plug $n = 3$ into the equation and work the steps of the question.

The equation becomes $2(3 + 5) = 3(3 − 2) + 8$, or $2(8) = 3(1) + 8$. This simplifies to $16 = 11$, which is false. Eliminate (B). Next, try (C). Plug $n = 4$ into the equation to get $2(4 + 5) = 3(4 − 2) + 8$, or $2(9) = 3(2) + 8$. This simplifies to $18 = 14$, which is false. Eliminate (C). Next, try (D). Plug $n = 8$ into the equation to get $2(8 + 5) = 3(8 − 2) + 8$, or $2(13) = 3(6) + 8$. This simplifies to $26 = 26$, which is true. Since (D) works, stop here. The correct answer is (D).

8. **C** The question asks for the value of the variable x in the given equation. Since the question asks for a specific value and the answers contain numbers in increasing order, plug in the answers. Begin by labeling the answers as x and starting with (C). Plug $x = 3$ into the equation and work the steps of the question. The equation becomes $3^{3+2} = 243$, or $3^5 = 243$. This simplifies to $243 = 243$, which is true. Since (C) works, stop here. The correct answer is (C).

7. **C** The question asks for the point that satisfies a system of inequalities. There are specific points in the answers, so plug in the answers. Test the ordered pairs in each inequality from the question and look for a pair that makes all three inequalities true. Start by plugging (A) into the first inequality to get $2(−4) − (−1) > −3$. This becomes $−8 − (−1) > −3$, or $−7 > −3$. Since this is not true, eliminate (A). Now plug the point in (B) into the first inequality to get $2(−3) − (−2) > −3$. This becomes $−6 − (−2) > −3$, or $−4 > −3$. Since this is not true, eliminate (B). Now plug the point in (C) into the first inequality to get $2(−1) − (−1) > −3$. This becomes $−2 − (−1) > −3$, or $−1 > −3$. This is true, but the point must work in all three inequalities. Plugging the point in (C) into the second inequality gives $4(−1) + (−1) < 5$. This becomes $−4 + (−1) < 5$, or $−5 < 5$. This is true, but test the third inequality as well. Plugging the point in (C) into the third inequality gives $−1 > −6$. This is also true. The point in (C) satisfies all three inequalities in the system. The correct answer is (C).

10. **D** The question asks for the value of the variable x in the given equation. Since the question asks for a specific value and the answers contain numbers in increasing order, plug in the answers. Begin by labeling the answers as x and starting with (C). Plug $x = \dfrac{1}{4}$ into the equation and work the steps of the question. The equation becomes: $\dfrac{24\left(\frac{1}{4}\right)}{4} + \dfrac{1}{\frac{1}{4}} = 5$. This simplifies to $\dfrac{6}{4} + 4 = 5$. Since $\dfrac{6}{4}$ will not simplify to a whole number, the left side of the equation cannot add up to a whole number and will not equal 5. Eliminate (C). Next, try (D). Plug $x = \dfrac{1}{2}$ into the equation to get $\dfrac{24\left(\frac{1}{2}\right)}{4} + \dfrac{1}{\frac{1}{2}} = 5$. This simplifies to $\dfrac{12}{4} + 2 = 5$, or $3 + 2 = 5$. This is true. Since (D) works, stop here. The correct answer is (D).

20. **A** The question asks for the value of the variable x in the given equation. Since the question asks for a specific value and the answers contain numbers in increasing order, plug in the answers. Begin by labeling the answers as v and starting with (B). Plug $v = −3$ into one of the equations and work the steps of the

question to solve for u. Plug $v = -3$ into the second equation because it does not contain fractions and will be quicker to solve than the first equation. The equation becomes $2(-3) = 7 + 5u$, or $-6 = 7 + 5u$. Solve for u to get $u = -\dfrac{13}{5}$. Next, plug the values for u and v into the first equation to see if the equation holds true. The equation becomes $-\dfrac{5}{7} - \dfrac{11}{7}\left(-\dfrac{13}{5}\right) = -(-3)$. This simplifies to $-\dfrac{5}{7} + \dfrac{143}{35} = 3$, or $\dfrac{118}{35} = 3$. This is not true, so eliminate (B). If it is not clear if a larger or smaller value is needed, just pick a direction to go in. Try (A) next. Plug $v = -4$ into the second equation to get $2(-4) = 7 + 5u$, or $-8 = 7 + 5u$. Solve for u to get $u = -3$. Next, plug the values for u and v into the first equation to see if the equation holds true. The equation becomes $-\dfrac{5}{7} - \dfrac{11}{7}(-3) = -(-4)$. This simplifies to $-\dfrac{5}{7} + \dfrac{33}{7} = 4$, or $\dfrac{28}{7} = 4$. This is true. Since (A) works, stop here. The correct answer is (A).

25. **C** The question asks for the range of values of x that would satisfy the parameters in the question. Since the question asks for a specific range of values and the answers are increasing order, plug in the answers. Before plugging in, however, find the desired amount of titanium in the final alloy. The question says that the final alloy must contain between 10 and 15% titanium and must weigh 10 kilograms total. If the alloy has 10% titanium, it contains $(0.10)(10 \text{ kg}) = 1$ kg of titanium. If the alloy has 15% titanium, it contains $(0.15)(10 \text{ kg}) = 1.5$ kg of titanium. So, the final alloy must contain between 1 and 1.5 kg of titanium. Start with (B). Choose a value for x that is within the given range and is easy to work with. Choose $x = 3$. x represents the weight of the 20% alloy, so there are 3 kg of the 20% alloy. Since the two alloys must add up to 10 kg, there are $10 - 3 = 7$ kg of the 5% alloy. Find the weight of titanium in each alloy. There are $(0.20)(3 \text{ kg}) = 0.6$ kg in the 20% alloy and $(0.05)(7 \text{ kg}) = 0.35$ kg in the 5% alloy. Therefore, there are $0.6 + 0.35 = 0.95$ kg of titanium in the final alloy. Since this is not within the desired range of 1 to 1.5 kg, eliminate (B). Also eliminate (A) because it has even smaller values of x. Try (C). Choose $x = 4$. There are 4 kg of the 20% alloy and $10 - 4 = 6$ kg of the 5% alloy. Find the weight of titanium in each alloy. There are $(0.20)(4 \text{ kg}) = 0.8$ kg in the 20% alloy and $(0.05)(6 \text{ kg}) = 0.3$ kg in the 5% alloy. Therefore, there are $0.8 + 0.3 = 1.1$ kg of titanium in the final alloy. Since this is within the desired range, (C) works, so stop here. The correct answer is (C).

Drill 3 (page 301)

a. 90
b. 320
c. 6
d. $x = 8$
e. 5
f. 3
g. 10
h. 120%
i. 108

j.   10%

k. $\dfrac{2,600}{18,600}$ = approximately 14%

The amount of money in a savings account after m months is modeled by the function $f(m) = 1,000(1.01)^m$
.

l.   *$1,000*

m.   *1%*

n.   *40*

o.   *1.5*

p.   *5 kPa*

2.   **D**   The question asks for an unknown value in relation to three known values. This relationship is a proportion, or direct variation, so set up two equal fractions, being sure to match the units. $\dfrac{10 \text{ pecks}}{2.5 \text{ bushels}} = \dfrac{x \text{ pecks}}{4 \text{ bushels}}$. Solve for x by cross-multiplying: $(4)(10) = (2.5)(x)$. Divide both sides of the equation by 2.5 to get $x = 16$. The correct answer is (D).

28. $\dfrac{5}{6}$ The question asks for a probability, which is defined as $probability = \dfrac{number\ of\ outcomes\ you\ want}{number\ of\ possible\ outcomes}$. Read the table carefully to find the right numbers. The question asks for the probability that a cell phone user in 2008 is a contracted user, so look at the row labeled 2008. In 2008, there were 225 contracted users, so that is the *number of outcomes you want*. There were 270 total cell phone users in 2008, so that is the *number of possible outcomes*. Therefore, the probability is $\dfrac{225}{270}$. Reduce the fraction to get $\dfrac{5}{6}$, or express it as a decimal, which is $0.8\overline{33}$. Grid in either the fraction or the decimal. When gridding in a repeating decimal, remember to include as many places as will fit, so grid in 0.833. The correct answer is $\dfrac{5}{6}$ or .833.

12.   **B**   The question asks for an expression that represents a specific situation. Use Bite-Sized Pieces to eliminate answer choices. The air squad is decreasing the size of the fire by a certain percent over time, so this question is about exponential decay. When the decay rate is a percent of the total, the decay formula is *final amount* = (*original amount*)$(1 - rate)^{number\ of\ changes}$. In this case, $F(t)$ is the final amount, and the question asks for the right side of the formula. The original amount is 10, so eliminate (D) because it does not include 10. The original amount must be multiplied by $(1 - rate)$, so eliminate (A) and (C), which use subtraction instead of multiplication. The only remaining answer is (B), and it matches the decay formula: the rate of 7%, or .07, is subtracted from 1, and this amount is raised to a power of $\dfrac{t}{12}$. In this case, t is the number of hours the fire has been burning, and the change happens every 12 hours. To see this, plug in $t = 24$. In 24 hours, there should be 2 changes, and indeed $\dfrac{24}{12} = 2$. The correct answer is (B).

15. **C** The question asks what must be true among three statements about a set of averages. For averages, use the formula $T = AN$, in which T is the total, A is the average, and N is the number of things. For the first three tests, 80 is the average and 3 is the number of things. The formula becomes $T = (3)(80) = 240$. Use the formula again for the last two tests, with 90 as the average and 2 as the number of things to get $T = (2)(90) = 180$. Now, use the formula one more time to find the average for all five tests. The total for all 5 tests is $240 + 180 = 420$, so the formula becomes $420 = A(5)$. Divide both sides by 5 to get $84 = A$. Now evaluate each statement and use Process of Elimination. The final two tests prove that the student must have scored more than 85 on at least one test. If the student scored the same on each of the second two tests, his score would be 90 on each. He could have also scored 0 on one test and 180 on the other test, or any other combination of two numbers whose sum is 180. No matter what, there's at least one test on which the student scored more than 85, so (I) must be true. Eliminate (B) and (D). No remaining answer choices include (III), so only consider (II). The student's average for all five tests was 84, which is less than 85. Statement (II) is true. The correct answer is (C).

19. **C** The question asks for a rate in terms of meters per second, so use the rate formula $D = RT$, in which D is the distance, R is the rate or speed, and T is the time. First, calculate the total distance that Maggie runs. She runs 1,200 meters before turning around and running another 1,200 meters to return home. She then runs 2,100 more meters after retrieving her iPhone. Therefore, she runs a total of 4,500 meters $(1,200 + 1,200 + 2,100)$. Next, find the total time that Maggie ran. Because she was at home for 3 minutes, the total time she spent running out of the 15 minutes shown on the graph was 12 minutes $(15 - 3)$. The question asks for speed in *meters per second*, so convert the 12 minutes to seconds by multiplying $12 \times 60 = 720$. Fill in the rate formula with the distance of 4,500 meters and time of 720 seconds to get $4,500 = R(720)$. To find the average speed or R, divide the total both sides by 720 to get $6.3 = R$. The correct answer is (C).

29. **45** The question asks for time it takes to do a certain amount of work at a certain rate, so use the rate formula and pay close attention to the units. The formula is $W = RT$, in which W is the amount of work done, R is the rate or speed, and T is the time. The question says that Marcia and David *work together*, so start by finding their combined rate. If Marcia types 18 pages per hour and David types 14 pages per hour, then together they will be able to type $18 + 14 = 32$ pages per hour. The total number of pages they need to type is 24. Use the rate formula with 32 as the rate and 24 as the work to get $24 = (32)T$. To find the time in hours that it takes Marcia and David to type 24 pages, divide both sides by 32 to get 0.75 hours $= T$. The question asks *how many minutes* the work will take, so multiply $0.75 \times 60 = 45$ minutes. The correct answer is 45.

22. **C** The question asks for a percent difference between two values. To find the percent change between numbers, use the formula $\frac{difference}{original} \times 100$. Read the table carefully to find the values. The question asks about *the number of registered Republicans who plan to vote for Candidate B*, which is 70, and *the number of registered Democrats who plan to vote for Candidate B*, which is 56. The question asks *what percent greater*, which means the *original* amount will be the smaller number. Put these numbers into the percent change formula to get $\frac{75 - 56}{56} \times 100 = 25$. The correct answer is (C).

25. **C** The question asks for the difference in the amount of time a certain trip takes at two different speeds. The question also asks about rates, so use the rate formula $D = RT$, in which D is the distance, R is the rate or speed, and T is the time. First, calculate the time it takes Everett's parents to make the trip. Fill in the formula with the distance of 200 miles and the parents' rate of 45 miles per hour to get $200 = (45)T$. To find the time the trip takes Everett's parents in hours, divide both sides by 45 to get $4.\overline{4}$ hours $= T$. Next, find the time it takes Everett to make the trip. There is a variable in the problem and in the answer choices, so plug in. Because the question is dealing with percentages, make $x = 100$. If Everett is driving at a speed 100% greater than his parents' speed, then he is driving at 90 mph. Fill this information into the rate formula to find Everett's time. The formula becomes $200 = (90)T$, so the time for Everett's trip is $T = 2.\overline{2}$ hours. The difference in the amount of time the trip takes for Everett versus his parents is $4.\overline{4} - 2.\overline{2} = 2.\overline{2}$. This is the target value; circle it. Now plug $x = 100$ into the answer choices to see which one matches the target value. Choice (A) becomes $\dfrac{-2(100)}{45\left(1+\dfrac{100}{100}\right)} = \dfrac{-200}{45(2)}$. Continue simplifying to get $\dfrac{-200}{90} = -2.\overline{2}$. Choice (A) is a negative value, which does not match the target, so eliminate (A). Choice (B) becomes $\dfrac{2(100)}{45\left(1-\dfrac{100}{100}\right)} = \dfrac{200}{45(0)}$. This becomes $\dfrac{200}{0}$, and because the denominator is 0, (B) is undefined. Eliminate (B). Choice (C) becomes $\dfrac{2(100)}{45\left(1+\dfrac{100}{100}\right)} = \dfrac{200}{45(2)}$. Continue simplifying to get $\dfrac{200}{90} = 2.\overline{2}$. This matches the target, so keep (C), but check (D) just in case. Choice (D) becomes $\dfrac{45\left(\dfrac{100}{100}\right)}{200\left(1+\dfrac{100}{100}\right)} = \dfrac{45(1)}{200(2)}$. Continue simplifying to get $\dfrac{45}{400} = 0.1125$. Eliminate (D). The correct answer is (C).

27. **A** The question asks for a statement supported by the data in a table. Read each answer carefully and use Process of Elimination. To determine how many people used both forms of transportation in Boston and New York, use the Group Equation: Total = Group 1 + Group 2 + Neither – Both. For Boston, this becomes $7,556 = 5,281 + 3,504 + 1,025 - B$. Combine like terms: $7,556 = 9,810 - B$. Subtract 9,810 from both sides: $-2,254 = -B$. Divide both sides by –1 to find that 2,254 people use both forms of transportation in Boston. Repeat the same process for New York: $7,789 = 2,476 + 5,738 + 1,459 - B$ becomes $7,789 = 9,673 - B$, and $-1,884 = -B$, so 1,884 people in New York use both forms of public transportation. Finally, determine whether 20% more people used both forms of transportation in Boston by using the percent change equation: $percent\ change = \dfrac{difference}{original} \times 100$. This equation becomes $\dfrac{2,254 - 1,884}{1,884} \times 100 = 19.6\%$. This is approximately 20%, so the statement in (A) is supported by the data. The correct answer is (A).

CHAPTER 13

Drill 1 (page 315)

3. **C**   The question asks for a certain form of the equation. There are many forms in which a quadratic can be written. To see x-intercepts or solutions, a quadratic must be in factored form, since factoring is used to find solutions. The factored form is $y = a(x - m)(x - n)$, where m and n are the x-intercepts. Only (C) is in this form. The correct answer is (C).

4. **C**   The question asks for the equation of a function. Notice that there are variables in the question and in the answer choices, so try to plug in. Since m represents months, plug in a number that works easily with the question. The number must be within the range $0 \le m \le 36$, so choose $m = 10$. After 10 months, the total amount paid will be: \$3,200 (the down payment) + \$380 × 10 months, or 3,200 + (380)(10) = \$7,000. This is the target value; circle it. Now plug $m = 10$ into each answer choice to see which one matches the target value. Choice (A) becomes $f(10) = 380 + 3,200(10)$. 3,200(10) is much larger than the target value, so eliminate (A). Choice (B) becomes $f(10) = 3,200 + 36(10)$, or 3,560. This does not match the target value, so eliminate (B). Choice (C) becomes $f(10) = 3,200 + 380(10)$. This matches the target value, so keep (C), but check (D) just in case. Choice (D) becomes $f(10) = 10,480 - 380(10)$, or 6,680. This does not match the target value, so eliminate (D). The correct answer is (C).

15. **3**   The question asks for the value of a function. In function notation, the number inside the parentheses is the x-value that goes into the function, and the value that comes out of the function is the y-value. Therefore, $x = a$ and $f(x) = f(a) = 10$. Plug $x = a$ into the function to get $f(a) = a^2 - a + 4$. Since $f(a) = 10$, replace $f(a)$ with 10 to get $10 = a^2 - a + 4$. To solve for a, subtract 10 from both sides of the equation and factor. The equation becomes $0 = a^2 - a - 6$, which can be factored into $0 = (a - 3)(a + 2)$. Set both factors equal to 0 to get $a = 3$ or $a = -2$. There are two possible solutions to this equation, but the question states that a is *non-negative*, so -2 cannot be a solution. The correct answer is 3.

9. **C**   The question asks for the value of the constant a. The question states that the number of bonus points increases by 25 when the number of purchases (p) increases by 4. To avoid working with multiple variables, pick a starting number for p. If $p = 0$, then the number of bonus points is: $B(p) = a(0) + 7$, or 7. When the number of purchases is increased by 4, the number of bonus points increases by 25. So if $p = 0 + 4 = 4$, then $B(p) = 7 + 25 = 32$. To find the value of a, plug $B(p) = 32$ and $p = 4$ into the equation and solve for a. The equation becomes $32 = a(4) + 7$, or $32 = 4a + 7$. This simplifies to $25 = 4a$, or $a = 6.25$. The correct answer is (C).

21. **D**   The question asks for the value of an expression made of two functions. To solve, first evaluate each function. In function notation, the number inside the parentheses is the x-value that goes into the function, and the value that comes out of the function is the y-value. Start with the top function. Plug $x = 8$ into the $f(x)$ function to get $f(8) = 8^{-\frac{2}{3}}$. Remember the rules of exponents: when a value is raised to a

negative exponent, take the reciprocal and make the exponent positive. So, $8^{-\frac{2}{3}} = \dfrac{1}{8^{\frac{2}{3}}}$. When dealing with fractional exponents, remember that the numerator raises the base to a power and the denominator takes a root of the base. So, $\dfrac{1}{8^{\frac{2}{3}}} = \dfrac{1}{\sqrt[3]{8^2}} = \dfrac{1}{\sqrt[3]{64}} = \dfrac{1}{4}$. Next, find $f(3)$. Plug $x = 3$ into the $f(x)$ function to get $f(3) = 3^{-\frac{2}{3}}$. This is equivalent to $\dfrac{1}{3^{\frac{2}{3}}} = \dfrac{1}{\sqrt[3]{3^2}} = \dfrac{1}{\sqrt[3]{9}}$. Simplifying this expression any further will give a complex decimal, so it is easier to leave it as a fraction. $\dfrac{f(8)}{f(3)} = \dfrac{\frac{1}{4}}{\frac{1}{\sqrt[3]{9}}} = \dfrac{1}{4} \times \dfrac{\sqrt[3]{9}}{1} = \dfrac{\sqrt[3]{9}}{4}$. The correct answer is (D).

23. **B** The question asks for a time when the temperature was 0°C. In the equation, $T(x)$ represents temperature and x represents time, so the question is asking for some value of x that makes $T(x) = 0$. Notice that the question gives an equivalent form of the first equation when $T(x) = 0$. Solve this equation for x to find a time at which $T(x) = 0$. First, subtract 100 from both sides of the equation to set the left side equal to 0. The equation becomes $0 = x^2 - 24x + 44$. This can be factored as $0 = (x - 22)(x - 2)$. To solve for x, set both factors equal to 0. There are two possible values of x: $x = 22$ and $x = 2$. Since x represents *the time in hours since midnight*, the temperature was 0°C at two times: 12:00 A.M. + 22 hours = 10:00 P.M. and at 12:00 A.M. + 2 hours = 2:00 A.M. Only 10:00 P.M. is an answer choice. The correct answer is (B).

12. **B** The question asks for the value of a variable in the table. Since the values in the table are part of a *linear function*, they must all lie on the same line. Recall that, in function notation, the number inside the parentheses is the x-value that goes into the function, and the value that comes out of the function is the y-value. Plug the x- and y-values into the slope formula to find the value of j. The slope formula is slope $= \dfrac{y_2 - y_1}{x_2 - x_1}$. Plug the two known points, $(-1, 2)$ and $(5, -6)$, into the equation. The equation becomes $slope = \dfrac{-6 - 2}{5 - (-1)} = \dfrac{-8}{6} = \dfrac{-4}{3}$. Now use the slope of the line and one of the known points to solve for j. Plug (j, j) and $(-1, 2)$ into the slope equation. The equation becomes $\dfrac{-4}{3} = \dfrac{2 - j}{-1 - j}$. Cross-multiply to get $-4(-1 - j) = 3(2 - j)$, or $4 + 4j = 6 - 3j$. Add $3j$ to both sides and subtract 4 from both sides to get $7j = 2$. Divide both sides by 7 to get $j = \dfrac{2}{7}$. The correct answer is (B).

30. **148** The question asks for a comparison between the values of two different functions. In function notation, the number inside the parentheses is the x-value that goes into the function, and the value that comes out of the function is the y-value. Since the question asks for the values of each function when $x = 12$, it asks for the y-values of each function at this point. First, plug $x = 12$ into the f function to get $f(12) = 12^2 - 4 = 144 - 4 = 140$. Now plug $x = 12$ into the g function to get $g(12) = -\frac{1}{3}(12) - 4 = -4 - 4 = -8$. At $x = 12$, $f(x)$ is $140 - (-8) = 148$ greater than $g(x)$. The correct answer is 148.

31. **8** The question asks for an x-coordinate. The question provides a lot of information, so take it in Bite-Sized Pieces. Line $h(x)$ is perpendicular to line $g(x)$ and the two intersect at the point $(-12, 0)$. Perpendicular lines have negative reciprocal slopes. Because the equation for line $g(x)$ is in slope-intercept form, the slope of line $g(x)$ is the coefficient of x (the m-value) in the given equation, or $-\frac{1}{3}$. The negative reciprocal of $-\frac{1}{3}$ is 3, so the slope of $h(x)$ is 3. The equation for $h(x)$ then becomes $h(x) = 3x + b$. Plug in $(-12, 0)$ to solve for b. The equation becomes $0 = 3(-12) + b$, or $36 = b$. Therefore, $h(x) = 3x + 36$. To find the point at which $h(x)$ intersects $f(x)$, set the function equations equal to one another: $x^2 - 4 = 3x + 36$. To solve for x, turn this into a quadratic equation by moving all terms to the left side and combining like terms: $x^2 - 3x - 40 = 0$. This equation factors to $(x + 5)(x - 8) = 0$. Therefore, the two solutions are $x = -5$ and $x = 8$. The question asks for a solution that is in Quadrant I—the upper right quadrant. In this quadrant, both x and y are positive, so $x = 8$ is the solution in this quadrant. The correct answer is 8.

Drill 2 (page 328)

3. **A** The question asks what value of t to use in the given equation to find the initial height of a projectile. The initial height of the projectile corresponds to the moment that it is launched before it ever moves, with t equal to the seconds since its launch. At that initial point, no time has passed, so $t = 0$. The correct answer is (A).

4. **B** The question asks for a value of t. Since the question asks for a specific value and the answers contain numbers in increasing order, plug in the answers. Begin by labeling the answers as t and starting with (B), -5. The equation becomes $12 - (-5 + 2)^2 = 3$ or $12 - (-3)^2 = 3$. This becomes $12 - 9 = 3$, which is true, so stop here. The correct answer is (B).

6. **B** The question asks for an equation that matches the graph. The answer choices are quadratic equations that have already been factored, so use the roots from the graph to eliminate wrong answers. The roots, or solutions, of a graph are where it crosses the x-axis: look at the graph to see that the correct solutions will be -3 and 1. Eliminate (C) and (D) which have a 4 in one of the factors instead of 1 and 3. To decide between (A) and (B), plug in a point from the graph. The vertex appears to be at $(-1, 4)$. Plug $x = -1$ and $y = 4$ into (A) to get $4 = -(-1 - 3)(-1 + 1)$. This becomes $4 = -(-4)(0)$ or $4 = 0$. This is not true, so eliminate (A), but check (B) just in case. Choice (B) becomes $4 = -(-1 + 3)(-1 - 1)$ or $4 = -(2)(-2)$. This simplifies to $4 = 4$. The correct answer is (B).

9. **A** The question asks for an equivalent form of an expression. There are variables in the answer choices, so plug in. Make $x = 3$ and $y = 2$. The expression becomes $3^4 - 2^4 = 81 - 16 = 65$. This is the target value; circle it. Now plug $x = 3$ and $y = 2$ into the answer choices to see which one matches the target value. Choice (A) becomes $(3 + 2)(3 - 2)(3^2 + 2^2) = (5)(1)(9 + 4) = (5)(1)(13) = 65$. This matches the target value, so keep (A), but check the remaining answers just in case. Choice (B) becomes $(3 + 2)^2(3^2 + 2^2) = (5^2)(9 + 4) = (25)(13) = 325$. Eliminate (B). Choice (C) becomes $(3 - 2)^2(3^2 + 2^2) = (1)^2(9 + 4) = (1)(13) = 13$. Eliminate (C). Choice (D) becomes $(3 + 2)(3 - 2)(3^2 - 2^2) = (5)(1)(9 - 4) = (5)(1)(5) = 25$. Eliminate (D). The correct answer is (A).

10. **C** The question asks for an equation with a vertex of $(-5, 2)$. There are variables in the answer choices, so plug in. Use the given point to make $x = -5$ and $y = 2$. Now plug $x = -5$ and $y = 2$ into the answer choices to see which one is true. Choice (A) becomes $2 = (-5 + 5)^2 - 2 = (0)^2 - 2 = -2$. Since $2 = -2$ is not true, eliminate (A). Choice (B) becomes $2 = (-5 - 5)^2 - 2 = (-10)^2 - 2 = 100 - 2 = 98$, which is not true. Eliminate (B). Choice (C) becomes $2 = (2)(-5 + 5)^2 + 2 = 2(0)^2 + 2 = 0 + 2 = 2$. Keep (C), but check (D) just in case. Choice (D) becomes $2 = 2(-5 - 5)^2 + 2 = 2(-10)^2 + 2 = 2(100) + 2 = 200 + 2 = 202$. Eliminate (D). The correct answer is (C).

14. **3** The question asks for the price per donut, x, that a donut shop should charge to maximize its profit, P. To see the maximum, the quadratic must be in vertex form since the vertex is that value. The vertex form is $y = a(x - h)^2 + k$, in which (h, k) is the vertex. The equation given in the question is $P = -4(x - 3)^2 + 2,000$, which is already in vertex form, so the vertex is $(3, 2{,}000)$. The x-coordinate is the price, so the shop should charge \$3. The correct answer is 3.

23. **B** The question asks for a value of the constant c in the given quadratic equation. Since the question asks for a specific value and the answers contain numbers in increasing order, plug in the answers. Begin by labeling the answers as c and starting with (B), 135. The equation becomes $x^2 + 24x + 135 = (x + 9)(x + p)$. The left side of the equation is a quadratic in standard form, and the right side is a factored quadratic; this means that 135 from the left side of the equation would equal $9p$ once the right side was expanded to standard form. Divide 135 by 9 to get $x^2 + 24x + 135 = (x + 9)(x + 15)$. Test whether this is the right answer by using FOIL to expand $(x + 9)(x + 15)$ into $x^2 + 15x + 9x + 135 = x^2 + 24x + 135$. The middle term is $24x$, which matches the value given on the left side, so stop here. The correct answer is (B).

26. **B** The question asks for an equation that models a specific situation. Translate the question in Bite-Sized Pieces and eliminate after each piece. One piece of information says that the correct equation should be a parabola. The standard form of a parabola equation is $y = ax^2 + bx + c$. The equation should include an x^2 term, so eliminate (D), which is a linear equation. The value of a tells whether a parabola open upwards (positive a) or downwards (negative a). Since the water from the fountain shoots up and then down, the parabola should open downwards and have a negative value for a. Eliminate (C), which has a positive value for a. Compare the remaining answers. The important difference between (A) and (B) is the c term. The question states that the fountain's spout is 8 feet above the ground. Since y is the height of the water and x is the time from the spout, $y = 8$ when $x = 0$. Plug $x = 0$ into (A) to see if whether becomes $y = 8$. Choice (A) becomes $y = -0^2 + 15 = 15$. This means $y = 8$ does not appear in (A), so eliminate (A). The correct answer is (B).

Drill 3 (page 337)

3. **D** The question asks for an equation that best models a specific situation. The question says that at a depth of 15 meters, the dissolved oxygen concentration is 0.0022. Plug $d = 15$ into the answers to see which one equals the corresponding oxygen concentration of 0.0022. Choice (A) becomes $\frac{1}{2} - \frac{1}{15^2} = \frac{1}{2} - \frac{1}{225}$. In decimal form, the expression is $0.5 - 0.00\overline{4} \approx 0.496$. This does not match the target number, so eliminate (A). Choice (B) becomes $\frac{1}{100(15)} = \frac{1}{1,500}$. In decimal form, this is equal to $0.000\overline{6}$. Eliminate (B). Choice (C) becomes $\frac{1}{15} = 0.0\overline{6}$. Eliminate (C). Choice (D) becomes $\frac{1}{2(15)^2} = \frac{1}{2(225)}$. Continue simplifying to get $\frac{1}{450} = 0.00\overline{22}$. This is a very close match for the target. The correct answer is (D).

6. **A** The question asks for the meaning of a number in context. Start by reading the full question, which asks for the meaning of the number 40. Then label the parts of the equation with the information given. The question states that P is the driver's net pay and d is the number of deliveries. Notice that the 40 is being subtracted from the rest of the equation, which means that there is a $40 reduction in the driver's net pay. Look for other information in the question that suggests some type of reduction. The only information on any type of reduction is that the shipping company *deducts a separate fee daily for the use of the company's delivery truck*. Therefore, it is reasonable to assume that the 40 represents this fee. Choice (A) matches this description. The correct answer is (A).

9. **B** The question asks for an expression representing a certain piece of information in the context of an equation. Start by reading the full question, which asks for an expression that represents *the total number of customers on a given day*. Then label the parts of the equation with the information given. The question states that R is the *total revenue* earned by the restaurant in one day, s is the *number of student customers*, and n is the *number of non-student customers*. Focus on the information that is needed to answer the question. The total number of customers is equal to the number of student customers, s, and the number of non-student customers, n. Add these two groups together to get the overall total. The calculation for this is $s + n$. The correct answer is (B).

7. **B** The question asks for the meaning of a quantity in context. Start by reading the full question, which asks for the meaning of the quantity ΔT. Then label the parts of the equation with the information given. The question states that the equation represents *the cooling of an object over time*. According to the question, *T is temperature in degrees Celsius, k is a rate constant, and t is time*. Next, use Process of Elimination to get rid of answer choices that are not consistent with the labels. Choice (A) refers to temperature, T, but it also includes time, t, so eliminate (A). Choice (B) refers to a difference between the *temperature* of the object and the *temperature* of its surroundings, so keep (B). Eliminate (C) because the question does not mention *Fahrenheit*. Eliminate (D) because it mentions a *constant factor*, which corresponds with the *constant rate*, k. By Process of Elimination, only (B) remains. Though it is not necessary to know this to answer the question, the symbol Δ (called "delta") is used to represent a change or *difference*. The correct answer is (B).

10. **D** The question asks for approximate *average yearly decrease in the number of Crucian carp* based on the line of best fit shown in the graph. In this graph, the slope of the line of best fit represents the average yearly change. To formula for slope is $\frac{y_2 - y_1}{x_2 - x_1}$. Choose two points from the graph to plug into the slope formula. On the graph, the number of carp in 2010 was 25,000 and in 2011, the number of carp was 22,500. Using these *x*- and *y*-values, the expression becomes $\frac{25,000 - 22,500}{2010 - 2011}$. Simplify the expression to get $\frac{2,500}{-1}$, or –2,500. Since the result is negative, it represents a decrease of 2,500 carp per year. The correct answer is (D).

8. **C** The question asks what can be deduced from the given function. Label the parts of the equation to determine what they represent. In this question, $N(c)$ is the net amount the students raised, and *c* is the number of cars washed. The question also says that the students paid for cleaning supplies. The number 0.40 is multiplied by the number of cars and subtracted, so it must have something to do with the cost of the cleaning supplies. Next, use Process of Elimination to get rid of answer choices that are not consistent with the labels. Choices (A) and (D) associate the number 8 with the cleaning supplies, so eliminate (A) and (D). Choice (B) says that the students paid a total of $40 for the cleaning supplies, but the number in the equation is 0.40, not 40, and it is multiplied by the number of cars, so it is not a total. Eliminate (B). Choice (C) matches the given function. The correct answer is (C).

12. **C** The question asks for a statement that is consistent with the data shown in a graph. Compare features of the graph to the answer choices and use Process of Elimination. Choice (A) is not supported by the graph because one employee had a linear decrease in energy, while the other employee's energy increased and decreased in an exponential fashion; eliminate (A). Choice (B) is also not supported; one employee had low energy after lunch, but the other employee had the highest energy level immediately after lunch. Eliminate (B). Choice (C) fits the employee who started with high energy and decreased throughout the afternoon; keep (C). Choice (D) fits neither employee: one employee's energy decreased throughout the afternoon, and the other employee's energy increased and then rapidly decreased. Eliminate (D). The correct answer is (C).

11. **D** The question asks for an inequality that represents a given situation. There are variables in the answer choices, so plug in. Plug in a value for *t* from the optimal temperature range (30–37) and use Process of Elimination. If *t* = 37, the correct answer will provide a statement that is true. Plug *t* = 37 into the answers and eliminate any answers that are not true. Choice (A) becomes $|37 + 7| \leq 37$ or $|44| \leq 37$. Since this statement is false, eliminate (A). Choice (B) becomes $|37 - 3.5| \leq 33.5$ or $|33.5| \leq 33.5$. Since this statement is true, keep (B). Choice (C) becomes $|37 - 30| \leq 7$, or $|7| \leq 7$. Since this statement is true, keep (C). Choice (D) becomes $|37 - 33.5| \leq 3.5$, or $|3.5| \leq 3.5$. Since this statement is true, keep (D). Next, plug in a value that is *not* in the optimal temperature range, such as *t* = 29, and eliminate any answers that provide a true statement. Choice (B) becomes $|29 - 3.5| \leq 33.5$ or $|25.5| \leq 33.5$. Since this statement is true, eliminate (B). Choice (C) becomes $|29 - 30| \leq 7$ or $|-1| \leq 7$. Since this statement is true eliminate (C). The correct answer is (D).

13. **B** The question asks for the meaning of an expression in context. Start by reading the full question, which asks for the meaning of the expression $a + k$. Then label the parts of the equation with the information given. The question states that S is the sum of a set of consecutive integers, and n is the number of integers in the set. None of the answer choices are clearly inconsistent with the labels, so plug in. Plug in 2, 3, and 4 as the consecutive integers. In this case, $S = 2 + 3 + 4 = 9$ and $n = 3$. The equation becomes $9 = \left(\dfrac{a + k}{2}\right)(3)$. Divide both sides of the equation by 3 to get $3 = \dfrac{a + k}{2}$. Multiply both sides by 2 to get $a + k = 6$. This is the target, circle it. Plug the correct values into each answer choice to see which one matches the target. Choice (A) becomes $2 + 3 = 5$. This does not match the target, so eliminate (A). Choice (B) becomes $2 + 4 = 6$. This matches the target, so keep (B), but check the other answers just in case. Choice (C) doesn't work because there is only one middle integer; eliminate (C). Choice (D) becomes $3 + 4 = 7$. Eliminate (D). The correct answer is (B).

23. **C** The question asks for the meaning of an expression in context. Start by reading the full question, which asks for the meaning of the expression $\dfrac{0.5}{12}$. Then label the parts of the equation with the information given. The question states that B is the balance of the account, and that t is the time in years. It also says that 250 is the beginning balance, and that the account has an annual interest rate of 5%, and that interest deposits are made to the account monthly. The 0.05 must have something to do with the 5% interest rate, and the 12 must have something to do with the 12 months in a year. Next, use Process of Elimination to get rid of answer choices that are not consistent with the labels. Eliminate (A) because 0.05 is the interest rate; it represents a percentage and cannot be the actual *amount of money* that is deposited. Eliminate (B) because $\dfrac{0.05}{12} \approx 0.004$; this is less than 1 cent. The beginning balance was \$250, and it doesn't make sense that there would be less money in the account after a deposit was made. Choice (C) refers to the *percentage* of the balance added during a *monthly interest deposit*, so keep (C). Eliminate (D) because 0.004 is too small to be a number of months. The correct answer is (C).

CHAPTER 14

Drill 1 (page 349)

a.   36
b.   24
c. $x = 10, y = 5$
d.   30
e.   22

4. **D** The question asks for the area of square *ABCD*. The lengths of the sides are given as variable expressions instead of numbers, so solve for *x* first. In a square, all sides are equal, so $2x + 1 = x + 3$. First, subtract 1 from each side so that $2x = x + 2$. Then subtract *x* from each side so that $x = 2$. Plug that value of *x* into the expression $x + 3$ to get $2 + 3 = 5$, which is the length of each side. The formula for the area of a square is $A = (length)(width)$, so the area is $(5)(5) = 25$. The correct answer is (D).

3. **D** The question asks for the pairs of angles that must have equal degree measures on a figure. Use the geometry basic approach. Start by labeling the figure with the given information. Mark lines *a* and *b* as parallel. In Statement (I), angles 1 and 5 do not have to be equal because a side of angle 1 is line *c*, which only intersects one parallel line in the figure; there is not enough information to determine whether any angle formed by line *c* is equal to one formed by line *b*. Thus, the angles in Statement (I) do not have to be equal; eliminate (A). Angles 2 and 7 are vertical angles (angles opposite each other when two lines intersect), and vertical angles must be equal. Therefore, the angles in Statement (II) have to be equal, so eliminate (C). Any time a line crosses two parallel lines, all of the small angles have the same measure and all of the big angles have the same measure. Angles 3 and 9 are both small angles formed where the same line (line *d*) crosses one of the parallel lines. Since the angles in Statement (III) must be equal, eliminate (B). Only Statements (II) and (III) are true. The correct answer is (D).

28. **60** The question asks for the area of rectangle *ABCD*. Use the geometry basic approach. Start by labeling the figure with the given information. The length of one side is 5, and the question states that the length of the diagonal, *BD* (or *AC*), is 13. The formula for the area of a rectangle is $A = (length)(width)$, so find the width first. Since the corner of the rectangle is a right angle, use the Pythagorean Theorem: $a^2 + b^2 = c^2$. Plug in *AB* for *a* and *BD* for *c* so that $5^2 + b^2 = 13^2$. Then solve for *b*, which will be *AD*, the length of the other side of the right triangle, and thus the width of the rectangle. First, simplify: $25 + b^2 = 169$. Then subtract 25 from both sides and take the square root: $\sqrt{b^2} = \sqrt{144}$. Then, $b = 12$. Since $AD = 12$, plug the length and width into the formula for the area of a rectangle to get $A = (5)(12) = 60$. The correct answer is 60.

9. **C** The question asks for the value of an angle on a figure. Use the geometry basic approach. Start by labeling the figure with the given information. Mark $\overline{BC}$ and $\overline{AD}$ as parallel. It may not be immediately obvious how to get the value of $\angle ACD$, so see what else can be determined. Any time a line crosses two parallel lines, all of the small angles have the same measure and all of the big angles have the same measure. The big and small angles are *supplementary angles*: the sum of the measure of any big angle plus any small angle equals 180°. In this figure, $\angle BCD$ and $\angle ADC$ are supplementary big and small angles. Because $\angle ADC$ has a measure given of 95°, subtract 95 from 180 to see that $\angle BCD$ must have a measure of 85°. Subtract 35 from 85 to see that $\angle ACD$ must have a measure of 50°. The correct answer is (C).

Drill 2 (page 362)

a. 24

b. 10

c. $\frac{6}{10}$, $\frac{3}{5}$, or 0.6

d. 20

e. $20\sqrt{5}$

f. $\frac{20}{20\sqrt{5}}$, $\frac{1}{\sqrt{5}}$, or $\frac{\sqrt{5}}{5}$

28. **7.5** The question asks for the value of x, the length of a side of a right triangle. The value of tan $a°$ is given, and the length of the side opposite to that angle is 7. SOHCAHTOA says that tangent $\theta = \frac{opposite}{adjacent}$. The needed side is adjacent to that angle, so set up a proportion: $\frac{14}{15} = \frac{7}{x}$. Cross-multiply to get $14x = 105$. Divide both sides by 14 so $x = 7.5$. The correct answer is 7.5.

14. **100** The question asks for the value of an angle on a figure. Use the geometry basic approach. Start by labeling the figure with the given information. Because $AB = BC$, ABC is an *isosceles triangle*, which has two sides that are equal. In an isosceles triangle, angles that are opposite equal sides must be equal. Therefore, $\angle A$ and $\angle C$ have the same measure, so $\angle A$ is also 40°. $\angle A$ and $\angle C$ have a combined measure of 80°. The sum of the angles inside a triangle must equal 180°. Subtract 80 from 180, and x must measure 100°. The correct answer is 100.

8. **C** The question asks for the perimeter of an isosceles triangle. Use the geometry basic approach. Start by labeling the figure with the given information. The question says that the triangle is isosceles, and there is a right angle present in the figure. An isosceles right triangle has angles that measure 45°, 45°, and 90°. Since $AB = 5$, that means $BC = 5$ as well. Using the 45°-45°-90° right triangle rule, $AC = 5\sqrt{2}$. Therefore, the perimeter of the triangle is $5 + 5 + 5\sqrt{2}$ or $10 + 5\sqrt{2}$. The correct answer is (C).

9. **B** The question asks for the minimum number of buckets of paint needed to cover the front of a barn's roof. To find the answer, solve for the total area. The formula for the area of a triangle is $A = \frac{bh}{2}$. The figure provides that the base, b, is 8 m. The two smaller right triangles both have angles of 30° and 90°, so the other angle must be 60° in both. Since they share a side (the height), the two triangles are the same size, and the 8 m base is equally split to be 4 m for each right triangle. To find the height, use the 30°-60°-90° right triangle rule: if the short side (opposite 30°) is h, the middle side (opposite 60°) is $h\sqrt{3}$. Make $4 = h\sqrt{3}$ and divide both sides by $\sqrt{3}$ to get $h \approx 2.4$. Then set $A = \frac{(8)(2.4)}{2} = (4)(2.4) = 9.6$. To cover 9.6 m², the owner will need $\frac{9.6}{5}$ buckets, which is 1.92. Since 1 bucket is not enough, round up to 2. The correct answer is (B).

10. **D** The question asks for a length of a line segment in a figure containing triangles. Use the geometry basic approach. Start by labeling the figure with the given information. When given two or more triangles and information about the lengths of the sides, look for similar triangles. Both triangles share $\angle DAE$ and each has a right angle. Since all triangles have 180°, the third angles in each triangle must also be equal. The two triangles must have the same set of angles, but they aren't the same size; they are *similar triangles*, so the sides of one triangle are proportional to those of the other. $BD = AD - AB$, and AB is given; find AD to get the answer. In the small right triangle, two sides are given, so use the Pythagorean Theorem to find the third: $a^2 + b^2 = c^2$. Plug in AB for a and AC for c so that $5^2 + b^2 = 13^2$. Then solve for b, which will be BC, the length of the other side of the right triangle. First, simplify: $25 + b^2 = 169$. Then subtract 25 from both sides and take the square root: $\sqrt{b^2} = \sqrt{144}$. Therefore, $b = 12$. Another way to solve for b would be to recognize the Pythagorean triple: 5-12-13. Since $BC = 12$, set up a proportion with corresponding sides: $\dfrac{AB}{AD} = \dfrac{BC}{DE}$ or $\dfrac{5}{AD} = \dfrac{12}{24}$. Cross-multiply: $(AD)(12) = 120$. Divide both sides by 12 to get $AD = 10$. Now solve $BD = AD - AB = 10 - 5 = 5$. The correct answer is (D).

13. **C** The question asks for an expression for the perimeter of a triangle. Use the geometry basic approach. Start by labeling the figure with the given information. Because $AB = BC$, ABC is an isosceles triangle, which has two sides that are equal. In an isosceles triangle, angles that are opposite equal sides must be equal. Therefore, $\angle A$ and $\angle C$ have the same measure, so $\angle A$ is also 35°. Indicate that in the diagram and draw a line from point B to AC to create two right triangles:

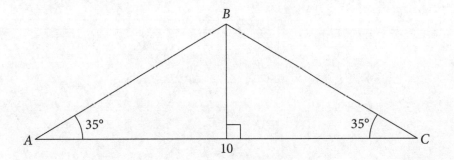

$\overline{AB}$ and $\overline{BC}$ are equal hypotenuses of the right triangles. Since the two triangles are congruent, the base of 10 is split equally so that each right triangle has a base of 5. The side adjacent to the 35° angle is known, so use cosine. SOHCAHTOA says that cosine $\theta = \dfrac{adjacent}{hypotenuse}$. Therefore, $\cos 35° = \dfrac{5}{AB}$. Solve to get $AB = \dfrac{5}{\cos 35°}$. Add $AB + BC + AC = \dfrac{5}{\cos 35°} + \dfrac{5}{\cos 35°} + 10 = \dfrac{10}{\cos 35°} + 10$ for the perimeter, but that's not an answer. Notice that two answer choices use a 55° angle, which is the angle at the top of each right triangle $(180 - 90 - 35)$. Another way of saying $\cos 35°$ is $\sin 55°$ because the side that is adjacent to the 35° angle is opposite the 55° angle. Replace $\cos 35°$ with $\sin 55°$. The correct answer is (C).

Drill 3 (page 372)

a. **16π** The question asks for the area of circle O. The given radius of the circle is 4. Since the equation for the area of a circle is πr^2, the area is $\pi(4)^2$. The correct answer is 16π.

b. **8π** The question asks for the circumference of circle O. Since the equation for circumference of a circle is $2\pi r$, the circumference is $2\pi(4)$. The correct answer is 8π.

16. **A** The question asks for the area of the circle. The parts of a circle are directly proportional to one another. In this circle, the fraction of the central angle of 360° is the same as the fraction of the arc length of the total circumference. Set up the proportion $\dfrac{central\ angle}{360°} = \dfrac{arc\ length}{circumference}$, then plug in the given information to get $\dfrac{60°}{360°} = \dfrac{2\pi}{circumference}$. Cross-multiply to get $60(circumference) = 360(2\pi)$. Divide both sides by 60 to get $circumference = 12\pi$. Since the formula for circumference is $2\pi r$, the radius of the circle is 6. Then, find the area using the formula πr^2. If $r = 6$, then the circle has an area of $\pi(6)^2 = 36\pi$. The correct answer is (A).

18. **C** The question asks for the perimeter of triangle ABC. Since no figure is provided, start by drawing the figure according to the description in the question. The figure should look like the following:

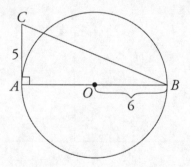

Next, write down the equations needed to answer the question. Since the area of the circle is 36π, and the formula is $A = \pi r^2$, the radius of the circle is 6. Therefore, the diameter of the circle is 12. Since a line that is tangent to a circle forms a 90° angle with the radius at the point of tangency, the side lengths of this right triangle are a 5-12-13 Pythagorean triple. To find the perimeter of the triangle, add the side lengths to get 5 + 12 + 13 = 30. The correct answer is (C).

12. **B** The question asks for the center of the circle with the provided circle equation. The equation of a circle in standard form is $(x - h)^2 + (y - k)^2 = r^2$, where (h, k) are the coordinates of the circle's center and r is the radius. Start by grouping terms with the same variable together to rewrite the equation as $x^2 - 2x + y^2 + 8y = -8$. In order to rewrite the given equation in standard form, you must complete the square. Take the coefficient of the first linear term, $-2x$, and divide the coefficient by 2 to get -1. Then, square this result to get 1. Add 1 to both sides of the equation to get $(x^2 - 2x + 1) + y^2 + 8y = -8 + 1$. Then, do the same with the coefficient of the other linear term, $8y$. Divide 8 by 2, which is 4, and then square that, which is 16. Add 16 to both sides to get $(x^2 - 2x + 1) + (y^2 + 8y + 16) = -8 + 1 + 16$. Finally, factor the groups of terms in parentheses on the left side and do the arithmetic on the right side to get $(x - 1)^2 + (y + 4)^2 = 9$. The coordinates of the center of the circle are given by (h, k) in the standard form, so, for this circle, the center is located at $(1, -4)$. The correct answer is (B).

29. **5.25** The question asks for the radius of the circle. Start by translating English to math. *Major arc PSR is* $\dfrac{4}{3}$ *the length of minor arc PQR* means $\overset{\frown}{PSR} = \dfrac{4}{3} \overset{\frown}{PQR}$. Since $\overset{\frown}{PSR}$ is 6π, substitute for $\overset{\frown}{PSR}$ to get $6\pi = \dfrac{4}{3} \overset{\frown}{PQR}$. Multiply both sides by 3 to cancel out the fraction to get $18\pi = 4\overset{\frown}{PQR}$. Divide both sides by 4 to get $\dfrac{18\pi}{4} = \overset{\frown}{PQR}$, or $\overset{\frown}{PQR} = 4.5\pi$. The two arcs, $\overset{\frown}{PSR}$ and $\overset{\frown}{PQR}$, add up to the circumference of the circle, so $C = 6\pi + 4.5\pi = 10.5\pi$. Since $C = 2\pi r$, the radius of the circle is 5.25. The correct answer is 5.25.

Drill 4 (page 376)

3. **B** The question asks for the value of an angle in the figure. There are variables in the answer choices, so plug in. Make $a = 90$. The third angle will be $60°$. Since the $60°$ angle and $b°$ are supplementary angles, $60 + b = 180$. Subtract 60 from both sides to get $b = 180 - 60 = 120$. This is the target value; circle it. Now plug $a = 90$ into the answer choices to see which one matches the target value. Choice (A) becomes $30 - 90 = -60$. This does not match the target, so eliminate (A). Choice (B) becomes $30 + 90 = 120$. Keep (B), but check (C) and (D) just in case. Choice (C) becomes $60 + 90 = 150$. Eliminate (C). Choice (D) becomes $80 - 90 = -10$. Eliminate (D). The correct answer is (B).

7. **B** The question asks about the ratio of the volumes of two cones with different radii. The question also describes a relationship between unknown numbers, so plug in. The relationship between the radii of the cones is provided, so plug in numbers that fit this relationship. Plug in $r = 6$ for Cone A and $r = 8$ for Cone B. Let $h = 3$. The formula for the volume of a cone is $V = \dfrac{1}{3} \pi r^2 h$, so plug in the values for r and h to determine the volume of each cone. The volume of Cone A is $\dfrac{1}{3} \pi (6)^2 (3) = 36\pi$, and the volume of Cone B is $\dfrac{1}{3} \pi (8)^2 (3) = 64\pi$. Therefore, the ratio of volume A to volume B is $36\pi{:}64\pi$, which reduces to $9{:}16$. The correct answer is (B).

5.   **A**   The question asks for the value of a trigonometric function. There are variables in the answer choices, so plug in. You are given a right triangle, so plug in for the sides of the triangle. Use the Pythagorean triple 3-4-5 to make the math easy. Add these side lengths to the figure as follows:

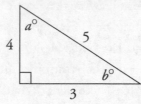

$sin\ \theta = \dfrac{opposite}{hypotenuse}$, so calculate $sin\ a° = \dfrac{3}{5}$. Let $x = \dfrac{3}{5}$. $cos\ \theta = \dfrac{adjacent}{hypotenuse}$, so calculate $cos\ b° = \dfrac{3}{5}$. This is the target value; circle it. Now plug $x = \dfrac{3}{5}$ into the answer choices to see which one matches the target value. Choice (A) becomes $\dfrac{3}{5}$. Keep (A), but check (B), (C), and (D) just in case. Choice (B) becomes $1 - \dfrac{3}{5} = \dfrac{2}{5}$. This does not match the target, so eliminate (B). Choice (C) becomes $\dfrac{1}{\frac{3}{5}} = \dfrac{5}{3}$. Eliminate (C). Choice (D) becomes $\dfrac{3}{5} - 1 = -\dfrac{2}{5}$. Eliminate (D). The correct answer is (A).

22.   **A**   The question asks for the area of a sector of the circle. There are variables in the answer choices, so plug in. Plug in $x = 3$. Write down the equations needed answer the question. The equation for area of a circle is $A = \pi r^2$, so the area of the circle is $\pi(3)^2 = 9\pi$. The equation for circumference is $C = 2\pi r$, so the circumference of the circle is $2\pi(3) = 6\pi$. The length of arc PQ is $\dfrac{\pi(3)}{18} = \dfrac{\pi}{6}$. The parts of a circle have a proportional relationship. In this circle, the fraction of the arc length out of the total circumference is the same as the fraction of the sector area out of the total area. Set up the proportion $\dfrac{arc\ length}{circumference} = \dfrac{sector\ area}{total\ area}$, then plug in the given information to get $\dfrac{\frac{\pi}{6}}{6\pi} = \dfrac{sector\ PQR}{9\pi}$. Divide the fraction on the left side of the equation to get $\dfrac{1}{36} = \dfrac{sector\ PQR}{9\pi}$. Cross-multiply to get $9\pi = 36(sector\ PQR)$, then divide both sides by 36 to get $sector\ PQR = \dfrac{\pi}{4}$. This is the target value; circle it. Now plug $x = 3$ into the answer choices to see which one matches the target value. Choice (A) becomes $\dfrac{\pi(3)^2}{36} = \dfrac{\pi}{4}$. Keep (A), but check (B), (C), and (D) just in case. Choice (B) becomes $\dfrac{\pi(3)^2}{18} = \dfrac{\pi}{2}$. This does not match the target, so eliminate (B). Choice (C) becomes $\dfrac{\pi(3)^2}{9} = \pi$. Eliminate (C). Choice (D) becomes $\dfrac{\pi(3)^2}{3} = 3\pi$. Eliminate (D). The correct answer is (A).

26. **C** The question asks for the volume of the space between the spheres and the rectangular box. Since no figure is provided, start by drawing the figure according to the description in the question. The figure should look like the following:

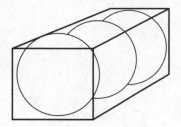

There are variables in the answer choices, so plug in. Make $r = 2$. Therefore, the diameter of the sphere is 4, which is also the width and height of the box. There are 3 spheres in a row, so the length of the box is $3(4) = 12$. The formula for volume of a rectangular solid is $V = lwh$, so plug in the values for the length, width, and height to get $(12)(4)(4) = 192$. The formula for volume of a sphere is $V = \frac{4}{3}\pi r^3$. So, the volume of each sphere is $\frac{4}{3}\pi(2)^3 = \frac{32\pi}{3}$. There are 3 spheres, so multiply this result by 3 to get a total volume of 32π. Therefore, the volume of the spaces between the balls and the box is $192 - 32\pi$. This is the target value; circle it. Now plug $r = 2$ into the answer choices to see which one matches the target value. Choice (A) becomes $(2)^3(3 - 4\pi) = 8(3 - 4\pi)$. Distribute the 8 to get $24 - 32\pi$. This does not match the target, so eliminate (A). Choice (B) becomes $4(2)^2(14 - \pi) = 16(14 - \pi)$. Distribute the 16 to get $224 - 16\pi$. Eliminate (B). Choice (C) becomes $4(2)^3(6 - \pi) = 32(6 - \pi)$. Distribute the 32 to get $192 - 32\pi$. Keep (C), but check (D) just in case. Choice (D) becomes $12(2)^2(2 - \pi) = 48(2 - \pi)$. Distribute the 48 to get $96 - 48\pi$. Eliminate (D). The correct answer is (C).

29. **160** The question asks for the surface area of a rectangular solid. The values of the side lengths are relative to each other, so write the side lengths using a single variable. Translate English to math to find that $l = \frac{1}{2}w$ and $w = \frac{1}{3}h$, or $h = 3w$. Since $V = lwh$, substitute the values for l, w, and h into the equation to get $96 = \left(\frac{1}{2}w\right)(w)(3w)$. Simplify the right side to get $96 = \frac{3}{2}w^3$. Multiply both sides by $\frac{2}{3}$ to get $w^3 = 64$, then take the cube root of both sides to get $w = 4$. Use this value for w to find the values of l and h. The length becomes $\frac{1}{2}(4) = 2$ and the height becomes $3(4) = 12$. The surface area is the sum of the areas of all the faces of the rectangular box, or $2lw + 2lh + 2wh$. Substitute the values for l, w, and h to get $2(2)(4) + 2(2)(12) + 2(4)(12) = 16 + 48 + 96$. Add these values to find that the surface area is 160. The correct answer is 160.

Part V
Practice Test 2

15   Practice Test 2
16   Practice Test 2: Answers and Explanations

Chapter 15
Practice Test 2

Reading Test

60 MINUTES, 47 QUESTIONS

Turn to Section 1 of your answer sheet to answer the questions in this section.

Each passage or pair of passages below is followed by a number of questions. After reading each passage or pair, choose the best answer to each question based on what is stated or implied in the passage or passages and in any accompanying graphics (such as a table or graph).

Questions 1–9 are based on the following passage.

This passage is adapted from Henry James, "The Beast in the Jungle," originally published in 1903. The passage describes the meeting, after many years, of John Marcher and May Bertram.

"You know you told me something I've never forgotten and that again and again has made me think of you since; it was that tremendously hot day when we
Line went to Sorrento, across the bay, for the breeze. What I
5 allude to was what you said to me, on the way back, as we sat under the awning of the boat enjoying the cool. Have you forgotten?"

He had forgotten and was even more surprised than ashamed. But the great thing was that he saw
10 in this no vulgar reminder of any "sweet" speech. The vanity of women had long memories, but she was making no claim on him of a compliment or a mistake. With another woman, a totally different one, he might have feared the recall possibly even of some
15 imbecile "offer." So, in having to say that he had indeed forgotten, he was conscious rather of a loss than of a gain; he already saw an interest in the matter of her mention. "I try to think—but I give up. Yet I remember that Sorrento day."
20 "I'm not very sure you do," May Bertram after a moment said; "and I'm not very sure I ought to want you to. It's dreadful to bring a person back at any time to what he was ten years before. If you've lived away from it," she smiled, "so much the better."
25 "Ah, if *you* haven't why should I?" he asked.
"Lived away, you mean, from what I myself was?"
"From what *I* was. I was of course [a boor],"

Marcher went on; "but I would rather know from you just the sort of [boor] I was than—from the
30 moment you have something in your mind—not know anything."

Still, however, she hesitated. "But if you've completely ceased to be that sort—?"

"Why I can then all the more bear to know. Beside
35 perhaps I haven't."

"Perhaps. Yet if you haven't," she added, "I should suppose you'd remember. Not indeed that *I* in the least connect with my impression the invidious name you use. If I had only thought you foolish," she explained,
40 "the thing I speak of wouldn't so have remained with me. It was about yourself." She waited as if it might come to him; but as, only meeting her eyes in wonder, he gave no sign, she burnt her ships. "Has it ever happened?"
45 Then it was that, while he continued to stare, a light broke for him and the blood slowly came to his face, which began to burn with recognition. "Do you mean I told you—?" But he faltered, lest what came to him shouldn't be right, lest he should only give himself
50 away.

"It was something about yourself that it was natural one shouldn't forget—that is if one remembered you at all. That's why I ask you," she smiled, "if the thing you then spoke of has ever come to pass?"
55 Oh then he saw, but he was lost in wonder and found himself embarrassed. This, he also saw, made her sorry for him, as if her allusion had been a mistake. It took him but a moment, however, to feel it hadn't

CONTINUE

been, much as it had been a surprise. After the first
50 little shock of it her knowledge on the contrary began,
even if rather strangely, to taste sweet to him. She was
the only other person in the world then who would
have it, and she had had it all these years, while the fact
of his having so breathed his secret had unaccountably
55 faded from him. No wonder they couldn't have met
as if nothing had happened. "I judge," he finally said,
"that I know what you mean. Only I had strangely
enough lost any sense of having taken you so far into
my confidence."

1

The point of view from which the passage is written
can best be described as

A) a first-person narrator telling his life story.

B) a disinterested reporter listing objective facts.

C) a critical observer who judges Marcher's actions.

D) a sympathetic chronicler who relates to Marcher's
feelings.

2

Over the course of the passage, the emotions of John
Marcher shift from

A) incredulity to begrudging acceptance.

B) confusion to disconcerted recognition.

C) disdain to unrequited love.

D) amazement to painful embarrassment.

3

Information in the passage suggests that John
Marcher and May Bertram are

A) comforting one another over mistakes made
during the previous ten years.

B) trusting one another with sensitive personal
information.

C) reminiscing about former times and
conversations.

D) expressing their true feelings for one another.

4

Which choice provides the best evidence for the
answer to the previous question?

A) Lines 1–6 ("You know . . . cool")

B) Lines 22–24 ("It's dreadful . . . better")

C) Lines 55–57 ("Oh then . . . mistake")

D) Lines 61–65 ("She was . . . him")

5

As used in line 12, "claim" most nearly means

A) application.

B) remark.

C) appeal.

D) demand.

6

In the second paragraph, the "loss" (line 16) Marcher
feels most likely refers to

A) a connection over an interest he has in common
with May.

B) a missed opportunity to compliment May.

C) his longing to return to the warm weather in
Sorrento.

D) May's rejection of his speech declaring love for
her.

7

The conversation between Marcher and May Bertram
suggests that Marcher had previously told May about
which of the following?

A) A troublesome puzzle

B) A romantic confession

C) A forgotten trifle

D) A personal belief

Which choice provides the best evidence for the answer to the previous question?

A) Lines 1–4 ("You know . . . breeze")

B) Lines 11–13 ("The vanity . . . mistake")

C) Lines 20–22 ("I'm not . . . to")

D) Lines 67–69 ("Only I . . . confidence")

As used in line 57, "allusion" most nearly means

A) reference.

B) image.

C) quotation.

D) apparition.

CONTINUE

Questions 10–18 are based on the following passage.

This passage is adapted from a speech delivered by Winston Churchill on May 13, 1940. Churchill became Prime Minister of Britain on May 10. This speech was his first address to the House of Commons, in which he asks the House to support his new administration.

I beg to move,

That this House welcomes the formation of a Government representing the united and inflexible resolve of the nation to prosecute the war with Germany to a victorious conclusion.

On Friday evening last I received His Majesty's commission to form a new Administration. It [w]as the evident wish and will of Parliament and the nation that this should be conceived on the broadest possible basis and that it should include all parties, both those who supported the late Government and also the parties of the Opposition. I have completed the most important part of this task. A War Cabinet has been formed of five Members, representing, with the Opposition Liberals, the unity of the nation. The three party Leaders have agreed to serve, either in the War Cabinet or in high executive office. The three Fighting Services have been filled. It was necessary that this should be done in one single day, on account of the extreme urgency and rigour of events. A number of other positions, key positions, were filled yesterday, and I am submitting a further list to His Majesty to-night. I hope to complete the appointment of the principal Ministers during to-morrow. The appointment of the other Ministers usually takes a little longer, but I trust that, when Parliament meets again, this part of my task will be completed, and that the administration will be complete in all respects.

I considered it in the public interest to suggest that the House should be summoned to meet today. Mr. Speaker agreed, and took the necessary steps, in accordance with the powers conferred upon him by the Resolution of the House. At the end of the proceedings today, the Adjournment of the House will be proposed until Tuesday, 21st May, with, of course, provision for earlier meeting, if need be. The business to be considered during that week will be notified to Members at the earliest opportunity. I now invite the House, by the Motion which stands in my name, to record its approval of the steps taken and to declare its confidence in the new Government.

To form an Administration of this scale and complexity is a serious undertaking in itself, but it must be remembered that we are in the preliminary stage of one of the greatest battles in history, that we are in action at many other points in Norway and in Holland, that we have to be prepared in the Mediterranean, that the air battle is continuous and that many preparations, such as have been indicated by my hon. Friend below the Gangway, have to be made here at home. In this crisis I hope I may be pardoned if I do not address the House at any length today. I hope that any of my friends and colleagues, or former colleagues, who are affected by the political reconstruction, will make allowance, all allowance, for any lack of ceremony with which it has been necessary to act. I would say to the House, as I said to those who have joined this government: "I have nothing to offer but blood, toil, tears and sweat."

We have before us an ordeal of the most grievous kind. We have before us many, many long months of struggle and of suffering. You ask, what is our policy? I can say: It is to wage war, by sea, land and air, with all our might and with all the strength that God can give us; to wage war against a monstrous tyranny, never surpassed in the dark, lamentable catalogue of human crime. That is our policy. You ask, what is our aim? I can answer in one word: It is victory, victory at all costs, victory in spite of all terror, victory, however long and hard the road may be; for without victory, there is no survival. Let that be realised; no survival for the British Empire, no survival for all that the British Empire has stood for, no survival for the urge and impulse of the ages, that mankind will move forward towards its goal. But I take up my task with buoyancy and hope. I feel sure that our cause will not be suffered to fail among men. At this time I feel entitled to claim the aid of all, and I say, "come then, let us go forward together with our united strength."

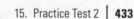
CONTINUE

10

Over the course of the speech, Churchill's focus shifts from

A) defeating Germany to reconstructing the government.

B) forming a War Cabinet to establishing war policy.

C) appointing an Administration to bolstering spirits.

D) reconciling differences to accepting defeat.

11

As used in line 4, "prosecute" most nearly means

A) fight.

B) litigate.

C) accuse.

D) enforce.

12

In the speech, Churchill claims that his administration must be formed more quickly than usual because

A) the king has told him to act with haste.

B) Parliament has been united under three party leaders.

C) the British Empire is in danger of losing the war.

D) the international political situation requires unusual measures.

13

Which choice provides the best evidence for the answer to the previous question?

A) Lines 6–7 ("On Friday . . . Administration")

B) Lines 18–20 ("It was . . . events")

C) Lines 53–57 ("I hope . . . act")

D) Lines 71–75 ("Let that . . . goal")

14

It can be inferred from the passage that Churchill's administration

A) is likely to be controversial.

B) will meet with approval from all members of the House of Commons.

C) is dominated by Opposition Liberals.

D) has some unfilled positions.

15

Which choice provides the best evidence for the answer to the previous question?

A) Lines 13–15 ("A war . . . nation")

B) Lines 24–28 ("The appointment . . . respects")

C) Lines 31–33 ("Mr. Speaker . . . House")

D) Lines 60–62 ("We have . . . suffering")

16

Churchill makes the statement "I have nothing to offer but blood, toil, tears and sweat" (lines 58–59) primarily to

A) convey his deep level of commitment to the war effort.

B) indicate that he believes Britain has little hope of winning the war.

C) suggest that there is not much he can offer in support of the military.

D) offer evidence of his dedication to a governing coalition.

CONTINUE

17

The primary rhetorical effect of the repetition of the words "victory" and "no survival" in the last paragraph is to

A) emphasize the hopeless nature of Britain's struggle.

B) clarify the administration's war strategy.

C) underscore the long-term implications of the outcome of the war.

D) maintain the sense of optimism introduced earlier in the speech.

18

As used in line 76, "suffered" most nearly means

A) endured.

B) allowed.

C) tolerated.

D) endorsed.

CONTINUE

15. Practice Test 2 | **435**

Questions 19–28 are based on the following passage and supplementary material.

This passage is adapted from Alex Kotlowitz, *Never a City So Real.* © 2004 by Alex Kotlowitz.

Fourteen miles southeast of the Loop, at the base of Lake Michigan, the city's easternmost corner, one finds a fistful of neighborhoods with hearty names
Line like Irondale, Hegewisch, The Bush, and Slag Valley.
5 This is South Chicago. Apart from Altgeld Gardens—a vast public housing complex virtually hidden from the rest of the world by towering mountains of garbage and often referred to as Chicago's Soweto—South Chicago is the city's most isolated community, its most
10 removed. The labor lawyer and author Tom Geoghegan has called it "a secret city." The vast majority of Chicagoans have never set foot here, and as if to ensure such detachment, above the compact redbrick bungalows with postage-stamp-size yards looms the
15 Chicago Skyway, a highway on stilts, which takes the prosperous to their cottages along the Indiana and Michigan shorelines. The neighborhoods below are modest in appearance, a collection of small homes and small taverns and diners with simple names like Steve's,
20 Pete's Hideaway, Who Cares?, Small World Inn, and Maria's Den. There's nothing fanciful about this area. As one observer wrote: "Streets named Commercial and Exchange offer testimony that people came here to make a buck, not admire the scenery."
25 And yet the scenery, so to speak, is awe-inspiring, the man-made equivalent of the Rockies. Dark, low-to-the-ground muscular structures, some three times the size of a football field, sprawl across the landscape, sprouting chimneys so tall that they're equipped
30 with blinking lights to alert wayward aircraft. These chimneys shoot full-bodied flames thirty feet into the sky; at night they appear almost magical, like giant torches heating the moon. Billows of smoke linger in the air like phantom dirges. It used to be, when the
35 steel mills were going strong, that these smokestacks spat out particles of graphite that would dust the streets and cars and rooftops like snow, catching the sun and setting the neighborhood aglitter. Suspended conveyor belts, pipes, and railroad overpasses weave in, out, and
40 over the behemoth buildings. The noise is crushing, the stench of sulfur so powerful that not even a closed car window can keep it at bay. Had Rube Goldberg lost his sense of humor, this is, I imagine, what he would have produced.

45 This is the heart of American industrial might, or what's left of it. The first of the mills was built in the 1850s, and within a hundred years more steel was produced in this stretch of land than anywhere else in the world. The freighters delivered iron ore
50 from Minnesota's Mesabi Range, and the mills turned the mineral into steel, shipping it west by rail and eventually east by the St. Lawrence Seaway. By the 1960s, the mills employed eighty thousand men and women; they cascaded in from Poland, from
55 Yugoslavia, from Mexico, and from the American South. Steel mills and refineries lined up along the dredged Calumet River and along the Lake Michigan shoreline, extending twenty-two miles from South Chicago to Gary, Indiana. This stretch of boiling steel
60 was the equivalent of an industrial mountain stream, the source for can openers and knives, refrigerators and cars, bridges and skyscrapers. It fed this country's insatiable hunger for consumption and comfort. It was, in short, the nation's lifeblood.
65 The local population is still so dependent on the mills that the daily newspaper in Hammond, Indiana, which is just over the Chicago border, runs a box score every Wednesday of the region's steel tonnage and capacity. Nonetheless, there are only fifteen
70 thousand working in the mills now; the owners grew complacent, so accustomed to their oligopoly that they forgot how to compete. Between the mills that still roll steel, there are hundreds of acres of vacant land littered with abandoned factory buildings stripped
75 of their exteriors, brick coke houses collapsing in on themselves, and railroad tracks and bridges that have turned a muddy brown from rust.

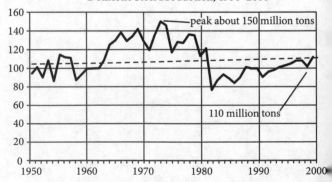

Domestic Steel Production, 1950–2000

Source: American Iron and Steel Institute

CONTINUE ▶

19

The author of the passage most likely believes South Chicago

A) should be a more popular vacation destination.

B) will soon have no working steel mills.

C) is isolated from the rest of the city.

D) embodies the dirty, smelly nature of American industry.

20

Which choice provides the best evidence for the answer to the previous question?

A) Lines 5–10 ("Apart from . . . removed")

B) Lines 25–26 ("And yet . . . Rockies")

C) Lines 40–42 ("The noise . . . bay")

D) Lines 45–46 ("This is . . . it")

21

The author includes a list of restaurant names (lines 19–21) primarily to

A) emphasize the modest nature of the neighborhood.

B) recommend places for visitors to have a meal.

C) suggest that there is little variety in the eating establishments.

D) explain why most people never visit South Chicago.

22

As used in line 38, "suspended" most nearly means

A) drooping.

B) hanging.

C) slumbering.

D) fixed.

23

In the context of the passage, the image of steel mills is compared to that of

A) the Rockies.

B) wayward aircraft.

C) a football field.

D) phantom dirges.

24

Which choice provides the best evidence for the answer to the previous question?

A) Lines 1–4 ("Fourteen miles . . . Valley")

B) Lines 11–17 ("The vast . . . shorelines")

C) Lines 25–30 ("And yet . . . aircraft")

D) Lines 49–52 ("The freighters . . . Seaway")

25

As used in line 63, "consumption" most nearly means

A) eating.

B) expenditure.

C) corrosion.

D) burning.

26

In the context of the passage as a whole, the primary purpose the last paragraph is to

A) criticize the steel mill owners.

B) lament the state of abandoned property.

C) explain the current status of the steel mills.

D) suggest changes to the steel industry.

CONTINUE

27

Which claim about domestic steel production is supported by the graph?

A) Between 1950 and 2000, production consistently increased.

B) Production was stagnant between 1950 and 2000.

C) Production peaked in the 1960s, followed by a steep decline in the 1970s.

D) Net production increased slightly from 1950 to 2000.

28

It can reasonably be inferred from the passage and the graph that

A) U.S. steel mills reached their greatest productivity in the mid-1970s.

B) the U.S. steel industry experienced growth followed by significant decline during the 20th century.

C) all domestic steel mills cut their workforces by over 75% between 1950 and 2000.

D) air pollution in communities surrounding steel mills was worse in the 1970s than in 2000.

CONTINUE

Questions 29–37 are based on the following passage and supplementary material.

This passage is adapted from E. Gene Towne and Joseph M. Craine, "Ecological Consequences of Shifting the Timing of Burning Tallgrass Prairie." © 2014 by E. Gene Towne and Joseph M. Craine. A forb is an herbaceous flowering plant.

Periodic burning is required for the maintenance of tallgrass prairie. The responses of prairie vegetation to fire, however, can vary widely depending upon
Line when the fires occur. Management and conservation
5 objectives such as biomass production, livestock performance, wildlife habitat, and control of specific plant species, often influence when grasslands are burned. In some prairie regions, timing of seasonal burns have been used to manipulate the balance of C_3
10 and C_4 species, control woody species, stimulate grass flowering, and alter the proportion of plant functional groups. Most grassland fire research, however, has focused on either burn frequency or comparing growing season burns with dormant season burns,
15 and there are few studies that differentiate effects from seasonal burning within the dormant season. In the Kansas Flint Hills, when prairies are burned is an important management issue, but the ecological consequences of burning at different times are poorly
20 understood.

The Flint Hills are one of the last remaining regions supporting extensive native tallgrass prairie in North America and frequent burning is integral to its preservation and economic utilization. Since
25 the early 1970's, recommendations have been to burn Kansas Flint Hills grasslands annually in late spring, typically once the dominant grasses have emerged 1.25–5 cm above the soil surface. Although frequent late-spring burning has maintained the Flint Hills
30 grassland, the resultant smoke plumes from en masse burning often leads to air quality issues in nearby cities. Concentrated smoke from grass fires produces airborne particulates, volatile organic compounds, and nitrogen oxides that facilitate tropospheric ozone
35 production. Burning in late spring also generates more ozone than burning in winter or early spring due to the higher air temperatures and insolation.

If the Flint Hills tallgrass prairie, its economic utilization, and high air quality are all to be
40 maintained, a good understanding of the consequences of burning at different times of the year is necessary. Burning earlier in spring has been regarded as undesirable because it putatively reduces total biomass production, increases cool-season [grasses] and
45 undesirable forbs, is ineffective in controlling woody species, and lowers monthly weight gains of steers compared to burning in late spring. Consequently, burning exclusively in late spring has become ingrained in the cultural practices of grassland
50 management in the Flint Hills, and local ranchers often burn in unison when weather conditions are favorable.

Despite long-standing recommendations that tallgrass prairie be burned only in late spring, the data supporting this policy is equivocal. Total biomass
55 production was lower in plots burned in early spring than plots burned in late spring, but the weights included grasses, forbs, and shrubs. It was not known if [grass] biomass was reduced by early-spring burning or if the differences were a site effect rather than a
60 treatment effect. Burning in early spring also shifted community composition in a perceived negative pattern because it favored cool-season grasses and forbs. This shift in community composition, however, may actually be desirable because many cool-season
65 grasses have higher production and nutritional quality than warm-season grasses at certain times of the year, and many forb species are beneficial to the diet of grazers. Burning in late spring has been considered the most effective time to control invasive shrubs,
70 but *Symphoricarpos orbiculatus* was the only woody species that declined with repeated late spring burning. Finally, average weight gain of steers was lower in an unburned pasture than in burned pastures, but there was no significant difference in monthly weight gain
75 among cattle grazing in early-, mid-, or late-spring burned pastures.

The historical studies that formed the foundation for time of burning recommendations in tallgrass prairie are inconclusive because none had
80 experimental replications and most were spatially limited to small plots. All of these studies were interpreted as suggesting that shifting the time of burning by only a few weeks would negatively influence the plant community. A more recent large-
85 scale replicated study that compared the effects of annual burning in autumn, winter, and late spring found that the timing of burning had no significant effect on grass production and no reductions in the composition of desirable warm-season grasses.

CONTINUE ▶

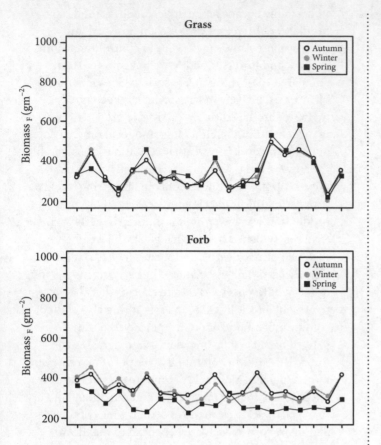

Grass

Forb

Changes in Upland and Lowland Grass (a) and Forb (b) Productivity Over Time for Autumn-, Winter-, and Spring-Burned Watersheds

29

The authors of the passage most likely believe that

A) burning should be done on a semiannual basis.

B) no burning should happen in the late spring.

C) late spring may not be the best time for burning.

D) changing burning schedules will negatively influence plants.

30

According to the passage, which of the following does NOT influence decisions on the timing of seasonal burns?

A) Biomass production

B) Control of specific plant species

C) Tropospheric ozone production

D) Weather

31

The passage suggests that the Kansas Flint Hills

A) are an ecologically sensitive area that must be treated with extreme caution.

B) must be regularly burned to remain economically viable.

C) have a unique composition of grasses and forbs that must be studied further.

D) will not support healthy livestock if the burning schedule changes.

32

Which choice provides the best evidence for the answer to the previous question?

A) Lines 21–24 ("The Flint . . . utilization")

B) Lines 38–41 ("If the . . . necessary")

C) Lines 42–47 ("Burning earlier . . . spring")

D) Lines 54–57 ("Total biomass . . . shrubs")

33

As used in line 49, "practices" most nearly means

A) traditions.

B) rehearsals.

C) accomplishments.

D) chores.

34

As used in line 54, "equivocal" most nearly means

A) wrong.

B) misleading.

C) ambivalent.

D) unclear.

CONTINUE

35

Based on the passage, it can be inferred that *Symphoricarpos orbiculatus* is

A) a forb species beneficial to grazers.

B) an invasive shrub.

C) a woody warm-season grass.

D) a late spring grass.

36

Which choice provides the best evidence for the answer to the previous question?

A) Lines 52–54 ("Despite long-standing . . . equivocal")

B) Lines 60–63 ("Burning in . . . forbs")

C) Lines 63–68 ("This shift . . . grazers")

D) Lines 68–71 ("Burning in . . . burning")

37

Which claim about grasses is supported by the graph?

A) Spring burning always results in higher biomass than does autumn or winter burning.

B) Over time, biomass will increase only in prairies burned in spring.

C) The timing of burning does not significantly affect biomass.

D) Biomass declined sharply in 2012 due to drastically lower rainfall.

CONTINUE

Questions 38–47 are based on the following passages.

These passages are adapted from KU Leuven, "Bacterium counteracts 'coffee ring effect.'" © 2013 and University of Pennsylvania, "Physicists undo the 'coffee ring effect.'" © 2011 Science Daily.

Passage 1

A team of University of Pennsylvania physicists has shown how to disrupt the "coffee ring effect"—the ring-shaped stain of particles leftover after coffee drops evaporate—by changing the particle shape. The
5   discovery provides new tools for engineers to deposit uniform coatings.

The research was conducted by professor Arjun Yodh, director of the Laboratory for Research on the Structure of Matter; doctoral candidates Peter Yunker
10 and Matthew Lohr; and postdoctoral fellow Tim Still.

"The coffee ring effect is very common in everyday experience," Yunker said. "To avoid it, scientists have gone to great lengths designing paints and inks that produce an even coating upon evaporation. We found
15 that the effect can be eliminated simply by changing the shape of the particle."

University of Chicago physicists Sidney Nagel, Thomas Witten and their colleagues wrote an influential paper about this process in 1997, which
20 focused mainly on suspended spherical particles, but it was not until the Yodh team's recent experiments that the surprising role played by suspended particle shape was discovered.

Yodh's team used uniformly sized plastic particles
25 in their experiments. These particles were initially spherical but could be stretched into varying degrees of eccentricity, to ensure the experiments only tested the effect of the particle's shape on the drying pattern. The researchers were surprised at how big an effect particle
30 shape had on the drying phenomenon.

"Different particle geometries change the nature of the membrane at the air-water interface," Yodh said. "And that has big consequences." Spherical particles easily detach from the interface, and they flow past one
35 another easily because the spheres do not substantially deform the air-water interface. Ellipsoid particles, however, cause substantial undulation of the air-water interface that in turn induces very strong attractions between the ellipsoids. Thus the ellipsoids tend to get
40 stuck on the surface, and, while the stuck particles can continue to flow towards the drop's edges during

evaporation, they increasingly block each other, creating a traffic jam of particles that eventually covers the drop's surface.

45   After experimenting with suspended particle shape, the researchers added a surfactant, essentially soap, into the drops to show that interactions on the drop's surface were responsible for the effect. With the surfactant lowering the drop's surface tension, ellipsoid
50 particles did not get stuck at the interface and flowed freely to the edge.

"We were thinking it would be useful if you could just sprinkle in a few of these ellipsoid particles to remove the coffee ring effect," Yodh said, "and we
55 found that sometimes this idea works and sometimes it doesn't."

Passage 2

Researchers from the Departments of Chemical Engineering and Chemistry at KU Leuven have now discovered how to counteract coffee rings with
60 'surfactants', i.e., soap. The key to the discovery was not a kitchen towel, but a bacterium that counteracts the coffee ring effect at the microscopic level.

When a coffee ring dries, its edges become noticeably darker and thicker. This occurs because the
65 coffee particles move toward the edge of the stain while the water in the liquid evaporates. At a microscopic level, this coffee ring effect can also be seen in liquids with particles of other materials such as plastic and wood.

70   In various industrial applications—applying an even coat of paint or varnish, for example—the coffee ring effect can be particularly troublesome and scientists have long been seeking ways to counteract it. Raf De Dier and Wouter Sempels (Departments
75 of Chemical Engineering and Chemistry) have now described a solution based on examples found in nature. De Dier and Sempels carried out experiments and calculations on nanomaterials as well as on a particularly promising bacterium, *Pseudomonas*
80 *aeruginosa*.

Pseudomonas aeruginosa is a dangerous bacterium that can cause infections in open wounds. "A *Pseudomonas aeruginosa* bacteria colony wants to find as large a breeding ground as possible. To avoid
85 overconcentration on the edges of a wound when spreading itself during the drying-out process, the

CONTINUE ▶

bacterium produces substances that counteract the coffee ring effect."

These surface-tension-disrupting substances are
90 called surfactants. Detergents such as soap are also surfactants. "Add soap to a stain—a coffee stain or any other stain—and you will still get a coffee ring effect. But at the same time the soap causes a counterflow from the edge back towards the centre of the stain
95 in such a way that the small particles—material or bacteria—end up in a kind of whirlwind. In this way, you get a more uniform distribution of particles as evaporation occurs."

38

The author of Passage 1 refers to a paper by University of Chicago physicists Sidney Nagel and Thomas Witten (lines 17–23) primarily to

A) imply that Nagel and Witten could have discovered the impact of ellipsoid particles.

B) describe an impediment to research on suspended spherical particles.

C) suggest that the study done by Nagel and Witten influenced the research by Yodh's team.

D) contrast the results of earlier, flawed research with the useful data obtained more recently.

39

Passage 1 most strongly suggests that Professor Yodh's team at the University of Pennsylvania assumed which of the following before their experiments?

A) The shape of the particles leads to detachment from the interface.

B) The shape of the particles has a minimal effect on drying patterns.

C) The shape of a spherical particle can't be changed to ellipsoid.

D) The shape of the particles is the only factor that affects the membrane.

40

Based on the passage, which choice best describes the relationship between Nagel and Witten's and Yodh's research?

A) Yodh's research challenges Nagel and Witten's.

B) Yodh's research builds on Nagel and Witten's.

C) Nagel and Witten's research contradicts Yodh's.

D) Nagel and Witten's research supports Yodh's.

41

As used in line 37, "undulation" most nearly means

A) attraction.

B) evaporation.

C) undertow.

D) ripple.

42

In lines 84–90 ("To avoid . . . surfactants"), what is the most likely reason the author of Passage 2 compares detergents and bacterium?

A) To justify research into surfactants from bacterium, since the surfactants in soap may cause some issues in industrial use

B) To alert companies that want surfactants for paint and varnish to the dangers of bacterium

C) To show that soap can help reduce the movement of particles to the edge of a stain, but can't stop it

D) To contend that soap is a better surfactant so it's best to avoid using *Pseudomonas aeruginosa* until further studies have been done

---

43

What does Passage 2 most strongly suggest about the coffee ring effect?

A) It generates many studies on ways to thwart it.

B) It sends microscopic particles into a whirlwind.

C) It can be eliminated with the use of surfactants.

D) It has various industrial applications.

CONTINUE ➤

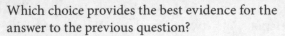

44

Which choice provides the best evidence for the answer to the previous question?

A) Lines 57–60 ("Researchers from . . . soap")

B) Lines 60–62 ("The key . . . level")

C) Lines 66–69 ("At a . . . wood")

D) Lines 70–74 ("In various . . . it")

45

As used in line 97, "uniform" most nearly means

A) spread thin.

B) similarly shaped.

C) evenly distributed.

D) wiped clean.

46

Is the main conclusion presented by the author of Passage 2 consistent with the properties of the coffee ring effect, as described in Passage 1?

A) No, since Passage 1 shows that surfactants can increase the coffee ring effect if ellipsoids are present.

B) No, since the study in Passage 1 describes how oblong spheres diminish the coffee ring effect.

C) Yes, since the study in Passage 2 explains that surfactants have an effect on the movement of particles.

D) Yes, since the study in Passage 2 concludes that bacteria can be genetically modified in order to produce surfactants.

47

One difference between the studies described in the two passages is that unlike the researchers discussed in Passage 1, the researchers in Passage 2

A) stretch the *Pseudomonas aeruginosa* until they become surfactants.

B) utilize biological organisms to disrupt the surface tension.

C) experiment on nanomaterials in order to breed *Pseudomonas aeruginosa*.

D) explore ways to increase evaporation and particle flow.

STOP
**If you finish before time is called, you may check your work on this section only.
Do not turn to any other section.**

No Test Material On This Page

Writing and Language Test

35 MINUTES, 44 QUESTIONS

Turn to Section 2 of your answer sheet to answer the questions in this section.

Questions 1–11 are based on the following passage.

Getting a CLOe

Imagine you go to a restaurant you've never tried before. Now, let's say you **[1]** had a bad experience. What next? For many, the answer is **[2]** simple, get on social media and tell the world. Aside from telling all your

1

A) NO CHANGE
B) have had
C) were having
D) have

2

A) NO CHANGE
B) simple get
C) simple: get
D) simple, hop

CONTINUE

friends and followers about the experience on Twitter and Facebook, [3] you would probably decide not to return to that restaurant. In fact, you might have used these services to find the restaurant in the first place. And really, if a place has two out of five stars on Yelp when you look it up, what's the chance you'll go there in the first place?

Companies, not just restaurants, are starting to see that their biggest business generators are not TV or Internet ads anymore. [4] Today, "buzz" gets created on social media, and it is more important than ever for companies to [5] insure that they are showing the best possible face to the world on social media. Maintaining that public face has created a new job: Chief Listening Officer. Where a Social Media Manager might be in charge of a [6] companies output on Facebook and other sites, a Chief Listening Officer is on the other side. A CLO scours blogs, Pinterest, tumblr, Facebook, Twitter, Google, Yelp, and whatever new site will be hot when you read this to make sure that a company's public image is under control.

3

Which of the following would best maintain the focus of this sentence and paragraph?

A) NO CHANGE

B) you might also go to a consumer-review site, such as Yelp, to tell future patrons.

C) it might make you feel better to tell your friends and relatives about the experience over the phone.

D) you could take the edge off by watching videos of animals doing funny stuff.

4

The author is considering deleting the phrase *not just restaurants* from the preceding sentence and adjusting the punctuation accordingly. Should the phrase be kept or deleted?

A) Kept, because it clarifies that the practice described in the essay is not limited to one industry.

B) Kept, because it encourages companies other than restaurants to hire Chief Listening Officers.

C) Deleted, because it incorrectly implies that patrons of other businesses discuss their experiences on social media.

D) Deleted, because the previous paragraph is all about restaurants, and this one is not.

5

A) NO CHANGE

B) assure the public

C) ensure

D) make insurance

6

A) NO CHANGE

B) companies'

C) company's

D) companys'

CONTINUE ➤

If a CLO sees a bad review on someone's blog, for instance, the CLO might contact a customer-service representative **7** and make it better to see if the situation can be remedied. On the other hand, if a company **8** unfurls a new advertising campaign and the ads are getting buzz on Twitter or many views on YouTube, the CLO might tell his marketing team to keep up the good work. The incredible **9** thing about this is that it is more detailed than market research has ever been before. People share their entire lives on social media, and a single post can reveal not only someone's positive or negative reaction but also **10** their age, gender, location, social status, friends, and so on.

7

A) NO CHANGE
B) and improve things
C) and say, "Get on it!",
D) DELETE the underlined portion.

8

A) NO CHANGE
B) rolls out
C) unrolls
D) roles out

9

A) NO CHANGE
B) thing about this kind of "market research"
C) thing
D) reality

10

A) NO CHANGE
B) they're
C) your
D) his or her

CONTINUE

Some criticize the CLO position as a fad, suggesting that companies are overreacting to the power of social media. **11** The fact of the matter is, however, CLOs will be needed as long as social media are around. After all, consumers are realizing that social-media reviews are often the purest of the pure—neither that of an overrefined food critic or tech geek nor that of someone in the pay of this or that company. The people are talking, and companies have at last made their "listening" official.

11

Which of the following most directly answers the criticism presented in the previous sentence?

A) NO CHANGE

B) They see social media as temporarily popular but not likely to endure.

C) Teachers say that students spend too much time on social media.

D) They say that some social media outlets are more effective than others.

CONTINUE

Questions 12–22 are based on the following passage and supplementary material.

Gimme Fever…Actually, Please Don't

Medical science has created some modern miracles, but it can be difficult to appreciate just how miraculous some of them are. The Spanish Flu hit the United States in the 1910s, and **12** polio rocked the foundations of America in the 1930s and 1940s, but it is difficult to imagine an epidemic like the Philadelphia Yellow Fever Epidemic of 1793. The official register listed over 5,000 deaths between August 1st and November 9th of that year. These figures are staggering when we consider that Philadelphia city, **13** the largest city in the country today, had a population of over 1.5 million, and its surrounding areas had only about 50,000.

Rank	Place	Population
1	New York city, NY *	33,131
2	Philadelphia city, PA*	28,522
3	Boston town, MA*	18,320
4	Charleston city, SC	16,359
5	Baltimore town, MD	13,503
6	Northern Liberties township, PA*	9,913
7	Salem town, MA	7,921
8	Newport town, RI	6,716
9	Providence town, RI*	6,380
10	Marblehead town, MA	5,661
10	Southwark district, PA*	5,661
12	Gloucester town, MA	5,317
13	Newbury town, MA	4,837
14	Portsmouth town, NH	4,720
15	Sherburne town (Nantucket), MA*	4,620
16	Middleborough town, MA	4,526
17	New Haven city, CT*	4,487
18	Richmond city, VA	3,761
19	Albany city, NY	3,498
20	Norfolk borough, VA	2,959
21	Petersburg town, VA	2,828
22	Alexandria town, VA*	2,748
23	Hartford city, CT*	2,683
24	Hudson city, NY	2,584
* See Notes for Individual Places.		
Source: U.S. Bureau of the Census		
Internet Release date: June 15, 1998		

Population of the 24 Urban Places: 1790

12

Which of the following would provide a detail that would best maintain the focus of this paragraph?

A) NO CHANGE

B) many people died from this flu, especially soldiers in World War I,

C) it's possible to get flu vaccinations at your local drug store now,

D) it just faded away even though doctors could never cure it,

13

Which of the following gives information consistent with the chart?

A) NO CHANGE

B) the second largest city in the country at that time, had a population of only about 28,000,

C) second only to New York and Boston, had a population of over 28,000 at the time,

D) was larger than its neighboring New York City by nearly 10,000 people,

CONTINUE

It was not ultimately medical science that saved the day during this epidemic. Doctors tried various **14** things, but they were stalled by their inability to figure out both how the disease originated and how **15** it was spreading. It therefore seemed a godsend when the frost came in November, and the number of deaths tapered off. Medical historians now know that the disease was spread by mosquitoes, but this was **16** pretty shady until nearly a century after the disease had come and gone.

14

A) NO CHANGE

B) options

C) management models

D) treatment approaches

15

A) NO CHANGE

B) it spread.

C) it had been spread.

D) its spread.

16

A) NO CHANGE

B) stupid idiocy

C) not verified

D) downright wrong

CONTINUE

[1] In 1793, Philadelphia was the second largest city in the new nation of the United States. [2] As a result, all of the quarantine and curfew measures that **17** they tried to impose had failed. [3] Panicked politicians blamed immigration. [4] The city's College of Physicians published a letter in the city newspapers that spoke to the confusion. [5] They recognized the epidemic for what it was, but their eleven measures for prevention were haphazard and confused and included the avoidance of alcohol, **18** hot sun, and night air. [6] Philadelphia didn't know what had hit it. [7] Dr. Benjamin Rush, one of the earliest and most brilliant physicians in all of American history, blamed a rotten shipment of coffee that had come into Philadelphia's port. **19**

17

A) NO CHANGE
B) one
C) city authorities
D) some

18

A) NO CHANGE
B) hot sun and night air.
C) hot sun, and also night air.
D) hot sun, and the air of the night.

19

The best placement for sentence 7 would be

A) where it is now.
B) at the beginning of the paragraph.
C) after sentence 1.
D) after sentence 3.

CONTINUE

It's difficult to imagine an epidemic on this kind of scale today. Moreover, Philadelphia's relative prominence and sophistication in that era should give us pause. The medical establishment sat back **20** helplessly: as the disease ravaged the city. The recent outbreak of the Ebola **21** virus, in West Africa, provides a terrifying reminder, of just how deadly certain diseases can be, when they are unchecked or inadequately understood. **22** By the same token, the Yellow Fever Epidemic provides a remarkable instance of a city's resilience in the face of adversity. As the population of the city was literally decimated, and other yellow-fever epidemics continued to ravage the city, Philadelphia persisted, and with it, the new nation grew stronger, just as it has in the face of crisis ever since.

20

A) NO CHANGE

B) helplessly,

C) helplessly

D) helplessly;

21

A) NO CHANGE

B) virus in West Africa provides a terrifying reminder of just how deadly certain diseases can be

C) virus, in West Africa provides a terrifying reminder, of just how deadly certain diseases can be

D) virus, in West Africa, provides a terrifying reminder of just how deadly certain diseases can be,

22

A) NO CHANGE

B) On the other hand,

C) Therefore,

D) Thus,

CONTINUE

Questions 23–33 are based on the following passage.

The Singing Brakeman

The early days of recorded music can be hazy. Many people find it difficult to believe that artists recording before the radio boom in the 1930s, or even before the rock and roll boom in the 1950s, could have had any success at all **23** seems doubtful. Despite this misconception, there is a treasure trove of recorded music from that era, and not only by the greats of bebop and swing. **24**

The circumstances of Rodgers's birth **25** is obscure, but legend has it that he was born in Meridian, Mississippi in 1897. Little is known for **26** sure, but his father was a foreman on the Mobile and Ohio Railroad in Meridian. Jimmie eventually became a brakeman, but **27** a health issue cut his career short. He stayed alive for a few years after his dismissal in 1927, but he could no longer work the rails.

23

A) NO CHANGE

B) strikes us as odd.

C) appears improbable.

D) DELETE the underlined portion and end the sentence with a period.

24

Which of the following would most effectively conclude this paragraph by introducing the main subject of the essay as a whole?

A) It takes a real music connoisseur to know who wa famous before Elvis Presley.

B) Most of the best-known names from the 1930s and 1940s are those of jazz singers.

C) One of these greats was Jimmie Rodgers, one of the first megastars of country music.

D) Some of the greats were Robert Johnson, Mississippi John Hurt, and Jimmie Rodgers.

25

A) NO CHANGE

B) are

C) has been

D) was

26

A) NO CHANGE

B) certain,

C) sure about his family,

D) sure about his mother, father, and siblings,

27

At this point, the writer wants to include a detail that provides specific information about Rodgers's illness. Which of the following would best fulfill that goal?

A) NO CHANGE

B) problems with his health

C) a bout of tuberculosis

D) one of the current diseases

CONTINUE

This inability to work, however, proved to be [28] fortuitous for Rodgers's great passion—music. At age 3, Rodgers had already secretly organized two traveling shows, only to be recovered and brought back to Meridian by his father. Once Jimmie could no longer work the [29] rails, however, he pursued his musical career in earnest. In Bristol, Tennessee, Rodgers organized his first band. That same year, the band was asked to record some songs for Ralph Peer of the Victor Talking Machine Company. The recordings survive today, though they feature a solo Jimmie Rodgers rather than his whole band, as a pre-recording quarrel led them to break up.

[28]

A) NO CHANGE
B) chancy
C) blessed
D) charmed

[29]

A) NO CHANGE
B) rails however
C) rails; however,
D) rails, however

The recording had moderate success, and it sparked Rodgers to pursue his music career in earnest. In October of that year, after Rodgers chased his dream, Victor released "Blue Yodel," better known as "T for Texas," which sold [30] all the way to New York City half a million copies. Rodgers quickly became a household name, and his trademark yodel would be known the world over. By this [31] time, Rodgers had become the famous "Singing Brakeman," and his influence would be felt for many generations to come.

This influence would not be felt only in country music either: blues singer Howlin' Wolf cited Rodgers as an early influence, [32] like Elvis Presley. Ultimately losing his battle with tuberculosis at age 33, Rodgers may have lived a short life, [33] so it's no surprise that his music is seldom remembered today.

30

If the punctuation were to be adjusted accordingly, the best placement for the underlined portion would be

A) where it is now.

B) after the word *year*.

C) after the word *dream*.

D) after the word *copies*.

31

A) NO CHANGE

B) time, when

C) time, as

D) time:

32

A) NO CHANGE

B) as did

C) similar to

D) much like that of

33

Which choice best concludes the essay by reinforcing its main idea?

A) NO CHANGE

B) but many of his family members attended his funeral and honor him today.

C) but he was able to work as both a train brakeman and a musician.

D) but if the history of American music is an indication, his influence is still alive and well.

CONTINUE

Questions 34–44 are based on the following passage and supplementary material.

Whale Grandmothers Know Best

We don't often think to apply gender differences to the animal kingdom. Certainly, males and females have [34] a distinct role, but these seem to be largely determined by biology and by the propagation of the species. As a result, many females do not live much beyond menopause, the phase after which females can no longer reproduce. The data below show that [35] only a handful of animals, such as the black-tailed prairie dog, have any post-reproductive life span at all. Some species, however, like humans, short-finned pilot whales, and killer whales, have females who typically live two or more decades after

[34]

A) NO CHANGE

B) a distinction,

C) a role that is distinct,

D) distinct roles,

[35]

Which of the following gives accurate data based on the graph?

A) NO CHANGE

B) most animals, including *homo sapiens*, tend to have some post-reproductive life span.

C) the common bottlenose dolphin has one of the shortest pre-reproductive life spans relative to other animals.

D) no rodent species has any post-reproductive life span at all.

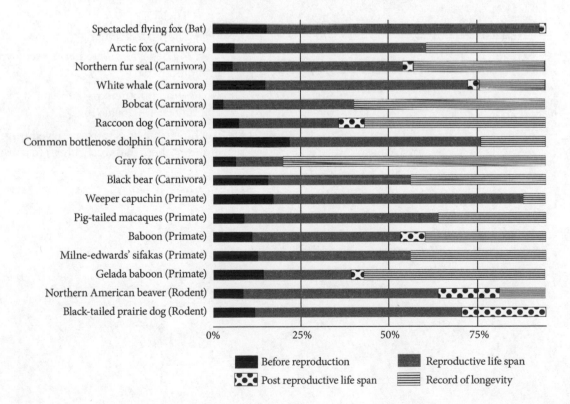

Relationship Between Reproductive Phase and Life Span Across Species

menopause. Scientists have long wondered why evolution has determined 36 they should live so much longer, sometimes to be as old as 90, than their counterparts in other species.

37 It seems that the social forces that define gender may apply to the animal kingdom as well, even though we consider animal behavior to be determined almost entirely by nature rather than nurture. After watching over 750 hours of video and observing the behaviors of pods of whales, 38 whale grandmothers were observed to have teaching behaviors by the scientists.

A) NO CHANGE

B) any of them

C) themselves

D) the female whales

37

Which of the following would provide the most effective transition from the previous paragraph to this paragraph?

A) The answer may have come from a recent study o killer whales.

B) Killer whales are some of the most fascinating marine species.

C) Pretty much everyone knows by now that whales are mammals, not fish.

D) Scientists will experiment and try new things unt they find something interesting.

A) NO CHANGE

B) scientists observed that many of the teaching behaviors were performed by whale grandmothers.

C) whale grandmothers were the most likely to exhibit teaching behaviors.

D) teaching behaviors were observed from whale grandmothers that were shown to scientists.

CONTINUE

[39] This knowledge is particularly useful for whale pods because the abundance of salmon is typically what determines whale life-cycles, both reproduction and mortality.

The scientists ascribe this behavior to what they refer to as the grandmothers' roles as "repositories of ecological [40] knowledge" in other words. Sharpened memories and long experience of learned behaviors make the older females extremely valuable to future generations. Without this knowledge, the younger whales would not be able to make the transition to maturity, and the species would not continue to propagate. The elder females have evolved this longevity because the species, simply put, needs it. [41]

At this point, the writer is considering adding the following true statement:

> The older female whales were the most likely to lead younger whales to salmon feeding grounds, particularly in the periods where the usually plentiful salmon were sparse.

Should the writer make this addition here?

A) Yes, because it clarifies some of the teaching behaviors mentioned in the previous sentence.

B) Yes, because it gives some credit to older whales, who were otherwise ignored in the study.

C) No, because the information conflicts with other information given later in the passage.

D) No, because the scientists' observations are not given as conclusive.

A) NO CHANGE

B) knowledge" in other words; sharpened

C) knowledge," in other words, sharpened

D) knowledge." In other words, sharpened

The writer is considering replacing the word *longevity* with the word *life* in the previous sentence. Should the writer make the change or keep the sentence as it is?

A) Keep the sentence as is, because "longevity" provides a more formal way of saying the same thing.

B) Keep the sentence as is, because the sentence refers to the length of whale life, not only the life itself.

C) Make the change, because "life" provides a more general way of articulating the point.

D) Make the change, because readers may not know the meaning of the word "longevity."

CONTINUE

42 From a gender perspective, these findings further break down the idea that gender roles are biologically determined. From an age perspective, the findings also show that societies that value youth and middle age to the detriment of old age may do so at **43** there own peril. Anyone with grandparents knows that these older relatives have experienced enough of life to know a thing or two. In whale pods as well as human communities, it seems, life may depend on the accrued knowledge **44** about the secrets of life that have been gathered by the old people who know about it.

42

Which of the following choices would introduce this paragraph most effectively?

A) Gender discrimination does not really exist in whale communities.

B) Whale grandmothers know things other than where to find the salmon.

C) There is a beautiful scene in Herman Melville's *Moby Dick* featuring whale families.

D) The findings are interesting to non-scientists as well.

43

A) NO CHANGE

B) their

C) it's

D) its

44

A) NO CHANGE

B) of some of the secret-knowing people whose long lives are long enough.

C) of those who have lived long enough to know the secrets of long life.

D) the longer-lived people who are more secret oriented.

STOP
**If you finish before time is called, you may check your work on this section only.
Do not turn to any other section.**

No Test Material On This Page

Math Test – No Calculator

25 MINUTES, 17 QUESTIONS

Turn to Section 3 of your answer sheet to answer the questions in this section.

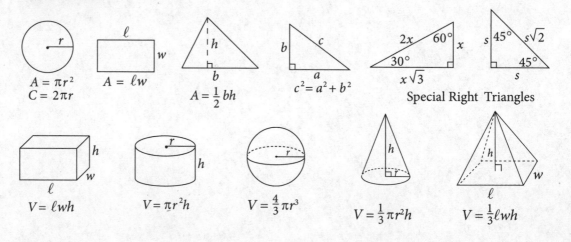

Which of the following ordered pairs (x, y) satisfies both equations $x = \frac{1}{2}y + 3$ and $y = x^2 - 5x + 6$?

A) $(0, 3)$

B) $(2, -2)$

C) $(4, 2)$

D) $(6, 12)$

2

Which of the following is an equivalent form of the expression $30y - 12cy$?

A) $(5 - 2c)y$

B) $(30 - 12c)y$

C) $18(c - 2y)$

D) $18cy^2$

3

The formula $F = ma$ is used to calculate the force on an object with a mass, m, and an acceleration, a. Based on this formula, what is the acceleration, a, in terms of F and m ?

A) $a = Fm$

B) $a = F + m$

C) $a = \dfrac{F}{m}$

D) $a = \dfrac{m}{F}$

4

$$-4j - 10k = 50$$
$$j - 3k = 4$$

If (j, k) is the solution to the system of equations above, what is the value of j ?

A) 13

B) −5

C) −7

D) −10

CONTINUE

5

The equation $y = 3{,}100x + 105$ models the relationship between the weight, y, in grams, of an average giant panda and the number of months, x, after it was born. If the equation is graphed in the xy-plane, what is indicated by the slope of the graph?

A) The weight, in grams, of an average giant panda at birth

B) The number of months it takes an average giant panda to gain weight

C) The age, in months, of an average giant panda when it is fully matured

D) The weight, in grams, that an average giant panda gains each month

6

Which of the following is a solution to the equation $3b^2 - 6b = 5 + 4b^2$?

A) –5

B) 0

C) 1

D) 3

7

A line is graphed in the xy-plane. If the line has an x-intercept of 4 and contains the point $(-2, 6)$, which of the following cannot be true?

A) The point $(-10, -6)$ is on the line.

B) The slope of the line is negative.

C) The y-intercept is positive.

D) The point $(10, -6)$ is on the line.

8

A patterned quilt uses 16 different squares of fabric. Each square of fabric must have an area of at least 34 square inches and no more than 360 square inches. What inequality represents all possible values of the total area of fabric, f, in square inches needed for the quilt?

A) $5{,}740 \le f \le 5{,}760$

B) $5{,}440 \le f \le 5{,}760$

C) $5{,}440 \le f \le 5{,}460$

D) $340 \le f \le 360$

CONTINUE

Christen wants to buy dishes that cost $17.30 each and bowls that cost $14.90 each. A 15% discount will be applied to the entire purchase and no tax is charged. If Christen buys 3 dishes, which equation relates the number of bowls purchased, n, and the total cost in dollars, x?

A) $51.90 + 14.90n = 1.15x$

B) $51.90 + 14.90n = 0.85x$

C) $1.15(51.90 + 14.90n) = x$

D) $0.85(51.90 + 14.90n) = x$

$$\left(a^{\frac{1}{3}}b^{\frac{1}{4}}\right)^3 \left(a^{\frac{1}{3}}b^{\frac{1}{4}}\right)^4 = a^{\frac{k}{3}}b^{\frac{k}{4}}$$

If the equation above, where k is a constant, is true for all positive values of a and b, what is the value of k?

A) 3

B) 4

C) 7

D) 10

11

A baker has $75 with which to purchase ingredients. The baker needs to buy at least 2 containers of flour and at least 3 containers of cocoa powder. Flour costs $3.99 per container, and cocoa powder costs $5.99 per container. If f represents the number of containers of flour and c represents the number of containers of cocoa powder, which of the following systems of inequalities models this situation?

A) $\begin{cases} f \geq 2 \\ c \geq 3 \\ 3.99f + 5.99c \geq 75 \end{cases}$

B) $\begin{cases} f + c \geq 5 \\ 3.99f + 5.99c \geq 75 \end{cases}$

C) $\begin{cases} f \geq 2 \\ c \geq 3 \\ 3.99f + 5.99c \leq 75 \end{cases}$

D) $\begin{cases} f + c \geq 5 \\ 3.99f + 5.99c \leq 75 \end{cases}$

12

If the equation $x = (y + 5)(y - 15)$ is graphed in the xy-plane, what is the y-coordinate of the parabola's vertex?

A) 5

B) 10

C) 25

D) 100

CONTINUE

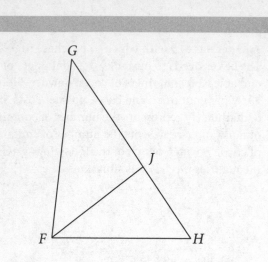

In the figure above, the ratio $\dfrac{FJ}{FH}$ has the same value as the ratio $\dfrac{FG}{GH}$. Which of the following angle measures must be congruent?

A) ∠FGH and ∠FHJ

B) ∠FJG and ∠FJH

C) ∠GFJ and ∠HFJ

D) ∠GFH and ∠FJH

r questions 14–17, solve the problem and
ter your answer in the grid, as described below,
the answer sheet.

Although not required, it is suggested that
you write your answer in the boxes at the top
of the columns to help you fill in the circles
accurately. You will receive credit only if the
circles are filled in correctly.

Mark no more than one circle in any column.

No question has a negative answer.

Some problems may have more than one
correct answer. In such cases, grid only one
answer.

Mixed numbers such as $3\frac{1}{2}$ must be gridded

as 3.5 or 7/2. (If  is entered into

the grid, it will be interpreted as $\frac{31}{2}$, not as

$3\frac{1}{2}$.)

Decimal Answers: If you obtain a decimal
answer with more digits than the grid can
accommodate, it may be either rounded or
truncated, but it must fill the entire grid.

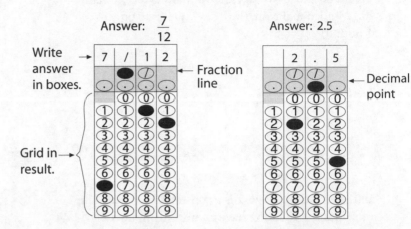

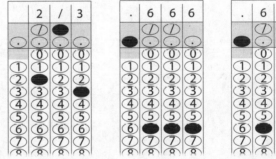

Acceptable ways to grid $\frac{2}{3}$ are:

Answer: 201 – either position is correct

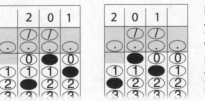

NOTE: You may start
your answers in any
column, space
permitting. Columns
you don't need to
use should be left
blank.

14

Monica sells home-made jams and she made half as many ounces of jam on Wednesday as she did on Thursday. She made a total of 3 pounds and 6 ounces of jam on those two days. How many ounces of jam did Monica make on Thursday? (Note: 16 ounces = 1 pound)

15

$$6(2y + z) = 12y + 18$$

In the equation above, z is a constant. For what value of z does the equation have an infinite number of solutions?

16

$$(gx^2 - 4y^2)(6x^2 + hy^2)$$

In the expression above, g and h are non-zero constants with a difference of 5. If the value of the coefficient on the x^2y^2 term is zero when the expression is multiplied out and the like terms are collected, what is the value of gh ?

17

$$8y^2 - dy - 15$$

If $2y - 3$ is a factor of the expression above, in which is an integer, what is the value of d ?

STOP
If you finish before time is called, you may check your work on this section only.
Do not turn to any other section.

No Test Material On This Page

Math Test – Calculator

45 MINUTES, 31 QUESTIONS

Turn to Section 4 of your answer sheet to answer the questions in this section.

For questions 1–27, solve each problem, choose the best answer from the choices provided, and fill in the corresponding circle on your answer sheet. **For questions 28–31,** solve the problem and enter your answer in the grid on the answer sheet. Please refer to the directions before question 28 on how to enter your answers in the grid. You may use any available space in your test booklet for scratch work.

NOTES

1. The use of a calculator **is permitted**.

2. All variables and expressions used represent real numbers unless otherwise indicated.

3. Figures provided in this test are drawn to scale unless otherwise indicated.

4. All figures lie in a plane unless otherwise indicated.

5. Unless otherwise indicated, the domain of a given function f is the set of all real numbers x for which $f(x)$ is a real number.

REFERENCE

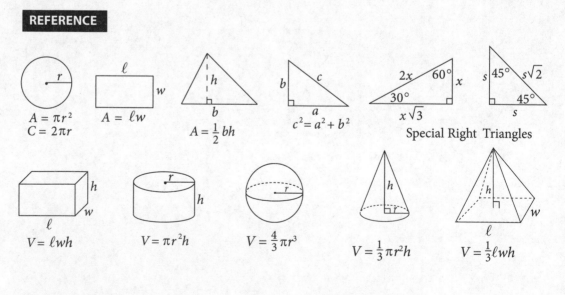

$A = \pi r^2$
$C = 2\pi r$

$A = \ell w$

$A = \frac{1}{2} bh$

$c^2 = a^2 + b^2$

Special Right Triangles

$V = \ell wh$

$V = \pi r^2 h$

$V = \frac{4}{3}\pi r^3$

$V = \frac{1}{3}\pi r^2 h$

$V = \frac{1}{3}\ell wh$

The number of degrees of arc in a circle is 360.
The number of radians of arc in a circle is 2π.
The sum of the measures in degrees of the angles of a triangle is 180.

CONTINUE

A college bookstore makes a profit of $0.75 for every 12 pencils it sells. Which of the following is the profit that the store makes for selling 20 pencils?

A) $0.75

B) $0.95

C) $1.25

D) $2.22

3

Sydney borrowed money from a friend and is paying back the loan. The remaining amount she owes, A, can be calculated by the equation $A = 870 - 30w$, where w represents the number of weeks since she took the loan. What does the number 870 represent?

A) The total amount of money Sydney has repaid

B) The amount of money Sydney repays each week

C) The number of weeks Sydney has been paying back the loan

D) The original amount that Sydney borrowed

A student planned to finish her summer reading assignment over the course of a 20-day portion of her summer vacation. Each day, she recorded the percent of her assignment she had left to read. The graph below shows the data for each day of the 20-day portion of her summer vacation.

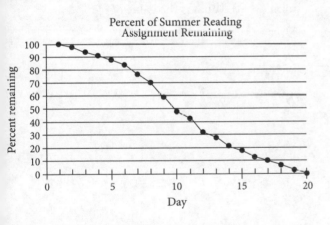

Percent of Summer Reading Assignment Remaining

During which of the following periods is the decrease in the percent of her remaining summer reading the least?

A) Days 1 though 5

B) Days 3 through 8

C) Days 7 through 12

D) Days 13 through 17

CONTINUE

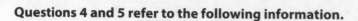

Questions 4 and 5 refer to the following information.

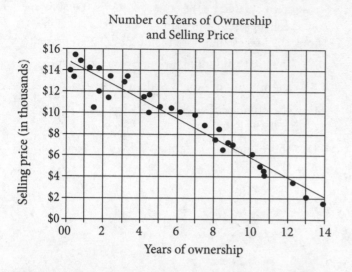

Number of Years of Ownership
and Selling Price

For 32 cars that were identical when new, the scatterplot above shows the number of years of ownership and the selling price when the first owner sold the car. The line of best fit is also shown.

4

Which of the following statements about the relationship between years of ownership and selling price is true?

A) As the number of years of ownership increases, the selling price decreases.

B) As the number of years of ownership decreases, the selling price decreases.

C) As the number of years of ownership increases, the selling price increases.

D) As the number of years of ownership decreases, the selling price remains constant.

5

For the car that was sold after exactly 7 years of ownership, the actual selling price of the car was approximately how much more than the selling price predicted by the line of best fit?

A) $650

B) $1,250

C) $2,150

D) $3,350

6

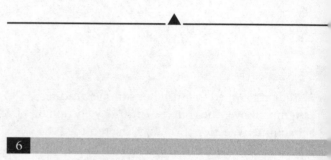

When the equation $y = 2x - b$, where b is a constant, is graphed in the xy-plane, the line passes through the point $(3, -1)$. What is the value of b ?

A) −5

B) −3

C) 1

D) 7

CONTINUE

Month	Balance
0	$1,400
1	$1,344
2	$1,290
3	$1,239
4	$1,189
5	$1,142

The table above shows the balance, in dollars, of a bank account. Which of the following best describes the model that fits the data?

A) Exponential, decreasing by approximately 4% per month

B) Exponential, decreasing by approximately 8% per month

C) Linear, decreasing by approximately $47 per month

D) Linear, decreasing by approximately $56 per month

A team of scientists is tracking a snail moving at a rate of 700 millimeters per minute. If there are 10 millimeters in a centimeter, at what rate does that snail move in <u>centimeters per hour</u>?

A)   4,200

B)   7,000

C)   42,000

D)   420,000

$$5\left(\frac{y}{2} + 5\right) = 2y + \frac{1}{2}y + 25$$

Which of the following describes the solution to the equation shown above?

A) The only solution is $y = 1\frac{1}{2}$.

B) The only solution is $y = 10$.

C) The equation has infinitely many solutions.

D) The equation has no solutions.

$$(2ab^2 + 5a^2 - 7a^2b) - (2ab^2 + 7a^2b - 3a^2)$$

Which of the following is equivalent to the expression above?

A) $4a^2b^4 - 21a^2b + 35a^2b$

B) $4ab^2 + 8a^2 - 14a^2b$

C) $2a^2 + 4ab^2$

D) $8a^2 - 14a^2b$

CONTINUE

11

Athletes in a School

	Left-Handed	Right-Handed
Varsity	11	98
Junior Varsity	17	144

The table above provides data about the 270 athletes in a particular high school. Approximately what percent of the athletes in the school are right-handed varsity athletes?

A)   6 percent

B) 36 percent

C) 53 percent

D) 98 percent

12

The table below shows the maximum weights that each of eight people at a gym can bench press.

Bench Press Weights

Person	Pounds
Aaron	40
Beth	30
Carey	110
Donna	230
Ethan	130
Fay	70
Gino	60
Helen	170

What is the difference between the maximum weight, in pounds, that Helen can bench press and the median weight, in pounds, of all eight people?

A) 10

B) 65

C) 70

D) 80

13

The table below shows the daily attendance of a Physics and a Biology class each day of a particular week.

Daily Attendance

Day	Physics	Biology
Monday	25	32
Tuesday	27	25
Wednesday	23	32
Thursday	31	21
Friday	25	28

Based on the information in the table, which of the following statements is true?

A) Both the mode and the range for the Physics class are less than the mode and range for the Biology class.

B) Both the mode and the range for the Physics class are greater than the mode and range for the Biology class.

C) The mode for the Physics class is less than the mode for the Biology class, but the range for the Physics class is greater than the mode for the Biology class.

D) The mode for the Physics class is greater than the mode for the Biology class, but the range for the Physics class is less than the mode for the Biology class.

14

A car company produces a particular model of car one at a time in its factories. If it takes one of the company's factories a total of 1,080 minutes to produce a single car, how many cars of that particular model can be produced by that particular factory in 540 <u>hours</u>?

A) 20

B) 25

C) 30

D) 35

CONTINUE

Questions 15–17 refer to the following information.

A major hospital conducted a study on a new experimental physical therapy method for some of its patients recovering from knee-replacement surgery. At the beginning of the study, 485 patients who had just had knee-replacement surgery were selected for the study; 194 of the patients were given the experimental physical therapy, and the remaining patients were put into conventional physical therapy. A summary of the recovery times for the patients who were in the study is shown in the table below.

Recovery Time for 485 Patients in the Study

Recovery Time	Experimental Therapy	Conventional Therapy
6 months or less	82	151
More than 6 months	112	140

15

What is the difference, to the nearest whole percent, between the percentage of patients in the experimental physical therapy with a recovery time of more than 6 months and the percentage of patients in the conventional physical therapy who had a recovery time of more than 6 months?

A)   10%

B)   8%

C)   6%

D)   4%

16

Of the patients in the conventional physical therapy, the ratio of those who had one knee replaced to those who had both knees replaced is approximately 3:7. Which of the following is the best approximation for the number of patients in the conventional physical therapy who had both knees replaced?

A)   58

B)   87

C)   125

D)   204

17

If a patient in the study is selected at random, which of the following is closest to the probability that the patient will have a recovery time of more than 6 months?

A)   0.28

B)   0.40

C)   0.52

D)   0.81

18

A circle is graphed in the *xy*-plane. If a circle has center (−3, 5) and a radius of 4, which of the following could be an equation of the circle?

A) $(x - 3)^2 - (y - 5)^2 = 4$

B) $(x - 3)^2 + (y - 5)^2 = 4$

C) $(x + 3)^2 - (y - 5)^2 = 16$

D) $(x + 3)^2 + (y - 5)^2 = 16$

19

A piano player charges a flat fee for an appearance plus an hourly rate based on the length of the performance. The equation $C = 100t + 50$ will relate the total charge *C*, in dollars, for a performance to the time *t*, in hours, of a performance. Based on this equation, how many additional hours will the length of the performance need to be for the piano player to charge an additional dollar?

A) $\dfrac{1}{100}$

B) $\dfrac{1}{50}$

C) 50

D) 100

20

Equal amounts of fencing are used to surround both an octagonal area and a square area. If each side of the octagon is 5 yards shorter than each side of the square, how many yards of fencing are needed to surround each area?

A) 20

B) 40

C) 60

D) 80

21

In the *xy*-plane, the graph of the function *f* is a parabola. If the graph of *f* intersects the *x*-axis at (*k*, 0) and (3, 0), and the vertex of *f* is at (5, −3), what is the value of *k* ?

A) 9

B) 7

C) 5

D) 1

CONTINUE

$$g(x) = \frac{3x + 9}{3x^2 - 3x - 18}$$

Which of the following is an equivalent form of rational function g that displays as constants or coefficients values that are not part of the domain?

A) $g(x) = \dfrac{1}{3x^2}$

B) $g(x) = \dfrac{1}{x - 2}$

C) $g(x) = \dfrac{x + 3}{x^2 - x - 6}$

D) $g(x) = \dfrac{3(x + 3)}{3(x - 3)(x + 2)}$

23

$$SA = 4\pi r^2$$

The formula for the surface area of a sphere with radius r is shown above. The radius of a volleyball is about 3 times the radius of a tennis ball. If a volleyball and a tennis ball are spherical, approximately how many times larger is the surface area of a volleyball than the surface area of a tennis ball?

A) 3

B) 9

C) 27

D) 36

A particle accelerates at a constant rate from a velocity of 20 meters per second to a velocity of 50 meters per second in 10 seconds. Which of the following expresses the velocity V, in meters per second, in terms of the time t, in seconds, after the acceleration began, for $0 \le t \le 10$?

A) $V = -50 + 3t$

B) $V = 20 + 3t$

C) $V = -20 - 3t$

D) $V = 50 - 3t$

25

If the function h is defined by $h(x) = 2x^2 - 7x - 3$, what is $h(x + 3)$?

A) $h(x + 3) = 2x^2 - 7x$

B) $h(x + 3) = 2x^2 - 7x - 6$

C) $h(x + 3) = 2x^2 + 5x - 6$

D) $h(x + 3) = 2x^2 - 23x + 15$

CONTINUE

26

$$10x - 62 = 9y$$
$$\frac{1}{4}x = y$$

The equations of two lines are shown above. If the lines are graphed on the *xy*-plane, which of the following ordered pairs represents the point of intersection of the two lines?

A) (8, 2)

B) (16, 4)

C) (24, 6)

D) (32, 8)

27

The amount of carbon-14 in a sample halves every 5,730 years. Which of the following best describes the type of decay that models the relationship between amount of carbon-14 and time?

A) Linear decay, because the amount of carbon-14 decreases by the same factor every 5,730-year period

B) Linear decay, because the amount of carbon-14 decreases by the same amount every 5,730-year period

C) Exponential decay, because the amount of carbon-14 decreases by the same factor every 5,730-year period

D) Exponential decay, because the amount of carbon-14 decreases by the same amount every 5,730-year period

CONTINUE

For **questions 28–31**, solve the problem and enter your answer in the grid, as described below, on the answer sheet.

Although not required, it is suggested that you write your answer in the boxes at the top of the columns to help you fill in the circles accurately. You will receive credit only if the circles are filled in correctly.

Mark no more than one circle in any column.

No question has a negative answer.

Some problems may have more than one correct answer. In such cases, grid only one answer.

Mixed numbers such as $3\frac{1}{2}$ must be gridded as 3.5 or 7/2. (If [3 1 / 2] is entered into the grid, it will be interpreted as $\frac{31}{2}$, not as $3\frac{1}{2}$.)

Decimal Answers: If you obtain a decimal answer with more digits than the grid can accommodate, it may be either rounded or truncated, but it must fill the entire grid.

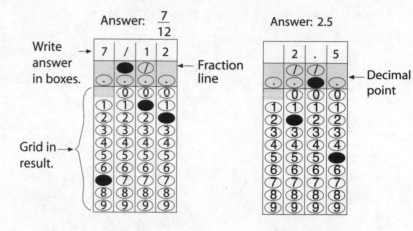

Answer: $\frac{7}{12}$

Write answer in boxes. — Fraction line

Grid in result.

Answer: 2.5 — Decimal point

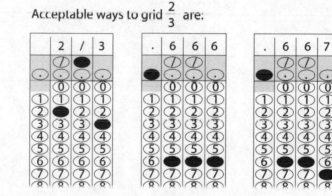

Acceptable ways to grid $\frac{2}{3}$ are:

Answer: 201 – either position is correct

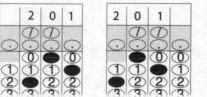

NOTE: You may start your answers in any column, space permitting. Columns you don't need to use should be left blank.

CONTINUE

28

$$y = x + 8$$
$$y = x^2 - x - 7$$

If (x, y) is a solution to the equations above, what is one possible value for the sum of x and y?

29

Type of Metal	Weight (ounces)	Price ($)
Gold	2	2,500
Platinum	5	7,500

A jewelry supply store sells boxes of sheet metal for gold and platinum at the weights and prices listed in the table above. A jeweler wants to purchase at least 9 ounces of metal and plans to spend at least $170,000. If she has already ordered 10 boxes of gold, what is the minimum number of boxes of platinum she can order to satisfy the requirements?

CONTINUE

Questions 30 and 31 refer to the following information.

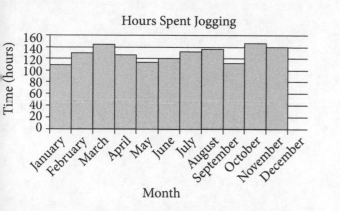

Hours Spent Jogging

The graph above shows the amount of time, in hours, that Robert spends jogging in each month through a particular year. The information for the month of December is not included in the graph.

30

In November, Robert jogged at an average pace of 8 miles per hour. In December, Robert ran for *h* hours at an average pace of 7 miles per hour. If the total distance that Robert jogged each of the two months was the same, what is the value of *h* ?

31

In June, Robert ran at a pace of 5 miles per hour at the beginning of the month before he increased in pace to 6 miles per hour toward the end of the month. If he spent 70% of this jogging time at the slower pace, and the rest at the faster pace, what is the total distance, in miles that Robert jogged during the month of June?

▲

STOP
If you finish before time is called, you may check your work on this section only.
Do not turn to any other section.

The Princeton Review®

COMPLETE MARK ● **EXAMPLES OF INCOMPLETE MARKS** ⊘ ⊗ ⊖ ◐ ● ◓ ⊘ ◑

It is recommended that you use a No. 2 pencil. It is very important that you fill in the entire circle darkly and completely. If you change your response, erase as completely as possible. Incomplete marks or erasures may affect your score.

■ TEST NUMBER

ENTER TEST NUMBER
For instance, for Practice Test #1, fill in the circle for 0 in the first column and for 1 in the second column.

```
    ⊔ ⊔
0  ○ ○
1  ○ ○
2  ○ ○
3  ○ ○
4  ○ ○
5  ○ ○
6  ○ ○
7  ○ ○
8  ○ ○
9  ○ ○
```

■ SECTION 1

	A B C D		A B C D		A B C D		A B C D
1	○○○○	13	○○○○	25	○○○○	37	○○○○
2	○○○○	14	○○○○	26	○○○○	38	○○○○
3	○○○○	15	○○○○	27	○○○○	39	○○○○
4	○○○○	16	○○○○	28	○○○○	40	○○○○
5	○○○○	17	○○○○	29	○○○○	41	○○○○
6	○○○○	18	○○○○	30	○○○○	42	○○○○
7	○○○○	19	○○○○	31	○○○○	43	○○○○
8	○○○○	20	○○○○	32	○○○○	44	○○○○
9	○○○○	21	○○○○	33	○○○○	45	○○○○
10	○○○○	22	○○○○	34	○○○○	46	○○○○
11	○○○○	23	○○○○	35	○○○○	47	○○○○
12	○○○○	24	○○○○	36	○○○○		

The
Princeton
Review®

PSAT/NMSQT PRACTICE TEST ANSWER SHEET

| | EXAMPLES OF | It is recommended that you use a No. 2 pencil. It is very important that |
| COMPLETE MARK | INCOMPLETE MARKS | you fill in the entire circle darkly and completely. If you change your response, erase as completely as possible. Incomplete marks or erasures may affect your score. |

■ SECTION 2

1 A B C D
2 A B C D
3 A B C D
4 A B C D
5 A B C D
6 A B C D
7 A B C D
8 A B C D
9 A B C D

10 A B C D
11 A B C D
12 A B C D
13 A B C D
14 A B C D
15 A B C D
16 A B C D
17 A B C D
18 A B C D

19 A B C D
20 A B C D
21 A B C D
22 A B C D
23 A B C D
24 A B C D
25 A B C D
26 A B C D
27 A B C D

28 A B C D
29 A B C D
30 A B C D
31 A B C D
32 A B C D
33 A B C D
34 A B C D
35 A B C D
36 A B C D

37 A B C D
38 A B C D
39 A B C D
40 A B C D
41 A B C D
42 A B C D
43 A B C D
44 A B C D

■ SECTION 3

A B C D
1 ○○○○

A B C D
2 ○○○○

A B C D
3 ○○○○

A B C D
4 ○○○○

A B C D
5 ○○○○

A B C D
6 ○○○○

A B C D
7 ○○○○

A B C D
8 ○○○○

A B C D
9 ○○○○

A B C D
10 ○○○○

A B C D
11 ○○○○

A B C D
12 ○○○○

A B C D
13 ○○○○

Only answers that are gridded will be scored. You will not receive any credit for anything written in the boxes.

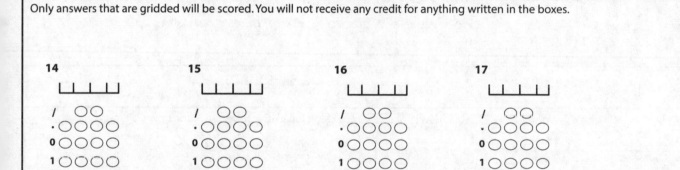

14   15   16   17

NO CALCULATOR ALLOWED

PSAT/NMSQT PRACTICE TEST ANSWER SHEET

COMPLETE MARK ● EXAMPLES OF INCOMPLETE MARKS

It is recommended that you use a No. 2 pencil. It is very important that you fill in the entire circle darkly and completely. If you change your response, erase as completely as possible. Incomplete marks or erasures may affect your score.

SECTION 4

1 A B C D	7 A B C D	13 A B C D	19 A B C D	25 A B C D
2 A B C D	8 A B C D	14 A B C D	20 A B C D	26 A B C D
3 A B C D	9 A B C D	15 A B C D	21 A B C D	27 A B C D
4 A B C D	10 A B C D	16 A B C D	22 A B C D	
5 A B C D	11 A B C D	17 A B C D	23 A B C D	
6 A B C D	12 A B C D	18 A B C D	24 A B C D	

Only answers that are gridded will be scored. You will not receive any credit for anything written in the boxes.

28	29	30	31
/	/	/	/
.	.	.	.
0	0	0	0
1	1	1	1
2	2	2	2
3	3	3	3
4	4	4	4
5	5	5	5
6	6	6	6
7	7	7	7
8	8	8	8
9	9	9	9

CALCULATOR ALLOWED

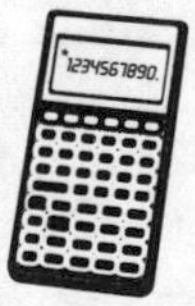

Chapter 16
Practice Test 2:
Answers and
Explanations

PRACTICE TEST 2 ANSWER KEY

Section 1: Reading		Section 2: Writing and Language		Section 3: Math (No Calculator)		Section 4: Math (Calculator)	
1. D	25. B	1. D	23. D	1. C	11. C	1. C	16. D
2. B	26. C	2. C	24. C	2. B	12. A	2. A	17. C
3. C	27. D	3. B	25. B	3. C	13. D	3. D	18. D
4. A	28. B	4. A	26. C	4. B	14. 36	4. A	19. A
5. C	29. C	5. C	27. C	5. D	15. 3	5. B	20. B
6. A	30. C	6. C	28. A	6. A	16. 24	6. D	21. B
7. D	31. B	7. D	29. A	7. A	17. 2	7. A	22. D
8. D	32. A	8. B	30. C	8. B		8. A	23. B
9. A	33. A	9. B	31. A	9. D		9. C	24. B
10. C	34. D	10. D	32. B	10. C		10. D	25. C
11. A	35. B	11. A	33. D			11. B	26. A
12. D	36. D	12. A	34. D			12. D	27. C
13. B	37. C	13. B	35. A			13. A	28. 2 or 18
14. D	38. C	14. D	36. D			14. C	29. 20
15. B	39. B	15. B	37. A			15. A	30. 160
16. A	40. B	16. C	38. B				31. 636
17. C	41. D	17. C	39. A				
18. B	42. A	18. A	40. D				
19. C	43. A	19. D	41. B				
20. A	44. D	20. C	42. D				
21. A	45. C	21. B	43. B				
22. B	46. C	22. A	44. C				
23. A	47. B						
24. C							

PRACTICE TEST 2 EXPLANATIONS

Section 1—Reading

1. **D** This question asks how to best describe the passage's *point of view*. Because this is a general question, it should be done after all the specific questions. In the second paragraph, the narrator refers to John in the third person: *He had forgotten and was even more surprised than ashamed.* Eliminate (A). In lines 45–47, the narrator says that *the blood slowly came to his face, which began to burn with recognition.* Since the author is using figurative language here, the point of view of the passage would not be described as *a disinterested reporter listing objective facts.* Eliminate (B). In the last paragraph, John is described as *embarrassed.* The narrator is not judging him here but instead is describing his emotions through the course of his conversation with May, so eliminate (C). Choice (D) is a good match because the narrator notes in the last paragraph that it was *No wonder they couldn't have met as if nothing had happened.* This line supports the notion that the narrator *relates to Marcher's feelings.* The correct answer is (D).

2. **B** This question asks how *the emotions of John Marcher shift* over the course of the passage. Because this is a general question, it should be done after all the specific questions. In the second paragraph, John Marcher is described as being *surprised* that he *had forgotten* a conversation with May. In lines 45–47, the text describes a shift in John Marcher's emotions: *Then it was that…a light broke for him…which began to burn with recognition. Incredulity* means disbelief, which does not match *surprised*, and there is no support for *begrudging acceptance* later in the passage. Eliminate (A). *Confusion* is a closer match to being *surprised* and having *forgotten*, and *disconcerted recognition* matches the description in lines 45–47, so keep (B). There is no evidence that John Marcher feels *disdain* nor *unrequited love*, so eliminate (C). While John Marcher is described as *embarrassed* (lines 55–56), the word *painful* is too extreme and isn't supported by the text, so eliminate (D). The correct answer is (B).

3. **C** This question asks about what the passage suggests about *John Marcher* and *May Bertram's* conversation. Because this is the first question in a paired set, it can be done in tandem with Q4. Consider the answers for Q4 first. In the lines for (4A), May Bertram says, "*…you told me something I've never forgotten…it was that tremendously hot day when we went to Sorrento,*" recalling a past conversation with John Marcher. Look to see whether these lines support any of the answers for Q3; they support (3C), which says they are *reminiscing about former times and conversations.* Draw a line connecting these two answers. The lines for (4B) don't support any of the answers for Q3, so eliminate (4B). The lines for (4C) discuss John feeling *embarrassed* and May feeling *sorry for him.* Choice (3B) is a Could Be True trap answer, since sharing *personal information* might make someone embarrassed, but John and May are discussing a conversation they had years before, not sharing new information. Therefore, the lines in (4C) don't support any of the answers in Q3, so eliminate (4C). The lines in (4D) don't support any of the answers in Q3, so eliminate (4D). Without any support from Q4, (3A), (3B), and (3D) can be eliminated. The correct answers are (3C) and (4A).

4. **A** (See explanation above.)

5. **C** The question asks what the word *claim* means in line 12. Go back to the text, find the word *claim*, and underline it. Carefully read the surrounding text to determine another word that would fit in

its place, based on the context of the passage. In line 12, the narrator notes that May *was making no claim* on John, and contrasts this with the fact that, with *another woman*, John *might have feared the recall…of some imbecile "offer."* Therefore, *claim* must mean something like "request." *Application* and *Remark* do not match "request," so eliminate (A) and (B). *Appeal* matches "request" more closely than *Demand*, which is too strong. Eliminate (D). The correct answer is (C).

6. **A**   The question asks what Marcher's *"loss"* refers to in line 16. Use the given line reference to find the window. Lines 15–18 state that John was *conscious…of a loss* and *already saw an interest in the matter of her mention*. This supports (A), so keep it. Line 13 states that May had made *no claim on him of a compliment*, but not that Marcher had *missed* an *opportunity to compliment* her, so eliminate (B). There's no discussion of Marcher *longing to return* to Sorrento, so eliminate (C). There's no evidence that Marcher's speech involved *declaring love for* May, so eliminate (D). The correct answer is (A).

7. **D**   The question asks what Marcher and May's *conversation* suggests *Marcher had previously told May*. Because this is the first question in a paired set, it can be done in tandem with Q8. Consider the answers for Q8 first. The lines for (8A) don't mention what Marcher told May, only that he told her *something* that May has *never forgotten*. These lines don't support any of the answers for Q7, so eliminate (8A). The lines for (8B) mention what was not said—neither a *compliment or a mistake*, but they don't discuss what March *told May*. Therefore, these lines don't support any of the answers for Q7, so eliminate (8B). The lines for (8C) don't discuss what was said, so they don't support any of the answers for Q7; eliminate (8C). In the lines for (8D), Marcher talks to May about *"…having taken you so far into my confidence."* This suggest that was he told her must have been *personal*, which supports (7D). Draw a line connecting (7D) and (8D). Without any support from Q8, (7A), (7B), and (7C) can be eliminated. The correct answers are (7D) and (8D).

8. **D**   (See explanation above.)

9. **A**   The question asks what the word *allusion* means in line 57. Go back to the text, find the word *allusion*, and underline it. Carefully read the surrounding text to determine another word that would fit in its place, based on the context of the passage. In lines 53–54, May asks Marcher *"if the thing you then spoke of has ever came to pass?"* Lines 55–57 indicate that Marcher feels *embarrassed* about what May asked, and May feels *sorry for him, as if her allusion had been a mistake*. Therefore, the word *allusion* must mean something like "mention" or "remark." *Reference* matches "mention," so keep (A). *Image* doesn't match "mention," so eliminate (B). What May mentioned was not a *quotation*, so eliminate (C). *Apparition* means "ghost" or "spirit," which doesn't match "mention." The correct answer is (A).

10. **C**   The question asks how the *focus* of the speech changes. Because this is a general question, it should be done after all the specific questions. The passage begins with an explanation of why and how Churchill formed a new government; he begins the description in lines 6–7, *On Friday evening last I received His Majesty's commission to form a new Administration*. Then in line 42, Churchill transitions to speaking of *one of the greatest battles in history*; in the last paragraph, he says the aim of the new government and the country is *victory*, and he urges the new government and country to *go forward together with…united strength*. Look for an answer choice that matches this prediction. Choice (A) references both of these topics but lists them in the opposite order; eliminate (A). Choice (B) is too narrow because it focuses only on the formation of the *War Cabinet*, as opposed to the government as a whole, so eliminate (B). The passage first discusses formation of a new government through

appointments and then goes on to rally that government to the shared cause of defeating Germany. This matches (C), so keep it. The passage does accept *defeat* but rather urges a dedication to *victory*, so eliminate (D). The correct answer is (C).

11. **A** The question asks what the word *prosecute* means in line 4. Go back to the text, find the word *prosecute*, and underline it. Carefully read the surrounding text to determine another word that would fit in its place, based on the context of the passage. The text says that there is a *united and inflexible resolve of the nation to prosecute the war with Germany to a victorious conclusion*. Therefore, to *prosecute* the war must mean something like "pursue" the war. *Litigate* and *accuse* both refer to another meaning of *prosecute*, "to bring legal action against," so eliminate (B) and (C). *Fight* the war matches the prediction of "pursue" the war, so keep (A). *Enforce* does not mean "pursue," so eliminate (D). The correct answer is (A).

12. **D** The question asks why Churchill claims *his administration must be formed more quickly than usual*. Notice that this is the first question in a paired set, so it can be done in tandem with Q13. Look at the answer choices for Q13 first. The lines for (13A) say only that Churchill *received His Majesty's commission to form a new Administration*, not why that administration needed to be formed. These lines do not support any of the answers to Q12, so eliminate (13A). The lines for (13B) say that *It was necessary that this should be done in one single day, on account of the extreme urgency and rigour of events*. This information matches (12D), indicating that the current *situation requires unusual measures*. Draw a line connecting (13B) and (12D). In the lines for (13C), Churchill asks for *allowances… for any lack of ceremony* due to the quick nature of the *political reconstruction*. However, these lines do not explain why his actions had to be quick; they don't support any of the answers to Q12, so eliminate (13C). The lines for (13D) discuss why the British need to prevail in their fight, not why Churchill needed to form his administration quickly. These lines do not support any of the answers for Q12, so eliminate (13D). Without any support in the answers from Q13, (12A), (12B), and (12C) can be eliminated. The correct answers are (12D) and (13B).

13. **B** (See explanation above.)

14. **D** The question asks what can be inferred about Churchill's administration. Notice that this is the first question in a paired set, so it can be done in tandem with Q15. Look at the answer choices for Q15 first. The lines for (15A) say that *A War Cabinet has been formed of five Members, representing…the unity of the nation*. Check the answers for Q13 to see if any of the answers are supported by these lines. At first, they may seem to support (14B), but this is a Mostly Right/Slightly Wrong trap answer: (14B) contains the word *all*, which is too strong to be supported by the passage. Eliminate (15A) because it does not support any of the answers for Q14. The lines for (15B) state that *the appointment of the other Ministers usually takes a little longer, but…when Parliament meets again…the administration will be complete in all respects*. This information matches (14D), indicating there are some unfilled positions. Draw a line connecting (15B) and (14D). The lines for (15C) mention that the Speaker took the necessary steps, but say nothing about Churchill's administration; these lines don't support any of the answers to Q14, so eliminate (15C). The lines for (15D) state that *We have before us many, many long months of struggle and of suffering*. This refers to the war with Germany, and doesn't support any of the answers from Q14. Eliminate (15D). Without any support in the answers from Q15, (14A), (14B), and (14C) can be eliminated. The correct answers are (14D) and (15B).

15.   **B**   (See previous explanation.)

16.   **A**   This question asks why Churchill makes the statement that he has *nothing to offer but blood, toil, tears and sweat.* Use the given line reference to find the window. In lines 60–65, Churchill states, *We have before us an ordeal of the most grievous kind. We have before us many, many long months of struggle and of suffering. You ask, what is our policy? I can say: It is to wage war, by sea, land and air, with all our might and with all the strength that God can give us.* His use of physical imagery serves to show the amount of exertion Churchill is willing to expend on fighting the war. Look for an answer choice that matches this prediction. The phrase *deep level of commitment to the war effort* matches the prediction, so keep (A). Eliminate (B) because it is contradicted by the remainder of the passage, as Churchill strongly speaks of *victory*. Choice (C) says that there is *not much* that Churchill can offer, but Churchill emphasizes his dedication; the reference is also not about military resources specifically, so eliminate (C). Choice (D) is a Mostly Right/Slightly Wrong trap answer—Churchill's statement is about his dedication to the war effort, not to the *governing coalition*. Eliminate (D). The correct answer is (A).

17.   **C**   The question asks for the *rhetorical effect* of repeating *"victory"* and *"no survival"* in the final paragraph, so read the last paragraph. Lines 67–73 state *You ask, what is our aim? I can answer in one word: It is victory, victory at all costs….for without victory, there is no survival. Let that be realized; no survival for the British Empire, no survival for all that the British Empire has stood for.* Churchill's message is that if Britain does not win the war, the British Empire will fundamentally change, and his repetition of the phrases serves to emphasize that point. Look for an answer choice that matches this prediction. Eliminate (A) because lines 75–76 state that Churchill has *hope* that their *cause will not be suffered to fail*. Eliminate (B) because these words are used for emphasis rather than to describe any specific *strategy*. Keep (C) because it is supported by the text; both of these terms are used to stress the importance of the outcome of the war for the British. Although Churchill ends the speech with optimism, that is not the purpose of these phrases; in these lines, Churchill declares that there would be *no survival* for Britain without *victory*; he is emphasizing what is at stake, so eliminate (D). The correct answer is (C).

18.   **B**   The question asks what the word *suffered* means in line 76. Go back to the text, find the word *suffered,* and underline it. Carefully read the surrounding text to determine another word that would fit in its place, based on the context of the passage. The text says that *mankind will move forward towards its goal. But I take up my task with buoyancy and hope. I feel sure that our cause will not be suffered to fail among men.* Therefore, *suffered* must mean something like "permitted"—Churchill believes that their cause (victory in the war) will not fail. Both *endured* and *tolerated* mean "withstood suffering"; these are Could Be True trap answers that do not match "permitted." Eliminate (A) and (C). *Allowed* matches "permitted," so keep (B). Eliminate (D) because *endorsed* means "approved," which does not match "permitted" to fail. The correct answer is (B).

19.   **C**   The question asks what the author believes about South Chicago. Notice that this is the first question in a paired set, so it can be done in tandem with Q20. Look at the answer choices for Q20 first. In the lines in (20A), the author describes South Chicago as the city's *most isolated community*. Check the answers for Q19 to see if any of the answers are supported by these lines. They support (19C), so draw a line connecting (20A) and (19C). The lines in (20B) mention the aesthetics of the area but do not go as far as to suggest it should be a *popular vacation destination* like (19A). The lines for (20B) don't support any of the answers for Q19, so eliminate (20B). Choice (20C) is a Deceptive Language

trap answer: the description *powerful stench* seems to match the phrase *smelly nature* in (19D), but (19D) says that South Chicago *embodies the dirty, smelly nature of American industry* in general, and the author does not make this comparison in the passage. Eliminate (20C). The lines for (20D) describe South Chicago as *the heart of American industrial might*, which does not directly support any answer choice from Q19. Eliminate (20D). Without any support from the answer choices in Q20, (19A), (19B), and (19D) can be eliminated. The correct answers are (19C) and (20A).

20. **A** (See explanation above.)

21. **A** The question asks why the author includes a list of restaurant names. Use the given line reference to find the window. Lines 19–21 provide examples of *small taverns and diners.* The author mentions such restaurants as a part of South Chicago's *modest* neighborhoods and says, *There's nothing fanciful about this area.* Choice (A) matches these lines, so keep (A). Eliminate (B) and (D), as the author does not discuss *visitors* to the area. Choice (C) can also be eliminated: the author does not discuss the *variety* of restaurants. The correct answer is (A).

22. **B** The question asks what the word *suspended* means in line 38. Go back to the text, find the word *suspended*, and underline it. Carefully read the surrounding text to determine another word that would fit in its place, based on the context of the passage. In the text, *suspended* is used to describe the *belts, pipes, and railroad overpasses* that go *in, out, and over* the buildings. therefore, *suspended* must mean something like "up in the air." *Drooping* means "hanging downward," which doesn't match "up in the air," so eliminate (A). *Hanging* matches "up in the air," so keep (B). *Slumbering* means "sleeping;" it doesn't match "up in the air," so eliminate (C). *Fixed* means "securely fastened," which does not match "up in the air," so eliminate (D). The correct answer is (B).

23. **A** The question asks for what comparison to the *image of steel mills* is made in the passage. Notice that this is the first question in a paired set, so it can be done in tandem with Q24. Look at the answer choices for Q24 first. The lines in (24A) discuss *neighborhoods*, and the lines in (24B) describe a *highway*. Neither of these windows mentions steel mills at all. Therefore, these lines don't support any of the answers for Q23, so eliminate (24A) and (24B). The lines in (24C) support (23A), describing the steel mills as *the man-made equivalent of the Rockies.* Draw a line connecting (23A) and (24C). Although these lines also reference *a football field*, they do not say that the steel mills are like football fields; they only say that some of the mills are *three times the size of a football field.* These lines also mention *aircraft*, but this reference is not part of a comparison. Choice (24D) describes the function of the steel mills but does not draw a comparison to any of the answer choices in Q23. Eliminate (24D). Without any support in the answer choices from Q24, (23B), (23C), and (23D) can be eliminated. The correct answers are (23A) and (24C).

24. **C** (See explanation above.)

25. **B** The question asks what the word *consumption* means in line 63. Go back to the text, find the word *consumption*, and underline it. Carefully read the surrounding text to determine another word that would fit in its place, based on the context of the passage. In the text, *consumption* refers to the use of modern comforts such as the *can openers and knives, refrigerators and cars, bridges and skyscrapers* produced by steel mills. The correct answer should mean something like "purchase" or "use." Choice (A) is a Could Be True trap answer: *eating* is a synonym of *consumption*, but it does not match "purchase"

or "use." Eliminate (A). Choice (B), *expenditure*, matches "purchase," so keep it. Neither *corrosion* nor *burning* means "purchase" or "use." Eliminate (C) and (D). The correct answer is (B).

26. **C** The question asks for the primary purpose of the last paragraph in the context of the passage. Read the last paragraph, which discusses how much the *local population still* depends on the steel mills, and states that *there are only 15 million working in the mills now*, and describes some of the mills as *abandoned* and *collapsing*. The passage as a whole discusses the *steel mills* of *South Chicago*, and the final paragraph describes what the mills are like *now*. Although the author describes the *mill owners* as *complacent*, the *primary purpose* of the paragraph is not to *criticize* them. Eliminate (A). Although this paragraph describes *abandoned factory buildings*, the primary purpose is not to *lament* the *abandoned property*. Eliminate (B). Choice (C) is supported by the descriptions in this paragraph. Keep (C). Eliminate (D), as the author never proposes specific *changes* for problems in the industry. The correct answer is (C).

27. **D** The question asks for a claim about *domestic steel production* that is supported by the graph. Work through each answer choice using the graph. Domestic steel production had periods of decrease as well as increase *from 1950 to 2000*; eliminate (A) and (B). Eliminate (C), as the peak of domestic steel production occurred in the 1970s, not *the 1960s*, and had *a steep decline* in the 1980s. Choice (D) is supported by the graph: the domestic steel production was just under 100 million tons in 1950 and just over 100 million tons in 2000, so the net production had *increased slightly*. The correct answer is (D).

28. **B** The question asks for an inference based on both the passage and the graph. First, work through each answer choice using the graph. According to the graph, domestic steel production reached a peak in the mid-1970s, so keep (A). Choice (B) states that *U.S. steel production* showed *growth followed by significant decline*. This is supported by the graph, which shows a general increase in steel production to about 1973, followed by a decline. Keep (B). The graph does not directly support any claims about either the size of the steel mill *workforces* or *air pollution*, so eliminate (C) and (D). Next, look for support in the passage for (A) or (B). Lines 52–54 mention the *1960s* as time when the steel mills employed large numbers, but the passage does not state that the mills reached their *greatest productivity* in the *mid-1970s*. Eliminate (A). Lines 45–56 discuss how *the first of the mills was built in the 1850s*. Within *one hundred years*, these steel mills produced *more steel…than anywhere else in the world*. This supports the claim that the steel industry grew from the 1850s to the start of the graph at 1950. The correct answer is (B).

29. **C** The question asks what *the authors of the passage most likely believe*. Because this is a general question, it should be done after all the specific questions. Work backwards from the answers to find evidence in the passage. The text never states that *burning should be done* semi-annually (which means twice a year), so eliminate (A). According to lines 24–30, *late spring* burning has been the recommendation since *the early 1970s* and *has maintained the Flint Hills grassland*, so eliminate (B). Lines 35–37 state, *Burning in late spring…generates more ozone than burning in winter or early spring*, and lines 52–54 state, *Despite long-standing recommendations that tallgrass prairie be burned only in late spring, the data supporting this policy is equivocal* (which means the data could be interpreted in more than one way). These lines support (C), so keep it. The last paragraph states that the *historical studies* on burning times *are inconclusive* and then cites a recent study which *found that the timing of burning had no significant effect*, so eliminate (D). The correct answer is (C).

30. **C** The question asks what *does NOT influence decisions on the timing of seasonal burns.* Because there is no line reference and the entire passage is about the timing of seasonal burns, this question should be done after the other specific questions. Pay attention to the word NOT in the question. Use Process of Elimination to eliminate three answer choices that do influence decisions on the timing of seasonal burning. Eliminate (A) and (B) since lines 4–8 say that *biomass production* and *control of specific plant species* do *influence when grasslands are burned.* According to lines 32–35, *Concentrated smoke from grass fires produces* particles *that facilitate tropospheric ozone production*; this is a consequence of *en masse burning* (many fires burning at once), NOT something that would *influence decisions on the timing of seasonal burns*, so keep (C). Lines 50–51 say that *ranchers often burn in unison when weather conditions are favorable*, so eliminate (D). The correct answer is (C).

31. **B** The question asks for something that is suggested about *the Kansas Flint Hills.* Notice that this is the first question in a paired set, so it can be done in tandem with Q32. Look at the answer choices for Q32 first. The lines for (32A) say that for *The Flint Hills…frequent burning is integral to its preservation and economic utilization.* Check the answers for Q31 to see if any of the answers are supported by those lines. They support (31B), so draw a line connecting (31B) and (32A). Consider the lines for (32B), which say that *a good understanding of the consequences of burning at different times of the year is necessary* to maintaining *the Flint Hills.* This answer does suggest *an ecologically sensitive area*, but it does not describe a need for *extreme caution*; these lines do not support any of the answers for Q31, so eliminate (32B). The lines for (32C) say that *Burning earlier in spring has been regarded as undesirable because it putatively…lowers monthly weight gains of steers compared to burning in late spring*, which may seem to support (31D). However, this is a Deceptive Language trap answer. *Putatively* means "supposedly," and lines 60–68 suggest that burning grasses in the early spring may support species that *are beneficial to the diet of grazers.* Therefore, (32C) does not support any of the answers to Q31, so eliminate (32C). The lines for (32D) mention *grasses* and *forbs*, but the text does not suggest that these *must be studied further.* These lines do not support any of the answers for Q31, so eliminate (32D). Without any support in the answers from Q32, (31A), (31C), and (31D) can be eliminated. The correct answers are (31B) and (32A).

32. **A** (See explanation above.)

33. **A** The question asks what the word *practices* means in line 49. Go back to the text, find the word *practices*, and underline it. Carefully read the surrounding text to determine another word that would fit in its place, based on the context of the passage. The text says that *burning exclusively in late spring* is one of the *cultural practices* of *the Flint hills.* Therefore, *practices* must mean something like "customs." *Traditions* matches "customs," so keep (A). Neither *rehearsals, accomplishments*, nor *chores* matches "customs," so eliminate (B), (C), and (D). The correct answer is (A).

34. **D** The question asks what the word *equivocal* means in line 54. Go back to the text, find the word *equivocal*, and underline it. Carefully read the surrounding text to determine another word that would fit in its place, based on the context of the passage. The text says that *the data supporting* burning grassland *only in late spring…is equivocal.* The rest of the paragraph describes examples of uncertain findings, such as that *It was not known if [grass] biomass was reduced by early-spring burning or if the differences were a site effect rather than a treatment effect.* Therefore, *equivocal* must mean something like "uncertain." *Wrong* and *misleading* do not mean "uncertain," so eliminate (A) and

(B). *Ambivalent* is another possible definition of *equivocal*, but it does not mean "uncertain;" this is a Could Be True trap answer because it doesn't match the meaning of the word in this context, so eliminate (C). *Unclear* matches "uncertain," so keep (D). The correct answer is (D).

35. **B** The question asks what *can be inferred* about *Symphoricarpos orbiculatus*. Look for the lead words *Symphoricarpos orbiculatus*, and read a window around the lines to find the answer in the passage. Lines 68–71 say that *Burning in late spring has been considered the most effective time to control invasive shrubs, but* Symphoricarpos orbiculatus *was the only woody species that declined with repeated late spring burning*. Therefore, *Symphoricarpos orbiculatus* is one of the *invasive shrubs*. Eliminate (A), (C), and (D), which do not match the prediction. The correct answer is (B).

36. **D** This question is the best evidence question in a paired set. Q35 was a specific question, so simply look at the lines used to answer the previous question. The lines used in the prediction were 68–71. The correct answer is (D).

37. **C** The question asks which *claim about grasses is supported by the graph*. Work through each answer choice using the figure. Eliminate (A) because *spring burning* does not always have a *higher biomass* than that of *autumn or winter burning*. Eliminate (B) because *biomass* increases and decreases similarly over time for areas burned in autumn, winter, or spring. Choice (C) is supported by the graph: the amounts of biomass shown for autumn, winter, and spring burning are similar, so keep (C). *Rainfall* is not represented in the figure, nor is it clear whether the graph depicts the year 2012, so eliminate (D). The correct answer is (C).

38. **C** The question asks why the author of Passage 1 mentions the *paper by University of Chicago physicists Sidney Nagel and Thomas Witten*. Use the given line reference to find the window. Lines 17–23 state that *University of Chicago physicists Sidney Nagel, Thomas Witten, and their colleagues wrote an influential paper about this process in 1997, which focused mainly on suspended spherical particles, but it was not until the Yodh team's recent experiments that the surprising role played by suspended particle shape was discovered*. It's clear that their paper was influential and that they used spherical particles, and their work preceded that done by Yodh's team. Look for an answer choice that matches this prediction. The passage doesn't mention any reason to think that *Nagel and Witten could have discovered the impact of ellipsoid particles*, so eliminate (A). Eliminate (B) because *impediment* means "obstacle," and Passage 1 doesn't indicate that Nagel and Witten's work in any way limited other studies. Choice (C) matches the prediction, so keep it. The passage does not state that their research was *flawed*, so eliminate (D). The correct answer is (C).

39. **B** The question refers to Passage 1 and asks what *Professor Yodh's team assumed* before they started *their experiments*. Because this is a general question, it should be done after all the specific questions about Passage 1. Lines 28–30 state that the *researchers were surprised at how big an effect particle shape had on the drying phenomenon,* so look for an answer about how the researchers didn't expect particle shape to have much of an effect on drying patterns. Choice (A) is a Deceptive Language trap answer; it looks similar to what is stated in lines 33–34—*Spherical particles easily detach from the interface*—but this was a discovery in the experiment, not something the researchers assumed before their experiments. Eliminate (A). Choice (B) matches the prediction because they had assumed shape wouldn't have a major effect; keep it. Lines 26–28 say that the *spherical* particles *could be stretched*;

the researchers planned this as part of their experiment, so eliminate (C). The passage indicates that the scientists didn't expect the *shape of the particles* to have much of an effect, so eliminate (D). The correct answer is (B).

40. **B** The question asks for *the relationship between Nagel and Witten's* research *and Yodh's research.* Use the lead words *Nagel and Witten* to find the window in Passage 1. Lines 17–23 state that Nagel and Witten *wrote an influential paper about this process in 1997, which focused mainly on suspended spherical particles, but it was not until the Yodh team's recent experiments that the surprising role played by suspended particle shape was discovered.* Therefore, Yodh's research builds on Nagel and Witten's. Look for an answer choice that matches this prediction. Eliminate (A) because the passage does not indicate that Yodh's work in any way proved Nagel and Witten's work wrong. Rather, it indicates that Yodh's team tried things that the earlier team had not. Choice (B) matches the prediction, so keep it. Choices (C) and (D) contradict the passage—Nagel and Witten's research came before Yodh's. The correct answer is (B).

41. **D** The question asks what the word *undulation* means in line 37. Go back to the text, find the word *undulation,* and underline it. Carefully read the surrounding text to determine another word that would fit in its place, based on the context of the passage. The text says that *spherical particles…do not substantially deform the air-water interface. Ellipsoid particles, however, cause substantial undulation of the air-water interface.* Therefore, *undulation* must mean some kind of "change of shape." Neither *attraction, evaporation,* nor *undertow* mean "change of shape," so eliminate (A), (B), and (C). A *Ripple* is a "change in shape," so keep (D). The correct answer is (D).

42. **A** The question asks why *the author of Passage 2 compares detergents and bacterium.* Although this question asks about a specific line reference, it asks about it in relation to the author's purpose in the passage as a whole. Because this is a general question, it should be done after all the specific questions about Passage 2. Lines 70–74 state, *In various industrial applications…the coffee ring effect can be particularly troublesome and scientists have long been seeking ways to counteract it.* Then the passage states that researchers have *described a solution based on…a particularly promising bacterium, Pseudomonas aeruginosa.* Lines 82–91 say that *Pseudomonas aeruginosa…produces substances that counteract the coffee ring effect. These surface-tension-disrupting substances are called surfactants. Detergents such as soap are also surfactants.* Therefore, the author compares the bacterium and soap as *surfactants* that may help solve the coffee-ring problem in *industrial* applications. Look for an answer choice that matches this prediction. Choice (A) mentions *research into surfactants* and *issues in industrial use,* so keep it. Eliminate (B) because the passage doesn't address the dangers of using the bacterium in industrial applications such as *paint and varnish*; it says it is dangerous in *open wounds.* Choice (C) is a Deceptive Language trap answer; the passage does mention *that soap can help reduce the movement of particles to the edge of a stain,* but this doesn't explain why the author of Passage 2 *compares detergents and bacterium.* Eliminate (C). The passage does not state that *soap is a better surfactant,* so eliminate (D). The correct answer is (A).

43. **A** The question asks what Passage 2 most strongly suggests *about the coffee ring effect.* Notice that this is the first question in a paired set, so it can be done in tandem with Q44. Look at the answer choices for Q44 first. The lines for (44A) say that *researchers…have now discovered how to counteract coffee rings.* Check the answers for Q43; none of the answers are supported by those lines, so eliminate

(44A). The lines for (44B) state that *the key to the discovery was…a bacterium that counteracts the coffee ring effect*; these lines don't support any of the statements about the coffee-ring effect in Q43, so eliminate (44B). The lines for (44C) say that the coffee-ring effect *can also be seen in liquids with particles of other materials such as plastic and wood.* These lines don't provide support for any of the answers in Q43, so eliminate (44C). The lines for (44D) say that *the coffee ring effect can be particularly troublesome and scientists have long been seeking ways to counteract it.* These lines support (43A). Draw a line connecting (43A) and (44D). Without any support from the answers in Q44, (43B), (43C), and (43D) can be eliminated. The correct answers are (43A) and (44D).

44. **D** (See explanation above.)

45. **C** The question asks what the word *uniform* means in line 97. Go back to the text, find the word *uniform,* and underline it. Carefully read the surrounding text to determine another word that would fit in its place, based on the context of the passage. This paragraph describes what surfactants such as soap do. Lines 93–98 say that *the soap causes a counterflow from the edge back towards the centre of the stain in such a way that the small particles—material or bacteria—end up in a kind of whirlwind. In this way, you get a more uniform distribution of particles as evaporation occurs.* Therefore, *uniform* must mean something like "the same throughout." *Spread thin* does not mean "the same throughout," so eliminate (A). Choice (B) is about similar shape, not *distribution*, so it doesn't match the prediction. Eliminate it. Keep (C) because *evenly distributed* matches "the same throughout." Eliminate (D) because *wiped clean* doesn't mean "the same throughout." The correct answer is (C).

46. **C** The question asks whether *the main conclusion* of Passage 2 agrees with Passage 1's description of *the properties of the coffee ring effect.* Consider one passage at a time. Choice (A) contradicts Passage 1 because lines 52–56 say *We were thinking it would be useful if you could just sprinkle in a few of these ellipsoid particles to remove the coffee ring effect…and we found that sometimes this idea works and sometimes it doesn't.* Eliminate (A). Eliminate (D) because Passage 1 does not discuss *bacteria.* Consider Passage 2 in relationship to (B) and (C). Eliminate (B) because Passage 2 focuses on surfactants and does not discuss the shape of particles. Lines 45–51 in Passage 1 say *the researchers added a surfactant* and the *ellipsoid particles did not get stuck at the interface and flowed freely to the edge.* Lines 93–98 of Passage 2 say that *soap causes a counterflow from the edge back towards the centre of the stain,* and *in this way, you get a more uniform distribution of particles as evaporation occurs.* This supports (C), so keep it. The correct answer is (C).

47. **B** The question asks for a *difference between the studies described in the two passages.* Consider one passage at a time. In Passage 2, the researchers do not stretch the *Pseudomonas aeruginosa* bacterium, so eliminate (A). The researchers in Passage 2 use a bacterium—a *biological organism*—to counteract the coffee ring effect, so keep (B). Choice (C) is a Deceptive Language trap answer because Passage 2 does reference experimenting on nanomaterials, but not *in order to breed Pseudomonas aeruginosa.* Eliminate (C). Lines 93–98 state, *the soap causes a counterflow from the edge back towards the centre of the stain in such a way that the small particles—material or bacteria—end up in a kind of whirlwind. In this way, you get a more uniform distribution of particles as evaporation occurs*; these lines support (D), so keep it. Consider (B) and (D) in relation to Passage 1. The researchers in Passage 1 do not use *biological organisms*, so (B) gives a *difference between* the passages; keep (B). Eliminate (D) because this statement is true of both studies; the researchers in Passage 1 also experiment with ways to change *evaporation* and the *flow* of particles. The correct answer is (B).

Section 2—Writing and Language

1. **D** Verbs change in the answer choices, so this question tests consistency of verbs. A verb must be consistent with other verbs in the sentence. Check for other verbs in the surrounding sentences. The verbs in the previous sentence, *imagine* and *go*, also refer to the subject *you* and are in present tense. Therefore, the underlined verb should be in present tense to be consistent. Eliminate (A), (B), and (C) because the verbs are not in present tense. Only (D) contains a present tense verb. The correct answer is (D).

2. **C** Punctuation changes in the answer choices, so this question tests STOP, HALF-STOP, and GO punctuation. Use the Vertical Line Test, and identify the ideas as complete or incomplete. Draw the vertical line between the words *simple* and *get*. The first part of the sentence, *For many, the answer is simple*, is a complete idea. The second part of the sentence, *get on social media and tell the world*, is also a complete idea. To connect two complete ideas, STOP or HALF-STOP punctuation is needed. Eliminate (A), (B), and (D) as commas and no punctuation are GO punctuation. The colon in (C) is HALF-STOP punctuation, which can be used to connect two complete ideas. The correct answer is (C).

3. **B** Note the question! The question asks which choice would *best maintain the focus of this sentence and paragraph*, so it tests consistency. Determine the subject of the sentence and paragraph, and find the answer that is consistent with that idea. The non-underlined part of the sentence discusses telling *about the experience on Twitter and Facebook*. The following sentences mention *these services* and *Yelp*. Look for an answer that is consistent with social media services. Eliminate (A) because there is no mention of social media. Keep (B) because it mentions *a consumer-review site*, which is consistent with the focus on social media. Eliminate (C) because, although it mentions *a phone*, it does not mention social media. Eliminate (D) because *watching videos of animals* is not consistent with the paragraph. The correct answer is (B).

4. **A** Note the question! The question asks whether a phrase should be deleted, so it tests consistency. If the content of the phrase is consistent with the ideas surrounding it, it should be kept. If not, it should be deleted. The first two paragraphs of the essay discuss using social media to talk about a restaurant experience. The phrase *not just restaurants* clarifies that other companies are related to the social media issue discussed in the first paragraph, which only discusses restaurants. The phrase is consistent with the essay and provides a transition between what is true for restaurants and how it is also true for other businesses, so it should be kept; eliminate (C) and (D). Keep (A) because it correctly describes the phrase's use in the sentence. Eliminate (B) because *Chief Listening Officers* are not introduced until later in the paragraph and do not provide a reason for keeping the phrase. The correct answer is (A).

5. **C** Vocabulary changes in the answer choices, so this question tests precision of word choice. Look for a word or phrase with a definition that is consistent with the other ideas in the sentence. The sentence says that *it is more important than ever for companies to* "make certain" *that they are showing the best possible face to the world on social media*, so the correct word or phrase should mean "make certain." Eliminate (A) because *insure* means to get insurance, or financial coverage, for something. Eliminate (B) because *assure the public* means to make people comfortable. Keep (C) because *ensure* is consistent with "make certain." Eliminate (D) because *make insurance* is similar to (A), and both are inconsistent with "make certain." The correct answer is (C).

6. **C** Apostrophes change in the answer choices, so this question tests apostrophe usage. When used with a noun, on the PSAT, an apostrophe indicates possession. In this sentence, the *output* belongs to a company, so an apostrophe is needed, and because the word *a* indicates that the noun is singular, the apostrophe should be placed before the *s*. Eliminate (A) because it does not contain an apostrophe. Eliminate (B) because the sentence is discussing one company, not companies. Keep (C) because it has the apostrophe in the correct place and a singular company. Eliminate (D) because the apostrophe is used incorrectly. The correct answer is (C).

7. **D** Phrases change in the answer choices, so this question tests precision of word choice. There is also the option to DELETE; consider this choice carefully as it is often the correct answer. Choices (A), (B), and (C) all contain phrases that mean the same thing in this context. The sentence already says *to see if the situation can be remedied*, which means "improved," so there is no need to repeat the idea. The underlined portion should be deleted to make the sentence precise and more concise. The correct answer is (D).

8. **B** Vocabulary changes in the answer choices, so this question tests the precision of word choice. Look for a word or phrase with a definition that is consistent with the other ideas in the sentence. The sentence discusses *a company* "launching" *a new advertising campaign*, so the correct word or phrase should mean "launches." Eliminate (A) because *unfurls* means "unroll" and is used for a physical object such as a piece of cloth. Keep (B) because *rolls out* means "launches" and need not refer to a physical object. Eliminate (C) because *unrolls* is similar to *unfurls* and is not consistent with "launches." Eliminate (D) because *roles* refers to "position" and is not consistent with "launches." The correct answer is (B).

9. **B** Phrases change in the answer choices, so this question tests precision and concision. Look for a phrase that is precise in meaning. The sentence says that *it is more detailed than market research has ever been before*, but the sentence does not clearly indicate what *it* refers to. Eliminate (A) because the word *this* does not clarify the word *it* later on in the sentence. Keep (B) because *this kind of "market research"* is more precise. It supplies a reference noun for the pronoun *it* and is consistent with the rest of the sentence. Eliminate (C) because it does not provide what *it* is. Eliminate (D) because *reality* does not explain what *it* refers to. The correct answer is (B).

10. **D** Pronouns change in the answer choices, so this question tests consistency of pronouns. A pronoun must be consistent in number with the noun it refers to. The underlined pronoun refers to the noun *someone's*, which is singular. Eliminate (A) and (B) because *their* and *they're* are both plural. Eliminate (C) because *your* is not consistent with *someone's*. Keep (D) because *his* and *her* are singular pronouns that work with *someone's*. The correct answer is (D).

11. **A** Note the question! The question asks which choice *most directly answers the criticism presented in the previous sentence*, so it tests consistency. Eliminate answers that are inconsistent with the purpose stated in the question. The previous sentence says that *some criticize the CLO position as a fad* and that *companies* may be *overreacting to the power of social media*. Look for an answer that responds to that criticism. Keep (A) because it states that *CLOs will be needed as long as social media are around*, suggesting the potential longevity of CLOs is tied to social media. Eliminate (B) and (D) because they continue the criticism of the previous sentence, and the question asks for a choice that *answers* the criticism. Eliminate (C) because *teachers* are not consistent with the previous criticism. The correct answer is (A).

12. **A** Note the question! The question asks which choice *best maintains the focus of this paragraph*, so it tests consistency of ideas. Determine the subject of the paragraph and find the answer that is consistent with that idea. The paragraph says *Medical science has created some modern miracles* and mentions the *Spanish flu* and the *Philadelphia Yellow Fever Epidemic of 1793*. Look for an answer that gives other examples of historical epidemics. Keep (A) because it mentions *polio*, which is consistent with the other epidemics mentioned. Eliminate (B) and (D) because they give extra and irrelevant details about the *Spanish Flu*. Eliminate (C) because it discusses the present, while the paragraph is about the past. The correct answer is (A).

13. **B** Note the question! The question asks which choice *gives information consistent with the chart*, so it tests consistency. Read the labels on the table carefully and look for an answer that is consistent with the information given in the graph. Eliminate (A) because the table shows populations in 1790, not populations today, so this information is not supported by the chart. Keep (B) because it correctly states that Philadelphia was the second largest city in 1790 and gives the correct population. Eliminate (C) because, according to the table, Philadelphia had a larger population than Boston. Eliminate (D) because Philadelphia did not have a population higher than that of New York City. The correct answer is (B).

14. **D** Vocabulary changes in the answer choices, so this question tests precision of word choice. Look for a word or phrase with a definition that is consistent with the other ideas in the sentence. The sentence says *Doctors tried various* "cures," *but they were stalled in their inability to figure out both how the disease originated and how it was spreading*, so the correct word should mean "cures." Eliminate (A) because *things* is imprecise. Eliminate (B) because *options* is also imprecise. Eliminate (C) because *management models* is not consistent with the work of doctors. Keep (D) because *treatment approaches* is consistent with "cures." The correct answer is (D).

15. **B** Verbs change in the answer choices, so this question tests consistency of verbs. A verb must be consistent with its subject and with the other verbs in the sentence. The underlined portion is part of a list of two things doctors were unable to figure out: *how the disease originated* and something about *spreading*. To be consistent, the underlined verb must be in the same form as *originated*, which is in past tense. Choice (A) is in past tense, but *spreading* is not in the same form as *originated*, so eliminate it. Keep (B) because *spread* is in past tense and in the same form as *originated*. Eliminate (C) because it is in the wrong tense. Eliminate (D) because it changes *spread* from a verb to a noun, which does not match with *originated*. The correct answer is (B).

16. **C** Vocabulary changes in the answer choices, so this question tests precision of word choice. Look for a phrase consistent in tone with the paragraph. The paragraph discusses *medical science*, and the first part of the sentence says *Medical historians now know that the disease was spread by mosquitoes*. The word *but* indicates a contrast between *now* and the past, which suggests that the idea was "not proven" until much later. Eliminate (A) because while *pretty shady* is somewhat similar to "not proven," it is too casual and thus not consistent with the tone of the passage. Eliminate (B) because *stupid idiocy* does not match with "not proven" and is also not consistent in tone with the paragraph. Keep (C) because *not verified* matches with "not proven." Eliminate (D) because *downright wrong* incorrectly changes the meaning of the sentence, suggesting that the idea was incorrect until later, whereas it merely wasn't proven until later. The correct answer is (C).

17. **C** Pronouns and nouns change in the answer choices, so this question tests precision. A pronoun can only be used if it is clear what the pronoun refers to. There is no noun in the sentence that indicates who *tried to impose*, so a pronoun cannot be used; eliminate (A), (B), and (D). Only (C) clearly states who *tried to impose*. The correct answer is (C).

18. **A** Commas and words change in the answer choices, so this question tests the four ways to use a comma and consistency. The sentence contains a list of three things: 1) *alcohol*, 2) *hot sun*, and 3) *night air*. There should be a comma after each item in the list. Eliminate (B) because it is missing a comma after *sun*. Additionally, all items in a list must be phrased the same way to be consistent with one another. Eliminate (C) because the word *also* isn't needed since that's implied by the word *and*. Eliminate (D) because it is less concise than (A), and the additional words don't make the meaning more precise. The correct answer is (A).

19. **D** Note the question! The question asks where sentence 7 should be placed, so it tests consistency of ideas. The sentence must be consistent with the ideas that come both before and after it. Sentence 7 mentions *blame* for something, so it should be placed near other sentences that discuss blame. Sentence 3 says that *politicians blamed immigration*, so this sentence should go either before or after sentence 3. Since before sentence 3 is not an option, sentence 7 should be placed after sentence 3. The correct answer is (D).

20. **C** Punctuation changes in the answer choices, so this question tests STOP, HALF-STOP, and GO punctuation. Use the Vertical Line Test and identify the ideas as complete or incomplete. Draw the vertical line between the words *helplessly* and *as*. The first part of the sentence, *The medical establishment sat back helplessly*, is a complete idea. The second part of the sentence, *as the disease ravaged the city*, is an incomplete idea. To connect a complete idea to an incomplete idea, HALF-STOP or GO punctuation can be used. Eliminate (D) because the semicolon is STOP punctuation. Eliminate (A) and (B) because there is no need to have any punctuation between the two parts of the sentence. The correct answer is (C).

21. **B** Commas change in the answer choices, so this question tests the four ways to use a comma. The underlined portion does not contain unnecessary information, a list, or two ideas that must be connected, so there is no reason to use a comma. Eliminate (A), (C), and (D). The correct answer is (B).

22. **A** Transitions change in the answer choices, so this question tests consistency of ideas. A transition must be consistent with the relationship between the ideas it connects. The sentence before the transition states that *the Ebola virus in West Africa provides a terrifying reminder of just how deadly certain diseases can be*, and the sentence that starts with the transition states that *the Yellow Fever Epidemic provides a remarkable instance of a city's resilience*. These are both about examples of deadly diseases, so a same-direction transition is needed; keep (A). Eliminate (B) because it contains an opposite-direction transition. Eliminate (C) and (D) because *therefore* and *thus* are used to show a conclusion, which is not consistent with how the ideas connect. Moreover, *therefore* and *thus* provide an identical meaning, so there is no reason to choose one over the other, which means they are both wrong. The correct answer is (A).

23. **D** Vocabulary changes in the answer choices, so this question tests precision of word choice. There is also the option to DELETE; consider this choice carefully as it is often the correct answer. Choices (A), (B), and (C)—*seems doubtful, strikes us as odd,* and *appears improbable*—all mean the same thing in this context. The sentence already says *Many people find it difficult to believe,* so there's no need to repeat the idea. The underlined portion should be deleted to make the sentence more concise. The correct answer is (D).

24. **C** Note the question! The question asks which choice *would most effectively conclude this paragraph by introducing the main subject of the essay as a whole.* Determine the subject of the paragraph and find the answer that is consistent with that idea. The paragraph says that *the early days of recorded music can be hazy,* but *there is a treasure trove of recorded music from that era.* The next paragraph describes the life of *Jimmie Rodgers.* The concluding sentence should introduce *Jimmie Rodgers.* Eliminate (A) and (B) because they do not mention Jimmie Rodgers. Keep (C) because it introduces *Jimmie Rodgers.* For (D), scan the rest of the passage. It only discusses Jimmie Rodgers and not any of the other musicians mentioned in (D), so mentioning those musicians wouldn't *introduce the main subject of the essay.* Eliminate (D). The correct answer is (C).

25. **B** Verbs change in the answer choices, so this question tests consistency of verbs. A verb must be consistent with its subject and with the other verbs in the sentence. The subject of the verb is *circumstances,* which is plural. To be consistent, the underlined verb must also be plural. Eliminate (A), (C), and (D) because they are singular. The correct answer is (B).

26. **C** Phrase length changes in the answer choices, so this question tests precision of word choice. Look for a phrase that is consistent with the ideas in the sentence and is precise. The second part of the sentence is about *his father.* Eliminate (A) and (B) because *for sure* and *for certain* are not precise. Keep (C) because *his family* is consistent with *his father* in the latter part of the sentence. Eliminate (D) because *his mother, father, and siblings* is a less concise way of writing *his family.* The correct answer is (C).

27. **C** Note the question! The question asks which choice would best fulfill the goal of including *a detail that provides specific information about Rodgers's illness,* so it tests consistency. Eliminate answers that are inconsistent with the purpose stated in the question. Eliminate (A), (B), and (D) because they do not give *specific* information about Rodgers's illness. Only (C) gives the name of the illness. The correct answer is (C).

28. **A** Vocabulary changes in the answer choices, so this question tests precision of word choice. Look for a word with a definition that is consistent with the other ideas in the sentence. The sentence says *the inability to work* was a good thing *for Rodgers's great passion,* so the correct word should mean "fortunate." Keep (A) because *fortuitous* means "fortunate." Eliminate (B) because *chancy* means "risky." Eliminate (C) because *blessed* means "holy." Eliminate (D) because *charmed* means "unusually lucky" or "privileged," which goes further than just "fortunate." The correct answer is (A).

29. **A** Punctuation changes in the answer choices, so this question tests STOP, HALF-STOP, and GO punctuation and the four ways to use a comma. Use the Vertical Line Test and identify the ideas as complete or incomplete. Draw the vertical line between the words *rails* and *however.* The first part of the sentence, *Once Jimmie could no longer work the rails,* is an incomplete idea. The second part of the sentence, *however, he pursued his musical career in earnest,* is a complete idea. To connect an incomplete idea to a complete idea, GO punctuation is needed. A semicolon is STOP punctuation,

so eliminate (C). The phrase *however* is unnecessary information, so it should have commas both before and after it. Keep (A) because it correctly places commas before and after *however*. Eliminate (B) and (D) because they do not have commas before and after *however*. The correct answer is (A).

30. **C** Note the question! The question asks for *the best placement for the underlined portion,* so it tests precision. The phrase *all the way to New York City* should come after the phrase it describes. Eliminate (A), (B), and (D) because the placement of *all the way to New York City* after *sold*, *year*, and *copies* does not make sense. Keep (C) because *chased his dream all the way to New York City* provides a precise meaning. The correct answer is (C).

31. **A** Punctuation and words change in the answer choices, so this question tests STOP, HALF-STOP, and GO punctuation. The first part of the sentence, *By this time,* is an incomplete idea. The second part of the sentence, *Rodgers had become the famous "Singing Brakeman," and his influence would be felt for many generations to come*, is a complete idea. To connect an incomplete idea to a complete idea, GO punctuation is needed. Keep (A) because a comma is GO punctuation and can be used between an incomplete idea and complete idea. Eliminate (B) and (C) because adding *when* or *as* makes the sentence incomplete. Eliminate (D) because a colon is HALF-STOP punctuation and can only be used after a complete idea. The correct answer is (A).

32. **B** Words change in the answer choices, so this question tests precision of word choice. The paragraph says *This influence would not be felt only in country music either* and that *blues singer Howlin' Wolf cited Rodgers as an early influence. Elvis Presley* also *cited Rodgers as an early influence.* Eliminate (A) and (C) because *like* and *similar to* are not precise and make the meaning of the sentence unclear (both make it sound like *Elvis Presley* was an influence, not that he was influenced). Keep (B) because *as did* makes the meaning of the sentence clear by adding a verb. Eliminate (D) because it is not precise and introduces an unnecessary possessive phrase. The correct answer is (B).

33. **D** Note the question! The question asks for a choice that best *concludes the essay by reinforcing its main idea*, so it's testing consistency. First, consider the main idea of the passage. The passage introduces *Jimmie Rodgers*, discusses his early life, explains how he began his country musical career, and evaluates Rodgers's significance, indicating that his influence *would be felt for many generations to come* and that his music influenced other non-country artists. Look for an answer choice that is consistent with these ideas. Eliminate (A) because it contradicts the passage's point that Rodgers was highly influential. Eliminate (B) because his influence on his *family* is not consistent with the passage's main idea—the passage focuses on his influence on the music industry. Eliminate (C) because it mentions only his careers and not his influence as a musician, so it's not consistent with the main idea. Keep (D) because the idea that *his influence is still alive and well* is consistent with the passage's main idea. The correct answer is (D).

34. **D** Nouns change from singular to plural in the answer choices, so this question tests consistency of nouns. A noun must be consistent in number with the other nouns or pronouns in the sentence. The sentence contains the nouns *males* and *females*, which are plural. To be consistent, the underlined noun must also be plural. Eliminate (A), (B), and (C) because they all contain the singular nouns *role* or *distinction*. Keep (D) because it contains the plural noun *roles*. The correct answer is (D).

35.   **A**   Note the question! The question asks which choice *gives accurate data based on the graph*, so it tests consistency. Read the labels on the graph carefully, and look for an answer that is consistent with the information given in the graph. Keep (A) because it gives information consistent with the graph, which shows that only a small number of species have a *post-reproductive life span* and that the *black-tailed prairie dog* is one of them. Eliminate (B) because it is not consistent with the graph as it does not show that *most* species have a *post-reproductive life span*, and humans are not on the graph. Eliminate (C) because the *common bottlenose dolphin* has the longest *pre-reproductive life span* of any species on the graph. Eliminate (D) because the two rodent species on the graph do have *post-reproductive life span*. The correct answer is (A).

36.   **D**   Pronouns and nouns change in the answer choices, so this question tests precision. A pronoun can only be used if it is clear what the pronoun refers to. *Scientists* are not the ones whom *evolution has determined should live so much longer*, so a pronoun is imprecise; eliminate (A), (B), and (C). Only (D) makes it clear that the *female whales* are the ones who *live so much longer*. The correct answer is (D).

37.   **A**   Note the question! The question asks which choice provides the *most effective transition from the previous paragraph to this paragraph*, so it tests consistency. Determine the subjects of the two paragraphs, and find the answer that is consistent with those ideas. The previous paragraph is about *gender differences* in the *animal kingdom*, specifically that *many females do not live much beyond menopause*. The paragraph ends by stating that *Scientists have long wondered why evolution has determined the female whales should live so much longer*. The current paragraph says that the *social forces that define gender may apply to the animal kingdom* and that scientists watched *over 750 hours of videos* and observed *the behaviors of pods of whales*. Keep (A) because it acknowledges the question at the end of the previous paragraph and connects to scientists studying whales in the current paragraph. Eliminate (B) and (C) because they do not connect to the information in the previous paragraph. Eliminate (D) because it does not mention *whales* at all. The correct answer is (A).

38.   **B**   Word order changes in the answer choices, so this question tests precision. Look for the phrase that makes the meaning of the sentence clear. The first part of the sentence says *After watching over 750 hours of video and observing the behaviors of pods of whales*. The first word after this phrase should indicate who did the *watching* and *observing*. The *whale grandmothers* are not the ones *watching* and *observing*, so eliminate (A) and (C). Keep (B) because it makes sense that the *scientists* are *watching* and *observing*. Eliminate (D) because *teaching behaviors* cannot watch and observe. The correct answer is (B).

39.   **A**   Note the question! The question asks whether a sentence should be added, so it tests consistency. If the content of the new sentence is consistent with the ideas surrounding it, then it should be added. The paragraph discusses *scientists* studying the *teaching behaviors* of *whale grandmothers*. The new sentence states that *the older female whales were the most likely to lead younger whales to salmon feeding grounds*, which describes a *teaching behavior* and is consistent with the paragraph. The new sentence should be added, so eliminate (C) and (D). Keep (A) because the sentence *clarifies some of the teaching behaviors*. Eliminate (B) because the *older whales* were not *ignored in the study*. The correct answer is (A).

40.   **D**   Punctuation changes in the answer choices, so this question tests STOP, HALF-STOP, and GO punctuation. Use the Vertical Line Test and identify the ideas as complete or incomplete. Draw the vertical line between the words *words* and *sharpened*. The first part of the sentence, *The scientists ascribe this behavior to what they refer to as the grandmothers' roles as "repositories of ecological knowledge"*

in other words, is an incomplete idea. The second part of the sentence, *Sharpened memories and long experience of learned behaviors make the older females extremely valuable to future generations*, is a complete idea. To connect an incomplete idea to a complete idea, GO punctuation is needed. STOP punctuation, like periods and semicolons, cannot be used to connect an incomplete idea to a complete idea; eliminate (A) and (B). Repeat the Vertical Line Test, drawing the line between the words *knowledge* and *in*. The first part of the sentence becomes a complete idea, and the second part of the sentence remains a complete idea. Only STOP punctuation can be used to connect two complete ideas; eliminate (C). Choice (D) correctly places STOP punctuation between two complete ideas. The correct answer is (D).

41. **B** Note the question! The question asks whether the word *longevity* should be replaced with the word *life* in the previous sentence, so it tests precision. The previous sentence states *The elder females have evolved this longevity because the species, simply put, needs it*. The word *longevity*, which means "living a long time" is more precise than the word *life*, which doesn't indicate the long period of time mentioned previously, so it should not be replaced; eliminate (C) and (D). *Longevity* is more specific, not more formal, than *life*, so eliminate (A). *Longevity* specifically refers to "life span," so keep (B). The correct answer is (B).

42. **D** Note the question! The question asks which choice *introduces the paragraph most effectively*, so it tests consistency of ideas. Determine the subject of the paragraph and find the answer that is consistent with that idea. The paragraph states that *the findings also show that societies that value youth and middle age to the detriment of old age may do so at* their *own peril* and that *in whale pods as well as human communities, it seems, life may depend on the accrued knowledge* of older relatives. Eliminate (A) because *gender discrimination* is not discussed in the paragraph. Eliminate (B) because there is no discussion of what else *whale grandmothers know*. Eliminate (C) because *Moby Dick* is not mentioned in the paragraph at all. Keep (D) because it mentions the study discussed in the previous paragraph and how it connects to society at large. The correct answer is (D).

43. **B** Pronouns change in the answer choices, so this question tests consistency of pronouns. A pronoun must be consistent in number with the noun it refers to. The underlined pronoun refers to the noun *societies*, which is plural. To be consistent, the underlined pronoun must also be plural. Eliminate (C) and (D) because they contain singular pronouns. In addition, the *peril* belongs to the *societies*, so the underlined pronoun must also be possessive. Eliminate (A) because *there* does not show possession. Keep (B) because *their* is plural and possessive. The correct answer is (B).

44. **C** Word order and number changes in the answer choices, so this question tests precision and concision. Look for the phrase that makes the meaning of the sentence clear in a concise way. Eliminate (A) because the phrase is not precise or concise. Eliminate (B) because *long lives are long enough* is not precise because it doesn't indicate what their lives are *long enough* for. Keep (C) because the meaning is clear. Eliminate (D) because the meaning is not clear, and a word is needed between *knowledge* and *the longer-lived people*. The correct answer is (C).

Section 3—Math (No Calculator)

1. **C** The question asks for the point that satisfies a system of equations. There are specific points in the answers, so use PITA. Test the ordered pairs in both equations from the question and look for a pair that makes both equations true. Start by plugging (A) into the first equation to get $0 = \frac{1}{2}(3) + 3$. This becomes $0 = \frac{3}{2} + 3$. Since this is not true, eliminate (A). Now plug the point in (B) into the first equation to get $2 = \frac{1}{2}(-2) + 3$. This becomes $2 = -1 + 3$ or $2 = 2$. This is true, but the point must work in both equations. Plugging the point in (B) into the second equation gives $-2 = (2)^2 - 5(2) + 6$, which becomes $-2 = 4 - 10 + 6$ or $-2 = 0$. Eliminate (B). Plug the point in (C) into the first equation to get $4 = \frac{1}{2}(2) + 3$. This becomes $4 = 1 + 3$ or $4 = 4$. This is true, but test the second equation as well. This gives $2 = (4)^2 - 5(4) + 6$, which becomes $2 = 16 - 20 + 6$ or $2 = 2$. This is also true. The correct answer is (C).

2. **B** The question asks for an equivalent form of an expression. There are variables in the answer choices, so plug in. Make $y = 2$ and $c = 3$. The expression becomes $30(2) - 12(3)(2) = 60 - 72 = -12$. This is the target value; circle it. Now plug $y = 2$ and $c = 3$ into the answer choices to see which one matches the target value. Choice (A) becomes $[5 - 2(3)](2) = (5 - 6)(2) = (-1)(2) = -2$. This does not match the target, so eliminate (A). Choice (B) becomes $[30 - 12(3)](2) = (30 - 36)(2) = (-6)(2) = -12$. Keep (B), but check (C) and (D) just in case. Choice (C) becomes $(18)[3 - 2(2)] = (18)(3 - 4) = (18)(-1) = -18$. Eliminate (C). Choice (D) becomes $(18)(3)(2)^2 = (18)(3)(4)$, which does not equal -12. Eliminate (D). The correct answer is (B).

3. **C** The question asks for an equation in terms of a specific variable. There are two good ways to solve. One is to solve for a. To begin to isolate a, divide both sides of the equation by m to get $\frac{F}{m} = a$. Another option is to plug in. Choose easy numbers that fulfill the equation $F = ma$, such as $m = 2$, $a = 3$, and $F = 6$. Now plug $m = 2$, $a = 3$, and $F = 6$ into the answer choices to see which one contains a true equation. Choice (A) becomes $3 = (6)(2)$. This is not true, so eliminate (A). Choice (B) becomes $3 = 6 + 2$. Eliminate (B). Choice (C) becomes $3 = \frac{6}{2}$. This is true, so keep (C), but check (D) just in case. Choice (D) becomes $3 = \frac{2}{6}$, which is not true, so eliminate (D). With either strategy, the correct answer is (C).

4. **B** The question asks for the value that satisfies a system of equations. There are specific values in the answers, so plug in the answers. The answer choices represent possible values of j. Test the values in both equations from the question and look for one that makes both equations the same. Start with (B). Plug the value into the first equation to get $(-4)(-5) - 10k = 50$. This becomes $20 - 10k = 50$. Subtract 20 from both sides to get $-10k = 30$ or $k = -3$. Then plug the value into the second equation to get $(-5) - 3k = 4$. Add 5 to both sides to get $-3k = 9$ or $k = -3$. This is the same as the first equation with this value. The correct answer is (B).

5. **D**   The question asks about the graph of the data representing a certain situation. Label the parts of the equation to determine what they represent. In this question, y represents the weight of the giant panda and x represents the number of months after the panda was born. The slope of a graph is defined as the change in y over the change in x, so the slope must relate to weight, not time. Eliminate (B) and (C) for this reason. The equation is in $y = mx + b$ form, where m is the slope of a graph, so here the slope is 3,100. Plug and play to determine what gives a value of 3,100. Make $m = 0$ to get the giant panda's weight after 0 months, or at birth. This becomes $weight = 3{,}100(0) + 105$ or $weight = 105$. Since the giant panda's weight at birth is not 3,100, eliminate (A). After one month, the giant panda will have a $weight = 3{,}100(1) + 105 = 3{,}100 + 105 = 3{,}205$. Therefore, in the first month, the panda gained $3{,}205 - 105 = 3{,}100$ grams in weight. The correct answer is (D).

6. **A**   The question asks for a solution to the given equation. Since the question asks for a specific value and the answers contain numbers in increasing order, use PITA. Begin by labeling the answers as b and start with (B), 0. The equation becomes $(3)(0)^2 - (6)(0) = 5 + (4)(0)^2$ or $0 - 0 = 5 + 0$. This isn't true, so eliminate (B). It may be difficult to see whether a larger or smaller number is needed to make the equation true, so just pick either direction. For (A), plug in $b = -5$ to get $(3)(-5)^2 - (6)(-5) = 5 + (4)(-5)^2$. Simplify this to get $(3)(25) + 30 = 5 + (4)(25)$ or $75 + 30 = 5 + 100$. This results in $105 = 105$, which is true, so stop here. The correct answer is (A).

7. **A**   The question asks for a statement that cannot be true about a graph. When given a description of a graph, make a sketch of the graph and use it to eliminate answers. This line crosses the x-axis at 4, so it contains the point (4, 0) as well as the given point (–2, 6). Draw the graph with these points, and then connect them like this:

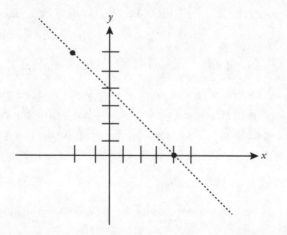

Now mark each answer as true or false. The slope and the y-intercept are easy to see, so start with those. The slope is negative, so (B) is true, and the y-intercept is positive, so (C) is true. The question asks for a statement that cannot be true, so eliminate (B) and (C). Choice (A) contains a point in the lower left quadrant of the graph, and (D) contains a point in the lower right quadrant. Since the line goes through only the lower right quadrant, only (D) can possibly be true. Eliminate (D). The correct answer is (A).

8. **B**   The question asks for an inequality that models a specific situation. Translate the question in Bite-Sized Pieces and eliminate after each piece. One piece of information says that each square of fabric must have an area of at least 340 square inches. Since the quilt uses 16 different squares of fabric, multiply 16 by 340 to get the minimum area of fabric needed for the quilt. This results in 5,440, so

eliminate (A) and (D), where this minimum value does not appear. Compare the remaining answers. The difference between (B) and (C) is the maximum value. The question states that each square of fabric must have an area of no more than 360 square inches, so multiply 16 by 360 to get the maximum. That value is 5,760, which does not appear in (C), so eliminate it. The correct answer is (B).

9. **D** The question asks for an equation that models a specific situation. Translate the question in Bite-Sized Pieces and eliminate after each piece. One piece of information says that a 15% discount will be applied. A 15% discount would be calculated with a multiplier of 0.85 (1–0.15), so eliminate (A) and (C), which multiply by 1.15 (an increase of 15%) instead. Compare the remaining answers. The difference between (B) and (D) is where the 15% discount is being applied. The question states that x is the total cost in dollars. The discount should be applied to the original purchase price of the dishes and bowls, so eliminate (B). The correct answer is (D).

10. **C** The question asks for the value of a constant that appears as part of a fractional exponent. When dealing with questions about exponents, remember the MADSPM rules. The MA part of the acronym indicates that Multiplying matching bases means to Add the exponents. The PM part of the acronym indicates that raising a base with an exponent to another Power means to Multiply the exponents. Use the order of operations to apply the exponents outside the parentheses to the bases inside by multiplying the exponents to get $\left(a^{\frac{3}{3}}b^{\frac{3}{4}}\right)\left(a^{\frac{4}{3}}b^{\frac{4}{4}}\right)$. Although it is possible to reduce some of these exponents, the next step will be to add them together, since the bases are multiplied. Leave the exponents in fractional form to make that easier, getting $a^{\frac{7}{3}}b^{\frac{7}{4}}$. According to the equation, this is equal to $a^{\frac{k}{3}}b^{\frac{k}{4}}$, so k must equal 7. The correct answer is (C).

11. **C** The question asks for a system of inequalities that models a specific situation. Translate the question in Bite-Sized Pieces and eliminate after each piece. One piece of information says that the baker needs to buy at least 2 containers of flour. Since f represents the number of containers of flour, one inequality should say $f \geq 2$, so eliminate (B) and (D), where this does not appear. Compare the remaining answers. The difference between (A) and (C) is the direction of the inequality sign. The question states that the baker has $75 dollars with which to purchase ingredients. Since the baker cannot spend more than this amount, the inequality should say that the total cost is ≤ 75. This does not appear in (A), so eliminate it. The correct answer is (C).

12. **A** The question asks for the y-coordinate of a parabola's vertex. The question gives the equation of a parabola in factored form, which makes it easy to determine the solutions, or y-intercepts in this case. Because parabolas are symmetrical about a central axis that runs through the vertex, the y-coordinate of the vertex will be halfway between the two y-intercepts. If $x = 0$, then the equation becomes $0 = (y + 5)(y - 15)$. Set each binomial equal to 0 to get $y + 5 = 0$ and $y - 15 = 0$, so $y = -5$ or 15. Eliminate (C) and (D), which aren't between the intercepts at all. To find the midpoint, average the y-intercepts to get $y = \dfrac{15 + (-5)}{2} = \dfrac{10}{2} = 5$. The correct answer is (A).

13. **D** The question asks for a pair of congruent angles in a figure containing triangles. When given two or more triangles and information about the ratios of the sides, look for similar triangles. Sides FJ and FH are both on the smallest triangle, while FG and GH are both on the largest triangle. Redraw the

two triangles side-by-side to better see the similarities. Start with triangle *FHJ*, redrawing it by itself with the same orientation it currently has, labeling the vertices. Then draw a bigger triangle next to it with the same shape as triangle *FHJ*, like this:

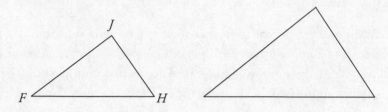

Since the ratio of $\dfrac{FJ}{FH}$ is equal to $\dfrac{FG}{GH}$, label the sides of this new triangle correspondingly. Make sure to keep $\angle FGH$ as the smaller angle and $\angle GFH$ as the larger one, like this:

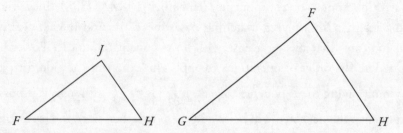

Now it is easier to check corresponding angles. Choice (A) gives the angles on the lower left of the big triangle and the lower right of the small triangle. These are not necessarily congruent, so eliminate (A). Choice (B) gives an angle that does not appear on either triangle and the angle at the top of the small triangle. These are not necessarily congruent, so eliminate (B). Choice (C) gives an angle that does not appear on either triangle and the angle on the lower left of the small triangle. These are not necessarily congruent, so eliminate (C). Choice (D) gives the angles at the tops of both triangles, so these angles are congruent. The correct answer is (D).

14. **36** The question asks for a measurement and gives conflicting units. Begin by reading the question to find information on the measurement. The question states that Monica made a total of 3 pounds and 6 ounces of jam on Wednesday and Thursday. There are 16 ounces in a pound, so set up a proportion to determine how many ounces of jam she made in total: $\dfrac{16\ \text{ounces}}{1\ \text{pound}} = \dfrac{x\ \text{ounces}}{3\ \text{pounds}}$. Cross-multiply to solve for x: $48 = x$. Add the remaining 6 ounces to get the total for both days: $48 + 6 = 54$ ounces in all. The question says she made half as many ounces of jam on Wednesday as she did on Thursday. The question asks how many ounces she made on Thursday alone, so set up an equation to find the answer, where x represents the ounces of jam Monica made on Thursday: $54 = \dfrac{1}{2}x + x$. Add $\dfrac{1}{2}x + x$ to get $54 = \dfrac{3}{2}x$. Then multiply both sides by $\dfrac{2}{3}$ to get $36 = x$. The correct answer is 36.

15. **3** The question asks for the value of z for which the provided equation will have an infinite number of solutions. First, isolate z. Distribute the 6 to get $12y + 6z = 12y + 18$. Subtract $12y$ from both sides to get $6z = 18$. Then divide both sides by 6 to get $z = 3$. If z is set equal to 3, the equation will have infinitely many solutions, because the y terms will always be eliminated. The correct answer is 3.

16. **24** The question asks about the product of two coefficients within a pair of binomials. When given a quadratic in factored form, it is often necessary to use FOIL to multiply the factors out to the standard form $ax^2 + bx + c$ to solve the question. The expression becomes $6gx^4 + ghx^2y^2 - 24x^2y^2 - 4hy^4$. It might be tempting to try to figure out what the values of g and h are, given the information that they have a difference of 5. However, make sure to read the full question, which asks for the value of gh, not g or h separately. The gh appears as the coefficient of one of the x^2y^2 terms, and the question states that the coefficient on that term when *like terms are collected* is zero. The second x^2y^2 term has a coefficient of -24, so the first one must have a coefficient of 24 in order to equal 0 when the two terms are combined. Thus, gh must equal 24. The correct answer is 24.

17. **2** The question asks for the value of one of the coefficients in a quadratic. When given a quadratic in standard form, which is $ax^2 + bx + c$, it is often necessary to factor it to solve the question. Here, the question supplies one of the factors, so use that to find the other factor. If $(2y - 3)$ is a factor, then the first part of the second factor must multiply by $2y$ to result in $8y^2$. Divide $8y^2$ by $2y$ to get $4y$ as the first term in the second factor. Similarly, the second term in the second factor must multiply by -3 to get -15. Divide -15 by -3 to get 5 as the second term of the second factor. Therefore, the second factor must be $(4y + 5)$. Now use FOIL on the two factors to both verify that these numbers give you $8y^2$ and -15 and to determine the coefficient on the y term, which will be the value of d. The expression becomes $(2y - 3)(4y + 5) = 8y^2 + 10y - 12y - 15$ or $8y^2 - 2y - 15$. Therefore, $d = 2$. The correct answer is 2.

Section 4—Math (Calculator Allowed)

1. **C** The question asks for the profit the store makes for selling 20 pencils. Because profits increase as pencils sold increase, set up a proportion: $\dfrac{12 \text{ pencils}}{\$0.75} = \dfrac{20 \text{ pencils}}{\$x}$. Cross-multiply to get $12x = \$15$. Divide both sides by 12 to get $x = \$1.25$. The correct answer is (C).

2. **A** The question asks for the period that shows the least decrease. Ballpark to find the answer. Choice (A) has a decrease of about one interval between horizontal gridlines. Choice (B) has a decrease of about more than two full intervals. Choice (C) has a decrease of about 4 intervals. Choice (D) has a decrease of about 2 intervals. Therefore, the correct answer is (A).

3. **D** The question asks for the meaning of a piece of an equation in context. Start by reading the full question, which asks for the meaning of the number 870. Then label the parts of the equation with the information given. The question states that A represents the remaining amount she owes and w represents the number of weeks since she borrowed the money. Because the number 870 is used to calculate A, the remaining amount owed, it must have something to do with money. Next, use Process of Elimination to get rid of answer choices that are not consistent with the labels. Choice (A) describes the total amount Sydney has repaid. However, the amount will change over time, so it cannot be represented by a constant. Eliminate (A). Choice (C) describes w and not 870, so eliminate (C). To check (B) and (D), plug in some numbers. If $w = 1$, then $A = 870 - 30(1) = 840$, so after 1 week, \$840 remains to be paid. If $w = 2$, then $A = 870 - 30(2) = 810$, so after 2 weeks, \$810 remains to be paid. Therefore, between week 1 and week 2, $840 - 810 = 30$ was repaid. Thus, 30 represents the amount Sydney repays each week, so eliminate (B). Only one choice remains. To confirm (D),

note that the original amount that Sydney owes is the amount that she owes after 0 weeks. If $w = 0$, then $A = 870 - 30(0) = 870$. The correct answer is (D).

4. **A** The question asks for the relationship between years of ownership and selling price. Look at the graph. There is clearly a downward trend in both the scatterplot and the line of best fit. Therefore, this is a negative correlation: as one variable increases, the other variable decreases. Eliminate (B), (C), and (D), which do not describe such a relationship. The correct answer is (A).

5. **B** The question asks how much more the actual selling price was compared to that predicted by the line of best fit for the car that was sold after it was owned for exactly 7 years. Find 7 on the horizontal axis and trace up to the point and the line of best fit. They lie between two gridlines on the vertical axis. Since each interval is $2,000, the difference must be less than $2,000. Eliminate (C) and (D). Since the difference makes up more than half the interval, the difference must be more than $1,000. Eliminate (A). The correct answer is (B).

6. **D** The question asks for the value of b in the equation when graphed and provides a point on the graph. Plug the point into the equation. Plug $x = 3$ and $y = -1$ into $y = 2x - b$ to get $-1 = 2(3) - b$. Simplify the right side to get $-1 = 6 - b$. Subtract 6 to both sides to get $-7 = -b$. Divide both sides by -1 to get $b = 7$. The correct answer is (D).

7. **A** The question asks for the model that best fits the data. Compare the answer choices. Two choices describe a linear decrease, which is a decrease by the same amount each month, and two choices describe an exponential increase, which is an increase by the same percent each month. Because linear decreases are easier to work with, first determine whether the relationship is linear with a consistent decrease. From month 0 to month 1, the decrease is $1,400 - $1,344 = $56. Eliminate (C), which indicates a decrease of $47. From month 1 to month 2, the decrease is $1,344 - $1,290 = $54.

Eliminate (D), since the decrease is not always $56. Therefore, the decrease must be exponential. To find the percent change between months, use the formula $\dfrac{difference}{original} \times 100$. From month 0 to month 1, the percent decrease is $\dfrac{\$1,400 - \$1,344}{\$1,400} \times 100 = \dfrac{\$56}{\$1,400} \times 100 = 0.04 \times 100 = 4\%$. The correct answer is (A).

8. **A** The question asks for the rate of the snail in centimeters per hour. Begin by reading the question to find information on the snail's pace. The question states that the snail moves at a rate of 700 millimeters per second. Convert the 700 millimeters into centimeters. Since there are 10 millimeters in 1 centimeter, set up the proportion $\dfrac{10 \text{ mm}}{1 \text{ cm}} = \dfrac{700 \text{ mm}}{x \text{ cm}}$. Cross-multiply to get $10x = 700$. Divide both sides by 10 to get $x = 70$. Therefore, the snail moves at a rate of 70 centimeters per minute.

Determine the number of centimeters travelled in 1 hour. Since there are 60 minutes in 1 hour, set up the proportion $\dfrac{10 \text{ cm}}{1 \text{ min}} = \dfrac{y \text{ cm}}{60 \text{ min}}$. Cross-multiply to get $y = 4,200$. Therefore, the snail moves at a rate of 4,200 centimeters per hour. The correct answer is (A).

9.   **C**   The question asks about the solutions to the equation. Two of the choices include numbers, and the other two are infinitely many solutions and no solutions. Plug in the easier of the choices with numbers. Plug in $y = 10$ to get $5\left(\dfrac{10}{2} + 5\right) = 2(10) + \dfrac{1}{2}(10) + 25$. The equation becomes $5(5 + 5) = 20 + 5 + 25$ or $5(10) = 50$. Since this is true, $y = 10$ is a solution. Eliminate (A), since $y = 1\dfrac{1}{2}$ cannot be the only solution, and eliminate (D), since there is at least one solution. It is still possible that there are infinitely many solutions. To test, plug in any other number. To make the math as easy as possible, plug in $y = 0$ to get $5\left(\dfrac{0}{2} + 5\right) = 2(0) + \dfrac{1}{2}(0) + 25$. The equation becomes $5(0 + 5) = 0 + 0 + 25$ or $5(5) = 25$. Therefore, $y = 0$ is also a solution. Since $y = 10$ is not the only solution, eliminate (B). The correct answer is (C).

10. **D**   The question asks for the difference of polynomials, so simplify and combine like terms. Do this in Bite-Sized Pieces. Find like terms, such as $2ab^2$ in the first polynomial and $2ab^2$ in the second polynomial. Subtract to get $2ab^2 - 2ab^2 = 0$. Therefore, the correct answer must not have an ab^2 term. Eliminate (B) and (C). Now, look at the a^2 terms. Subtract $-3a^2$ from $5a^2$ to get $5a^2 - (-3a^2) = 8a^2$. Eliminate (A), which does not include this term. Only one choice remains. The correct answer is (D).

11. **B**   The question asks for a percent based on data. Set it up, then find the numbers on the table. The question asks what percent of the athletes in the school are right-handed varsity athletes, so the percent is $\dfrac{\text{right-handed varsity}}{\text{total athletes}} \times 100$. The table indicates that there are 98 right-handed varsity athletes, and the question states that there are 270 athletes in the school. Plug the two values into the percent to get $\dfrac{98}{270} \times 100 \approx 36.296$. The question says *approximately*, so select the closest choice. The correct answer is (B).

12. **D**   The question asks for the difference between the maximum weight that Helen can lift and the median, so find the median. The median of a list of numbers is the middle number when all values are arranged in order. In lists with an even number of items, the median is the average of the middle two numbers. Put the maximum weights in order from least to greatest: 30, 40, 60, 70, 110, 130, 170, 230. Find the middle number by crossing out numbers in pairs starting from the outside. Cross out 30 and 230. Cross out the next least and next greatest: 40 and 170. Cross out the next least and next greatest: 60 and 130. Only 70 and 110 remain. Since there is no single middle number, find the average of the middle two to get $\dfrac{70 + 110}{2} = 90$ as the median. Find the difference between this value and the maximum weight that Helen can lift. The maximum weight that Helen can lift is 170 pounds, so the difference is $170 - 90 = 80$. The correct answer is (D).

13. **A**   The question asks which statement is true, and the statements refer to mode and range. Begin with the easier statistic, which is mode. By definition, the mode of a list of numbers is the number that appears the most often. For the Physics class, 25 is the only number that appears more than once, so 25 is the mode. Similarly, for the Biology class, 32 in the only number that appears more than once, so 32 is the mode. Since the mode for Physics is less than the mode for Biology, eliminate (B) and

(D). Now check the range, which is, by definition, the difference between the greatest and least number in a list. For the Physics class, the range is 31 − 23 = 8. For the Biology class, the range is 32 − 21 = 11. Since the range for the Physics class is less than the range for the Biology class, eliminate (C). The correct answer is (A).

14. **C** The question asks how many cars the factory can produce in 540 hours. The rate is given in minutes, so convert the 540 hours into minutes, using the proportion $\frac{60 \text{ minutes}}{1 \text{ hour}} = \frac{x \text{ minutes}}{540 \text{ hours}}$. Cross-multiply to get x = 32,400. Since the factory can produce 1 car in 1,080 minutes, set up the proportion $\frac{1,080 \text{ minutes}}{1 \text{ car}} = \frac{32,400 \text{ minutes}}{y \text{ cars}}$. Cross-multiply to get 1,080y = 32,400. Divide both sides by 1,080 to get y = 30. The correct answer is (C).

15. **A** The question asks for the difference between the percentage of patients in the experimental physical therapy with a recovery time of more than 6 months and the percentage of patients in the conventional physical therapy with a recovery time of more than 6 months. Find both percentages. There was a total of 82 + 112 = 194 patients in the experimental physical therapy, 112 of whom had a recovery time of more than 6 months. Therefore, the percentage is $\frac{112}{194} \times 100 \approx 57.731$. There was a total of 151 + 140 = 291 patients in the conventional physical therapy, 140 of whom had a recovery time of more than 6 months. Therefore, that percentage is $\frac{140}{291} \times 100 \approx 48.11$. To find the difference, subtract to get 57.731 − 48.11 = 9.621. The question asks for the difference rounded to the nearest percent, so the correct answer is (A).

16. **D** The question asks for the number of patients who had both knees replaced. The ratio of those who had one knee replaced to those who had both knees replaced is 3:7. Add the parts of the ratio together to determine the number of people in one group, which is 3 + 7 = 10. Now use the chart to determine the actual number of people. The question only refers to those *in conventional physical therapy*. According to the chart, there is a total of 151 + 140 = 291 patients in the conventional physical therapy. If there are 10 people in a group and 291 people total, divide 291 by 10 to find that there are 29.1 groups. This multiplier can be applied to both parts of the ratio to find the actual numbers. The question asks about those with *both knees replaced*, which is the 7 in the ratio. Multiply the ratio by the multiplier to find that there were 7 × 29.1 = 203.7 people in conventional therapy that had both knees replaced. The question asks for the *best approximation* of this number, so round the number to 204. The correct answer is (D).

17. **C** The question asks for the probability a patient in the study selected at random will have a recovery time of more than 6 months. Probability is defined as $\frac{\text{\# of outcomes that fit the requirement}}{\text{total \# of possible outcomes}}$. Read the table carefully to find the right numbers to set up the probability. Because the question states that *a patient in the study is selected at random*, the *total # of possible outcomes* is the total number of patients in the study, which is 485. Because the question asks for the probability that the patient *will have a recovery time of more than 6 months*, the *# of outcomes that fit the requirement* is the total number of patients with a

recovery time of more than 6 months. Make sure to include both those in experimental physical therapy and those in conventional physical therapy to get a total of 112 + 140 = 252. Therefore, the probability is $\frac{252}{485} \approx 0.5196$. The question says *is closest to*, so select the closest choice. The correct answer is (C).

18. **D** The question asks for the equation of a circle. The equation of a circle can be written in the form $(x - h)^2 + (y - k)^2 = r^2$, where (h, k) is the center of the circle and r is the radius of the circle. Eliminate (A) and (C), which have subtraction between the binomials instead of addition. Look at the two remaining choices. The choices differ both in the center and in the radius, so eliminate one choice using any of this information. Since the center is (–3, 5), $h = -3$ and $(x - h) = (x + 3)$. Also, since the radius is 4, $r^2 = 16$. Using either of those pieces, eliminate (B). The correct answer is (D).

19. **A** The question asks how many additional hours a performance will need to be for the piano player to charge an additional dollar. Although there are numbers in the answer choices, plugging in the answers is not the ideal approach here because they represent the difference rather than a value in the equation. Instead, since there is a relationship between the two variables, this can be solved using Plugging In. Let $t = 2$. If $t = 2$, then $C = 100(2) + 50 = 250$. The question asks about the piano player charging an additional dollar. Since the amount charged is C, let $C = 250 + 1 = 251$. Plug $C = 251$ into the equation to get $251 = 100t + 50$. Solve for t. Subtract 50 from both sides to get $201 = 100t$. Divide both sides by 100 to get $2.01 = t$. The question asks for the *additional* hours, so subtract the two values of t to get $2.01 - 2 = 0.01$. This is equivalent to $\frac{1}{100}$, so the correct answer is (A).

20. **B** The question asks how many yards of fencing are needed to surround each area. There are numbers in the answer choices, so plug in the answers. Start with one of the middle choices. Try (B). If 40 yards of fencing are needed for each area, then the perimeter of each area is 40 yards. Begin with the square area. If the perimeter of a square area is 40 yards, then each side is 40 ÷ 4 = 10 yards. The side of the octagon is 5 yards shorter than this, which is 10 – 5 = 5. The perimeter of the octagon must match the perimeter of the square, so find the perimeter of the octagon, which is 8 × 5 = 40. Since this is equal to the perimeter of the square area, the correct answer is (B).

21. **B** The question asks for the value of k, which is the x-coordinate of one of the x-intercepts. According to the question, the graph of f is a parabola, which means it has vertical symmetry. In a parabola, the axis of symmetry goes through the vertex. Since the vertex is at (5, –3), the axis of symmetry is $x = 5$. Since one of the x-intercepts is (3, 0), the other must be equidistant from the axis of symmetry. Since the distance from 3 to 5 is 2, the distance from 5 to k must also be 2. Therefore, $k = 5 + 2 = 7$. The correct answer is (B).

22. **D** The question asks for an equivalent form of the function that displays values not included in the domain as constants or coefficients. Determine what is not in the domain. In a rational function, a value of x is not in the domain if it makes the denominator equal to 0. To find these values, set the denominator equal to 0 to get $3x^2 - 3x - 18 = 0$. To get the roots of the quadratic, put the quadratic in factored form. Therefore, the correct answer must have the denominator written in factored form. Factor 3 from $3x^2 - 3x - 18$ to get $3(x^2 - x - 6)$. Now factor $(x^2 - x - 6)$ to get $3(x - 3)(x + 2)$. Therefore, the denominator must be written in the form $3(x - 3)(x + 2)$. Eliminate (A), (B), and (C), which don't include this. The correct answer is (D).

23. **B**   The question asks how many times larger the surface area of the volleyball is compared to the surface area of the tennis ball. Because the question does not ask for either surface area but only for the relationship between the two, this can be solved by plugging in. Plug in the radius of the tennis ball as 2. If $r = 2$, then $SA = 4\pi r^2 = 4\pi(2)^2 = 16\pi$ for the tennis ball. The radius of the volleyball is three time the radius of the tennis ball, so, for the volleyball, plug in $r = 3 \times 2 = 6$. If $r = 6$, then $SA = 4\pi r^2 = 4\pi(6)^2 = 144\pi$ for the volleyball. Translate the question into an equation. The term *how many* translates to the variable. Use y. The word *times* translates to "multiplication." The term *the surface area of the tennis ball* translates to 16π. The word *is* translates to "equals." The term *the surface area of a volleyball* translates to 144π. Solve the equation $y \times 16\pi = 144\pi$. Divide both sides by 16π to get $y = 9$. The correct answer is (B).

24. **B**   The question asks for the velocity, in terms of t. There are variables in the answer choices, so plug in. According to the question, the particle accelerates from 20 to 50 meters per second in 10 seconds, so when $t = 10$, the velocity is 50. Let 50 be the target number, and plug $t = 10$ into each of the choices, eliminating any that are not equal to 50. Choice (A) is $V = -50 + 3(10) = -20$, so eliminate (A). Choice (B) is $V = 20 + 3(10) = 50$, so keep (B), but check the other answers just in case. Choice (C) is $V = -20 - 3(10) = -50$, so eliminate (C). Choice (D) is $50 - 3(10) = 20$, so eliminate (D). The correct answer is (B).

25. **C**   The question asks for $h(x + 3)$. There are variables in the answer choices, so plug in. Let $x = 2$. If $x = 2$, then $h(x + 3) = h(2 + 3) = h(5) = 2(5)^2 - 7(5) - 3 = 2(25) - 35 - 3 = 50 - 38 = 12$. Therefore, the target is 12. Plug $x = 2$ into each choice and eliminate any for which $h(5)$ is not equal to 12. In (A), $h(2 + 3) = 2(2^2) - 7(2)$, so $h(5) = 2(4) - 14 = 8 - 14 = -6$. Eliminate (A). In (B), $h(2 + 3) = 2(2^2) - 7(2) - 6$, so $h(5) = 2(4) - 14 - 6 = 8 - 20 = -12$. Eliminate (B). In (C), $h(2 + 3) = 2(2^2) + 5(2) - 6$, so $h(5) = 2(4) + 10 - 6 = 8 + 4 = 12$. Keep (C). In (D), $h(2 + 3) = 2(2^2) - 23(2) + 15$, so $h(5) = 2(4) - 46 + 15 = 8 - 31 = -23$. Eliminate (D). The correct answer is (C).

26. **A**   The question asks for the point of intersection, which is the point that satisfies both equations. There are specific points in the answers, so plug in the answers. Test the ordered pairs in both equations from the question and look for a pair that makes both equations true. Start with the simpler equation. Plug in each choice into the second equation. For (A), $\frac{1}{4}(8) = 2$, so keep (A). For (B), $\frac{1}{4}(16) = 4$, so keep (B). For (C), $\frac{1}{4}(24) = 6$, so keep (C). For (D), $\frac{1}{4}(32) = 8$, so keep (D). Since all four choices are solutions to the second equation, plug them into the first equation. For (A), the equation becomes $10(8) - 62 = 9(2)$. This simplifies to $80 - 62 = 18$ or $18 = 18$. This is true, so keep (A). Since the coordinates in (A) work in both equations, (A) must contain the intersection of the two lines. The correct answer is (A).

27. **C**   The question asks for the model that best describes the decay of the amount of carbon-14 over time. Compare the answer choices. Two of the choices describe linear decay and two describe exponential decay. Linear decay describes a relationship in which the decrease is by a constant amount. Exponential decay describes a relationship in which the decrease is by a constant factor or percent. Eliminate (A) and (D), which reverse the definitions. According to the question, the amount of carbon-14 halves every 5,730 years. This is a reduction by the same factor. To better see this, plug in. If there are 100 grams of carbon-14 to start, then in 5,730 years, there will be 50 grams. In another 5,730 years, there will be 25 grams. Since the amount of the decrease was not constant, eliminate (B). The correct answer is (C).

28. **2 or 18** The question asks for the sum of x and y and provides a system of equations. Since both equations are set equal to the same value, setting the right sides of the two equations equal will be the best method to solve the system for x. The new equation becomes $x + 8 = x^2 - x - 7$. Because this is a quadratic equation, get one side equal to 0. Subtract 8 from both sides to get $x = x^2 - x - 15$, and subtract x from both sides to get $0 = x^2 - 2x - 15$. Factor the right side. Find two numbers with a product of –15 and a sum of –2. These are 3 and –5. Therefore, the equation can be written as $0 = (x + 3)(x - 5)$. Set each factor equal to 0 to get $x + 3 = 0$ and $x - 5 = 0$. The question asks for one possible sum of x and y, so it is necessary to get only one value of x. Therefore, one possible solution is to subtract 3 from both sides of $x + 3 = 0$ to get $x = -3$. Plug this value of x into the first equation to get $y = -3 + 8 = 5$. Therefore, one possible sum of x and y is $-3 + 5 = 2$. Alternatively, to get the other possible solution, add 5 to both sides of $x - 5 = 0$ to get $x = 5$. Plug this value of x into the first equation to get $y = 5 + 8 = 13$. Therefore, the other possible sum of x and y is $5 + 13 = 18$. The correct answer is either 2 or 18.

29. **20** The question asks for the least number of boxes of platinum that the jeweler can order to satisfy the requirements. Translate the English into math in Bite-Sized Pieces. Let the number of gold boxes purchased be g and the number of platinum boxes purchases be p. Since there are two ounces of gold per box, the total weight of the gold purchased is $2g$. Since there are five ounces of platinum per box, the total weight of the platinum is $5p$. Therefore, the total weight of the metal is $2g + 5p$. The jeweler wants to purchase at least 90 ounces of metal, so $2g + 5p \geq 90$. Similarly, a box of gold costs $2,500, so the total cost, in dollars, of the gold is $2,500g$. A box of platinum costs $7,500, so the total cost, in dollars, of the platinum is $7,500p$. Therefore, the total cost of the metal is $2,500g + 7,500p$. This must be *at least* $170,000, so $2,500g + 7,500p \geq 170,000$. According to the question, the jeweler already ordered 10 boxes of gold, so plug in $g = 10$ to get $2(10) + 5p \geq 90$ or $20 + 5p \geq 90$ for the first inequality and $2,500(10) + 7,500p \geq 170,000$ or $25,000 + 7,500p \geq 170,000$ for the second inequality. Solve each inequality. Subtract 20 from both sides of $20 + 5p \geq 90$ to get $5p \geq 70$. Divide both sides by 5 to get $p \geq 14$. Now look at the other inequality. Subtract 25,000 from both sides of $25,000 + 7,500p \geq 170,000$ to get $7,500p \geq 145,000$. Divide both sides by 7,500 to get $p \geq 19.\overline{3}$. The least value of p that satisfies both inequalities is $p = 20$. The correct answer is 20.

30. **160** The question asks for the value of h, which is the number of hours jogged during the month of December. The question says that the total distance jogged each of the two months was the same. Find the distance jogged in November. The question says that Robert jogged at an average pace of 8 miles per hour, and the chart says that he jogged for 140 hours. To find the total distance, multiply the rate by the time to get $8 \times 140 = 1,120$ miles. In December, the rate is 7 miles per hour and the total distance is also 1,120. To find the time, set up the equation $1,120 = 7h$. Divide both sides by 7 to get $h = 160$. The correct answer is 160.

31. **636** The question asks for the total distance jogged during June. According to the graph, Robert spent 120 hours jogging. The question says that Robert spent 70% his jogging time at the slower pace, which was 5 miles per hour. Therefore, he spent $\frac{70}{100} \times 120 = 84$ hours at 5 miles per hour. To find the distance, multiply the rate by the time to get $84 \times 5 = 420$ miles. He spent the rest of the time at the faster pace. The remaining time is $120 - 84 = 36$, so he spent 36 hours at 6 miles per hour for a distance of $36 \times 6 = 216$. Thus, the total distance traveled for the month is $420 + 216 = 636$ miles. The correct answer is 636.

RAW SCORE CONVERSION TABLE SECTION AND TEST SCORES

Raw Score (# of correct answers)	Reading Test Score	Writing and Language Test Score	Math Section Score	Raw Score (# of correct answers)	Reading Test Score	Writing and Language Test Score	Math Section Score
0	8	8	160	25	22	26	510
1	9	8	180	26	23	26	520
2	10	9	200	27	23	27	530
3	11	9	210	28	24	28	540
4	12	10	220	29	24	28	550
5	12	10	240	30	25	29	560
6	13	11	260	31	26	29	570
7	13	11	280	32	26	30	580
8	14	12	300	33	27	30	590
9	14	13	320	34	28	31	600
10	15	14	330	35	28	32	610
11	15	15	350	36	29	33	620
12	16	15	370	37	30	33	630
13	16	16	380	38	30	34	640
14	17	17	400	39	31	34	650
15	17	17	410	40	32	35	660
16	18	18	420	41	33	36	670
17	18	19	430	42	33	37	680
18	19	20	440	43	34	37	690
19	19	21	450	44	35	38	700
20	20	22	460	45	36		710
21	20	22	470	46	37		730
22	21	23	480	47	38		740
23	21	24	490	48			760
24	22	25	500				

CONVERSION EQUATION SECTION AND TEST SCORES

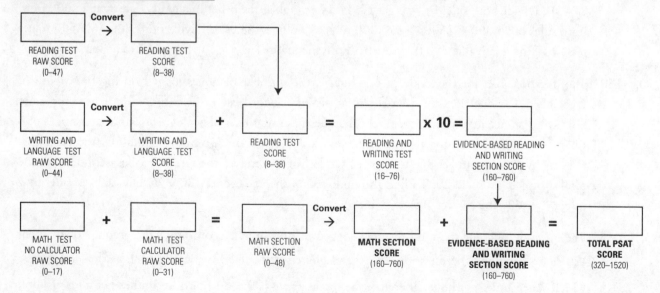

NOTES